COLLECTIVE BARGAINING
IN THE
PUBLIC SECTOR:
CASES IN PUBLIC POLICY

COLLECTIVE BARGAINING IN THE PUBLIC SECTOR: CASES IN PUBLIC POLICY

by

Frank H. Cassell
Professor of Industrial Relations
Graduate School of Management
Northwestern University

and

Jean J. Baron
Research Associate
Graduate School of Management
Northwestern University

TABLE OF CONTENTS

INTRODUCTION

By 1980, some seventeen million Americans will work for government. This will be nearly 20 percent of total employment. Between 1965 and 1980, government employment will have increased by seven million. Nine out of ten people who will go to work for government will be employed in state and local government, the fastest growing employment sector in the nation.

Employment growth encourages unionization. The Bureau of Labor Statistics reports that during the two year period, 1966 to 1968, union membership in the public sector jumped nearly 900,000. Federal employment union membership is now close to 1.5 million, and union membership is growing rapidly at the state and local levels.

The cases in this book deal with this area of growth, change and uncertainty. These are real life cases. They concern the worker and his work in relation to his employment in the public service. They concern the influence of public policy and politics upon the work he does and his conditions of work. They concern human beings whose lives are shaped by public policy in a manner which is different from those in the private sector. They concern the processes whereby the employee and his public employer work out arrangements in an environment at once highly complex and charged with political implications. They concern conflict, not only between labor and management, but among the conflicting claims and values of the various segments of a community.

All labor-management relationships involve ways employer and employee can come to some sort of arrangement — accommodation and adaptation — satisfactory to both. To redress an imbalance of power, employees sometimes organize into unions and seek advantageous legislation. In the process, employees attempt to define in their own terms what wages, hours, and working conditions mean. In the public sector particularly, the definition of such conditions may intrude upon public policy. Conversely, when citizens and their representatives define their own needs, they may intrude upon the workers' conditions of work.

A teachers' union may, for example, demand shorter hours of work to improve the lot of the teacher or to keep pace with other employees. This may be interpreted by parents and school administrators as an attempt by the union to decide for them how the schools should be managed. It is this intertwining of interests and viewpoints which makes public sector bargaining more complex than that in the private sector.

Some of the cases in the book concern three basic questions of labor-management relations:

1. Do public workers have a right to form organizations such as unions to protect their special interest?

2. If they are granted participation through their union, what issues should be decided jointly, through negotiations, and what issues should be kept away from the bargaining table?

3. If management and union fail to reach agreement on the bargainable issues, how is conflict to be resolved?

For the most part, the answers to these questions are being borrowed from the private sector, which has had longer experience with collective bargaining. The same questions were asked in the private sector more than forty years ago. They were answered with the passage of the Wagner Act in 1935 and with interpretations of the act since then. In essence, public policy has given these answers to the collective bargaining questions in the private sector:

1. Strong unions and free collective bargaining are encouraged.

2. The function of government in regard to bargaining is to encourage the parties to settle their disputes themselves without government intervention; negotiation of the substantive terms of the labor agreement are left almost entirely to the parties involved.

3. The appropriate subject matter of bargaining includes wages, hours and working conditions. But no government machinery is provided to solve differences over wages, hours and working conditions which may arise between the parties.

4. The government should not intervene in labor disputes to prevent strikes, boycotts, or picketing. These rights are guaranteed to workers, within certain guidelines. If third parties are injured in the process of collective bargaining, that is the price of the right to organize and to engage in free collective bargaining.

5. Employers are legally compelled to bargain with any union designated by a majority of employees in an appropriate unit. Procedures are provided to determine the appropriate unit and to assure impartial determination of the majority's choice of bargaining agent.

6. Collective bargaining is considered the best means for achieving industrial peace without unduly reducing the personal freedoms of the individual. The collective bargaining relationship is expected over time

to lead to better communications, more informed judgments by the parties, and to evolve from a stage of conflict to a stage of cooperation.

There have been some modifications of these basic principles in regard to strikes tinged with a strong public interest and there are proposals for more alterations, but for most private sector collective bargaining these ideas prevail.

When we note that the public sector has been borrowing these ideas from the private sector, some further comments are necessary. The borrowing process isn't always peaceful or amicable; in many cases, the ideas are being forced upon public employers very much against their will. In some ways, public sector collective bargaining is repeating the history of private sector bargaining and is repeating some of the same bitter fights.

The borrowing process is an uneven one. It is far advanced in some states, barely started in others. Federal labor law does not apply to state and local governmental units and the states that have passed labor legislation have answered differently the questions raised by collective bargaining. Some states haven't answered them at all.

Despite the likelihood that the borrowing process will continue, there is a basic enigma in the transference of techniques from the private sector to the public. The enigma is related to the central fact that private bargaining is rooted in the economic system and public bargaining, although it has economic aspects, is rooted in the political system.

Scholars have described five components of public sector negotiations:
* The mood, needs, and demands of the community constituency.
* The mood, needs, and demands of the political establishment.
* The limitations, restrictions, and requirements of state constitutions, statutes, ordinances, civil service, education laws, municipal charters.
* The mood, needs, and demands of the employer.
* The mood, needs, and demands of the employees.

The first three of these components are either not present in private sector negotiations or, if present, are of major significance only with respect to disputes which affect the health and safety of the nation.

In the final analysis, the governmental unit makes policy, subject to its grant of power from the state. An important element of policy is its implementation through the allocation of revenues. The union is only one claimant upon those revenues. How can the union's claims be fairly balanced against other community groups' claims to limited resources? To whom does the governing unit owe primary responsibility? If the resources are too limited to allow payment of competitive wages, how can they be increased? If not increased, how can capable people be attracted into government? How can workers receive justice? How can citizens be protected from destructive strikes to enforce demands which cause reallocations of revenues contrary to their wishes? Because of the inherent difference in the bases of the public and the private sector, some of the answers to these questions must inevitably be different.

Even without unions, these forces are at work. The union often institutionalizes latent dissatisfactions and aspirations of workers. There is ever present in a democratic society the desire of workers to receive justice in the work place comparable to the justice they receive outside work. This is often achieved informally by individual workers and groups of workers, as one of the cases suggests. The union structure formalizes procedures and provides protections for workers. But even with a union present, how can a worker receive just treatment if the governing unit and citizens refuse it?

The contrasts between public and private sectors are perhaps the greatest in regard to strikes. The strike is considered legitimate in the private sector, but public anxiety over public sector strikes is intense, so much so that most states prohibit public strikes. The prohibition raises the crucial need for adequate strike substitutes that can resolve impasses, but successful forms of strike substitutes have not been forthcoming, either from the private models or from those public jurisdictions which have attempted experiments. Strikes, though prohibited, take place anyway and often don't resolve the public issues that gave birth to them.

It might be fairly said that in these areas of labor-management relations, public management is in crisis. The cases in this book examine the crisis in various dimensions. In the process, they deal with many of the critical issues and confrontations of our time. These include questions such as how we shall govern ourselves, how we shall live together as people, how power can be distributed so that it enhances the lives of all our citizens and preserves their individual freedoms, and how labor and management can accommodate each other in ways which benefit both the workers and the public.

ISSUES IN PUBLIC SECTOR COLLECTIVE BARGAINING

There has been a tendency for collective bargaining procedures that appear to work effectively in the private sector to be incorporated into bargaining in the public sector. Some of these procedures are appropriate and should be borrowed. But there are such basic differences in the nature of the two sectors, private and public, that not all such procedures are transferable.

The most significant difference is that private sector bargaining is rooted in the economic system, whereas bargaining in the public sector is rooted in the process of political representation, with a public agency ultimately accountable to the public for its performance and financing.

The differences between the two sectors are illustrated most dramatically by their relationships to strikes by employees. It is legimate in the private sector, with its economic base, for management and labor to use economic pressures, including the strike. In the public sector, however, with its base of political responsibility and accountability, some of these economic pressures may be unacceptable. In this context, the costs of a strike are not borne merely by the employer and the employees but by various segments of the public to whom the public employer is accountable for service. If police strike, the public safety may be at stake. If teachers strike, the children are the losers. If hospital workers strike, the costs of the strike are borne directly by the patients whose health and life may depend upon uninterrupted service and by that part of the public which finances the strike through their taxes. The strike in the public sector may fulfill its function of bringing about agreement but it may be at a cost which many feel is too high.

Largely because of the impact of public employee strikes on the public, more than half of the states have passed legislation regulating collective bargaining in the public sector. The legislation varies considerably but most states have outlawed public strikes and provide some kind of impasse procedure, such as fact-finding or arbitration, to lead to agreement without a strike.

These state laws on public collective bargaining usually provide a range of procedures covering recognition of bargaining agents for all public employees or for certain groups of employees, establishment of appropriate bargaining units, the subject matter of bargaining, grievance procedures, unfair labor practices, and other aspects of bargaining. Many of these procedures have evolved over the years in the private sector and have been transferred to the public sector with few alterations.

Other states have not yet legislated on public collective bargaining, sometimes because the political pressure is lacking, sometimes because of a deep-seated disapproval of any kind of public union, sometimes because both the employing agencies and the unions have lobbied against legislation, feeling they are better off without state regulation of the bargaining process, particularly if it includes a no-strike requirement.

Whether or not state law exists with respect to collective bargaining, the parties or potential parties have the opportunity to influence long term relationships by the decisions they make at each step of the way, beginning with the coverage of employees by a union and the level of recognition.

And whether or not state law exists, most of the same issues must be dealt with by the parties. Often they are issues that generate considerable heat, such as recognition of a bargaining agent, the scope of bargaining, and the right to strike.

The rest of this chapter deals with a range of issues that must be resolved by parties to bargaining, whether in the public or private sector and whether there is or is not relevant legislation.

Recognition of Employee Bargaining Agents

For much of our industrial history, employee unions or associations were viewed as criminal conspiracies and almost any kind of action opposing them was condoned. It was not until passage of the Wagner Act — labor's bill of rights — in 1935 that employee unions were fully legalized and became protected in their legitimate activities by public policy.

But the Wagner Act did not apply to public employees, at any level of government, and organization of public employees into unions lagged far behind organization in the private sector. The prevailing feeling was that public employment was a privilege and that anyone who did not wish to accept the terms and conditions of public employment could look elsewhere for a job rather than to seek collectively to alter the terms and conditions.

Some unions and some public employees began pushing against these restrictions and seeking some form of employee participation in decisions regarding the work place. Firemen were among the pioneers, partly because of the long hours historically associated with their jobs. Police organization was much slower, perhaps because of the paramilitary structure of police departments and the strong emphasis on the chain of command. Teachers and nurses began adapting their professional associations to include bargaining activities. Other employees began to show interest.

Public employee bargaining received a major boost from President John F. Kennedy's Executive Order 10988, issued in 1962 to allow certain bargaining activities by employees of federal agencies. The years since 1962 have brought a tremendous growth in public employee unions, not only at the federal level but at every level of government. These years, too, have brought confusion by government agencies about how to deal with these new employee organizations.

Some local government agencies have refused to recognize and deal with employee organizations at all, stating that public employees have no right to organize and make demands of a governmental body which exists to try to serve the public. Some have contended — and still contend in many places — that a public agency has no legal authority to share decision-making power with employees and that such sharing is an unlawful delegation of their statutory power to run their agencies.

Passage of state laws in some states has answered this question, but only in part. Many of the states have granted the right to organize only to certain groups of employees, leaving out other groups. Not all the states which have granted the right to organize have provided procedures for recognition of the organization by the government employer. And not all the states that provide for employee organization and recognition have granted the right to bargain collectively; some provide only that employee groups have a right to present proposals or a right to "meet and confer."

For many large groups of public employees, then, the right to organize, the right to union recognition, and the right to bargain collectively remain burning issues. These groups include many in the states with no bargaining legislation at all and others in the states where not all public employees are covered.

The absence of state legislation on bargaining does not always mean the absence of collective bargaining in public agencies. Court cases and attorney general opinions in some states have established the right of government agencies to recognize and bargain with employee groups if they wish to and many have found it either wise or expedient to do so.

In any case, with or without supporting laws, recognition of a bargaining agent must be accompanied by solution of some of the issues that follow.

Inclusion or Exclusion of Employees in Collective Bargaining

Inclusion or exclusion of supervisory employees is one of the first questions that must be answered in the development of the collective bargaining relationship. Does the role of supervisors as part of management place them in a position different from other employees? On what basis, if any, can supervisors be denied rights that are extended to other employees?

In federal government employment, operating under executive orders, supervisors are excluded (Executive Order 11491, Section 1(6) 1969), but state jurisdictions have varying practices regarding the bargaining rights of supervisory employees. Depending on state laws or absence of laws, a governmental unit may have three options:

1. It may state that supervisory employees are not covered by agency policies establishing collective bargaining rights.
2. It may include supervisory employees under agency policies and permit supervisors to be members of a common bargaining unit with non-supervisors.
3. It may recognize the right of supervisory employees to bargain through a separate unit.

The first option: Why exclude supervisory employees from bargaining rights? The basic reason is a belief transferred from experience in the private sector that supervision is an integral part of management accountable to the agency and its top executives. The crucial question of management accountability has sometimes been blurred where collective bargaining has been established for supervisors. The process of bargaining, even at its most constructive and cooperative, involves basic differences between the parties: different points of view, different goals, different interests. Bargaining tends to cast the parties in the roles of adversaries. If supervisors are viewed as an integral part of management, thinking of themselves as adversaries of management is a contradiction.

Option two would permit supervisors to bargain collectively but as members of a broader unit. Where supervisors are in the same unit with non-supervisors, there would appear to be a conflict of interest. There are likely to be differences between the interests of the institution and the interests of its non-supervisory employees on such issues as wages, hours, benefits and discipline. Supervisors may, for example, be required to impose discipline upon subordinates who are also their fellow union members. There is, in addition, the possibility of employer domination, through its supervisors, of the bargaining agent. Besides legal considerations, extensive employer influence or domination of the union can unstabilize the union. This unsettling impact can readily be seen within present associations of teachers and registered nurses.

Option three includes supervisory employees under collective bargaining policies but requires them to form a separate bargaining unit. Although this may be more suitable than a common unit with non-supervisory personnel, the problem might remain of a single union representing both units, supervisory and non-supervisory. Supervisory domination could persist. In addition, this option clearly places levels of management in adversary positions with each other possibly disrupting their common interest in quality management and diluting accountability. Permitting separate units for supervisors could lead to increased conflict. In the non-profit hospitals of New York State, for example, not only are supervisors permitted to bargain, but different levels of supervision can form separate units. The resulting "tribalization" has led directly to the whipsawing (in which one group plays off its own special interests against another) so characteristic of unstable collective bargaining.

Level of Recognition; Exclusive Representation; Obligations of the Parties

Basic to the decision of establishing collective bargaining is the necessity to make a choice between two levels of union recognition:

1. An employer can informally recognize and negotiate with a union, on behalf of employees the union shows are members. This is an informal process, without any formal contractual relationship or test of actual representative status. With respect to the craft employees, this type of informal recognition and negotiation is often a practical recognition of current realities.
2. At a second level, an employer may seek to define an appropriate bargaining unit — a cluster of job classifications — and then bargain for that entire unit only with a union that shows it represents the majority of employees in the bargaining unit. Whichever union is shown to have majority support, usually through a carefully conducted election, is granted exclusive representation for that unit and bargains for all the employees in the unit, whether they are members of that union or not. Exclusive representation means that only one union may negotiate the terms and conditions of employment for the entire unit.

This second approach has characterized the system of collective bargaining in the private sector since the passage of the Wagner Act in 1935. In fact, it is one of the key differences between the American industrial relations system and the industrial relations system of Western Europe.

The granting of exclusive bargaining rights to a union that represents the majority of employees in a unit contributes significantly to stabilizing the collective bargaining process. It eliminates the confusion and jockeying for position that are inevitable where several unions contend that they speak for the same group of employees.

Granting exclusive representation creates certain obligations for both sides. On a continuing basis, management of an agency is obligated to deal only with the designated union. The union, in turn, is obligated to effectively represent all employees of the unit, whether they favor the union or not. Employees are obligated to bargain and seek redress of grievances only through procedures established by the employer and the bargaining agent, rather than individually or through another union.

This process places a limit on individual rights within the unit and on the rights of employee groups other than the recognized union. When the union is granted exclusive representation status, then the rights of the individual to determine for himself wages, hours, and working conditions become mute.

There is thus a tradeoff, the kind of tradeoff that exists in many other areas of collective bargaining. Certain individual rights are subordinated to collective rights. This tradeoff is necessary in building stability into the bargaining process and is one of the key elements in the American collective bargaining system.

The introduction of the race issue into union-member relations poses special problems for the majority and minority in the unit in that the minority, black or brown, may have interests and goals which may not be consistent with or welcomed by the elected exclusive bargaining agent. What has previously been the submerging of individual interests could become the submerging of the interests of a class, a race, an ethnic group. There is thus a clash of interests of groups and races; a submerging of individual interests in favor of order and greater predictability in the labor management relationship.

Once a union attains exclusive representation within the bargaining unit, little remains of individual employee freedom of choice concerning his terms and conditions of employment. These aspects of employment can only be altered through negotiations between the bargaining agent and the management. The issue of compulsory union membership has led to extensive emotional and philosophical debate, when in fact, given exclusive representation, individual freedom is diminished.

Determination of an Appropriate Bargaining Unit

No element of collective bargaining is more complex than the structuring of an appropriate bargaining unit and no other phase has so great an impact on the ongoing relationship between the parties. This issue is not one that captures public attention, in contrast to the

extensive debate about whether or not public employees should have
the right to strike. However, in many ways, the composition of bargaining units is a more fundamental and more crucial issue. It is,
indeed, rarely understood by management of agencies.

A bargaining unit is a group of people working in jobs classified
according to craft or common skill, or product or service produced,
or working for a common employer; the group of people is combined
for the process of collective bargaining. The bargaining unit is the framework within which the bargaining agent is chosen by the employees
and it is the basic framework for the conduct of negotiations and the
processing of grievances for all employees within that unit. It is a basic
building block in union-management relationships. At times, a bargaining unit can be joined with other bargaining units for a specific purpose, such as negotiation of issues common to each unit. At other
times, the unit can be dealt with separately for issues that relate
only to that unit. The building block concept allows for some future
flexibility in negotiations; there is the possibility of combining units
in different ways for specific bargaining purposes. There is less flexibility to alter the composition of the bargaining unit once it is established; its composition is difficult to change over time.

Determination of the bargaining unit is a knotty problem because it
involves so many different parties, each with interests that may conflict. For example, employees may want a unit which will give them the
maximum amount of self-determination together with the greatest
amount of bargaining power with which to gain their objectives. A
union is interested in organizing employees and seeks a unit which it
thinks it can most successfully organize. The employer is concerned
with stability and efficiency and usually prefers a larger bargaining
unit, fearing the competition which might result from fragmentation
into many narrowly-defined units. The public is interested in the
availability and cost of services.

The agency's task is the difficult one of accommodating these interests. Its objective must be long-run stability in union-management
relationships which permit the agency to concentrate on its major
objective, the efficient delivery of services.

If broad units are formed, then the task of bargaining tends to be
simplified and the agency is better able to achieve a goal of con-
sistency in administration and equity among employees. Broad units
allow more stable negotiations on such basic issues as work standards,
pensions, and insurances, where solutions must be common to all employee groups.

If many narrow units are formed, the agency would likely find itself negotiating the same issue over and over again with different unions,

leading to a range of contractual agreements that provide different answers to the same problem. Institution-wide job evaluation plans or a uniform program of job benefits would be difficult if not impossible. A balanced wage structure, relating wages to the value of job content, would be difficult to attain. Revisions of organizational structure, important to the development of an effective organization, would be close to impossible. "Pyramiding" of contract settlements would probably occur, as one union sought to use another union's settlement as the base for its own demands. Fragmentation leads to more work in negotiating, to more competing interests, more reopening dates, a greater variety of objectives and a greater frequency of strikes.

There is a relationship between the size of the bargaining unit (the number of job classifications included within the unit) and the scope of bargaining (the range of issues which are open to negotiation). If an agency can establish broad units, then it can allow a wider scope of bargaining, giving its employees a greater share of power to bargain economic issues. If the agency allows the formation of many narrow units, it will need to place stricter limits on the scope of bargaining.

Union Security

A union traditionally seeks some form of union security to maximize its dues-paying members and to stabilize day-to-day aspects of collective bargaining. Unions particularly feel the need for some kind of membership guarantee where they have been granted exclusive representation. There is always concern by a union about bargaining unit employees who derive benefits from the union's activities but in no way contribute to its financial support (which is the practical consequence of the union being required to represent all employees in the bargaining unit). The union claims these employees are "free riders." To keep them at a minimum and to increase the efficiency of dues collection, bargaining agents seek to have one or more of these forms of security stipulated in the contract:

1. A union shop clause which requires union membership as a condition of continued employment after a specified period of time following initial employment, usually within thirty to ninety days. A union shop clause assures the bargaining agent full membership among regular full-time and part-time employees within the unit.

    Opposition to the union shop rests on the premise that no one should be compelled to join an organization against his will and as a condition for continued employment. Employer opposition to the union shop can also be evaluated as means to restrict union income and generally weaken union control within the bargaining unit and in general alter the balance of economic power. Except for the states which have enacted "right-to-work" laws under Section 14B of the Taft-Hartley Act, the union shop is legal and widely established in private enterprise.

The legality of the union shop in public employment has not been broadly determined. In a few scattered instances, public jurisdictions have agreed to union shop clauses. The latest Executive Order (11491) revising collective bargaining procedures for federal employees does not provide for the union shop, nor does the new collective bargaining procedure for postal employees.

2. An agency shop clause requires employees who are a part of the bargaining unit, but who are not union members, to pay the union a "service fee" in lieu of union dues, for the benefits they receive from union representation. Employees are not required to join the union as a condition of continued employment. However, employees of the unit who refuse to become union members or pay the "service fee" may be discharged. There has been limited experimentation with the agency shop in public employment.

3. A maintenance-of-membership clause provides that employees who agree to join a union must maintain their membership (as a condition of continued employment) during the life of the contract. A specified "escape period" is provided, usually at the end of a contract period, during which time employees may withdraw from the union if they choose. Therefore, employees who do not initially join the union, or who leave the union during the "escape period," may continue working without payment of any fees or dues to the union. This form of union security is becoming increasingly popular in public employment.

4. A dues checkoff clause simply stipulates that upon authorization by the individual employee, the employer withholds the amount of union dues from union members' paychecks, for payment directly to the union. Such a provision is obviously beneficial to the union in solving the nettlesome and expensive problem of collecting dues each month. The dues checkoff clause may provide for the payment of a service fee by the union to the employer to cover the cost of this additional payroll work. Dues checkoff is a common form of union security in both public and private sector collective bargaining.

Scope of Bargaining and Management Rights

A commitment to collective bargaining means commitment to joint determination of certain issues. But a commitment to collective bargaining does not necessarily mean that all issues of common concern to the public agency and its employees need be negotiated at the bargaining table. Some issues can be directed away from the traditional procedures of collective bargaining, with their attendant pressures.

Prior to establishment of collective bargaining relations with a union, the agency has unilateral administrative authority, subject only to some external requirements such as those imposed by regional planning agencies and licensing agencies. With the establishment of collective bargaining, however, certain aspects of its authority come to be shared with the union. This is what is meant by joint determination. The issues that used to be determined unilaterally and which are now jointly determined make up the scope of bargaining.

State laws frequently define the issues that are bargainable. In the absence of labor legislation, the scope of bargaining covers only those matters which management agrees to jointly determine. Depending upon how management views its function and its legal responsibility, management will likely seek to keep some issues out of bargaining, retaining them in an area in which management alone will make the final determination. This is called management's reserved authority. The issues within this reserved authority will not be negotiated — jointly determined — with the union. This concept is important to management because, in order to perform its role, it must remain flexible enough to make basic decisions about how it will manage.

To remain effective and efficient, management must be able to act, to introduce new technology and new methods that will improve productivity, to decide what jobs should be created or discontinued, to change work assignments and promote its most effective employees, to decide how the resources of the institution are best to be used. These add up to management's right to manage. But in its efforts to maintain its reserved authority, management may often find itself in conflict with the union over the subjects that should be included within the scope of bargaining.

Most labor legislation defines bargainable issues as wages, hours, and working conditions. Although these terms sound precise and limited, they actually are not. When it comes to details of a contract, it is difficult to think of any employee interest that is not in some way directly or indirectly related to wages, hours, or conditions of employment. There has been a tendency, in the years since the passage of the Wagner Act, to interpret these terms in a broader and broader fashion. Even such issues as professional practices, and the extent and quality of public services, whether education or hospital care or policing of the streets, are only in theory reserved entirely to the management of the unit of government. In practice, these interests collide with those of the employees, for what may be to the agency head a prerogative of management may be to the employee a condition of his work over which he should have some say. To extend this back a step, the collision could very well be with a hospital board, a school board, the mayor, or a community group which believes it should decide such matters as how medical care should be provided, or how many children in a classroom are desirable. But to change class sizes or health procedures is to also change conditions of work which, under a labor agreement, are bargainable matters.

Despite the difficulties, employing agencies do seek to keep out of the scope of bargaining a range of issues they believe should be retained for management decision-making. The issues assigned to one area or the other are determined pragmatically; they are dependent upon the nature of the institution, the power relationships between the parties, applicable legislation, and the way the parties view their own interacting roles. Management-union relationships can take many forms, from generally antagonistic, at one extreme, to genuinely cooperative, at the other.

To suggest that an agency should retain its authority to make final decisions on management-related issues is not to say that it will never discuss such issues with a union. An agency may refuse to discuss some of them. It may agree to discuss some of them in channels outside collective bargaining. It may even choose to discuss some of them in negotiations, without giving up its right to reach a final decision unilaterally.

The existence of alternate channels for discussion of some issues, particularly professional issues relating to the function of the agency and employees' legitimate professional interest in that function, is one very important method of limiting the scope of bargaining.

Another method of limiting the scope of bargaining exists where there is a merit system, or civil service system, covering the employees in a bargaining unit. Issues that come within the merit system — often promotions and sometimes wages — can then be resolved within that system rather than at the bargaining table.

Forces that tend to expand the scope of bargaining include:

Legislative changes, decisions of administrative agencies that enforce labor legislation, court decisions, and interpretations of this body of law by arbitrators. All of these have tended through the years to broaden the meaning of wages, hours and working conditions.

Day-to-day practices in the work place. No matter how careful a management is in choosing the issues on which it will bargain, no matter how careful it is in the wording of contract language, it may dissipate its decision-making authority through its daily operations. When agency policies are not clear or are not consistently followed by supervisory employees, an arbitrator may decide that the day-to-day practices really constitute the policy, not the written ones.

Collective Bargaining and the Budgetmaking Process

Cost elements of the negotiated contracts, when incorporated into the budget proposal, are often viewed as joint recommendations from the agency and the unions to the ultimate decision maker, the holder of the purse strings, the taxing authority, whether a local or state board, or a legislature or city council. Although the parties may have reached agreement, joint recommendation means the labor agreements cannot be finalized until the budget is approved. In this instance, the parties would not be approaching the taxing body or board as adversaries, but as parties who have agreed to the fairness and adequacy of the proposals. They will have a common interest in the approval of the budget appropriation. This gives a different dimension to the bargaining concept and makes it unlike bargaining in the private sector.

Involvement of Broader Interests in Public Sector Collective Bargaining

A public institution, such as a school or police department or a hospital system serves a broad community with many special interest groups, both internal and external to the institution. In the allocation of scarce community financial resources, it is important to realize that employee demands upon those resources are not the sole claim. Union representation tends to give the special interests of employees a concentration and forcefulness not usually available to other special interest groups. The public nature of the collective bargaining process requires some method for hearing spokesmen and taking into account the interests of the community and groups within the community who may have special knowledge which could be of value to the bargaining process. Public hearings have been employed to enable various special interest groups to make known to the agency (and to the unions) their ideas and proposals regarding allocation of community financial resources. For collective bargaining purposes, this enables negotiators to develop a rationale for stating that other interests, besides those of employees, must be considered in the budget-making process.

This need for a relationship with the larger community is one of the fundamental differences between private sector and public sector collective bargaining. In private sector bargaining, decisions in the marketplace provide rough justification for the allocation of resources. In the absence of a market mechanism to restrain demands at the bargaining table, allocations are often made largely on the basis of union power. This poses a conflict with other claimants and participants in the decision-making process, including patients or students, the community, taxpayers and governing boards who themselves are concerned with efficient and economic operations and use of resources.

The Grievance Procedure

A grievance procedure is a formal method, established in a collective bargaining agreement, through which employees may seek to have certain problems related to the workplace resolved in a fair and equitable manner. It is a way of handling disputes that arise out of interpretation of the collective bargaining agreement and the policies and practices management adopts under that agreement. The existence of a grievance procedure implies recognition of certain employee rights and recognition of the agreement as a governing mechanism, establishing these rights and establishing the processes for fair treatment.

Typically, the matter in dispute is processed through a series of steps of the grievance mechanism, each step representing a higher level of union and management hierarchy, with emphasis placed on settling the dispute by mutual agreement at any step. Where the issue is not resolved by mutual agreement, the final step usually is binding arbitration by an outside third party.

A grievance procedure of some sort is a characteristic component of the American system of industrial relations. It might be viewed as the means to relieve the pressures which often lead to work stoppages that develop out of contractual disputes if there were no other established method of resolving these disputes. The process is important in both private and public sectors of collective bargaining, but seems particularly important in public employment, where work stoppages (strikes) are typically viewed as unacceptable because they may place a greater burden on a third party, the public, than on the parties to the dispute.

Because a grievance procedure terminating in binding arbitration is an alternative to a work stoppage over a dispute, such a grievance procedure is usually closely associated with a no-strike pledge by the union during the duration of the agreement. The union, in return for a commitment to arbitrate unresolved grievances, agrees not to engage in any form of work stoppage during the term of the contract. Where management is unwilling to engage in a binding arbitration as a

final step of the grievance procedure, usually because it is unwilling
to turn over to an arbitrator its decision-making authority on certain
matters, the union will likely assert, in turn, that it must retain the
right to strike on those matters.

Establishment of a grievance procedure does not mean that there
will be no differences or disputes between management and union.
There will be. But it does mean — and it is an important advantage
for both parties — that there will be an orderly method for reaching
a solution without unduly upsetting the ongoing stability of the relationship between management and union.

Another advantage of the establishment of a grievance procedure is
that it provides a form of two-way interaction between management and
union. It provides a safety valve, a way to defuse tension over problems
before it leads to serious difficulties in the workplace. It is an informational process for the exchange of ideas from both points of view.

The most important advantage to the employee is that the grievance
procedure gives him the sense that he will be fairly and equitably
treated. It offers him a guarantee of due process in the workplace.

The Strike in Public Sector Collective Bargaining

A strike is both a manifestation of conflict and a method that has
arisen over time for the resolution of a dispute that has not been settled
at the bargaining table. Collective bargaining and strikes are not
necessarily inseparable; the right to strike is not an essential and
integral part of collective bargaining.

Collective bargaining is a mechanism which enables employee participation in decision-making on certain aspects of the relationship of
the worker and management. It is in fact a negative check on the
unilateral authority of management. It allows joint determination
of wages, hours, and working conditions, and it thus permits employee
participation in decisions which affect workers' lives. Where such
participation exists, conflict can arise between the participants over
differences in objectives, goals and interests. The need in collective
bargaining is for methods to resolve such conflicts. The strike is one
tool, or method. There are other tools. The strike or the threat of a
strike can be a useful, effective and acceptable tool. But in situations
where the strike cannot fulfill its function, substitute procedures have
to be developed for the resolution of conflict.

It should be noted that the strike is usually viewed as a union tool,
but this is not always a correct view. A strike may be provoked by
management action, actually desired and encouraged by management,
which may make a series of moves which leave workers no recourse
but to strike. Management may itself engage in a version of a strike,

locking out its employees so they cannot come to work. More often, where management perceives that it has something to gain in collective bargaining as a result of a strike, management may act in such a way that it brings on an employee strike.

The view that a strike is a tool for resolving specific conflict at the bargaining table is in many ways uniquely American. In Europe, strikes often take on political and ideological overtones. In the United States where most collective bargaining experience has been in private enterprise, the strike has emerged as a method appropriate to the economic forces of the private enterprise, competitive system. It allows the worker a share of power in determining the allocation of the fruits of production.

In considering the strike as a functional tool in collective bargaining, the following points seem relevant to understanding why, in certain situations, the strike performs its function more adequately than any substitute procedure, and why, in other situations, the strike is inappropriate because it does not fulfill the function for which it was intended:

1. The function of a strike in the private sector is to impose an economic cost on management through lost income to the firm. A lockout, in contrast, is designed to impose a cost on employees through loss of wages.

   In the vast number of collective bargaining situations, the mere threat of economic loss during contract negotiations is sufficient to induce concessions leading to agreement. But for this process to work effectively, the primary impact of the strike must be upon the parties directly involved.

2. The effectiveness of the strike is diminished when the larger impact of the work stoppage is upon third parties — the public. When the third party is unwilling or unable to tolerate this adverse impact, political pressures on government officials develop to eliminate or restrict the strike as a tool.

3. The concept of collective bargaining in the private sector is built around the assumption that finally the consumer exerts an influence through the product marketplace. If negotiations at the bargaining table result in cost increases which are translated into price increases, theory holds that the consumer may respond to an unacceptable price increase by refusing to buy at all, by postponing his purchases or by substituting one good for another. Threat of unemployment or going out of business restrains decisions at the bargaining table.

   This process cannot work effectively, though, unless the marketplace is substantially competitive. If competitive elements are weak or nonexistent, then the restraints of the marketplace disappear. In considering the public sector, the influence of a product marketplace as a constraint on excessive demands at the bargaining table is lost and there is only an imperfect substitute, the allocation of funds via the political process.

4. The public sector mechanism for allocation of resources has its roots in representative government. Elected representatives or appointees of elected representatives make decisions regarding shares of resources. The rightness or wrongness of allocations are thus related to political influence. Strongly organized public sector unions bring a new dimension to this allocation process. Where public employees are organized into strong unions, the allocation of limited public resources is forced to respond to the coercive pressure which public unions can exert and to the needs and priorities of the community as the union defines them.

5. Public employment, in contrast to private employment, generally entails services which are broadly considered essential to the ongoing stability of a society — police and fire protection, sanitation services, schools, medical care and the like. Some services provided by private employment may also be considered essential. Whether you are talking about public or private employment, the impact of a work stoppage may be harmful in a public police department or a private electric utility, in a public sanitation service or a private railroad. But it is generally true that public employment is more apt to deal with what society considers essential service. It is not likely that consumption of essential public services can be postponed or substitutes found for these services. Besides, the ultimate constraint in private enterprise — the possibility of a firm's going out of business — is not operative in governmental services. The government is not about to go out of business. A more likely result is the deterioration in the quality of public service. Increasing taxes is another possible result.

6. Collective bargaining in private enterprise assumes that the negotiators — particularly the employer — have the authority to conclude the final agreement and the authority to generate revenue to fulfill the contractual commitments it reaches in bargaining. Moving from private to public enterprise, we find public employers who have the responsibility for negotiating and concluding contracts but may not have the power to produce the revenue to finance the pay increases; that power resides at a higher political level such as a state legislature. Thus one of the most fundamental questions of public collective bargaining, a question not relevant in the private sector is: Where does final decision-

making authority lie? In the public sector, when a strike occurs, against whom is it directed?

It is not sufficient to say, however, that since the strike may not fulfill its function as it does in the private sector, it can be discarded. The differences between the objectives of the employing agency and the union would still remain and must be resolved in some fashion. The challenge, then, is not merely to consider the legality or desirability of strikes, but to take a further step and consider what alternative means for resolving conflict might be better than the strike.

Alternative Procedures to the Strike

The states have variously answered the question of the strike. New York law prohibits strikes by all public employees. Pennsylvania allows them except where a court may decide that the detrimental impact of a strike warrants its termination by court order. But making public strikes illegal does not necessarily prevent them. A union may choose to strike anyway and pay the penalties (if any) exacted by law. And whether the strike is outlawed or not or whether it can be prohibited by the courts or not, the critical question remains: How do you resolve conflict that persists?

In public sector collective bargaining, with its multi-party nature, the long term goal becomes one of finding decision-making processes which can take into account and balance the diverse interests involved: those of the agency, the employees, the recipients of service, the tax-payers, the union. A special aspect of an agency's responsibility is to represent the interest of the public as well as its own management interests during negotiations.

There are two basic ways in which procedures designed to be alternatives to the strike can be made available to the parties to a public sector dispute: those originated by the parties themselves and those originated outside the immediate parties.

When the parties feel the need for such procedures, they may, by mutual agreement, request the help of some appropriate unit of government or they may, by mutual agreement, invite intervention by a third party outside government.

In the absence of such voluntary alternatives to the strike, government may, on its own initiative if authorized by statute, intervene in disputes affecting local and state governmental units.

The interventions, whether originating from the initiative of the parties or an appropriate agency of government, may include such procedures as conciliation, mediation, fact-finding, or arbitration, either individually or in combination.

In the case of fact-finding, the facts may be made available to the parties only, or they may be made public, depending on the wishes of the parties or the statutory procedures, whichever applies.

In the case of arbitration, the parties may agree voluntarily to arbitrate the terms to be included in an agreement or the meaning and interpretation of the agreement. They may decide whether the arbitration result is to be advisory or binding. If such action by agreement is not taken, government may elect to provide compulsory or voluntary arbitration. The results may be considered either advisory or binding on the parties, depending upon the legislation.

Among the alternatives to the strike which have been developing in the private sector and which may serve as models for the public sector are intervention procedures which combine some of these ideas:

* Government-ordered mediation and fact-finding have developed under the Railway Labor Act.

* The Taft-Hartley revisions of the Wagner Act called for presidential intervention in strikes considered to be national emergencies; the intervention combines a cooling-off period, mediation and fact-finding, and a requirement that strikers cast secret ballots on the employer's last offer.

* A more recent proposal, popularly dubbed "Russian Roulette," is a form of compulsory arbitration in which a board studies the final offers of both parties and selects one of them as the final settlement.

Also available to the public sector are these other models of private sector efforts to adjust differences and reach solutions short of a strike situation. These, like voluntary arbitration, are procedures arrived at by joint agreement short of government intervention:

* Ongoing Human Relations Committees composed of union and company people whose object it is to learn from the parties' experience with the agreement and to jointly develop solutions to be laid on the bargaining table at the termination of the agreement.

* Continuing joint technical committees in areas such as job evaluation and wage incentive administration.

* The "living document," a contract which can be changed by mutual consent at any time during the term of the agreement and as the parties feel the need.

All of the procedures discussed in this section are designed to be impasse procedures, to settle differences without a strike. The law may prohibit or enjoin a strike but the problems will remain unless some other method resolves the impasse.

The lockout in public sector employment is not generally considered a viable part of the collective bargaining process, although this action has been threatened by some school boards.

In the absence of the coercive element characteristic of the strike or lockout, the remaining "coercive tool" to move the parties toward agreement is information — economic facts. These include the cost of living, productivity, and comparisons of wages by occupation, by area and by governmental unit. The ability to pay is omitted from this procedure because only the representatives of the citizens can decide this since it involves making decisions as to taxing and allocation of resources.

As statistical resources and economic data are developed at both the state and federal level, the possibility exists of economic fact-finding as an ongoing process, acting on the parties and available to the public, to encourage decision-making based on fact and in advance of the labor dispute.

Such economic fact-finding may be considered as a strike alternative, as a supplement to ad hoc fact-finding, conciliation, mediation and arbitration, and as a guide to the public as to what is reasonable and competitive with respect to wages and other conditions of employment for the people who provide their services. It cannot, however, serve to solve all the very complex disputes involving non-wage questions such as seniority, merit employment, crew sizes and other conditions of work, but if the economic part of the collective bargaining process can be made subject to objectively determined data, chances for agreement on at least the wage issue can be improved, and perhaps the incidence of strikes over this issue can be reduced.

A VERY PUBLIC BUSINESS: II
THE BELL TELEPHONE SYSTEM
STRIKES OF 1968

Introduction

The Bell System case was selected as the initial case for three reasons:

1. Development of collective bargaining in the Bell System reflects the evolution of labor-management relations in the private sector over a period of nearly seventy years and includes development of public policy on bargaining.

2. Bell System operations resemble those in both the public and private sectors. Internal decision-making processes are characteristic of private enterprise management. When these decisions intersect with the public interest, the decision-making processes become profoundly political in nature, resembling those of a public agency.

3. The case illustrates union and corporate bargaining strategies at a very basic level.

During the period covered by the case, public attitudes and policy changed from a stance which discouraged the growth of unions to one which encouraged their growth. The Bell System response to these changes was, in microcosm, a reflection of private business behavior over the span of years. It is a reflection of the evolution of union-management relations, the strategies employed by both labor and management, and the evolution of the law.

An example of the hybrid character of the Bell System is collective bargaining over rates of pay which result in increased costs which may or may not be absorbed into the consumer's rate structure, depending upon the decision of a public rate-making body which has access to the company's financial record. This process is similar to that of a purely public agency which must secure public approval of its budget and has special problems if that budget includes increased taxes to the public. The need for increased taxes by a public agency, like the telephone utility's need for increased rates, may arise out of a collective bargaining agreement. In both cases, there may be considerable consumer or taxpayer opposition.

The characteristic which most distinguishes the Bell System or any public agency from private enterprise is the degree of freedom which

it has to alter the price of its product — the degree to which
a free market is operative. The private firm, in normal circumstances,
prices its product according to market advantage. The public agency
and a utility must persuade public bodies that proposed changes in
rates are needed by the organization and can be borne by the citizens.

Although the Bell System is highly complex, the bargaining process
illustrated in the case is rather straightforward and is typical of the
private sector collective bargaining that is so profoundly influencing
public sector labor-management relations at present.

For each of these reasons, the Bell System case serves as a bridge
between collective bargaining practices developed in the private sector and the more recent introduction of collective bargaining in the
burgeoning public sector.

Chronology

January, 1968	Communications Workers of America's Collective Bargaining Policy Committee met to set goals for bargaining with the Bell System. The emphasis was on a wage increase to keep up with the rising cost of living. A strike appeared likely from the mood of the membership.
	In the same month, the Bell Telephone Council of International Brotherhood of Electrical Workers met to set goals. The IBEW represents a smaller group of workers in some of the Bell Telephone Companies. Goals, in addition to a large pay increase, included an effort to end the pattern system of bargaining which has meant that IBEW members have to go along with the key bargain determined by the CWA.
February, March, 1968	Bargaining between the CWA and Western Electric, an AT&T subsidiary, chosen to negotiate the pattern settlement for the industry, proceeded without agreement.
March 7, 1968	Bargaining began between Illinois Bell Telephone Company and the IBEW locals which represented a majority of Illinois Bell's employees. Similar bargaining sessions, devoted largely to local issues not related to the key bargain, were underway in other Bell companies. In Illinois, no progress was made, and a strike was authorized.
March 12, 1968	Western Electric installers, CWA members in the key bargaining unit, rejected the company's final offer and indicated willingness to strike. The strike deadline was twice postponed while informal talks continued but they too failed.
April 18, 1968	CWA went on strike against all Bell Telephone Companies, the first coast-to-coast strike against the Bell System in 21 years.
May 5, 1968	CWA officials announced the end of the strike after 18 days, when a majority of members across the nation accepted the settlement.

May 6,
1968
Illinois Bell offered IBEW locals a new three-year contract, based on the pattern settlement with CWA. The
unions rejected the offer.

May 8,
1968
IBEW struck Illinois Bell. Federal mediators sought,
in May and June, to end the strike but failed.

June,
July,
1968
Because the IBEW strike threatened television coverage
of the Democratic National Convention in Chicago,
Mayor Richard J. Daley entered negotiations, but
succeeded only in salvaging convention coverage.

August 31,
1968
IBEW members voted to reject the three-year contract
based on the pattern settlement with CWA.

September 7,
1968
IBEW members voted to reject an 18-month contract
offer that was essentially the same as the proposal union
negotiators turned down the previous April.

September 21,
1968
IBEW members finally voted for acceptance of the three-
year contract, ending a 137-day strike, the longest in
Bell history.

Communications Workers of America

1

"The voice with the smile will be gone for a while," Joseph Anthony Beirne said to newsmen as he joined a Washington, D.C., picket line at 3 p.m., April 18, 1968.* His gesture marked the start of the first coast-to-coast strike in 21 years against the giant Bell Telephone System, the nation's biggest business.

The basic issue was money, the complicated wage structure for the 400,000 men and women employed by 21 Bell System companies under contracts with Beirne's union, the AFL-CIO Communications Workers of America. The solution would affect up to one million American workers: the CWA members, Bell System employees in other unions and in no unions, plus men and women employed by telephone companies outside the Bell System, which have little choice but to go along with the Bell wage settlements.

Spiraling costs of living (up almost 7 percent since the last wage negotiations) sparked the controversy. In Beirne's union — and in others in the Bell System — there were increasingly restive employees who were demanding more money, convinced that the Bell System's offer just wasn't enough to let them keep up with their expenses. But the companies had made their biggest offer in their history and were, in turn, under pressure from government economists not to get too far out of line on wages, thus adding to the powerful inflationary trend.

Beirne was a man in the middle, caught between the pressures of his own membership and the power of the richest corporation in the world. History had put him there, this 57-year-old son of Irish immigrants, who had welded together a strongly centralized union, shaped carefully to correspond to the strongly centralized Bell industry.

Beirne had been president of the Communications Workers of America for a quarter of a century, since he was in his early 30's, and is a powerful voice in the top leadership of the AFL-CIO. In some ways he's an old-fashioned labor loyalist, in other ways he's a modernist, who's learned to accommodate to the vast automation of the industry

---

*Joseph A. Beirne resigned as head of the CWA in 1974, after this case was written. He died September 2, 1974.

and who urges constant modernization of the labor movement to keep up with changing economic and social conditions.

"Joe Beirne probably keeps his organization as modern as the Bell System keeps its own," commented a labor department observer before the start of the strike. CWA headquarters in Washington, D.C., include busy computers and a staff of costly consultants in labor-management relations who advise Beirne and his people on economic policy and bargaining strategy.

The modern methods have helped Beirne compensate for the lack of traditional muscle in his tightly run organization. A healthy proportion of the members are women telephone operators — "the voice with the smile" — and the industry is so highly automated that no strike can have any immediately devastating effect. Beirne himself had once said that a strike against the Bell System had become about as meaningful as "throwing pebbles at the Queen Mary while it steamed down New York harbor." Why, then, was he engaged in a strike, when he felt it an increasingly ineffective weapon in the telephone industry? One reason was the strong rank and file pressure for militant action to get more money, a pressure that had been growing in many other well-established unions throughout the country in the 1960s. Sometimes a strike fills a need of a union membership, and this one had been brewing for months.

Beirne himself has long sought other ways of bringing pressure on the industry, among them modern public relations and advertising techniques. A good example is his national advertising campaign during the months before the 1968 strike. The CWA spent three-quarters of a million dollars on image-building newspaper ads in about 40 major cities, in Time and Business Week magazines, and on spot ads on about 80 radio stations. Their message was that "CWA is a reasonable union" and is seeking only a fair share of the Bell System's immense revenue. The ads were aimed at company stockholders and public officials, at people who help make opinion, and were meant to show that a strike by such responsible union members could only mean that the company must be wrong. The campaign was a brand new kind of economic pressure on management, and an interesting parallel to the Bell System's own heavy campaign of image-building advertising.

Behind the wage issue that brought on the 1968 strikes lies the complex question of how to bargain with so many people in such an intricate network of companies. The system of bargaining that has evolved is part of an unfinished story that starts, perhaps, as far back as 1876, when Alexander Graham Bell was issued patent No. 174,465 for his new gadget.

Illustration I. One of the series of advertisements run in newspapers and magazines by Communications Workers of America in a three-quarters of a million dollar ad campaign, a new kind of union economic pressure.

From its earliest days, managers of the growing Bell System kept tight control of its patents, granting their use in return for a stake in the newly organizing operating companies. The outlines of the present system had taken shape by 1900 when American Telephone & Telegraph Company became the top holding company in the structure.

The growth of the American Telephone & Telegraph Company from those early days to the electronic marvel of today is certainly one of the great success stories of American business. (The Telegraph in the name has been retained although it no longer has anything but historical meaning. AT&T once owned 30 percent interest in Western Union, but got rid of it in 1913 when public sentiment against monopolies was building and a trust-busting suit against AT&T was being talked about.)

"We have the world's largest computer," states a Bell System advertisment of 1968. "It is our nationwide communications-switching network.

"The switching network connects 102 million telephones and other telecommunications devices. It permits you to reach any of these phones or devices at will.

"That is its distinguishing feature — the 'at your demand' interconnection of 'stations' anywhere in the country — for messages involving information of any kind — video, written, drawn, data and voice. Today, there are about five million billion possible different connections."

Bell telephone users average 304 million local calls and 18 million long distance calls in one day.

AT&T is at the peak of the pyramid that runs this complex system, a system that underlies almost every function of modern society. It includes 24 operating companies which it refers to as "consolidated companies" or "subsidiaries" in its annual report. (See Appendix I) AT&T owns 100 percent of the stock of 16 of the companies, controlling interest (up to 99.3%) in five, and a minority interest in three. Together the companies own 88 million telephones.

In addition, AT&T is the sole owner of the Western Electric Company, which manufactures the equipment for all the operating companies and is itself one of the biggest businesses in the nation, with sales in 1968 of $4,032,000,000 and earnings of $192,120,000. About three-quarters of Western Electric's sales are to Bell System companies. Most of the rest are to the United States government, whom Western Electric serves as prime contractor on the Sentinel missile defense system and an important supplier to the Atomic Energy Commission and the National Aeronautics and Space Administration.

AT&T and Western Electric jointly own the prestigious Bell Laboratories, Inc., which conducts basic research and works on new developments for the system, work such as research on laser beams as a step toward a future system of carrying information on light waves, perhaps someday carrying hundreds of thousands of conversations simultaneously. With 6,500 scientists and engineers, Bell Labs makes up the largest research system in the United States.

The tightly-unified AT&T organization has assets of more than $40 billion, more than any other company in the world. Gross income for 1968 was $14.5 billion — more than the combined yearly revenues of the four most populous states in the union. In 1968, the system employed 872,018 people.

Who owns AT&T? As of the end of 1968, 3,142,075 shareholders, so widely diffused that the largest holder owns less than one-tenth of one percent. Such diffusion of such a tremendous organization inevitably means means strong management control.

The center of the management complex is AT&T headquarters in New York (at 195 Broadway, abbreviated by Bell people to just "195"), with a staff of 3,200. Headquarters serves as banker for the operating companies, provides central consulting and managerial services to coordinate the vast system, and operates the long lines department. That's long distance. The long lines department is the link between the phones of each Bell company and the independent phone companies; in addition, it handles all overseas long distance calls.

Staff at 195 includes specialists in every area of the business: accounting, public relations, finance, engineering, personnel. Close consultation with these specialists and intercompany conferences help the operating companies achieve the uniform quality of service on which the Bell System prides itself.

Observers of the system sometimes wonder to what extent the uniformity is due to dictation from headquarters. A nationwide policy, once arrived at, certainly allows little room for deviation, but perhaps it's more significant that Bell executives don't seem to have any great desire to deviate from a policy. Bell officials in the operating companies see themselves as part of a nationwide industry and say that through frequent conferences — and, of course, telephone calls — they have a voice in the formulation of policy. They tend to talk of industry-wide "guidelines" rather than of directives from New York.

AT&T links operating companies in other ways, too, chiefly through considerable interchange of personnel at many levels of management. A company executive who has always worked for the Bell System, for example, may have come up the management ladder in a series of jobs in different operating companies. Parallel operating practices make this interchange easy and aid in intercompany communication. The interchange has been facilitated in recent years through establishment of central assessment centers to appraise candidates for first-level supervisory positions. Sixty-three of the centers across the country evaluate about 11,000 employees a year to pick those with the kind of management and personnel skills that are hard to observe in day-to-day jobs.

In many ways the companies make up a strongly inbred system; most executives have come through the ranks and know intimately the details of many jobs under their direction. Every president of AT&T, for example, has risen in this fashion.

For the complex of reasons, the Bell System is a unified whole, with considerable uniformity of policy in all areas of operation. Whether guidelines or directives, the messages come through clearly, along well-defined chains of command. Students of management structure are impressed with the efficiency of the process.

Some wonder about it, though. Commented one observer in another utility industry, "Bell is a good place to work, but it's frustrating. If the answer is not in the book, you can't get it."

The extent of the uniformity is important because of its effect on labor-management relations.

Labor Organization in the Bell System

The welding of the nation's telephone system into a powerful business organization through the last two decades of the 19th century and the beginning of the 20th was not matched by a comparable mushrooming of labor organizing. The tumultuous job of forging labor unions was left to the hardier folk in the mines and heavy industry. Not until the days of the Wagner Act in the 1930s did unionism take any real hold in the telephone industry.

But the idea was there and there was some sporadic early organizing chiefly by one of the big trade unions, the International Brotherhood of Electrical Workers, founded in 1891. In Indianapolis, in Buffalo, in Cleveland, in Detroit, and in other places, electricians who got telephone jobs formed locals. In Illinois in 1910, the IBEW formed a unit of Illinois Bell electricians and attached it to a big local of building trades electricians, a union that was to play a major role in the Bell System's 1968 troubles.

The IBEW even tried organizing women telephone operators, forming a local in Boston in 1912. But many of the craft-oriented electricians worried about that; they didn't want women dominating their union and it was eventually split off into a separate department. ("We think there can be no rule of ethics or of human right which requires men handling the sting of electricity," read their executive board report in 1918, "to submit forever to the rule of telephone operators in their methods and conditions of work because they have tried that arrangement for a while.")

In many ways the relationship between AT&T and the gradually-developing unions of its employees parallels those relationships in any other big American enterprise. Nowhere were unions accepted with enthusiasm. Even the basic idea of unionism, that employees have a right to some say in the determination of wages and working conditions, was hard fought by business and industry. The greater the threat of union strength, the greater was the employer opposition, reaching its peak in opposition to the National Labor Relations Act of 1935 (the Wagner Act), labor's bill of rights.

The labor market prior to the Wagner Act was very different from today's labor market. Most of the workers in the large basic industries were unorganized or were members of associations dominated by management. There were only about four million union members, concentrated in construction, transportation, mining, and the clothing industry. Employers made no secret of their hostility to unions and they resorted to lockouts, intimidation, blacklists, yellow-dog contracts and various kinds of spying and discrimination to keep union organizations out of their plants.

There were bitter strikes and lockouts in some Bell companies, too, and employees who wanted to join unions might face demotion, suspension or dismissal. But the record is not one of great militancy on either side. Women workers, particularly office workers, were often hard to organize. And the Bell companies were in many ways progressive employers; a good pension system, for example, was started in 1913.

The story of Bell System unions has been told in considerable detail in a controversial United States Senate subcommittee investigation, in 1950 and 1951, into labor-management relations in the Bell System. The subcommittee report details the historical background this way:

". . . no really successful labor organizing occurred in the Bell System until after the National Labor Relations Act had been held to be constitutional by the United States Supreme Court in 1937. Prior thereto, employee organizations in the system were, for the most part, employee representation plans and associations sponsored by the Bell companies. These plans and associations had their beginnings in a directive issued in 1919 by the Postmaster General, under whose direction the telephone industry had been placed during World War I. The directive appears to have resulted from a telephone strike caused, at least in part, by the firing of telephone employees for union activity. The directive ordered that employees in the telephone industry be given the right to bargain, either individually or collectively, with the telephone companies.

"Immediately after the issuance of the Postmaster General's directive, and the recognition of unionism embodied therein, the vice president of American Telephone & Telegraph Company announced the formation of the American Bell Association. For 16 years thereafter, the company-formed and -fostered employee representation plans and associations continued in the system. The purpose of these organizations was to improve working conditions and discuss grievances which the employees might have with the company. Each Bell company provided the funds, services, and control for its association, and all employees of the company automatically became members.

"When the National Labor Relations Act was about to be passed in 1935, certain changes were made in these company-sponsored employee plans and associations in anticipation of the passage of the act, such as initiating the collection of dues from members, but basically the structure and officers appear to have remained much the same.

"In the two-year period between passage of the National Labor Relations Act and the Supreme Court's holding of the act to be constitutional, the attitude of the Bell System companies appears to have been one of hope and conviction that the statute would be declared unconstitutional, and this philosophy was imparted to the system's employees.

"After the Supreme Court's decision in 1937, upholding the constitutionality of the Labor Act,[1] the representation plans and associations in the companies were replaced by some 184 unions, which sprang up within the unusually short space of a few months all over the telephone industry. Recognition of these unions by Bell System companies appears to have been quickly secured, and contracts easily negotiated. Methods for handling grievances were immediately established. Some of these unions were charged before the National Labor Relations Board, and found by that Board to be company dominated.[2]

"In 1939, 25 or more of the unions in the Bell System formed the National Federation of Telephone Workers, a loose confederation in which each union remained autonomous, with no limitation on its right to negotiate contracts. Each union sent delegates to a national assembly and paid dues on the basis of its membership. None of the Bell companies raised any question of recognition when NFTW was formed, and delegates had no difficulty in getting time off to attend NFTW national conventions. NFTW grew in strength in the years that followed, although from time to time unions withdrew their membership. By 1947, there were 49 independent Bell unions in NFTW.

"As the years passed, whatever domination or influence the Bell System companies had over the independent unions in NFTW disappeared, and a struggle between the companies and the unions began to develop. Experiences in the 1945-46 and 1947 bargaining negotiations demonstrated the basic weakness in NFTW's structure resulting from the complete autonomy of its unions, and showed the need for a more unified approach to bargaining.

"In December, 1945, NFTW had agreed upon certain wage and other demands to be sought by all the member unions, but by February, 1946, 32 of its unions, acting independently of one another, had signed contracts for less than the agreed-upon demands. The remaining 17 NFTW unions continued to press for the demands that had been agreed upon, but being confronted with the wage pattern that had emerged through contracts negotiated by the other unions, they failed to reach agreements with their companies and a strike deadline was set for March 7, 1946. The wage agreement for the system, reached shortly before the strike deadline, between AT&T's Vice President, C.F. Craig, and NFTW's President, Joseph A. Beirne, . . . not only averted the strike, but accomplished a wage increase in the space of a few hours for all the employees in the system, which was higher in amount than any which the other 32 NFTW unions had been able to negotiate in their individual company bargaining negotiations. It became necessary to reopen the contracts of these 32 unions, as well as those of other unions not affiliated with NFTW, in order to accord all system employees the full benefits of the Craig-Beirne agreement and maintain uniformity in the system's wage structure.

"In the light of this effective system-wide bargaining from one central point, NFTW set up a policy committee to coordinate the bargaining of its unions in the 1947 negotiations. But the Bell System companies were determined not to have the national bargaining of 1946 repeated. The demands of the NFTW unions in 1947 included ten national items (wages, union security, narrowing of area differentials, reduction in the number of town classifications, shortened wage progression schedules, service assistant's title and job description, jurisdiction of work clause, provisions for treatment of union officers and representatives, improved vacation plan, and improved pension provisions) which the unions believed affected all Bell System employees. In the first months of bargaining negotiations in 1947, none of the Bell System companies would bargain on any of the 10 items, and AT&T officials likewise refused to make any commitments with respect to them. Finally, the telephone workers voted to authorize their officers to call a strike, and the central policy committee of NFTW was empowered to set a strike date upon a favorable referendum of the members. The strike was set for April 7, 1947, and on that day, some 375,000 Bell System employees went on strike.

"Just prior to, and during the early weeks of the strike, the companies agreed to take a position on wages, one of the 10 national items, but the uniform position of the companies was that no wage increases were justified, although they would all agree to local state arbitration by persons selected by the governors of the States, providing the arbitrators based their findings on the companies' community wage theory. The unions rejected arbitration on the terms specified by the companies.

"After the strike had been in progress some six to seven weeks, the Governor of Minnesota pressured the Northwestern Bell Telephone Company into making a wage increase offer. But before the company would make any offer, it required the union with which it was bargaining to withdraw from the policy committee which had been set up by the NFTW to deal with the dispute. Identical action was taken by every company in the Bell System. The effect of this uniform action was to divide NFTW into segments and thereby weaken the effectiveness of union bargaining.

"When the Northwestern Company finally made its wage increase proposal, NFTW disbanded its policy committee, and shortly thereafter all the associated companies began offering the same increase. The strike was settled on the uniform pattern of $2, $3, and $4 per week in all the companies throughout the Bell System.

"The long duration of the 1947 strike (44 days) left NFTW prostrate. The strike demonstrated again the weakness of NFTW's internal structure, for as the strike wore on, NFTW's autonomous union members began to break away and sign contracts, resulting in the collapse of the strike.

"The 1946 convention of NFTW had laid the groundwork for curing this structural defect when it voted a change in its internal structure, subject to ratification by referendum. A new constitution was adopted abolishing the loose federation of autonomous unions, and creating increased centralized powers in a single international union under the new name of Communications Workers of America. The individual unions were to be known as divisions, retaining the power to negotiate contracts, which would be subject to the approval of CWA's executive board."

The union affiliated with the CIO in 1949 and has since further centralized its activities, matching more closely the organization of the companies.

The new union set about lobbying in Washington, too, and won a signal victory in getting the senate subcommittee to conduct an investigation into labor management relations in the Bell System. Beirne, who was looking for government support for nationwide negotiating with AT&T, was chief witness for CWA and testified for five days, stressing AT&T control over the operating companies and insisting that labor relations were very bad.

Company witnesses took strong issue with Beirne; they denied, for example, that AT&T controls labor relations policies and collective bargaining in its associated companies. They said there is a plan of decentralized operation in the Bell System, under which each company operates as a separate corporation, managing its own affairs independently of the American Telephone & Telegraph Company. They said they didn't think labor relations were particularly bad but, if they were, Beirne was helping to make them so.

The subcommittee dwelt at length on the question of autonomy of individual Bell System companies. The facts, it claimed, "demonstrate that any description of the local associated Bell companies as autonomous corporations is theoretical and can only be justified in the strictest legal sense, for . . . these companies function as parts in a closely integrated corporate system completely and directly controlled by the AT&T management. This AT&T control flows from its stock ownership of most of the associated companies, from license contracts which it has with all the operating associated companies in the system, and from the long continued control which AT&T executives have exercised through the years over promotions and salary increases of administrative officers in the associated companies."

The subcommittee claimed that under "this controlling influence . . . there have developed among the various Bell companies uniform bargaining strategies and approaches which have slowed and thwarted the collective bargaining process on the local company level" and that the resulting integrated wage structure has caused poor labor-management relations at the local level.

It dealt at length with the license contracts under which the Bell System companies act. The report stated: "These contracts serve as the medium through which AT&T ties together the Bell System into one complete operating whole. Under the terms of these contracts each operating company is given a specified territory within which to operate, and is licensed to use all telephones, telephone devices, apparatus, methods and systems needed for its telephone business which are covered by patents owned or controlled by AT&T, or which AT&T may have the right to authorize it to use. AT&T, under the contracts, coordinates the physical operations of the system through its maintenance of proper connections between the transmission lines of the licensed associated companies, as well as between places within the territory of the licensed associated company which the latter is not authorized to connect. To make the operation of the system complete, the contracts also provide for the maintenance by AT&T of a source of supply for standardized Bell System telephones and related equipment to be manufactured under its patents and sold to the associated companies . . .

"The greatest impact of these license contracts upon labor-management relations in the Bell System results from the provisions in the contracts under which AT&T furnishes to the operating associated companies functional services essential to the operation of the system. These services, which the Bell System management considers indispensable, pertain to all phases of the business of the operating companies, including labor-management relations, and are furnished by AT&T through a central organization which . . . relieves the individual operating companies from the necessity of attempting to perform the services themselves . . .

"The management witnesses maintained at the hearings that the services performed by AT&T under these license contracts are in the form of information, advice, and suggestions which are merely advisory and do not affect the responsibility of the associated company to make its own decisions. But, as long ago as 1939, the Federal Communications Commission, after an exhaustive four-year investigation of the Bell System, found that the influence of the AT&T executives upon actual details of administration within the associated companies could be carried to any degree considered desirable by the AT&T management . . .

"This controlling influence of AT&T, as the evidence shows, has had a direct effect upon the course of labor relations in the system. Much of this effect, under present bargaining conditions, is disruptive. For instance, there have developed among the various Bell companies uniform bargaining strategies and approaches which have slowed and thwarted the collective bargaining process on the local company level, until bargaining has steadily become less and less effective, and strikes and threats of strikes throughout the system are becoming more and more common . . .

"The integrated wage structure that has been established in the system is another factor resulting from this closely coordinated control which has complicated collective bargaining at the local company level and engendered poor labor-management relations. Management insists that Bell System wage rates are based on the prevailing wage rates in each community, and that, therefore, bargaining on wage increases is a purely local matter which must take place on the local company level. But the evidence shows that the closely woven Bell System reflects itself in a wage policy extending beyond the local labor market areas in which the telephone exchanges exist, and as a means of maintaining stability in the system's wage structure, wage differentials have been established between the various Bell companies, as well as between different wage areas within each company. These differentials are therefore factors for consideration in any bargaining on wage changes, and this fact prompted the national telephone panel, in applying the wage-stabilization policy of World War II to the telephone industry, to conclude that 'any realistic application of wage policy to the telephone industry must take into account the existence of the Bell System itself.' . . ."

Government Regulation of the Bell System

Nothing really came of the Senate subcommittee hearings and report in 1950 and 1951, but the very fact that the hearings were held points up one important aspect of AT&T's existence: the extent of government involvement in the affairs of the holding company and all its subsidiaries. In many ways the operation of the system is a very public business. The chairman of the board, H.I. Romnes, in the 1969 annual report, referred to AT&T as "a public trust under public regulation."

AT&T stock is privately owned, of course; its more than half a billion shares are owned by more than three million shareholders. But the nature of the business is of such concern to the public and to the very operation of national life that many agencies of government, at all levels, have developed regulatory proceedings to deal with different aspects of AT&T operation. It's a complex network.

The federal government concerns itself with AT&T in a number of ways, among them:

1. The Federal Communications Commission, which has jurisdiction over AT&T's interstate and foreign long distance operations and approves or disapproves of new types of service the company wants to offer in interstate commerce. It has the power to review all financial aspects of this area of the business in order to set rates to allow the company a fair return on its investment.

    In the setting of rates to allow a fair return on shareholders' investment in the business, the FCC might concern itself to some extent with wage rates, which make up a large share of the operating costs of the business.

2. Congress, which determines the policies of regulation. Committees of both houses of Congress have concerned themselves with anti-trust proceedings and with rate setting, as well as with employee relations.

3. The Justice Department, whose anti-trust division has from time to time been concerned with the relationship between AT&T and its wholly-owned manufacturing subsidiary, Western Electric.

4. The Defense Department, with whom Western Electric has large contracts.

5. The General Services Administration, which has a Transportation and Public Utility section with authority to represent the federal government in rate negotiations.

6. The Comptroller General, whose office audits such areas of AT&T business as the use of leased lines by the Air Force.

7. The Labor Department, which was deeply involved in negotiation of the 1968 contracts with AT&T unions because of government efforts to hold the line on inflationary wage settlements in all basic industries.
8. The President's Council of Economic Advisers, which has sought during the 1960s to establish guidelines on reasonable wage and price increases.

In addition to federal regulation, each state government, except Texas, has some sort of public utilities commission with the power to set rates, based on the investment of the local operating company within its jurisdiction. Most of these are considered rather weak regulatory agencies, and the inter-relationships in the system are so complex as to be largely beyond their scope.

Some municipalities also concern themselves with telephone system operation and regulation, which further relates AT&T and its operating companies to public policy.

An industry in which government is such a day-to-day partner has a particular concern for public opinion and is, more than most big industries, susceptible to public pressure. This was certainly illustrated in the 1968 labor negotiations, in which the labor department played an important role.

"The Federal Mediation and Conciliation Service and the Department of Labor — at the highest level — were involved," said an executive of one of the operating companies. "They were very interested in the wage relationships being preserved, the relationships between wages of telephone workers and other big groups, like auto workers, rubber workers and so on."

The Growth of Pattern Bargaining

In the years since the 1947 nationwide strike against the Bell System and the 1951 Senate subcommittee attempt to require nationwide bargaining with the CWA, a kind of pattern bargaining developed between the AT&T companies and the Communications Workers of America and other Bell System unions.

In the early 1950s, the union had to submit to the corporation's demand for individual bargaining with the major subsidiary companies. But at the same time, the union was strengthening its national structure and was seeking ways to implement national union goals. The pattern system that has evolved allows the CWA to concentrate its bargaining on major issues at one location; when agreement is reached there, union members in all bargaining units vote on that major settlement, which is incorporated in separate contracts with the operating companies. The system is, indeed, a kind of nationwide bargaining.

While the pattern negotiations on major issues, including wages, are going on, CWA bargainers in local units are meeting with negotiators for the other AT&T companies, if their contracts are approaching an expiration date. They talk about strictly local issues and settle nothing definitely until word comes down — on both sides of the table — that the pattern has been set. The pattern is then translated into local terms (there are some wage differentials based on geographic locations) and is usually quickly accepted by the local bargainers.

Obviously, the pattern has to be acceptable to AT&T as well as to the pattern-setting company. And what is going to be acceptable to AT&T is generally fairly well established long in advance. Labor negotiators for the companies meet with AT&T officials during the year and present local wage surveys, Bureau of Labor Statistics figures, and other pertinent material for general discussion. The exact pattern that would be acceptable is not set at those meetings, but participants have said they had a general idea "about where it would end up."

When the pattern is set, the negotiating is about at an end. There is some leeway for local adjustments in some areas within the pattern, but there is no freedom to alter the outer limits. Some years it's been a dollar pattern, with certain increases across the board; some years it's been a percentage pattern.

It seems to be a system that suits both management and the CWA. Neither has any desire for basically different contracts in the different operating companies. Both sides use the word "chaos" to describe a totally free system of local bargaining. It's a solution tailor made to suit the realities of bargaining in the Bell System — at least with the CWA, the union that represents the largest proportion of employees, about 68 percent.

"I just can't see how anything else would work," one Bell insider commented.

The 1968 Negotiations

The 1966 contracts between CWA and the Bell System companies provided for a wage reopening midway through the contract period. The Collective Bargaining Policy Committee met in January, 1968, in Washington, D.C., to set its goals. There was strike talk even then. Before the end of the month Beirne sent a letter to each union member, stating:

"On March 6, 1968, we will have an agreement on a wage increase or we will be in negotiating trouble.

"The Western Electric Installers have been selected as our wage pattern setters. Their contract wage reopener has the March 6th effective date. I know many of you are covered by contracts which have a much later effective date but negotiating procedure in the Bell System makes the Installers' settlement the one which will affect you. The Installers' pattern settlement will be the kind of wage increase you will get when your contract reopener is discussed."

The letter went on to outline 11 contract demands related to wages. The first demand was for "a substantial general wage increase and eliminating merit wage systems. We know our productivity has averaged 7.4% for years. We know the profits of the Bell System topped all previous records in the past year. In fact, the most recent 3 month net profits were almost $537 million; a 7.5% increase over the same quarter in 1966. We know that wage settlements in other industries require us to receive a much greater increase in wage benefits than ever before. We know the increases in living costs require a substantial wage catch-up by us. We know our wage demand can be easily met without any price increase."

Beirne repeated, as CWA was saying in its ad campaign, that the demands were "reasonable and just," then said:

"It is proper for me to honestly report . . . the great pressure we will all be under — from the company management . . . from the various federal and other governmental agencies . . . from the general public. The pressures will take the form of telling us we are helping to cause inflation. We know the wage level is not as high as our very important jobs demand. We know there are great inequities in our wage conditions which should be corrected. Other people will not care about our problems. They will try to belittle our just claims and will try to destroy our unity. There will be a time when even you will have doubts.

"Let us all prepare now to work together, being strengthened by the knowledge we are reasonable people with a just claim.

"How can we all work together? As openers we can start *to think* in a positive way. Let's begin by saying and believing (because it's true) 'My Union is a strong defender of our nation and its communities. It will do nothing harmful to the industry or the country.'

"Or — 'My Union is and has been most reasonable and sagacious. Its demands are never wild or immoderate.'

"Or — 'If there is any trouble or if a strike is necessary, I know my Union has done everything possible to avoid the difficulty. Hence, the blame must be properly placed on management's back.'

". . . I sincerely hope we don't have to strike. If we do, however, I think each of you should know that our Defense Fund has $9,772,384 in it. This is a great deal of money in anybody's language. How far will it stretch? Well, if the Installers picket we expect all Members to observe the picket lines. By April 16th there will be 12 other bargaining units representing approximately 144,000 members involved for their own contract. About a quarter of a million people can be affected.

This means less than $40 per affected Member. A strike, however, involves great sums of money for other costs. It can be reasonably figured therefore, there is *not* $25 per affected Member for the duration of a

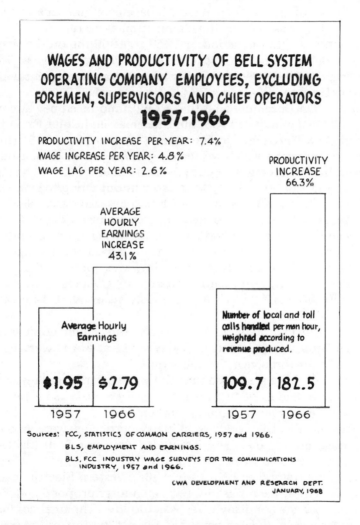

WAGES AND PRODUCTIVITY OF BELL SYSTEM OPERATING COMPANY EMPLOYEES, EXCLUDING FOREMEN, SUPERVISORS AND CHIEF OPERATORS
1957-1966

PRODUCTIVITY INCREASE PER YEAR: 7.4%
WAGE INCREASE PER YEAR: 4.8%
WAGE LAG PER YEAR: 2.6%

PRODUCTIVITY INCREASE 66.3%

AVERAGE HOURLY EARNINGS INCREASE 43.1%

Average Hourly Earnings

Number of local and toll calls handled per man hour, weighted according to revenue produced.

$1.95 $2.79   109.7   182.5

1957   1966   1957   1966

Sources: FCC, STATISTICS OF COMMON CARRIERS, 1957 and 1966.
BLS, EMPLOYMENT AND EARNINGS.
BLS, FCC INDUSTRY WAGE SURVEYS FOR THE COMMUNICATIONS INDUSTRY, 1957 and 1966.

CWA DEVELOPMENT AND RESEARCH DEPT.
JANUARY, 1968

Illustration II. One of a series of charts prepared by Communications Workers of America development and research department to back up the union's economic goals. Wage demands in 1968 were keyed strongly to increased productivity, more so than to cost of living increases. Productivity changes are part of an extensive story of automation prepared by The Diebold Group and paid for by the union.

strike. I put this matter in its proper focus because some believe they should get money from the Union to strike. This is not possible and will not be done. If a just strike is necessary there will be great sacrifices by everyone. I believe you should know this now so you can save your money or prepare in some other way."

The policy committee prepared a 16-page economic analysis to back up its demands. Among the claims it made were:

Productivity: "In the period of 1957 to 1966 the productivity increase in Bell was 66.3%. This represents a yearly average of 7.4%. Associating the productivity in Bell with the wage treatment we find the period 1957 to 1966 had a 23.2% lag in wages.

Profits: "On December 21st the AT&T announced new income records . . . On January 4, 1968, the Chairman and Chief Executive Officer of AT&T predicted an increase in revenues for 1968. This is excellent information which we certainly hope proves to be true. It reflects additional strength to our position concerning the closing of the wage gap and the ability to do so without any price increase.

*"It has been 18 months since our last general increase. Since that time agreements have been reached in three major areas:

"1. The Rubber Worker settlements following a three-month strike against major producers in the rubber industry, averaged more than 44.2 cents for three years in wages only.

"2. The governmental Board — created by Congress — in the railroad shopcraft dispute unanimously awarded 48.14 cents for two years.

"3. The Auto Workers' settlement with the leading companies in the industry, following a 47-day strike at Ford, averaged 58.5 cents for three years in wages only."

CWA officers have said since that the wage offer from Western Electric would have had to be "fantastic" to avert a strike, so great was the pressure from younger union members.

The Western Electric installers, skilled electricians, were among the union's most militant members. They also were among its highest-paid, averaging $154 a week.

Between February 5 and March 6, 1968, Western Electric made four offers to the CWA. Each was met with a counter proposal and the contention that the company offer was too low. The final company offer was termed by the company its "biggest, best offer" in history; it represented, company spokesman said, a 5.6 percent increase in the wage schedule. CWA said it really was only a 5.4 percent increase, and was holding out for 7 percent annually.

On March 12, CWA announced that the Western Electric installers had rejected, by a 15-1 majority, the company's final offer and had indicated their willingness to strike.

The strike deadline was twice postponed while informal talks continued, but they brought no agreement. Beirne offered to take the settlement to arbitration but Western Electric turned down the proposal. The April 18 strike deadline grew closer and there was talk of perhaps negotiating a whole new three-year contract, opening up issues other than wages for bargaining, too, but nothing seemed to be happening.

The Bell System companies "have made every effort to avoid a strike," H.I. Romnes, AT&T Board chairman, told the corporation's annual meeting in Boston, Mass., on April 17. Other companies besides Western Electric were involved because contract deadlines had expired in some of them and Western Electric installers would be picketing most of the rest.

The system was clearly ready for the strike. It had even had a little practice. The New Jersey Bell Telephone Company had been struck on April 15, earlier in the week, by members of the International Brotherhood of Electrical Workers (who hold jobs like the Western Electric installers, but are represented by IBEW instead of CWA). There, executives were manning switchboards and the techniques being worked out there for keeping the phones in operation were under study for the whole Bell System.

Western Electric did make a last-ditch move to avert the strike. It was April 17, the day before the strike deadline, the day Romnes was speaking to assembled stockholders in Boston, telling them of record monthly earnings in March, a big increase in long distance calls, and a record rate for installation of new phones.

In the last-ditch move, Western Electric told CWA it would be interested in exploring a new three-year agreement and would be willing to discuss details at the convenience of the union. It was interpreted by some observers as a significant management concession.

"Too late," said Beirne (who'd been able to deal with last-ditch offers in the past). "We have, regretfully, reached the point of no return. Despite lengthy attempts by both sides, I am convinced it is too late to avoid the strike." He went on to say, with apparently no hint of hostility, that informal talks would continue and the union remained available for talks any time.

Minutes before the strike began on April 18, Beirne insisted at a news conference that the union's position "isn't frozen" and that he and other negotiators were "still trying very hard to find a way to convince the management of the Bell System that our proposals are reasonable." He went from the news conference out to the street to join the picket line.

In New York, at the start of the big strike, Ben S. Gilmer, president of AT&T, called the strike "regrettable and unnecessary." He repeated Romnes' position stated at the stockholders' annual meeting that Western Electric and the other Bell companies "have already made the largest wage offers ever made" by the system.

(No news media account mentioned what CWA insiders say is a fact, that Beirne and Gilmer met face to face a number of times before the start of the strike. One added, "The only way to effectively bargain with the Bell System is to bargain with 195 Broadway. Management tells us frankly they can't make a move on big issues without an okay from 195.")

Bell companies had pointed out consistently that their offer was in line with increases in other industries and was already straining the 5 percent a year level that government economists considered "not wildly inflationary" at that point. The government guidelines had been stated by the President's Council of Economic Advisers (CEA), which was urging wage and price restraint to put a brake on inflation.[3] AT&T, of course, is particularly sensitive to such government demands and the whole question of its rates and earnings was then under review by the Federal Communications Commission.

An editorial in the New York Times on the day the strike started pointed up the economic enigma. It noted that Beirne had been under strong rank and file pressure for militant action. It stated, on the other hand, that the company's offer of about 5.5 percent a year "strains the informal anti-inflation ceiling recommended by the CEA."

But, "even so," the editorial continued, "the substantially higher settlements won in recent months by workers in automobile, construction, copper and other key industries have a much greater impact on the thinking of the telephone unionists than the company's insistence that a greater increase would aggravate the wage-price spiral, to everybody's detriment."

The Times, apparently sympathizing with both sides, noted that Beirne was "the last union leader anyone would accuse of being strike-happy" and that he was well aware that the extent of automation in the telephone industry has made the strike obsolete as an effective instrument for resolving labor-management disputes. The Times concluded that "arbitration represents the sound method for ending this exercise of futility on a basis that will protect everybody involved."

Beirne had suggested arbitration and New York Times endorsement of the idea was valuable support. AT&T companies had uniformly proposed arbitration years before, seeking to avert the 1947 nation-wide strike, but had since then consistently rejected the idea of arbi-

trating contract items, claiming it was no substitute for bargaining.
In 1968, AT&T did not respond to the arbitration suggestion. Both
sides, of course, take a certain risk in arbitration, the risk that they
may lose decisions on matters that they consider important. The
advantage, on the other hand, is that a work stoppage can be averted.

Some observers believe that neither AT&T nor CWA really wanted
to avert the strike, that the strike might actually have had a certain
value as a tool for defusing the tempers of the most militant members
of the CWA. A strike, if it's not too long, can sometimes be to the
advantage of a union.

It is worth considering, at this point, some of the background causes
of strikes, not the surface issues of the bargaining process, but the
kind of underlying forces that can sometimes make a strike inevitable.
Lloyd G. Reynolds has dealt at length with these causes:[4]

"Between 98 and 99 percent of the contract negotiations carried
out in the United States each year result in agreement without a
strike. The possibility of a strike, however, is a central feature of the
bargaining process and the main force making for ultimate agreement.
Where a strike does occur, this usually means either (1) that the true
minimum terms of the parties failed to overlap even under the pressure
imposed by a strike threat, or (2) that one or both parties miscalculated
the true position of the other side. One party, firmly convinced that the
other will improve its final offer, may refuse concessions which it would
have been willing to make had it accurately estimated the other's
intentions. Thus there may occur a strike which nobody wants."

There is also a possibility, Reynolds continues, that one of the
parties does want a strike. He cites some historical examples, stating
that an employer may think a strike is a good way to break a union,
or a radical union may want to build up revolutionary fervor against
the company.

Another background cause, Reynolds says, is "inability of the
parties to compromise their positions." Even where the negotiators
themselves would be willing to compromise, they may be prevented
because they are not free agents. "An absentee corporation president
or board of directors, sitting in the head office and looking at the
balance sheet, may order a plant manager to take a position which
leads inevitably to a strike." On the other hand, "pressure from the
membership may force union negotiators to maintain a position
which they know the company cannot accept.

"Even where compromise is possible, one side may be unwilling
to compromise because it has a low opinion of the other's strength
and thinks it can win its point." The employer may underestimate
the membership, solidarity and financial strength of the union; the

union may underestimate the determination of the employer to resist further concessions.

Beirne added another thought on the subject. "When you have to go on strike," he said, "it means the bargainers have failed. And I'm the bargainer here. The strike is a failure on my part." He added, as might be expected, that management also had failed.

The strike lasted 18 days, with about 220,000 CWA workers out in most areas of the country except New England (where an independent union was soon to conduct its own strike). Supervisors, working long hours, kept the nation's telephones operating so that the strike had little impact on the public.

Negotiations continued during the strike, centered about a new three-year contract instead of sticking to wage reopening talks to cover the final 18 months of the existing contract. The three-year contract had been talked about before, but had not been agreed upon. Beirne had suggested it before the strike started. And an offer to bargain a three-year contract had been the last-ditch attempt by Western Electric to avert the strike, an attempt Beirne said came "too late."

"Renegotiating the contracts permits bargaining on non-wage items such as pensions, subjects which aren't covered under a wage reopener," Beirne said. "This has given us many things to talk about that the CWA Collective Bargaining Policy Committee has long called for."

On April 30, formal bargaining resumed between CWA and Western Electric, in New York, and between CWA and Bell companies in 16 other cities. On May 2, the third day of the new negotiations, a tentative settlement was reached on the key bargain between Western Electric and CWA negotiators. The pattern settlement was then submitted by other Bell companies. The union was to vote across the country on the weekend of May 4 and May 5.

The tentative settlement provided wage increases and additional benefits totalling 8 percent the first year, 6.7 percent the second, and 4.9 percent the third. The average of about 6.5 percent a year was above the CEA guidelines. It was also somewhat higher than other major industrial contract settlements during the preceding year, but not higher than major settlements that came later in 1968. Continuing inflation would seem to account for the difference.

The package increase of 19.6 percent for three years wasn't all money-in-the-pocket because the fringe benefits were a significant part of the settlement. In terms of wages, the settlement meant increases for top-rated employees of $12 a week the first year, $6 the second and $6 the third. As a percentage, the first year wage increase was slightly more than the cost of living increase since the 1966 negotiations.

Not everyone was due for a $12 a week increase, of course. The wage schedule provides many levels of pay, depending upon the nature of the job, the progression schedule for each job, and the geographical wage differentials designed to take into account the differing living costs in differing kinds of areas. For top level operators, for example, the increase was $8 a week and the schedule ranged downward to $4 a week for operators and clerical employees who had not been working long enough to reach the top of their job categories.

Other contract changes affected pension, night differentials, increased overtime for holidays, five weeks of vacation after 25 years, and an increase in the number of paid holidays. These are areas that were opened up to bargaining by agreement to a new three-year contract, instead of sticking to the wage reopening.

The acceptance by Beirne's negotiating committee and the executive board undoubtedly reflected Beirne's own long-time enthusiasm for fringe benefits. There is some opposition to this point of view in his union, and it's probably growing. Most unions were experiencing the same trend in the 1960s; younger members are being called the "pork chop generation." They want more wages now and care less about fringe benefits that will pay off in the future. Particularly do they care less about such issues as job security and union security, issues that were important in past decades. The young members weren't around during the days of labor's struggle to get organized and they aren't much interested in hearing about them.

Many of the pork chop generation had little enthusiasm for the tentative agreement and many did, indeed, vote against the settlement on that first weekend in May. Voting took place in CWA locals concerning contracts with 17 Bell System units; the total vote was to determine whether the whole wage package was accepted or rejected.

Just before midnight on May 5, CWA officials announced that the strike was over because the settlement had been accepted by a vote of 54,680 to 30,721. Fifteen of the units accepted the settlement, but two voted it down: the Western Electric installers, the key bargainers, and the unit at Michigan Bell. Those units were instructed to vote again, after some local contract improvements were made, improvements that did not affect the nationwide package. The later votes did ratify the agreement, but perhaps did not stop the rumbling of discontent among the young members. The strike had cooled them off some, but not entirely. ("Maybe the strike should have been a little longer," one CWA officer has since stated, a bit ruefully.)

So the strike ended after 18 days and the voice with the smile was heard again at the other end of the line — in most places. There were other, smaller strikes still going on against Bell companies in some areas and CWA members were honoring those picket lines — for a while.

What were the results of the strike?

To the average telephone user, it meant little. For him, the highly automated industry operated almost in a normal fashion, much more so than in the 44-day strike in 1947, when automation was less extensive. In 1947, only 59.8 percent of Bell-owned phones were dial-operated; the rest required an operator to complete the call. In 1947, there was no long distance dialing. But in 1968, local calls were 99.8 percent automated, and about 90 percent of long distance calls could be dialed directly. The automated equipment is so sophisticated that it can even police itself to some degree by spotting specific troubles and giving off signals that tell human monitors where the trouble is. If a line fails to function properly, the equipment can also transfer calls automatically to an alternative line.

The only disruptions in service during the 1968 strike were in those services that required manpower, such as person-to-person calls, credit card calls, information, and installation and repairs. Even these were not totally affected because management personnel was able to take over. Because Bell is an up-through-the-ranks industry, these executives knew what to do because they themselves had done the technical jobs before.

AT&T stockholders didn't suffer either. Board Chairman Romnes, reporting on the three-month period that ended May 31, 1968 — the period that included the strike — stated that AT&T had attained the highest revenues and earnings in its 83-year history during that time. Operating revenues for the three-month period were $3.460 billion, compared to $3.233 billion for the same period in 1967; net income was $546.98 million, compared to $495.8 million. Bell companies added more than 700,000 phones during the period, despite the strike, and the number of long distance calls was up 10 percent.

In the annual report at the end of the year, AT&T mentioned the strike only briefly, saying:

> New contracts with the unions, most of them for three-year periods, provided for increases in wages and benefits that come to about 6.5% annually. These agreements were reached after work stoppages lasting from 18 days to five months. The cost was high but not above the levels previously arrived at in other major industries and was necessary to enable the Bell System to continue to attract capable employees in competition with other companies.

The same annual report told stockholders that earnings per share were down a little, but that that was due to the 10 percent federal

CWA Stacks Up Best

COMPARISON OF RECENT MAJOR THREE YEAR SETTLEMENTS

(TOTAL WAGES AND FRINGES)

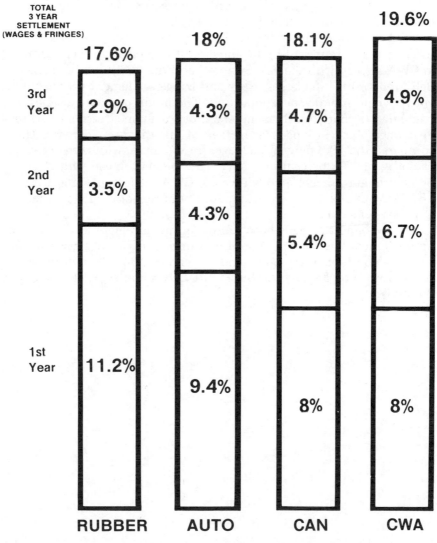

TOTAL
3 YEAR
SETTLEMENT
(WAGES & FRINGES)

	RUBBER	AUTO	CAN	CWA
Total	17.6%	18%	18.1%	19.6%
3rd Year	2.9%	4.3%	4.7%	4.9%
2nd Year	3.5%	4.3%	5.4%	6.7%
1st Year	11.2%	9.4%	8%	8%

Source: Contract Settlements as Publicly Reported CWA Development & Research, May 1968

Illustration III. One of a series of graphs prepared by Communications Workers of America to interpret its 1968 package settlement with Bell.

income tax surcharge. The dividend paid went up. (See Appendix II)

What of the union? Where did its members stand at the end of the strike? They had lost 18 days of pay, with no strike benefits from the defense fund — as they had been forewarned at the end of January. But they did win a pay package somewhat larger than the original offer of slightly more than 5 percent a year.

CWA literature termed the settlement a real victory, stating, "These wage increases represent by far the largest pay package ever bargained in CWA history with the Bell System" and the "2 billion bonanza at Bell" represents "the largest wage and fringe settlement ever negotiated with a single American corporation." The union prepared a series of comparative charts for its members, most of them stressing the three-year wage-plus-fringe package instead of just the wage increase. They compared the 19.6 percent package, for example, with three-year packages of 17.6 percent in rubber, 18.1 percent in can, and 18 percent in auto (negotiated before the CWA settlement), and with 18.5 percent and 18.7 percent in aluminum (negotiated after the CWA settlement).

Still on hand to plague both union and management after the catch-up settlement was the problem of continuing inflation. Between the time the contracts were signed and the end of 1968 the consumer price index, prepared by the Bureau of Labor Statistics, climbed another 3.8 percent.

APPENDIX I

The American Telephone and Telegraph Company

Operating Companies	% of stock held by AT&T
1. New England Telephone & Telegraph Co.	69.5
2. The Southern New England Telephone Co.	17.9
3. New York Telephone Co.	100.0
4. New Jersey Bell Telephone Co.	100.0
5. The Bell Telephone Co. of Pennsylvania	100.0
6. The Diamond State Telephone Co.	100.0
7. The Chesapeake and Potomac Telephone Companies	100.0
Chesapeake & Potomac Telephone Co. (D.C.)	
Chesapeake & Potomac Telephone Co. of Maryland	
Chesapeake & Potomac Telephone Co. of Virginia	
Chesapeake & Potomac Telephone Co. of West Virginia	
8. Southern Bell Telephone & Telegraph Co.	100.0
9. South Central Bell Telephone Co.	100.0
10. The Ohio Bell Telephone Co.	100.0
11. Cincinnati & Suburban Bell Telephone Co.	26.7
12. Michigan Bell Telephone Co.	100.0
13. Indiana Bell Telephone Co.	100.0
14. Wisconsin Telephone Co.	100.0
15. Illinois Bell Telephone Co.	99.3
16. Northwestern Bell Telephone Co.	100.0
17. Southwestern Bell Telephone Co.	100.0
18. The Mountain States Telephone & Telegraph Co.	86.8
19. Pacific Northwest Bell Telephone Co.	89.2
20. The Pacific Telephone & Telegraph Co.	89.7
Bell Telephone Co. of Nevada (wholly owned by Pacific Telephone & Telegraph Co.)	
21. Bell Canada	2.1

Western Electric Company   100.0
(one engineering research center and a network of manufacturing plants, service centers and regional centers for engineering and service and for equipment installation)

Bell Laboratories
(jointly owned by AT&T and Western Electric Co., with 15 locations.)

Source: AT&T Annual Report, 1968

APPENDIX II

Selected Figures from a Ten-Year Review of AT&T and Its Telephone Subsidiaries

000 omitted from dollar amounts except amounts per share

INCOME AND EARNINGS	1968	1967	1966	1959
Operating revenues	$ 14,100,014	$ 13,009,204	$ 12,138,265	$ 7,392,997
Operating expenses	8,442,226	7,816,414	7,260,861	4,479,495
Operating taxes	3,300,010	2,875,935	2,713,493	1,690,289
Operating income	2,357,778	2,316,855	2,158,911	1,223,213
Other income	314,531	274,836	281,165	147,197
Income before interest deductions	2,672,309	2,591,691	2,440,076	1,370,410
Interest deductions	560,405	481,421	402,818	221,641
Net income before minority interests	2,111,904	2,110,270	2,037,258	1,148,769
Net income applicable to AT&T Co. shares	2,051,765	2,049,405	1,978,943	1,113,152
Earnings per share	$ 3.75	$ 3.79	$ 3.69	$ 2.61
Dividends per share	2.40	2.20	2.20	1.57½
Return on average equity	9.26%	9.73%	9.86%	9.77%
Return on average total capital	7.50%	7.77%	7.91%	7.55%
OWNERSHIP AND CAPITAL				
AT&T share owners	3,142,075	3,110,074	3,089,648	1,736,681
Shares outstanding	546,688,000	540,312,000	536,107,000	426,806,000
Equity per share	$41.30	$39.83	$38.23	$27.16
Total Capital	$ 36,858,383	$ 34,484,610	$ 32,016,537	$ 18,892,016
Proportion of debt in total capital	36.44%	35.36%	33.35%	36.26%

APPENDIX II (continued)

TELEPHONE PLANT, SERVICE EMPLOYEES				
Construction expenditures	$ 4,742,144	$ 4,309,620	$ 4,192,564	$ 2,249,143
Total plant, end of year	44,974,991	41,475,671	38,354,182	22,205,475
Telephones in service	88,007,000	83,762,000	79,903,000	57,944,000
Average conversations per day	322,664,000	306,873,000	295,187,000	208,042,000
Overseas conversations per year	15,200,000	12,332,000	9,932,000	3,089,000
Employees at end of year	872,018	841,241	833,559	729,035
Wages and pension and benefit costs	$ 7,651,325	$ 7,124,688	$ 6,724,941	$ 4,323,821

Source: AT&T Annual Report, 1968

Footnotes

1. The decision, a milestone in the nation's labor relations, came in National Labor Relations Board v. Jones & Laughlin Steel Corp. It upheld the 1935 National Labor Relations Act on all contested constitutional grounds and placed interstate manufacturing operations within the pale of the federal commerce power. On the same day, the Supreme Court handed down decisions in four companion cases, all of them upholding the constitutionality and coverage of the act.

2. Labor Board v. Southern Bell Telephone Company, 319 US 50.

3. The Council of Economic Advisers' guidelines, never accepted with wholehearted enthusiasm by either management or labor, had been evolving since they were first stated in a specific fashion in the CEA's annual report of January 1962. The CEA had long been concerned that prices kept creeping upward, with no clear relationship to supply and demand factors in the marketplace, and had made repeated appeals for responsibility and moderation in wage-making and price-making.

The 1962 standards sought to tie wage and price increases to productivity, in the belief that not all wage increases are inflationary, but only those which exceed the rate of increase of productivity. They stated:

"1.   The general guidepost for wages is that the annual rate of increase of total employee compensation (wages and fringe benefits) per man-hour worked should equal the national trend rate of increase in output per man-hour.

"2.   The general guidepost for prices is that prices should remain stable in those industries where the increase of productivity equals the national trend; that prices can appropriately rise in those industries where the increase of productivity is smaller than the national trend; and that prices should fall in those industries where the increase of productivity exceeds the national trend."

The CEA, in its 1969 report, looked back over the period since 1962 and stated: "Between 1962 and 1965, decision makers with discretionary powers generally conformed to the pattern envisaged by the guideposts. There were occasional departures, however. In particular, some industries with higher-than-average productivity gains did not reduce prices as unit labor costs fell. The extent to which the satisfactory performance was enhanced by the efforts of the Administration to urge the observance of the guideposts cannot be precisely assessed. But the history of key wage and price decisions during this period indicates that these efforts did exert a distinct and significant influence."

During this period, consumer prices advanced at "a moderate annual rate of 1.2 percent," the report states. "The first significant break in relative price stability occurred early in 1965. Farm and food prices began a sharp upward climb, spurred by special and erratic factors affecting supply at home and abroad. More pervasive inflationary pressures started in the second half of 1965 when the military buildup in Vietnam began. The rise in prices of consumer services accelerated as firms found it increasingly difficult to recruit and keep workers in the traditionally lower paying service jobs. With consumer prices rising more rapidly and with stronger demand for labor, upward pressures on wages mounted.

"These developments show up clearly in the price and wage record. Between the second quarters of 1965 and 1966, consumer prices rose 2.7 percent. During the same period, average hourly compensation in the private nonfarm economy jumped 6 percent, well above the growth of productivity; as a result, unit labor costs rose nearly 3 percent." The rate slowed for a while, "then higher costs built into the economy during 1965 and 1966 again accelerated prices and wages when the economy picked up speed in the second half of 1967. Union settlements, which had lagged in the initial stage of the advance, rose especially sharply in late 1967 and in 1968.

"The blemished price-wage record of the past three years reflects primarily an excessive growth of demand. Indeed, the initial departures from the path of price and cost stability were concentrated in farm products, raw materials, and services where guideposts have little, if any, applicability. The same forces also influenced price and wage decisions in areas of discretionary market power. Once consumer prices started to move up sharply, increases in compensation no larger than the productivity trend would not have led to any improvement in real income. Workers could not be expected to accept such a result, particularly in view of the previous rapid and consistent rise in corporate profits. Recognizing this situation, the Council, in its 1967 and 1968 reports, did not suggest that wage increases should be limited to the trend growth of productivity. It did, however, continue to urge maximum possible restraint in both wage settlements and price adjustments, and it continued to maintain the validity of the basic productivity principle for long-run price stability."

Other economists have pointed out that the guideposts did not have much real influence after 1966 because of the inflation rooted chiefly in the Vietnam war, but predicted that the guideline experience might be the basis for either compulsory or voluntary wage and price restraints later.

During the Bell System negotiations of 1968, the government economists had abandoned the specific guideposts, but were strongly urging "maximum possible restraint."

4. Lloyd G. Reynolds, *Labor Economics and Labor Relations* (3rd edition). 1959. Prentice Hall.

Discussion Questions

1. To what extent is the bargaining structure between Communications Workers of America and the Bell System a product of (a) technology; (b) power accretion; (c) public necessity; (d) managerial efficiency; (e) drive for profits; (f) organization of the Bell System; (g) other? Specify by example.

2. It has been argued that modern technology neutralizes the effect of a strike. Evaluate this contention (a) on the basis of information in this case; (b) on the basis of other experiences in American industry.

3. In what respects does the Bell System resemble a publicly managed enterprise? A privately managed enterprise? The Post Office? Tennessee Valley Authority? Atomic Energy Commission? COMSAT?

4. In the light of the nature of Bell's activities which affect individuals and the public, what should be public policy respecting strikes in this industry?

5. Industry-wide or nation-wide bargaining brings into play power which can be aligned against the Bell System, itself a unified organization. In terms of the public interest, should these aggregate powers be permitted to continue without government regulation to prohibit or ameliorate the effect of strikes on the public? What forms of regulation would seem to be feasible and appropriate? Why regulations at all?

6. Wages are traditionally based on such criteria as productivity, ability to pay, comparative wages, and cost of living. Using data in the case and elsewhere, what criteria can be selected to make the union's best case for a wage increase? What criteria can be selected to make management's best case on a wage increase?

7. To what extent does organization structure affect the behavior of individuals in this case?

8. Is pattern bargaining, as it is described here, a kind of nation-wide

bargaining? What are its advantages? Defects?

9. How do you account for the Western Electric installers, the key bargainers in this case, turning down the settlement?

The International Brotherhood of Electrical Workers Refuses the Pattern Settlement

2

"Let us simply say that the year was most unusual . . ."

Those were the opening words of the Illinois Bell Telephone Company's annual report for 1968. And Illinois Bell had, indeed, an unusual story to tell. It was in Illinois that the Bell system pattern of bargaining met the severest test in its history because the skilled workers there simply would not buy the pattern settlement. Their refusal led to a strike of 137 days, the longest strike in Bell System history. It was the strike that for many weeks threatened a blackout on television coverage of the tense Democratic National Convention in Chicago, a threat that brought tremendous political pressure on the negotiating process.

One key to the conflict lies in the fact that other unions were involved. At Illinois Bell, the technicians that deal with the complicated installation and maintenance of telephone equipment are not members of the Communications Workers of America, as they are in most other Bell system jurisdictions. They are members of the International Brotherhood of Electrical Workers, which is also an AFL-CIO union but with a far different orientation. The IBEW is an old craft union and was affiliated historically with the American Federation of Labor, while the Communications Workers were originally part of the Congress of Industrial Organizations, shaped along broad industrial lines rather than by specific crafts.

The IBEW has its own ideas of what a wage settlement should be and finds the idea of accepting a pattern dictated by the CWA distasteful, at best. IBEW members picked 1968 as the year to express that long-smoldering resentment.

To them, "the other side" is not just the Bell System but the Bell System plus Joe Beirne's Communications Workers. They see Beirne as the company's man and are publicly scornful of him. The settlement that ended the CWA's nationwide strike was promptly labelled "a sweetheart contract" by Robert Nickey, chief negotiator for the IBEW members at Illinois Bell.

When Illinois Bell negotiators presented to the IBEW bargaining team a package of proposals based on the CWA pattern settlement,

the IBEW flatly turned it down. For one thing, the IBEW felt the
wage settlement was inadequate. But perhaps more important in
the rejection was the feeling of IBEW negotiators that the company
wasn't bargaining in good faith by offering the pattern settlement.
They wanted to bargain for themselves on the issues as they saw them
and they claimed the company was refusing to bargain.

Illinois Bell spokesmen, on the other hand, explain that the "Bell
System views itself as a large industrial system" and "from the point
of view of the system, you just can't give Chicago people $23 a week
more" than those in other areas. They point out that there is considerable local bargaining on such local issues as upgrading of jobs from
one wage rate to another, upgrading of towns from one cost-of-living
zone to another, and starting rates. There is room within the general
pattern settlement for strictly local adjustments, they explain, but
the adjustments must be within the "fairly narrow framework" of
system-wide coordination.

IBEW negotiators in past years had agreed to buy the package based
on the pattern settlement, but there had been a growing reluctance
to do so. The year 1968 was different — it was a showdown year. It
was different for a complex of reasons:

1. For the first time there was some coordinated effort by IBEW
   locals in different parts of the country to deal with Bell System
   companies on their own terms, rather than on the CWA's.
2. The IBEW leadership in Illinois had undergone a change and
   included more militant people, with different views of the
   relationship between the company and its union employees.
   The chief union negotiators were men who were in this position of power for the first time.
3. There is increasing rivalry between CWA and IBEW for bargaining power with the Bell System, and IBEW people were particularly
   anxious to show they could do better than Beirne. Somewhat
   paradoxically, at the local level in Illinois there was a bit more
   cooperation between the two unions than there had been in the
   past; each side helped the other for the first time.
4. Illinois Bell management had also undergone a reorganization,
   so its chief negotiators, too, were in this position of power for
   the first time. The men who faced each other across the bargaining table, then, were men who had a somewhat different view of
   their relationship than their predecessors had and who had almost no past experience in dealing with each other, with no personal backlog of understanding and trust on which to draw.
5. The entire economy, not only in the Bell System, has been tending
   toward greater and greater centralization of power and decision-
   making, with accompanying changes in bargaining structure. The

process, while it promotes greater organizational efficiency, can produce considerable tension in certain local areas.

6. There are basic changes in the nature of union members in the decade of the 1960's, changes as disturbing to union leaders, in some cases, as they are to management. The new "pork chop generation" cannot be discounted as part of the equation.

Because each of these reasons is fundamental to understanding the Illinois Bell strike in 1968, each will be more fully considered.

IBEW Locals Join Forces

The International Brotherhood of Electrical Workers dates back to 1891. In 1968, with about 875,000 members, it was one of the six largest unions in the nation. But it doesn't really speak with one voice as some of the other big unions do. One reason is the diversity of its membership. IBEW members don't all work in one big industry, as the United Automobile Workers do, for example. Only a fraction of its members, less than 10 percent, work with electrical equipment manufacturing and installation in the telephone industry. Other members are building trades electricians, railroad shop electricians, shipyard electricians; they are electricians in many kinds of shops of many different sizes. They do not always have common problems on which to bargain. Another reason for the lack of a single voice by the IBEW is the ancient tradition of local autonomy. Historically IBEW locals, wherever they are, have sought to solve their own problems, with less direction from the international union than exists in such industrial unions as the Auto Workers and the Steel Workers. Advice has been available, of course, and the international has an impressive strike fund, but IBEW locals, historically, have been responsible for their own bargaining.

With the great growth and the shifts in the kinds of labor organizations during the 1930's, the IBEW has branched out and organized factory workers on an industrial basis, but the old philosophy of local autonomy still has great strength. There is certainly no coordinated overall bargaining posture, nation-wide, for the IBEW.

But individual IBEW locals have been gradually developing a policy of working together on common problems, a trend seen throughout the labor movement. One facet has been the development of local councils, on a geographical basis, to pool strength in bargaining. One such council exists in the Illinois Bell picture; the strikers were members of five different IBEW locals, with varying problems and some old animosities, but they bargain together as System Council T-4.

Another facet of the growing policy of working together has been the development of nation-wide IBEW conferences, organized accord-

ing to the industries where members were working. IBEW launched
a national telephone conference in the early 1960s, with representatives
of locals in different telephone companies meeting together once a year
to think about national goals. In 1966, the national telephone conference was further divided into three separate councils "to try to up-
date our aims and keep contracts in line." One is the Bell System
Council, another is the General Telephone Council representing members who work for the second largest telephone company; the third
is a council concerned with the small independent telephone companies.

"We're coming to realize that we must have coordinated effort to
meet the power of an immense monopoly," explained Donald Servatius, an Illinois Bell electrician who worked part time for the telephone
company and part time for one of the IBEW unions that struck Illinois
Bell in 1968. His role during the 1968 negotiations was as an unofficial
public relations man, a role for which he had no particular training but
a certain flair. He had a liking for strategy, too, and was involved in
developing the union's bargaining position in 1968.

The Bell Telephone Council of the IBEW held a meeting in January,
1968, not long before the Illinois Bell negotiations started. Robert
Nickey, the chief negotiator for the IBEW locals at Illinois Bell, was
a strong figure in the Council meetings; he had traveled widely, working with other IBEW locals, in the months between the 1966 negotiations and the January, 1968, meeting of the Bell Telephone Council.

"The 1968 meeting was part of a 10-year plan to get real bargaining
in the Bell System, instead of just taking the pattern," Servatius explained. "We see it as long-term strategy, and it's going to take years.
In 1966, for example, we made some noises — threatened a walkout —
but it really started with 1968. We do realize that we need more
cooperation with our people in other states, and we're beginning to
get it. But we still have some problems, like the whole idea of local
autonomy."

One of the goals set, but without a specific figure or percentage,
was to get more money. IBEW people felt the spiraling cost of living
had more than consumed the 1966 increases and that catch-up pay
was crucial. They also felt that the rates the Bell System pays electricians had been falling farther and farther behind wage schedules
for electricians in other industries. The other major goal, more vague
in terminology but very real in the minds of the men, was to have real
bargaining with the Bell companies. The pattern settlement was the
target; the IBEW was determined to destroy it.

The IBEW in Illinois

The International Brotherhood of Electrical Workers was one of the pioneer organizers in the Bell System and has been part of the bargaining picture at Illinois Bell since 1910. In that year a group of equipment installers who had worked for the company as independent contractors joined the IBEW and were attached to IBEW Local 134, a big and powerful union primarily of electrical workers in the construction trades. The long-time power in that union was a legendary figure in the Chicago labor movement named Mike Boyle, nicknamed "Umbrella Mike" because of an often-repeated but impossible-to-document story that he always carried an umbrella, into which an employer slipped a pay-off when he wanted to guarantee labor peace. Boyle dominated Local 134 negotiations for more than 50 years.

There's a story around Illinois Bell that Mike Boyle had once promised that his local would "never strike Bell." It's rooted in the fact that the union electricians certainly were better off under a contract with management than they had been as independent workers. They were on the payroll every day, year around, no matter what the weather. Before, on a day-to-day employment basis, they would have no work and thus no pay when cold or wind or rain meant their heavy outdoor work could not be done.

Whether Boyle ever made that promise or not may be disputed, but it is true that in 58 years of bargaining, the Local 134 members never did strike Bell — until 1968.

The structure of Local 134 remains much the same. The Bell segment is still part of the same local, and it's had a union shop agreement since 1910, one of only two union shops in the entire Bell System. But the Bell electricians in Local 134 are still only a small part of the local, with their 1500 members making up only about 10 percent of the local. The fact that the Bell members of the local have a lower wage scale than the construction-worker members was one of the real irritants in the 1968 strike picture.

Bell members of Local 134 have their own business agent; he is appointed by the business manager of the whole local, who is elected. Traditionally, this group of Bell technicians, with its long heritage of craft unionism, held itself somewhat aloof from other Bell technicians who joined the IBEW much later. Those groups which came into the IBEW fold later were for a while independent unions which, in turn, had grown out of company-sponsored employee associations.

These IBEW locals began to take shape in 1946 and 1947, the same time the Communications Workers of America was consolidating many of the independent locals on a national basis. But the CWA's particular emphasis at the time was on organizing the operators who

put through the calls in the complex system. In Illinois, IBEW
organizers beat the CWA to the plant people, the electrical workers.

The Bell System is divided into three general areas, based on function: plant, commercial, and traffic. Plant is concerned with equipment, both installation and maintenance. Traffic is concerned with
getting calls from one phone to another. Commercial is concerned
with selling services, billing and other strictly business office details.
A whole complex of unions is involved. In some of the operating companies, all union-eligible employees are members of the CWA. In some,
they are all still members of independent unions. In none of them,
are they all members of IBEW. In some, all three kinds of unions are
represented; Illinois Bell is one of these. Illinois Bell negotiates six
different kinds of contracts:

Two kinds with CWA unions, one representing the operators in
Chicago and one the operators in suburban and state-wide areas.

One kind with an independent union representing commercial
workers in state and suburban areas.

One kind with an independent union in Chicago, representing commercial employees, including the marketing department.

One kind with an IBEW local representing accounting employees
throughout the company.

One kind with the group of IBEW workers in the plant department
in the whole state.

Thus it is obvious that contract negotiations in Illinois Bell are far
more complex than in many other operating companies, particularly
those where the strongly-centralized CWA speaks for all union members. (See Chart I.)

The developing IBEW locals at first worked somewhat independently
of each other, although they had a jointly-negotiated contract. Gradually they began to feel the need for more consolidation and coordination of their efforts. In the late 1950's the five locals tightened their
organization by forming Systems Council T-4, which bargains jointly
for all five. Each of the five has a representative on the bargaining team.
Changes in these representatives have obviously meant changes in the
character of negotiations; different men view the issues and their own
roles in different ways, and sometimes they view management in different ways, too. In the ten years before the 1968 strike, the Systems
Council gradually grew more militant. In order to see how this happened, there needs to be some consideration of the changing role and
power position of each of the five participating locals. They are:

Local 399, whose 2000 members work outside of the Chicago and
suburban area. They were represented by Delbert Brown, a rather
taciturn man in negotiations who had recently lined up with, but not
led, the more militant negotiators.

Local 336, whose 3900 members work on construction and maintenance of the system in the vast suburban area around Chicago. The local also includes electricians who are not Bell employees. It was headed at the time of the strike by William Bartelt, who had formerly been chief negotiator for the System Council before Nickey won the role. Bartelt's relationships with Bell negotiators were cordial over the years and tended more toward cooperation than toward militancy. Bartelt was in the minority in 1968.

Local 165, whose 4000 members work on installation and maintenance within the Chicago city limits. Their representative was Robert Nickey, who took a hard line in negotiations and was outspokenly scornful of the company's point of view.

Local 315, a small local of 400 members who do heavy construction work, such as setting poles and stringing cables, within the city of Chicago. They were represented by Joseph O'Rourke.

Local 134, the construction trades local which has the long-time union shop agreement with Bell. The 1500 Bell employees in this local install the complicated multiple key equipment, chiefly business phones, in Chicago and Cook County, and do all Bell work in buildings under construction. Their representative, appointed by the Local 134 business agent, was Frank Cunningham, another hard-liner. Cunningham brought the traditionally aloof local solidly into the Systems Council and brought it in on the militant side. In the 1966 negotiations, he and Nickey voted against the final Bell settlement. The settlement was accepted anyway because three of the five members voted for it, but that was the first time in Illinois Bell's dealings with the System Council that the contract was accepted without a unanimous vote.

Nickey and Cunningham don't always agree, but they line up solidly together against the company. Their position prevailed when they won the vote of Delbert Brown in reorganizing the System Council, with Nickey succeeding William Bartelt as chief negotiator.

Thus, in the 1968 negotiations, Nickey was the chief negotiator for the first time. He was still dissatisfied with the 1966 settlement, he had been working actively to promote a stronger stand against the Bell System by all IBEW locals, and he spoke of the Bell System (and of Joseph Beirne and the CWA) with considerable hostility. He was determined to break the pattern system of contract negotiation which he was convinced had made the IBEW people at Illinois Bell consistently lose ground in the local labor market.

Nickey is a powerfully-built, big man, with a deep resonant voice and a firm jaw. He went to work for Illinois Bell in 1941 and worked in commercial and plant divisions for almost 20 years before he was

elected president of Local 165. He is not, as some negotiators are, a
man trained in broad labor relations policies, but has accumulated
his ideas and experience by coming up through the ranks of Bell labor.

To one former Bell negotiator, Nickey's rancor and scornful attitude
toward management was a major reason for the 1968 strike.

"It's pretty nearly impossible to establish any kind of rapport with
him," the former negotiator said. "He believes that if you're sitting
on the management side, you're automatically a son of a bitch. He
doesn't believe in compromise. When I'd come in to bargain, he'd say
things like, 'Here comes the office boy from New York.' Now you
can just take so much of that."

Rivalry Between IBEW and CWA

The animosity that IBEW leaders in Illinois express toward Beirne's
CWA has old historical roots. The IBEW does not intend to forget
that it did the pioneer labor organizing in the Bell System, when that
organizing was rough work and there was no Wagner Act to give it
legal blessing. And for a number of years the CWA and IBEW fought
each other to take in the newly-independent unions in the Bell System.
Since both unions have been part of the AFL-CIO structure, they are
bound by the no-raid pact that prohibits trying to purloin each other's
members, but they are still strong opponents wherever independent
unions still exist and where there are no unions.

The IBEW was not able to keep all its pioneer units in the Bell
System partly because employer pressures against any unions were so
great in those early days and partly because it continued to think of
itself as primarily a craft union, of and for electricians, and apparently
never really thought in terms of organizing the whole industry. It was
noted in Part I, for example, that IBEW electricians in New England
fretted under the threat of domination by the female operators.

But historical forces from the mid-1930's on tended to encourage
the industrial form of organization over the craft type. And the CWA
emerged as the dominant labor organization in the Bell System, with
about 68 percent of the union members in the system as compared
to about 12 percent in the IBEW. Throughout the Bell System, among
the men who hold jobs like those of IBEW members in Illinois, more
are members of the CWA than are members of IBEW. This poses a
particular problem in Illinois Bell, where the biggest single group of
union employees is in IBEW. And in the company where they represent a majority, they are particularly hostile to buying a pattern
settlement negotiated by another union.

Illinois Bell IBEW members contend they want one of two things:

1. Real local bargaining with Illinois Bell, without regard to the

pattern settlement, or

2. Some kind of national bargaining for IBEW members in Illinois and other states, perhaps coordinated with CWA's brand of nationwide bargaining.

But both of these aims seem to IBEW members to be blocked, not only by the companies but by the CWA. Gordon Freeman, former president of the IBEW - who was still president at the time of the 1968 strike - on several occasions approached Joseph Beirne to suggest that the unions work together on a proposal to AT&T and negotiate together on a coordinated basis, similar to the coalition of 13 unions that bargain together with General Electric Co.

"Beirne told Freeman to get out of the telephone industry," said Robert Nickey, the IBEW chief negotiator in Illinois. "Freeman told him he was in the telephone industry before CWA was born and he'd still be in it when Beirne was gone."

On the other hand, IBEW sees itself as blocked on getting active local negotiations because the industry is committed to the pattern settlement in which IBEW has no part.

On April 29, 1968, Gordon Freeman, the IBEW president, sent a telegram to Ben S. Gilmer, AT&T president. The big IBEW local in New Jersey was out on strike and the Illinois group was close to a strike date. The pattern settlement was just being worked out.

Freeman's telegram read:

"Since over many years the American Telephone and Telegraph Company has not engaged in nationwide or systemwide collective bargaining, the International Brotherhood of Electrical Workers, AFL-CIO, insists that reports of contract talks allegedly being held in New York City between the American Telephone and Telegraph Company and another union have no effect on the outcome of negotiation between Brotherhood Local unions and various of the telephone companies and Western Electric with whom we have a contractual relationship.

"The insistence of the individual telephone companies that bargaining take place at the local level must be pursued or nation-wide bargaining must be entered into by the American Telephone and Telegraph Company with this international union.

"We have no intention of accepting the bargaining results arrived at in secret meetings and between persons who are not conversant with our position. We insist that free collective bargaining be entered into between our local unions and the companies with whom we have contracts."

Freeman received an answering telegram from W. C. Mercer, personnel vice president of AT&T.

"In reply to your telegram of April 29 to Mr. Ben S. Gilmer, the

negotiation of labor contracts continues to be a function and responsibility of each of the telephone operating companies, Western Electric,
and other units of the Bell System. We concur that free collective
bargaining should be entered into between your local union and the
companies with whom you have contracts."

But Nickey felt it was clear that Illinois Bell was not free to bargain
with IBEW and said, "When they come in to bargain with us, they
have to get that package."*

There is a local contradiction in Illinois, however, to the continued
tension between the two international unions. In 1968, for the first
time, there was cooperation — at least to some extent — between CWA
and IBEW groups at Illinois Bell. Relations between them had been
cool over the years since 1947, when the CWA group was involved in
its first nationwide strike and the IBEW locals were just getting organized. IBEW members did not honor the CWA picket lines in 1947. But
in 1968, with strikes looming for both, officers of the two labor groups
at Illinois Bell held some joint meetings early in the year. The IBEW
members did honor the CWA picket lines during the 18-day strike, and
the CWA operators did stay out - for a while - when the IBEW strike
against Illinois Bell followed. IBEW blames a "company threat" for
the operators' return to work while the IBEW strike continued.

Despite the semblance of local rapport, IBEW resentment of CWA
and what it considers CWA's favored place in the industry cannot be
discounted as an important factor in the 1968 strike at Illinois Bell.

Changes in the Illinois Bell Bargaining Team

The start of the strike year, 1968, marked the start of a labor relations reorganization within Illinois Bell management, so that new people
were responsible for reaching a contract agreement with the IBEW
locals. The newcomers had had long experience with the company,
coming up through the ranks as most Bell System executives have done,
but had not been primarily concerned in the past with labor negotiations.

The changes were at two levels, that of the personnel vice president
and that of the chief negotiator.

Jennings N. Stanbery, long-time personnel vice president of Illinois
Bell, retired in January, 1968. Stanbery had been personnel vice president for more than 20 years and had been personnel manager before
that, so that he had been in close touch with the developing CWA and
IBEW locals at Illinois Bell.

Taking Stanbery's place as vice president was Jack B. Gable, who
had started with Illinois Bell as a plant craftsman in Peoria, Illinois,
and had worked his way through the Bell hierarchy. Before becoming
personnel vice president, he had been vice president and general manager

*In 1974, AT&T announced that it would initiate nationwide bargaining with the
Communications Workers of America and the International Brotherhood of
Electrical Workers. National bargaining will cover basic wages, budgets, and length
of contract. Certain local issues will still be bargained separately at the local level.

of suburban operations for the sprawling, fast-growing area around Chicago. A lean, articulate, forthright man, Gable is squarely in the Bell System tradition, stating that the system "views itself as a large industrial system," and "from the point of view of the system, you just can't give Chicago $23 a week more." He had a lively interest and deep concern in the collective bargaining procedures at Illinois Bell, but as vice president, did not sit in himself on most negotiations with representatives of any of the Bell unions. He did take part, however, when federal mediators came from Washington to help reach a solution after the strike had started. And he did take part in seeking a solution when talks moved away from the bargaining table and into the office of Mayor Richard J. Daley, who grew increasingly concerned that the telephone strike threatened his long-awaited Democratic National Convention.

The main burden of carrying on negotiations went to Clyde C. Boylls, who talks of his job with understanding, patience and frankness. He has a considerable affinity for dealing with people, something he discovered early in his career when he abandoned his original aim to be an accountant. He went from college into the army during World War II, then to Western Electric as an auditor.

"I worked at it three months," he says, "and that was enough. I came over to Illinois Bell and asked them to put me anywhere but accounting." Bell put him in traffic and then, through a period of more than 20 years, into other jobs in all three areas of operations - traffic, commercial, and plant. His personnel background, he says, comes from these years of direct experience in dealing with people as a supervisor at many levels. His "first brush with organized labor," he recalls, was in Rock Island, Illinois, with a strong CWA local of women telephone operators. By 1963, he was a supervisor in the plant department and thus took some part in the negotiations with IBEW that concerned his particular area.

Boylls was named general personnel manager in 1967, succeeding Frank Braden, who had been with Illinois Bell for 42 years and had been in charge of negotiating union contracts since he "went upstairs" in 1952.

Braden was an affable, folksy sort of man who had immensely enjoyed his dealings with the Illinois Bell unions and had developed a close, personal, cooperative kind of relationship with many of the union representatives who sat across the bargaining table.

The company's labor relations function was further reorganized at the beginning of 1968, the strike year. The job of general personnel manager was divided into two separate areas, with Boylls head of a new labor relations department, no longer concerned with other personnel aspects such as salary administration, training, and appraisals. And the

bargaining system was made more centralized, with Boylls, as head of
the department, chairing all negotiations.

Boylls explains that before January, 1968, bargaining was carried on
with each union by the department head whose employees were represented by that union. Braden, as general personnel manager, worked
with them but the department heads had considerable responsibility.

The new centralized bargaining, launched in 1968, shifted the major
responsibility to the labor relations department head - Boylls - who was
then to be assisted by a series of teams representing the different departments, taking part in the bargaining on parts of the contracts that
applied to them. There were three teams, for plant, traffic, and commercial departments. The plant team, which negotiated with IBEW,
consisted at first of Boylls, a recorder, the Chicago plant personnel
manager, and representatives of plant managers for suburban and downstate areas. Later, a sixth member of the team was added: a public
relations department representative. He was added after the IBEW
team brought in Don Servatius, who frequently served as a public
spokesman for the IBEW negotiators.

(The union also had as an active participant an IBEW international
representative, Don Mahoney, of whom Boylls said, "We hadn't known
him before but did know something of his background, including the
fact that he's adept at running a strike.")

Thus, at the beginning of 1968, when a nationwide CWA strike was
already being threatened and tension was high throughout the industry,
when the IBEW team in Illinois was in the hands of new and more militant men, Illinois Bell had a new vice president of personnel, a new chief
negotiator and a new system of bargaining. For management, too, it
was "a whole new ball game." The men who would sit around the
bargaining table - all of them on both sides with long experience and
knowledge of Illinois Bell but not primarily in collective bargaining and
not in the catbird seat - had no backlog of past dealings or trustful
relationships on which to lean. It seems unlikely that either side could
have known just how firm the other's stand would be.[1]

The Trend Toward Centralization

The trend toward centralization has dominated American economic
life, and is perhaps as inevitable a result of the industrial revolution as
the organization of workers into labor unions. Wherever it has been
feasible to combine, in order to protect markets or promote greater
economies in production or administer enterprises with greater efficiency, the drive has been toward increasing centralization. Obviously
centralization seems to have made economic sense. But there has been
growing realization in the past two decades that centralization, no matter

how efficient, leaves in its wake some nagging social problems . . .people problems. Some of modern man's frustrations seem to be due to his sense of remoteness, his lack of ability - or his feeling that he lacks ability - to act in any way to affect his own circumstances. Often, he feels that all he is able to do is kick the vending machine.

It's a nebulous kind of problem, this frustration, but it may have had a bearing on the Illinois Bell strike.

American Telephone and Telegraph Company is as good an example as can be found of the evolution of a vast and centralized enterprise, dedicated to efficiency, to supplying all the links in an extremely complex civilization, to anticipating new needs and new products and new markets, to devising new techniques of management in every area in order to continue operating smoothly and successfully, at a profit.

Throughout its developments, it has reached into every area of the nation, linking small independent companies and incorporating many of them, growing, consolidating, centralizing.

Part I has illustrated that the Communications Workers of America has developed, in its own way, along similar lines. A plethora of independent local unions, jealous of their autonomy, just didn't work very well and they gradually, and sometimes painfully, welded themselves into a nationwide organization as strongly centralized as the Bell system.

The International Brotherhood of Electrical Workers had some of the same impulses and showed traces of joint action in the telephone industry as early as the turn of the century. More recently, as we have noted, the IBEW telephone workers have begun the process of joining together for greater strength, with the organization of the Bell Telephone Council within the union and the plans for similar approaches to the Bell companies in the 1968 bargaining. The suggestions for possible coordinated bargaining at the national level with CWA are another aspect of the same trend.

Bell company officials tend to look with some approval on the centralized efficiency of the CWA.

"CWA has strong leadership at the national level," Jack Gable of Illinois Bell states. "Beirne is personally involved in bargaining for the Bell System. And the union party line comes down clearly. The union has good communications. The leadership makes a deal, and the rest live with it."

But there were indications in 1968 that the CWA's centralization

was posing problems. The crack in the facade was particularly apparent
in the rejection of the pattern settlement by Western Electric and
Michigan Bell and the need to take a later mail poll to get ratification
in those units.

"Beirne may have to change his stance toward the company," Gable
said, "and have much more local involvement in bargaining."

Whatever local restiveness there may be among CWA members at
the local level is multiplied in the IBEW, which feels left out of the
whole process and sees itself as the victim of the pattern settlement
between CWA and the Bell System. IBEW leaders in Illinois even believe
that the CWA nationwide strike of 1968 was a joint plan of management
and the union.

"When the CWA talks opened on the 18-month reopener, it was
apparent that the company would make an inadequate offer," Nickey
conjectured. "Beirne realized he was in trouble then. His people were
angry. The whole thinking was planned in a closed door session. A
strike - but a quick end to it. It was meant to take the heat off Beirne.
They had to save Beirne. He's their man because he can rule that union.
When CWA rejected the 18-month offer, to feed him a little more they
came up with the three-year contract."

Bell companies that deal only with CWA have tended to have fewer
labor relations problems with their employees because the union as
well as the company buys the industry-wide approach. But in Illinois,
as we have noted, the biggest employee group is represented by IBEW.

Illinois Bell has found ways, Gable says, to make the agreement in
Illinois local, providing different terms within the framework of the
overall pattern. "There is a lot of local bargaining on details of the
contract," he explained. Local bargaining deals with such monetary
matters as upgrading jobs from one wage group to another (there are
ten wage groups in craft jobs, for example), with upgrading towns
from one class to another (there are six classes, based on differing
costs of living), with starting and progression rates for employees who
have not been in the company long enough to reach the top rate for
their wage groups. So there are local variations, but the pattern is
always there too; it is the company's intent not to exceed the pattern
settlement, which sometimes has been a dollar amount and sometimes
a percentage.

But it is that overall pattern that is the target of the IBEW, particularly since it is a pattern the IBEW plays no part in setting. All other
efforts to localize the agreement apparently have not answered the
sense of frustration in the IBEW.

"They kept telling us we could move it around within the package,"
said Don Servatius, "but that there's no more money. We could change
upgrades, for example, and trade that for something else. Well, that

would satisfy one group and then 200 other guys would cut you up."

The Pork Chop Generation

The growing restiveness of younger members of labor unions, and their impatience with traditional union practices and techniques as well as their determination to get more money in the pay envelope today, has been noted in Part I. This group played a major role in the CWA's nationwide phone strike and seems to be at least as significant among the members of the IBEW locals.

The restive group of workers is made up of men who have entered the labor force since the mid-1950's, a group which has been hard hit by increasing inflation. They've heard a lot about the affluent society but feel it is passing them by. Their standard of living has climbed, but not as much as they want it to. They don't really question the system; they just want a bigger share.

Observers have listed a number of differences in the young workers entering the labor force since the 1950s, in comparison with those who started working earlier in the century. Most are American born, since the great immigration period has ended. Better educated, they have grown up in a time of full employment and they take a rising standard of living for granted. They are often skeptical about both management and unions and feel free to express dissatisfaction, by frequent absenteeism and by wildcat strikes. They feel less bound to some long-time union aims, such as pensions and union security, and they often show little loyalty to the union bargaining committee; they vote to turn down settlements the bargainers have agreed to. Their lack of docility poses new problems for unions as well as management and will doubtless lead to changes in the way unions are run.

Perhaps one reason that the pork chop group has felt so free to indicate its displeasure with union leadership as well as with management is that the unions themselves have changed and may well have lost some of the fire and vigor that attracted loyal memberships in earlier decades.

The younger workers feel acutely aware, too, of the difference in age - and perhaps in interest - between themselves and top leadership in most unions, where many of the long-time leaders are in their sixties and seventies and view the labor scene from another perspective.

The restlessness of the younger workers is as much a problem for the union leadership as it is for management. One aspect of the problem is that unions must, of course, try to reflect the needs and demands of this growing group. Another is the difficulty of trying to carry out a union's obligations under a contract. Wild cat strikes are increasingly frequent, indicating that the younger workers are as unhappy with the unions as with management and don't hesitate to show it. But union

leaders who can't maintain discipline among the rank-and-file members
are placed in a poor bargaining position with management, which has
a reasonable right to expect that a contract will be enforced.

All these underlying factors seem to have been significant in the
Illinois Bell Strike of 1968. They help to show what was different in
that year and why the peace that had prevailed between Illinois Bell
and IBEW for 58 years was shattered in 1968.

The 1968 Negotiations

Before the first bargaining session between Illinois Bell and System
Council T-4 of the IBEW was held on March 7, 1968, the union prepared a long position paper, chiefly the work of Don Servatius, the
part-time telephone employee with a liking for strategy, and Don
Mahoney, the IBEW international representative whose reputation for
skill in strike situations had already reached Illinois Bell officials.

Divided into four chapters, the union's document dealt with the
financial condition of the company, employee contributions to productivity, wage comparisons, and a conclusion that "we need at least
a minimum of a 20 percent increase in wages just to catch up to 1968
without giving consideration to the future."

The company, the union said, is "flying higher than ever before in
its history," adding, "in the 10-year period, 1957 through 1966, the
company has had an increase of 47.6 percent in telephones; an increase
of 71.4 percent in operating revenue, and a profit increase of 128 percent. Mother Bell, of course as usual, was taking care of itself to the
tune of 151 percent increase in dividends and the net worth of the
company rose 112.9 percent."

At the same time, the union continued, there has been a 14.5 percent
decrease in employment and only a 36.2 percent increase in wages
and related costs.

"It is self evident to the employees," said the union document,
"that the only thing they got was to dig up the road and make it
possible for Illinois Bell Company to pave the road to 195 Broadway
with gold. They . . . want their share of the gold."

Illinois Bell called the IBEW's financial analysis "statistical sleight
of-hand." Referring to the same 1957 to 1966 period, a company
analysis made these points:

The net worth of the business did double but the union neglected
the fact that the required investment, to meet the growing service
commitment, also almost doubled. The number of shares outstanding increased by 91 percent.

As profit (net income) was increasing by 128 percent, the net increase per share — because of the expanded number of shares — was increasing only 25 percent.

As total dividends paid out were increasing 151 percent, this again was related to the increase in the number of shares outstanding. Dividends paid per share did not increase by 151 percent, but by 37.5 percent.

Relating the increase in wages and related costs to the decreased number of employees, the figures show that these costs per employee increased 59.5 percent, not 36.2 percent. (See Appendix III.)

The union placed particular emphasis on comparative wage rates paid by Commonwealth Edison Company, the electric power utility company in Northern Illinois. The fact that Commonwealth Edison's wage rates have been pulling farther and farther ahead for work the union feels is comparable is a particularly sore point with the IBEW. And because of its autonomous bargaining position and stress on wage rates in the local labor market instead of in a nationwide industry, the sore point is even more vexing. ("The Bell companies that don't have craft unions don't get comparisons with local labor rates," said one Illinois Bell official. "That means less problem for the company.")

Commonwealth Edison bargains with 18 different IBEW unions, but none of them are the same locals that bargain with Illinois Bell.

The union position paper selected the Commonwealth Edison lineman's pay scale for comparison with Illinois Bell's linemen (a wage group 2 position at Illinois Bell, $5 a week under the top-rated wage group 1). In 1957, the Commonwealth Edison lineman earned $120 a week and the Illinois Bell lineman $112.50. By 1967, the power company's lineman earned $180.40 a week and the telephone lineman, $155.50. The union presented this hourly wage comparison for the two wage scales:

Year	Commonwealth Edison lineman	Illinois Bell lineman (wage group 2)
1957	3.00	2.8125
1958	3.14	2.90
1959	3.30	3.025
1960	3.46	3.05
1961	3.60	3.1875
1962	3.72	3.2625
1963	3.87	3.4125
1964	4.00	3.5625
1965	4.10	3.6875
1966	4.28	3.8875
1967	4.51	3.8875
Percent change	50.3	38.2

(Whether the work of the two linemen is comparable is, of course, relevant to the question. Illinois Bell officials claim the power company work is harder because the linemen deal with high tension wires, making the work "higher, hotter and heavier." "Yeah, I know they say that," replied Frank Cunningham of the IBEW, "and we say ours is lower, lousier, and lesser."

"Edison is a very direct corollary," Nickey added, "but the company is so rigid, it can't accept that." The 10-year history is a serious problem to the men, Cunningham went on, stating "Our men feel loss of dignity in their position.")

Another local wage comparison that rankles among the IBEW members is that of the construction trade electricians who make up 90 percent of the membership of IBEW Local 134. In 1967, a journeyman electrician in the local earned $5.40 an hour and the journeyman who worked for Bell as a PBX installer earned $3.9875 an hour. Historically, construction trade workers have earned a higher rate because they've never been guaranteed work for each day. Actually, in Chicago — considered by labor people to be a "good union town" — many journeyman electricians do work full time and full-time city electricians, thanks to Mayor Richard J. Daley, receive the top rate.

Whatever the historic or economic justifications for the differing wage rates, it seems clear that the Illinois Bell electrical workers saw themselves as getting farther and farther behind. Nor were they encouraged by comparing themselves with other large employee groups in the city. In their analysis, for example, they included weekly earnings of Chicago policemen, whose pay had climbed from about $100 a week in 1957 to $173.07 in 1968, while top-rated Wage group 1 at Illinois Bell went from $117 a week to $160.50.

It is in this area, the area of what set of wage rates you choose for comparative purposes, that the issue between Illinois Bell and the IBEW was clearly drawn. The union, with a long history of autonomy and no dictation from its national office, related its wage demands to the local labor market, comparing its rates with others paid in the area for jobs it believes are comparable; it didn't want to hear the industry-wide rates, particularly since the personnel vice president of AT&T had assured IBEW officers that "the negotiation of labor contracts continues to be a function and responsibility of each of the telephone operating companies."

The company, with its close relationship to the entire Bell System, tied its wage figures into the industry-wide approach because, as Jack Gable, Illinois Bell personnel vice president, puts it, "The Bell System views itself as a large industrial system." Bell officials can see no reasonable justification for paying electricians in one Bell company an entirely different schedule of wages from that paid in another Bell company. "Chaos" is the word used by official after official whenever they contemplate that idea. There are differences in the schedules now, based on the different cost of living zones and thus related somewhat to other rates in the local labor market, but the overall pattern must be consistent, officials believe. Complicating the picture is the fact that IBEW is distinctly a minority in the Bell System-union relationship. Throughout the industry, more electricians with jobs like those of the IBEW members in Illinois are members of the Communications Workers of America than are members of IBEW. Paying one set of union members higher rates than another set, for comparable work, makes no more sense, in the view of management, than does paying significantly higher rates in one operating company than in another.

Bell officials believe that the pattern system of establishing an overall wage structure and then negotiating strictly local issues within the pattern does allow sufficient flexibility to adjust to local needs.

At first, when negotiations opened between Illinois Bell and IBEW System Council T-4, the topic of the talks was just the wage reopening for the final 18 months of the contract. Talks started March 7, 30 days before the date when contract agreement was supposed to be reached. The union presented its demands first: the 20 percent wage increase proposed in its position paper, job and town upgrades, differential adjustments, and a 35-hour work week.

Four more negotiating sessions were held before the company made its first offer, on March 28, concerning only wages. The union promptly turned it down, claiming it was unsatisfactory and incomplete. Both sides made counter-proposals that were rejected. Late in the afternoon of April 6, the tenth time the negotiating teams had met and the day before the contract date, Illinois Bell made a final offer: a wage increase of $12 a week at the top, ranging down to $4 a week; one job upgrade and six town upgrades, neither as numerous as the union wanted.

The midnight contract deadline was extended to allow union consideration of the proposal, but it is doubtful anyone expected it to be accepted. It wasn't. The start of the nationwide CWA strike was still almost two weeks off, its settlement almost a month away.

On April 8, when the IBEW negotiators told the company they had rejected the offer, they announced that, under their contract, they would be free to strike in 30 days.

The threat of a strike brought the Federal Mediation and Conciliation Service into the picture. Both sides met with Commissioner Arthur W. Luchs in his Chicago office to review the status of negotiations on April 10. They met again, sometimes separately and some-

times together, on April 12 and 17 and were meeting on April 18
when the CWA strike began and IBEW announced its members would
honor the picket lines. Both sides met again with the commissioner
on April 19, 20 and 23, when the company offered some more job
upgrades. On April 25, the union made a new proposal, modifying
the flat 20 percent increase it had sought. It asked, instead, a two-
step wage increase: $19.50 a week for the first year (about 12 per-
cent) and an additional $10 a week (about 5 percent more) for the
remaining six months of the contract. The company rejected the
proposal, and the union began to set up strike machinery. Another
meeting with Commissioner Luchs on May 4 brought no change from
either side, and another session was scheduled for May 6, two days
before the strike deadline.

At the May 6 meeting, the day CWA members went back to work
after voting to end their strike, Illinois Bell offered the IBEW a new
three-year contract, based on the pattern settlement with CWA. The
union rejected the offer the next day and left the meeting to start
its strike on May 8.

These were "record-breaking proposals," said an Illinois Bell spokesman, "which would please most reasonable men."

They were inadequate, replied Robert Nickey, adding, "We've had
58 years of labor peace here, but it appears that the company is
not willing to sit down and bargain with us." He was referring, of
course, to the offer of the pattern settlement, a kind of bargaining
he was determined to overthrow.

APPENDIX III

Selected Figures from Illinois Bell Telephone Company Annual Reports

000 omitted from dollar amounts except amounts per share

	1968	1967	1966	1957
INCOME AND EARNINGS				
Operating Revenues	$ 865,529	$ 819,259	$ 763,804	$ 445,540
Operating Expenses	479,400	473,945	431,860	284,407
Operating Taxes	237,717	200,221	189,282	98,251
Operating Income	148,412	145,512	142,663	62,883
Other Income	3,999	4,419	2,108	1,017
Income Before Interest	152,411	149,512	144,771	63,900
Interest Deductions	23,526	20,157	15,900	7,397
Net Income applicable to shares	128,885	129,354	128,872	56,503
Earnings per share	2.49	2.60	2.70	2.16*
Dividends per share	2.20	2.20	2.20	1.60*
Return on average equity	9.53	10.04	10.53	9.56
Return on average total capital	8.13	8.50	8.89	7.84
OWNERSHIP AND CAPITAL				
I.B.T. Share Owners	2,306	2,155	2,115	964
Shares Outstanding	53,932,709	49,784,309	49,784,309	26,123,765*
Equity per share	25.95	26.15	25.62	22.93*
Total Capital	1,956,265	1,836,152	1,693,413	862,520
Debt Ratio	28.46	29.10	24.67	30.56
TELEPHONE PLANT, SERVICE AND EMPLOYEES				
Construction Expenditures	244,384	250,140	220,368	150,283
Total Plant, year end	2,584,929	2,400,149	2,220,522	1,170,940
Telephones in Service	5,584,866	5,445,512	5,243,213	3,552,177

APPENDIX III (continued)

Average con- versations per day	18,247,000	17,368,000	16,651,000	11,153,000
Employees, year end	37,849	38,421	37,084	43,422
Wages and pension and benefit costs	333,852	349,662	315,989	231,947

*Adjusted for 5-for-1 stock split April 1, 1960

Footnotes

1. Joseph Beirne of the CWA made a speech at a college seminar in November, 1968, on "Factors that Create Breakdowns in Collective Bargaining." As a guideline to more effective bargaining, he suggested:

"It is essential that the . . . negotiators know and understand each other. It has been my observation that in the collective bargaining process — at least in the big corporations — the weight of negotiations eventually lands on the shoulders of one man on each side of the table. It is essential that these men know each other well, and indeed develop an almost intuitive understanding of each other's problems. Each must learn to believe the other. That doesn't mean just believing in the factual truth of the words; it goes beyond that, to accepting and comprehending the other man's appraisal of his position, of his strengths, of his weaknesses, of his compulsion, of his options. Sensitivity is a key factor at the negotiating table, which can produce either industrial peace or a breakdown in the bargaining process.

"I have noticed an interaction between the personalities of the leaders of negotiating teams in big corporations. We develop each other, in some form of non-scientific mutual evolution. The kind of man one side gets will tend to be reflected in the kind of man the other side produces to negotiate with him. In the big leagues of bargaining, you tend to get the kind of man you deserve." (From the text of an address at St. Bonaventure University, Olean, New York, November 16, 1968.)

Discussion Questions

1. IBEW negotiators in past years had agreed to buy the package based on the pattern settlement. Why did they refuse in 1968?

2. In light of the changing technology, speculate on the future relationships among the unions having bargaining relationships with the Bell System and Illinois Bell.

3. In their introduction to the Harvard cases, *Problems in Labor Relations*, the authors identify eight "structures of institutional relationships" between parties: containment-aggression, ideology, conflict, power-bargaining, deal-bargaining, collusion, accommodation, cooperation. How would you characterize the employer-union relationships in Illinois Bell in 1968? In prior years?

4. Trace the process whereby the bargaining structure has come to be what it is, including size and scope of bargaining units, distribution of decision-making power.

5. Compare the "pork chop generation" as this case discusses it with
the Lordstown Syndrome (Ohio General Motors plant) of boredom
and alienation. Is this the same generation?

6. If the pork chop generation distrusts union leadership as much as
it does management, what changes can you foresee in collective bargaining?

7. Set the various arguments of System Council T-4 and Illinois
Bell against each other for bargaining purposes. Which are appropriate
or inappropriate to the bargaining situation? Evaluate each argument
and prepare counter arguments.

8. Is it reasonable in bargaining that an increase in wages for a worker
be equated with an increase in return on investment to the shareholder?
How does this then, relate to productivity increases of the worker, the
firm's ability to pay, comparative wages, cost of living?

9. Based on information in the case, develop a wage policy for Illinois
Bell; for System Council T-4. If you were called in to arbitrate this
dispute what would be the bases upon which your decision would be
made?

10. Why do both industrial and craft unions exist in the Bell System?
How do they relate to worker self-interest? To protection of the
unions' interests? To the protection of the employer's interest?

11. In view of the craft-industrial conflict between IBEW and CWA,
what are the possible strategies to unify the interests of the two
unions?

The long weeks of the strike were marked by bitterness and frustration on both sides, by charges and counter-charges of unfair labor practices filed with the National Labor Relations Board, by increasing political efforts both in Chicago and Washington to find a solution to the strike before the Democratic National Convention was affected, by a hassle over arbitration, and by painstaking efforts by federal mediators that seemed to lead nowhere.

At one point, the mediation service's top troubleshooter commented, "This is the toughest strike I've ever been exposed to."

Each side charged the other with certain kinds of violent behavior. Considerable damage was done to Illinois Bell telephone cables, for example, and company spokesmen strongly suggested that strikers were responsible. More than 100 cables were slashed, some of them serving large areas in residential communities and some serving large downtown office buildings.

Charles L. Brown, Jr., operations vice president who later became Illinois Bell president, told the press the company had no evidence the IBEW was involved but "it doesn't happen when there is no strike on." Throughout the summer the company ran many advertisements offering rewards of $10,000 each for information leading to the arrest and conviction of the persons responsible for specific cable damage.

Union spokesmen consistently disclaimed any knowledge of the cable-cutting and said the union does not condone it. Servatius once added, though, "If the company had been honest and just with us at the bargaining table, we're sure these incidents never would have happened."

The company reported, too, that acid had been thrown at employees seeking to repair damaged lines and that someone was pouring liquid solder into the payslots of downtown telephones.

On the other hand, the union signed assault charges against Bell supervisors who, members said, had driven cars and trucks into picket lines, injuring strikers. And the union claimed that the company was hiring suburban police to break up legal picketing activities and was highly indignant when some of their pickets were sprayed with chemical Mace in one suburb.

When emotions are at a high pitch, perhaps some such acts are inevitable. Some observers think that the extensive automation of the industry was a contributory cause. The union was running a tough, militant strike, seeking to shut down the industry, yet it seemed to have little effect on the operation of the telephone business. When a strike is that frustrating, individuals perhaps seek other ways to lash out at what frustrates them.

Increasing tensions showed in other ways, too: in terser language, in more summary refusals, in more and more vehement accusations of unfairness, of inhumanity, of double-dealing. Illinois Bell ran a series of frequent full-page ads in the Chicago newspapers, suggesting with increasing acidity that the union leaders didn't really speak for the membership of the unions and were, indeed, leading the membership astray.

The union mimeographed and handed out strike bulletins, usually one or two a week, that were increasingly belligerent in tone, that charged the company with "back door bargaining" (for communicating directly with the strikers rather than going through union leadership) and with strikebreaking (Bell System employees from other areas were brought in to keep the phones operating), and suggesting that Illinois Bell should "go to hell."

During May, the first month of the strike, further meetings were held with federal mediators, but the two sides were far apart. Illinois Bell negotiators were offering the three-year contract and union negotiators were insisting on an 18-month agreement to finish out the current contract. The union people were convinced — and still are — that a three-year contract, particularly one with a major increase the first year and smaller increases in the second and third years, is not in their best interests.

"It means we get farther and farther behind," Nickey explained. "This was an issue that had been building up. In 1966 all the companies had gotten similar contracts — three years with one wage inreopener. Before that we had had wage reopeners every year. At that time our union was angry. The men didn't like the contract; they thought 18 months between wage talks was too long. The vote to accept that contract was very close, about 53 percent in favor. Anger has kept on building up. We believed we'd be better off in the long run if we got increases for the rest of the contract, then went into new negotiations when the contract ran out."[1]

Union negotiators were reluctant at first even to talk about the three-year proposal because they did not want to give up the option of bargaining for 18 months.

That was a major headache for the company negotiators, partly because some of the fringe benefits negotiated in the nationwide settlement with the CWA were contingent upon those benefits (chiefly pension changes) going into effect in all operating companies at the same time.

"Sure, we wanted the three-year contract," said Clyde Boylls, chief negotiator for Illinois Bell. "It was a matter of labor peace. And it had a lot of goodies in it the 18-month contract didn't have, things like additional vacation time and improved pensions. But they just didn't want to follow the CWA pattern. What they really want is to take the CWA base and then improve on it. That's intolerable for us because we have the rest of the industry to think about."

On May 27, Illinois Bell ran one of its full-page ads, summarizing its position.

"The latest telephone strike concerns everyone — us, our employees, and you (especially if you're waiting to have a telephone installed)," the ad stated. "If you have wondered what Illinois Bell is doing to bring about a reasonable settlement, here is the story.

"The latest strike: Background and issues:

"Illinois Bell currently is being struck by 11,800 employees of our Plant department represented by the International Brotherhood of Electrical Workers. They include installers, repairmen, cable splicers, and some clerical workers.

"This strike officially began on May 8. But most of the strikers have been off their jobs since April 18 because they refused to cross picket lines during the earlier strike by members of the Communications Workers of America.

"Our current general contract with the IBEW, which extends to October 18, 1969, called for a discussion of wages only at this time. Negotiations began on March 7.

"What has the company offered?

"After considerable bargaining the company made a proposal which calls for the largest increase ever offered these employees. It would have immediately increased the top pay for craftsmen by $12 a week in Chicago. The union bargaining committee turned it down.

"Next we proposed a package similar to the one that had resolved the earlier CWA strike. It provides for total increases of nearly 20 percent to be paid within two years — and a new three-year contract.

"Some 300,000 Bell System employees across the country have accepted this offer; including 70,000 who have the same kinds of jobs as our craftsmen. Other union leaders have hailed the package; it surpasses the settlements in other major industries such as auto, can, and rubber. Yet the IBEW bargaining committee in Illinois studied it briefly and flatly rejected it.

"What's the latest offer made by the company?

"A few days ago we altered the package and offered the IBEW even higher basic wage increases with somewhat less in fringe benefits.

"Top craftsmen in Chicago, for example, would get increases totaling $26 a week within the next two years, including an immediate increase of $14 a week.

"This means each man getting these increases would collect more than $3,000 in additional pay over the next three years.

"In addition, they would enjoy all the benefits listed in the box at right.

"Again, the IBEW bargaining team in Illinois showed no interest in the offer.

"Where can we go from here?

"We believe that our craftsmen do deserve substantial increases. And we think our latest offer is substantial by any standard.

"We feel, however, that we have gone as far as we can to settle the dispute without being unfair both to our customers and our other employees.

"Our three-year package offer, when fully in effect and applied to all employees, would add $56 million a year to our costs. And, of course, the money for these increases ultimately must be paid by our customers.

"We stand ready to meet with the union around the clock to settle this dispute. But it takes two to negotiate.

"Our management people, along with some 6,800 craft employees who are on the job, are working hard to give you service that is as near normal as possible while the strike continues. Meanwhile, we ask for your continued patience and cooperation and hope you understand our position in trying to end the strike."

The "box at right" referred to in the ad states:

"Here are the kinds of benefits IBEW members could be enjoying now:

1. Three wage increases totaling $26 over two years for top craftsmen; $16 for top clerical people.
2. Payment of double time for weekly hours beyond 49, starting after the second year of the contract.
3. An additional 10 percent payment for night work, after the first year of the contract.
4. Minimum pensions increased, effective June 1, 1969.
5. Starting June 1, 1969, Social Security adjustments on pensions will be eliminated. In effect, this increases pensions by one-quarter of the individual's Social Security benefits.

6. Pension vested, so that anyone at least 40 years old with 15 or more years of service can leave the company and still get a pension at age 65. Effective June 1, 1969.
7. The company will pay the full cost of hospital and surgical insurance after the second year of the contract; will pay 75 percent immediately.
8. The Extraordinary Medical Expense plan paid in full by the company, will cover additional medical expenses beyond three percent of the employee's basic pay.
9. The employee's share of group life insurance premiums is reduced 12½ percent immediately. The company will pay the full cost after the second year of the contract.
10. Five weeks' vacation after 25 years of service beginning next year.
11. Sickness or off-the-job accident disability pay, ranging from 52 weeks of half-pay for employees with as little as six months of service up to a full year of full pay for employees with 25 years of service. Effective June 1, 1969.

"Overall, these wage increases and benefits which become effective over the next two years add up to nearly a 20 percent increase in compensation."

The only official comment from the union came in the next mimeographed Strikers' News: "Illinois Bell is spending a fortune in advertising and on the news media to explain their position. Also, how normal everything is in phone service. Phooey — if they would get to the table and use this money wisely in wage increases, etc., they could get a contract now. But alas, no — Illinois Bell must preserve their image (public, that is) and to hell with you and me."

The same strike bulletin commented on a company mailing to individual employees, covering the material in the ad: "The company is trying backdoor bargaining again. All of us have received the company handbill which purports to tell what a marvelous offer they have made to you . . . telling everyone how crazy we must be and how wonderful they are. Well, we strongly urge you to return this bit of propaganda to your union office with a note on the back telling the company to see your bargaining representative."

At the end of May, the IBEW called on Chicago's Mayor Richard J. Daley to intervene in the strike. It's a common role for Daley. In many taut labor disputes, particularly those with a considerable public interest, Daley calls both sides together and keeps them together — frequently all day and all night — until some kind of agreement, at least temporary, is reached.

During the next few days, Daley met separately with both union and company spokesmen, and then promised to act if he found it necessary. But the next move came from Washington.

William Simkin, Federal Mediation Director, called Illinois Bell officials and IBEW negotiators to Washington for talks June 5, 6 and 7. Also summoned were negotiators for IBEW locals in Western Electric plants across the country; they also had not reached agreement. But the Washington talks were recessed without reaching any solutions.

Early June brought a new headache for the IBEW. CWA telephone operators, who had been honoring the electricians' picket lines, returned to work after receiving notices from Illinois Bell that, after June 6, their service dates would be moved forward one day for each day of unauthorized absence from work, thus affecting such fringes as vacations and pensions. The IBEW promptly accused the company of threatening strikers with loss of seniority and filed a charged of unfair labor practice. The company contended that such adjustment of service dates was an established company practice that was uniformly applied. The issue sounds fairly simple but there were some complex legal points involved; there were lengthy hearings. The question was not resolved — in the company's favor — until months after the strike.

Further meetings with federal mediators in Chicago during June brought no progress in solving the strike issues.

The Democratic National Convention

Chicago's Mayor Richard J. Daley reentered the picture at the end of June. He had been growing increasingly nervous about the threat the strike posed for the Democratic National Convention, scheduled to begin in Chicago August 26. Time was growing short to begin the installation of complex electronic equipment in the city's International Amphitheatre, where the convention would be held. The equipment, necessary to news and television coverage of the convention, was to be installed by Illinois Bell, but it couldn't be done if the strike continued.

Daley had fought hard, against powerful pressure, to have the convention held in his city and the Democratic National Committee had finally made that decision, but without much enthusiasm. Many feared that black residents of the city would seek to disrupt the convention, which was to be in a black neighborhood; they argued it would be safer to hold the convention on the Miami island where the Republicans were to hold their convention. Network television executives pressured for Miami, too, to save the vast amounts of money needed to install different equipment in Chicago. Though Daley had won the Chicago decision, many of the pressures to hold the convention in Miami — or anywhere else — still continued. And it would be bitter irony for the mayor, who has strong labor support, to lose out on his long-time dream because of a telephone strike.

Illinois Bell executives believe that the IBEW had seen the convention as a powerful weapon from the very beginning of negotiations. The union is scornful of that suggestion.

"We didn't go out in May with any thought of the convention in August," said Don Servatius. "We're reasonable men. That was never our thought. If it had been, we'd have extended negotiations until July. No one believed the strike would go on so long. We'd never been on strike, you know."

But all agree that as the August date neared, the convention did become a weapon. Perhaps it turned out to be a two-edged sword.

It was first mentioned in the mimeographed Strikers' News on June 3, with the comment, "If things continue, there will be many events not held in Chicago this summer. We think of one major event that is fast going down the drain, and that is the Democratic National Convention. Unless the telephone workers are back on the job soon, no communication links (TV, radio, telephones) will be available to the politicians in the Amphitheatre."

It was surely on Mayor Daley's mind when he called representatives of Illinois Bell and the striking IBEW to meet with him in his office on June 28.

James W. Cook, Illinois Bell president, was interviewed on the way to the mayor's office and, referring to the convention issue, called the strike "legalized extortion. I don't intend to submit to that."

Nickey was interviewed, too. "We, as a group, do not necessarily threaten the convention," he said. "We only point out there could be a disruption."

Daley, also asked about the threat to the convention, snapped back, "No one threatens the Democratic Convention."

With Cook for the company in the mayor's office were Clyde Boylls, the chief negotiator, and Jack Gable, the personnel vice president. The five-man negotiating team was there for the IBEW. The groups met with the mayor on June 28, again on June 29, and again, for six hours, on June 30.

During the talks, company officials talked of perhaps increasing the offer at the top level if other parts of the contract were modified. The union replied that was the "old game of 'you can move it around within the framework'," and turned it down. The talks ended, and no more were scheduled.

Cook announced after the meeting that the company would ask the Federal Mediation Service to poll the union rank-and-file on the latest company offer. Nickey replied he would oppose the poll, that the company offer was the same one made May 25, which had already been rejected by the union.

Nothing had been accomplished to solve the problem of equipment installation for the convention. TV executives began to talk of asking the Democratic National Committee to switch the convention to another city. The company estimated that about 79,000 man hours of work needed to be done before August 26 to complete the installation work and that it should be started by July 8. To be installed were 6,000 telephones, 400 teletype machines, 20 switchboards, and 56 TV network channels. All the cables and wires had been assembled near the amphitheatre, company officials said. There had been some talk of having company supervisors install the equipment, but Nickey had replied, "We will have picket lines any place where management people try to take our jobs." Then the Amphitheatre management had asked that supervisors not install the equipment because other craftsmen would not cross the IBEW picket lines.

Said Nickey, "Unless they agree to bargain, we will have an old-fashioned convention, with news carried by runner."

Early July brought extraordinary political pressure. Labor Secretary W. Willard Wirtz talked to Mayor Daley. Undersecretary James J. Reynolds conferred with Cook, Illinois Bell president, in Washington, and said the Democratic National Committee was thinking of switching the convention. Illinois Bell officials told the labor department it was reluctant to grant the IBEW terms for fear the nationwide Bell pattern would be upset.

The Chicago newspapers began to pressure the strikers. Said the Sun-Times, normally rather sympathetic to labor, "No doubt the electrical workers believe they have the telephone company and the citizens of Chicago over a barrel because they can prevent the Democratic Convention being held here. If they do drive it off to another city, they will only prove that union power can be abused to the detriment of everyone . . . If the convention is moved, the electrical workers will lose not only the good will of their fellow Illinoisians, but the big gun they are now holding at the telephone company's treasury. We hope their friends and neighbors will persuade the electrical workers that they and everyone else will be benefitted if they settle now."

In Washington, Democratic leaders went to Joseph Keenan, international secretary of the IBEW, pleading with him to intervene in Illinois and settle the strike. Keenan turned them down with the reply that the union had complete control.

Daley said city workers might be used to install convention equipment. Illinois Bell suggested private contractors be allowed to make the installations. System Council T-4 said they would picket in either case.

There was talk of arbitration of the differences (it will be dealt with in another section) and extraordinary pressure was put upon Illinois Bell to agree. The company said "No."

It was Daley, with his bank of past favors to labor, who found a way around the installation impasse. In a series of tense meetings with top labor officials in Chicago, with Illinois Bell people, and with the striking IBEW, Daley worked out this plan:

*An all-Chicago Labor Committee was formed to act as contractor for the Amphitheatre installation work.

*Illinois Bell would pay for the work (at top electricians' rates, not at the lower Bell rates for electricians), with the money going to the all-Chicago Labor Committee.

*The committee would turn the money over to the IBEW strike fund.

*The IBEW would find 300 strikers who would volunteer to install the equipment for no compensation other than the regular strike bene-fit of $25 a week.

*Through it all, Daley and the labor leaders would continue to support the striking IBEW workers and to urge Illinois Bell to arbitrate the issues in the strike.

A beaming Daley, flanked by 24 top labor leaders, announced the plan July 22, and stated, "The solution to this problem came from within the labor movement. I was always optimistic about a solution in a labor matter, because my father was a labor man and my mother was an optimist."

A Chicago Sun-Times reporter who had been watching the proceed-ings confirmed that Daley had indeed been optimistic through it all. "Shuttling among the smoke-filled rooms was the non-smoking Daley, sometimes grim-faced, usually beaming, forever confident. Last week, when there seemed to be no hope, Daley saw 'great brightness in the skies'."

What did Nickey think of the agreement? He told reporters, "The mayor told us that the prestige of the city was at stake. He told us how much holding the convention meant to business. He convinced us to make this concession."

He told his union people they'd have to go along with the agree-ment because there really was no alternative, but he had some trouble at first lining up the 300 volunteers. The Strikers' News announce-ment of the plan stressed that the installation of the equipment would be at the Amphitheatre *only*, and then explained the reason:

"Because we have an ironclad commitment from all of labor in Chicago to back the rest of our strike 100 percent — wherever we have or put up picket lines; these lines will be honored by all of labor. None of the hotels, businesses, etc., will be provided with any communication

facilities unless we can get Illinois Bell to settle our strike on terms
acceptable to us. Also, in all other areas around the state, this cooperation will be present. Our fight with Illinois Bell is too vital to allow
them to force the convention out of Chicago, which would hurt not
only us, but all of labor in Chicago and Illinois. Our strike effort will
continue even stronger in all other areas. Sometimes, it is necessary
to sacrifice in one area in order to gain more for everyone on the long
haul. This, the system council has decided, is the way this must be
done. They realize all of the implications involved in this action and
ask for the patience and the cooperation of all the members throughout
the state."

The agreement was viewed by many observers as a turning point
in the long strike. More precisely, as the moment at which the IBEW
lost the strike. Asked about that later, Nickey still contended that he
never really had a choice but to go along with the plan, particularly
since the labor movement had joined in the appeal.

"The big club was really Miami," he reminisced. "A lot of powerful people wanted the convention there, anyway, and were looking
for an excuse. Bell wanted it there. The networks wanted it there. If
the convention had been switched to Miami, it would have gone down
in the books as our fault. By our action, we had the public with us.
It was one of the few times we did."

The agreement did leave some unsolved problems. TV officials
were unhappy and explained convention coverage was still seriously
limited because the agreement covered only the Amphitheatre and not
the hotels. As it later turned out, television crews were hampered by
this fact in trying to cover the tumultuous events that occurred around
the Hilton Hotel and in the parks during the days of the convention.

But for the mayor, the agreement was a victory. It surely didn't
solve all his problems. There was the revolt within his beloved party
to claim his attention. And a cab strike looming for convention week.
And a strike by black bus drivers that was to hamstring hotel service
for convention delegates because the hotel service people couldn't
get to work. And his worry over the growing threat from thousands
of young rebels to come and destroy Chicago during the convention.

Back on the strike front, both Nickey and Illinois Bell officials
announced that the Amphitheatre agreement in no way changed their
positions on any strike issues.

Proposal to Arbitrate

During those same July days when politics so dominated the Illinois
Bell strike news, there were other developments of interest and significance to students of labor-management relations. One of them was

the proposal by the IBEW System Council T-4 to submit the disputed contract issues to binding arbitration.

It was an unusual proposal because American labor leaders as far back as Samuel Gompers, the founder of the American Federation of Labor, have usually insisted on their right to bargain collectively on the terms of labor contracts, without any outside interference or assistance. So opposed was Gompers to any kind of governmental tampering with labor relations that he even objected to the establishment of government facilities for mediation. He feared that might eventually lead to compulsory arbitration.

Labor opposition to arbitration does not apply, of course, to arbitration as the final step in the grievance procedure, a step that is provided for in about nine of every 10 union contracts. In these cases of disagreement about contract rules and how they are enforced, arbitration is a long-accepted practice. But arbitration of the terms that go into the contract is something very different.

"We knew it was an unusual proposal," Nickey said later when asked about his suggestion. "But we were dealing with an unusual employer."

"It came out of the utter frustration of our bargaining," added Frank Cunningham of the IBEW System Council T-4. "We felt we just couldn't get anywhere." The proposal was made on July 13, a Saturday night, at the end of a fruitless day-long bargaining session with top federal mediators from Washington.

It came at the end of a week when feelings ran high, partly because the political pressure was building. On the Saturday before, the IBEW had held a rally for the strikers in Hansen Park stadium, on Chicago's Northwest side. Illinois Bell officials had been pushing for a rank-and-file vote on its latest proposal. Nickey had asked President Cook if he'd like to make that request at the rally. Cook said no, that he didn't think that was appropriate, but he gave Nickey a letter to read.

Nickey spoke to about 6,000 strikers in the stadium. He said Cook was either "too big or too tight" to go the stadium to speak for himself. Then he read the letter, asking for a membership vote. When he finished the letter, he tore it into pieces, then told the rally, "The company proposals are worth as much as that paper I tore up."

Then he asked the strikers whether they wanted to take a secret ballot on the company offer. The crowd howled, "No." The union later estimated that only about 50 members had stood up to demand a vote or acceptance of the best offer by the negotiating team.

During the week, Nickey met again with Mayor Daley and told him the unions would modify their wage demands. He indicated they would settle for an immediate increase of $17.50 and another $8 after a year, instead of $19.50 immediately and $10 after a year. The unions still wanted an 18-month contract. But the demands were still a long way from the company offer of a three-year contract with wage increases of $14, $6 and $6.

The modification did not bring any progress at the day-long Saturday session with the mediators from Washington. And it wasn't until after that meeting broke up that Nickey made his offer to submit the dispute to binding third-party arbitration. It got headlines in the Sunday morning papers, apparently one of the reasons it was made after the mediation session broke up. IBEW people felt they had not had a fair chance to tell their story in the press.

Besides the wage issue, Nickey said, arbitration would also decide problems involving union demands for reclassification of towns to increase the basic salaries of some downstate workers, for upgrading some jobs and to "clean up problems all around the state." Nickey said the unions wouldn't be willing to submit the three year contract proposal to an arbitrator; they still wanted the 18-month contract.

The following day, Sunday, July 14, Illinois Bell agreed to take the proposal under consideration. Mayor Daley sent the company a telegram, urging it to accept arbitration, saying "Surely, this is the American way."

The next day, without yet giving an answer, the company asked whether Nickey had a legal right to commit the unions to arbitration without a vote by union members. Nickey told reporters the union was conferring with lawyers, but said, "We feel the membership has given us authority to work out a satisfactory agreement, and arbitration is one way of doing it." Later that day, Gordon Freeman, the international president of the union, sent the company a telegram saying the negotiating committee was authorized to submit the membership to binding arbitration and assuring the company the international union would stand by the offer.

The IBEW put out another issue of its Strikers' News, explaining the proposal:

"This means the unions are willing to have an arbitrator examine the economic positions and make a decision on what should be given to the strikers on wages and the related items. The System Council does not relish the idea of doing this, but when you are forced to deal with the adamant Bell System, drastic action such as binding arbitration may be the only way to end this strike. What does this mean? It means both parties in the strike must agree on a neutral third party to arbitrate the economic issues on our present contract dispute. When the arguments are complete, the arbitrator will make a decision on how much will be awarded in wages, etc., to the IBEW strikers.

"Any back to work agreement will be handled separately from the arbitration. The System Council does not want to hinder in any way getting everyone back to work as quickly as possible — so we did not clutter up the arbitration offer with anything else. It's simply a straight question to IBT. "Will you or will you not accept binding arbitration?'

"The IBEW is sincere in trying to end this strike. We wonder about the company's sincerity most of the time."

On Tuesday, July 16, Illinois Bell rejected the proposal to arbitrate. Cook, the president, said the company felt a referendum among union members would be needed before arbitration could be binding on the strikers.

"The best legal opinion we have is that the arbitration decision is not binding on the membership until ratified by it. This makes the union offer an empty one, which is, in effect, binding only on the company."

Cook also stated that no subsidiary of AT&T had ever submitted a labor dispute to arbitration, a factor that was undoubtedly important in the minds of company officials. (AT&T had proposed arbitration on the local level for each operating company back in 1947, in an effort to avert the first nation-wide strike, but the Communications Workers of America had turned it down.)

Mayor Daley said he was greatly disappointed at the management decision and added, "It is a sad commentary when management will refuse to sit down." He continued to push the arbitration idea during the coming weeks of negotiations over the Amphitheatre installation.

On the same day that Illinois Bell rejected the arbitration offer, officials announced they would make a new three-year proposal to the union and urged that this time it be taken to a union vote. Illinois Bell people had long been convinced that their message wasn't getting through to the membership and that the negotiating team was not really speaking for the membership.

On that day, too, another full-page Illinois Bell ad (obviously in preparation earlier, before the arbitration argument) appeared in the Chicago papers.

"89 days," read the headline, in big type. "When a strike lasts this long, someone is out of step. IBEW workers have been off the job since April 18. What's holding up a settlement? Is Illinois Bell offering too little, or is the union demanding too much? Look at the facts and decide for yourself.

"fact:

Nationwide, the Bell System has reached contract agreements with 60 union locals this year, 17 of them in the IBEW. Another union in New England is preparing to submit a company proposal to union members for their approval. However, one local union — the IBEW

System Council T-4 here in Illinois — even though it has been offered its choice of the terms which 60 locals have accepted, is demanding more. This union just says 'We want more — more than anyone else.'

"fact:

We have offered the union a choice of two substantial packages: (1) an 18-month contract with wage increases of 7.5 percent — a pattern set in bargaining with the IBEW, or (2) a 36-month contract involving increases in wages and fringe benefits of more than 19 percent — a pattern set in bargaining with another union (CWA), but selected by 8 IBEW locals. Nationally, 11 locals have said 'yes' to the 18-month contract; 49 have said 'yes' to the 36-month contract. 60 union locals in all have agreed. But IBEW T-4 union leaders say 'no!' To both patterns they say, 'We want more — more than anyone else.'

"fact:

400,000 telephone workers across the country — including 50,000 in the IBEW — are now at work and will enjoy substantial increases under these new contracts — the same kind of contracts we are offering in Illinois. But still the IBEW T-4 leaders say 'no.' They say, 'We want more than anyone else.'

"fact:

Leaders of other unions have hailed the package as outstanding; it surpasses the settlement reached in the auto, rubber and every other basic industry. And still the IBEW T-4 leaders say 'no.' They say, 'We want more than anyone else.'

We are sure that if the 11,800 members of IBEW T-4 would be allowed to voice their opinion by secret ballot tomorrow, they would agree with 400,000 fellow workers across the country and say 'yes.' But even to voting, IBEW T-4 leaders say 'no.' "

On July 17, the following day, Illinois Bell did make a new three-year contract offer to the IBEW. In wages, it provided $1.50 more a week than the last offer, with wage increases for top level craftsmen totaling $27.50 over three years ($14.50 the first year, $6 the second, $7 the third). Boylls, the chief negotiator, explained that the offer was not an increase in the total package, but a rearrangement of the offer in order to provide more money at the top. Certain fringes, he said, were reduced to keep the offer within the guidelines established by AT&T for new contracts between electrical workers and members of the Bell System.

Union negotiators promptly replied that this was the same old story; no new money, just the same package redistributed. They rejected the offer and refused to submit it to a membership vote. They further announced that they would file an unfair labor charge, saying that the company was refusing to bargain in good faith. (The charge will be considered in the next section).

It is worth noting here, however, that this offer, rejected on July 17 was basically the offer that was finally accepted by the membership; but not until three votes had been taken, the tumultuous convention had come and gone, and the strike had continued for two more months.

The company's refusal to arbitrate did not end that clamor. The proposal gained considerable support, both in Chicago and elsewhere. Daley renewed his urging to arbitrate and he was joined by the Democratic National Committee and its top leadership, the Chicago Convention Bureau, and the Chicago Federation of Labor, whose president, William Lee, said, "The entire labor movement of Chicago is disturbed and upset. It is almost unheard of for any company to refuse arbitration."

Responding to Lee in a statement, Illinois Bell said, "Arbitration in a wage dispute is still a one-way street. Once the convention issue is removed from our wage negotiations, collective bargaining will resolve the dispute."

The New York Times joined in editorially:

". . . As usual, the rights and wrongs in this dispute are not easily apportioned between the strikers and the company. Although the difference between the union's latest demand and the company's latest offer is comparatively small, the Chicago employees are seeking more than the pattern of wage settlements reached by the union and the Bell companies in other sections of the country.

". . . the union has asked arbitration . . . the company has questioned whether it can be binding . . . A more compelling motive appears to be the traditional reluctance of companies in the Bell System to surrender their freedom of action to outside arbiters.

"This reluctance is understandable, but it cannot be controlling. No public utility can legitimately place its private preference above the needs of the public it exists to serve . . . Submission of the dispute to an arbiter is the responsible course of action for Illinois Bell."

The Chicago Sun-Times didn't agree and stated on its editorial pages that Illinois Bell would not arbitrate for reasons "most business executives can appreciate. Arbitrators usually offer a settlement which is a compromise between the latest offer of the company and the demand of the workers. Such a compromise often happens without arbitration, but it should happen as a consequence of the company's own ability and willingness to pay.

"Illinois Bell is concerned with the effect any settlement with the IBEW will have on the national wage-price upsurge and with contracts already signed with 367,000 workers in the national telephone system.

"The strikers say their pay has not kept pace with that of electrical workers in other utilities. But it has kept pace with wages paid within the national telephone industry and is even slightly better. Eight years ago the strikers' average wage was $106.28 weekly. Today it is $136.44, up 28.37 percent. The increase for all telephone workers has been 26.49 percent.

"The strikers are asking a 10.88 percent increase now and another 4.73 percent a year hence, with a contract to end six months after that with presumably another wage demand to be made then. This is higher than the 6 to 7 percent increases that have been current throughout American industry in the past few months. One Illinois Bell offer is 7.5 percent in the next 18 months." The *Sun-Times* urged the strikers to vote and end the dispute.

On July 21, IBEW leaders said they would submit the company offer to a vote if Illinois Bell would agree to arbitration in case the membership rejected the offer. The company said "No," that it could not accept arbitration. That brought another heated blast in the Strikers' News and a charge that the company was "afraid of arbitration":

"If their 'pattern' is so good for the country, why, then, are they afraid? An arbitrator would only look at both sides and decide what is just. Evidently, the company is in mortal fear of justice being given to their employees around the nation. The company spokesmen even sound like they're ashamed of what they are being forced to say. They should be!"

It may be that the IBEW leaders never really expected the company to agree to arbitration and didn't much want it themselves, that the offer was largely a public relations gesture. Nickey has said since that only then and at the time of the Amphitheatre agreement did the strikers feel the public was with them. And the public is an important factor in the outcome of any big strike.

Charges of Unfair Labor Practices

When Illinois Bell turned down the arbitration proposal, the IBEW filed a charge with the NLRB that the company was not bargaining in good faith. It based the charge on the contention that the company was bargaining from a predetermined position, from which it was unwilling or unable to deviate, because the position was imposed upon the company by its parent company, the American Telephone & Telegraph Co.

Specifically, the IBEW locals charged both Illinois Bell and the

AT&T with two separate violations of the National Labor Relations Act—Sec. 8 (a) (5), which provides:

"It shall be an unfair labor practice for an employer . . . to refuse to bargain collectively with the representatives of his employees . . ."

Illinois Bell, "by its officers, agents and employees," the complaint stated, "has refused to bargain in good faith with System Council T-4, IBEW, in that said employer has bargained from a predetermined position that allowed no variance in its offer from the national pattern of wage increases imposed in the telephone industry by the American Telephone & Telegraph Company."

AT&T was charged with imposing the package on Illinois Bell so "the negotiators for Illinois Bell when meeting with System Council T-4 were without authority to bargain on behalf of their company."

Robert E. Fitzgerald, Jr., attorney for the IBEW group, wrote a series of letters backing up the claims to Ross M. Madden, NLRB regional director in Chicago.

". . . The American Telephone & Telegraph Company and its policy of negotiating with the Communications Workers of America for its Western Electric subsidiary and then requiring that all its subsidiary companies offer only that package to the various unions bargaining with the companies is, in reality, the cause of the bad faith bargaining by Illinois Bell," one of the letters stated. "Thus, although System Council T-4 does not bargain directly with AT&T it (and all other unions attempting to bargain with subsidiaries of the AT&T) is required to face the economic power of AT&T. The evidence of this in the instant case is that Illinois Bell Telephone Company has from the beginning of the strike received supervisory personnel from various companies throughout the country to perform the struck work that would be done by the Illinois Bell employees who are workers of the local unions in System Council T-4."

In another letter, summing up material presented to Madden, Fitzgerald wrote, "the union submitted its wage demands based upon economic surveys conducted for both Illinois Bell Telephone Co. and the AT&T. The Illinois Bell negotiators failed to respond to the Illinois survey, except to ultimately admit that they were limited in the amount of money that they were able to offer because of the package imposed upon them by AT&T. It is submitted that this additional evidence further exemplifies the 'take-it-or-leave-it' attitude of the Illinois Bell negotiators, which reached its culmination in their admission that they were unable to vary their offer from the national package of AT&T."

Fitzgerald then referred to the NLRB ruling in the General Electric case: "In practical effect, respondent's 'bargaining' position is akin to that of a party who enters into a negotiation with a predetermined resolve not to budge from an initial position, an attitude inconsistent with good faith bargaining. . . It placed itself in a position where it could not give unfettered consideration to the merits of any proposal that the union might offer." Fitzgerald contended that the facts in the two cases were comparable.

Fitzgerald then cited what he termed evidence of AT&T's overriding control," including almost total ownership of Illinois Bell by AT&T, the transfer of chief executive officers from one company to another within the system, the industry-wide pension and benefit system, the sending of supervisors from other companies to do the struck work, and:

"Finally and most clearly the fact that all subsidiaries of AT&T have offered the same nationwide package is evidence of the complete control by AT&T of the telephone industry. This control of the bargaining of its subsidiaries is not merely a situation where AT&T engages in permissible pattern bargaining. The pattern bargaining situation, to be valid, must occur only where the subsidiary company or local union involved has the ability to vary the terms of the pattern when local circumstances require, and thus possess other than a 'take-it-or-leave-it' attitude. The evidence previously submitted clearly shows that the Illinois Bell negotiators were unable to vary the nation-wide package in spite of (1) being presented with an economic survey justifying higher wages than the national pattern, (2) having to endure a lengthy strike which required the importation of supervisory personnel from throughout the country and which placed in jeopardy the Democratic National Convention and (3) being offered the alternative of voluntary arbitration. There is absolutely no reason to believe that the Illinois Bell Telephone Co. and its bargaining agents were able to vary the national pattern and thus possessed the open mind required for good faith bargaining. Therefore, the subsidiary company directly involved in these charges was not engaging in what might be considered permissible pattern bargaining.

"Finally, by the admission of the Illinois Bell negotiators that subsidiary was not allowed to vary from the national package."

At the time the charges were filed with the NLRB, Illinois Bell President Cook replied that they were "totally without merit and we welcome the opportunity to show them up for the contrived accusations that they are." The company contended, of course, that it did bargain locally with its employees, that it was free to alter the package to meet local needs, and that it had indeed done so in the series of offers that it had made to the strikers.

On August 6, the NLRB dismissed the charge that the company had not bargained in good faith, and later ruled that other evidence submitted did not substantiate the charge. There had been no formal contract negotiations during the three-week period, but there had been informal talks. In these talks, Jack Gable, Bell Vice President of Personnel, contended the IBEW had "displayed an unbending attitude." Indeed, it was the feeling of company officials that the union had been more bound to a predetermined position than the company had.

There were other charges filed, by both sides, with the NLRB. They led to NLRB and court orders that forced the union members to alter some of their picketing practices. Other charges submitted were later withdrawn. But the very fact they were filed is significant; the filing of such charges is increasingly a tactic in any complex strike, part of the arsenal of coercive measures each side tries to summon against the other. The fact that the charges may later be withdrawn, when the need for a coercive measure is past, is part of the same picture; neither side is really out after total victory because they still have to work together when the dispute is over. The filing of charges and counter-charges with the NLRB indicates, too, the large role such a third party plays in umpiring the process of collective bargaining.

Later, before the end of the strike, the IBEW would make another effort to bring in a third party to help resolve the issues.

The Final Phase of the Strike

The beginning of August brought little change in the deadlocked negotiations. The strike had been in progress since May 8. The company estimated the strikers were losing wages totalling $1,600,000 a week. Some, but not all, had found other jobs. Those who weren't working were getting strike benefits of $25 a week from the international union's strike fund. That weekly benefit was paid 18 times and cost the union $5 million. There were rumors of a back-to-work move.

The Strikers' News of August 1 summed up the positions this way: "*Negotiations*: Illinois Bell has not changed its offer since April 23 on the 18-month wage reopener. On the 3-year package--no change since May 25. Council never agreed on the 3-year negotiations. Members want to finish out the current contract. Union has modified proposals--company only says, "You can move the money around within the total package or framework.'
"*Union Position:* 2-step wage increase of $17.50 a week now; $8.00 a year from now (top wages). Reduce town classification to 4 (now 6). Upgrade 5 jobs. Reduce money spread between towns.
"*Company Position:* Increase $4.00 to $12.00--variations of this by removing other items below surface. Upgrade 6 towns only. Job upgrades used as bargaining point. Spread money further between towns."

A few days later, Illinois Bell ran another advertisement:

Illinois Bell
Offers Still More

Now the Union Says
"All or Nothing"

What Does Bargaing Mean to
The Leaders of System Council T-4, IBEW?

They Made it Quite Clear Last Week

It Means: They Will Accept Nothing Less
Than Everything They Demand.

"With the Democratic Convention issue out of the way, we resumed informal negotiations with the union on July 26.

"In an all-out effort to end ths strike, we discussed significant additions to a contract we already considered eminently fair.

"We offered to try and bridge the difference between our last offer of July 17 and the union's last three-year contract position handed to us in Mayor Daley's office on June 29.

"But the union representatives would listen to nothing but complete capitulation.

"Why?

"Because they are betting they can disrupt your phone service so much that you will want us to give them all they ask — anything — just to end this strike.

"How much is fair?

"Who knows. But . . .

"How would you like to get $3,200 more pay over the next three years?

"Weekly wage increase of $14 now and another $13.50 within the next two years.

"Sound fair?

"That's what our formal three-year offer of July 17 would give 2 out of 3 of the workers involved.

"They would also enjoy these improvements in fringe benefits, starting at various dates during the contract: full payment by the company of hospital, surgical and group life insurance premiums; 5 weeks vacation after 25 years; increased pensions and disability payments.

"Similar contracts already have been accepted by half a million other telephone employees here and across the country.

"Without any additions, our July 17 offer surpasses the wage agreements reached in all other major industries this year . . .

"Despite the obvious merits of our July 17 offer, we concluded we should make one more determined effort to reach a settlement.

"That's when we indicated our willingness to try and bridge the difference between offer and demand.

"But the union leaders showed no interest. They want all or nothing.

"Now the question is: How much more is more? . . ."

On August 8, the same day the ad appeared, cables in a big downtown office building were severed, apparently with a power saw, knocking out phone service on 23 floors. Vandalism continued for several more days. The union continued to denounce it and claim no connection. A company statement said, "This concerted drive of criminality extending several days certainly removes any possibility of sheer coincidence or accident."

With all the tension, talks were going on, however. When the NLRB charges were cleared away, the Federal Mediation and Conciliation Service came back into the picture, scheduling negotiations for August 12, the first formal negotiations since July 13, the day of the arbitration offer. At the suggestion of the mediator, negotiators divided into two groups, one to go on talking about money, the other to talk about a back-to-work agreement. It was at one of those sessions that Gilbert Seldin, a top trouble-shooter from Washington, made his comment that "this is the toughest strike I've ever been exposed to."

Intensive negotiations continued for several days, sometimes with federal mediators, sometimes without them. One of the disagreements during this period centered around the new three-year contract proposals the company said it intended to make — the "bridge" referred to in its ad. Company negotiators wanted an agreement from Nickey and the other union men that they would recommend a membership vote in favor of it; they wanted such an agreement before they formally put the offer on the table. Nickey was opposing the idea and said he couldn't be bound to agree to recommend an offer he hadn't been able to see. There were other disagreements, over some of the back-to-work provisions and over retroactivity. The union wanted the offer retroactive to April, the date of the wage reopener; the company wanted June.

On August 28, the IBEW agreed to submit the new three-year proposal to a vote by the membership on Saturday, August 31. It called for an increase of $14.50 a week for top craftsmen, retroactive to June 2 (up 50 cents from the previous offer), $6 on June 1, 1969 (down 50 cents from the previous offer), and $7 on May 31, 1970.

The two sides disagreed on what Nickey promised on August 28. A company official recalls that Nickey said he'd remain neutral, that he wouldn't recommend a vote for the contract, but that he wouldn't recommend against it. "Then 15 minutes later he was on television calling the contract a lousy deal and saying he was going to recommend a vote against it," the official said later. Nickey says he made no promises. He was quoted in the press as saying that he was dissatisfied with the contract, but if the union members voted for it, he'd go along. "I'm going to vote against it," he said, "but I think it will be a close vote."

The vote was held, with union officials supervising, in strike headquarters in Chicago, in six suburbs, and in several other locations throughout the state. Union members, to the considerable suprise of Illinois Bell, voted down the offer, 4,761 to 3,991. In three of the five locals, those located chiefly in Chicago, the majority voted to reject the offer. The votes were:

Local 134 — 251 to accept, 1,122 to reject
Local 165 — 1,199 to accept, 1,251 to reject
Local 315 — 110 to accept, 147 to reject

In the suburban and the downstate locals, the majority voted acceptance, in Local 336 (suburban) by 1,484 to 1,479, and in Local 399 (downstate) 947 to 762.

"It is impossible for us to make any further concessions," a company spokesman said the next day. "We know that this $56,000,000 pact is the best possible offer that could be put together."

A union spokesman said the vote meant the membership "is honestly sick and tired of the dictates of AT&T."

Early the next week, Illinois Bell invited the 3,991 who voted for the contract to return to work, and charged union officials brought about rejection of the contract by failing to inform strikers where to vote.

The union negotiators then agreed to have the membership vote again the following Saturday, September 7, on the 18-month contract offer, essentially the same proposal that union leaders had turned down April 23, before the start of the strike.

Don Servatius was quoted in the newspapers as saying, "We don't want the three-year contract. What we would gain in the first year would be lost in the second and third."

The next issue of the Strikers' News seemed to suggest that the members vote in favor of the 18-month contract. "It's your decision," it stated. "Do we stand firm on our principles and insist on honoring the contract that was signed by the company as well as us? Or do we allow AT&T to dictate new terms, new contracts, and now pre-set wages for three years? Maybe next time they can look in their crystal ball and decide our future wages for 5, 6 or even 10 years. This is the basic decision to be made *now*. Be sure to vote this Saturday, September 7.''

Clyde Boylls, Illinois Bell negotiator, said a vote to accept would be "absolutely incredible," that the union would be giving up $8,500,000 in wages and benefits. "It is the least attractive proposal we have made since the IBEW left their jobs, and will be voted down by any members who understand the alternatives." He added that five wage and benefit offers had been made since April 23, "all superior."

When the votes were counted, it was 6,667 to 1,511 to reject the offer. The proposal lost in each of the five locals; in the suburban and downstate locals, it lost by more than 10 to 1. Nickey said the vote meant the union wanted an improved 18-month offer. He then renewed the proposal for arbitration and added a new suggestion: appointment of a fact-finding board to examine the issues and then recommend a settlement which would have to be approved by both parties.

The fact-finding proposal led nowhere. A union chronology of the strike said that members were getting "edgy." The IBEW then proposed another membership vote, to be held September 21, with a three-way choice for the members:

1. Accept the three-year contract, the same one rejected on August 31.
2. Accept the 18-month contract, the same one rejected on September 7.
3. Continue the strike and continue bargaining.

So the members went again to vote, and this time they accepted the three-year contract. The vote was:

Local	18-month Contract	Three-Year Contract	Strike
134	33	427	902
165	103	1,564	616
315	8	133	107
336 (suburbs)	27	2,191	770
399 (downstate)	21	1,208	467
TOTALS	192	5,523	2,862

"The people got to the point where they had to receive some money," Nickey told the press. "The feeling was that no hope was left."

CHART I
ILLINOIS BELL LABOR-MANAGEMENT RELATIONSHIPS

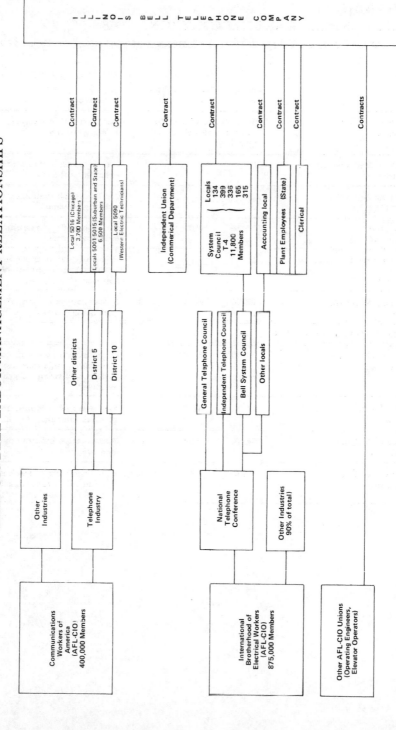

NOTE: UNION MEMBERS TOTALLED 28,261 OF ILLINOIS BELL'S 37,849 EMPLOYEES AS OF DECEMBER 31, 1968

CHART II
ILLINOIS BELL WAGE NEGOTIATIONS, 1968
(Proposed rates for top-skilled technicians at top level of experience)

	1st year	2nd year	3rd year	Comments
IBEW demands March	20% increase across the board (about $32 a week at the top)			for 18-month remainder of existing contract
Illinois Bell first offer March 28	$10			for 18-month remainder of existing contract
Illinois Bell offer April 6	$12			for 18-month remainder of existing contract
IBEW offer April 25	19.50	10.00		for 18-month remainder of existing contract
Pattern settlement with CWA May 5	12.00	6.00	6.00	Combined with fringe benefits, total package equalled 19.6% increase over 3 years
Illinois Bell offer May 6	12.00	6.00	6.00	3-year contract, with other package benefits
STRIKE STARTED MAY 8				
Illinois Bell offer May 24	14.00	6.00	6.00	Company said package totaled same percentage increase as pattern settlement. 3-year package.
IBEW offer July	17.50	8.00		for 18-month remainder of existing contract
Illinois Bell offer July 17	14.00	6.00	6.00	Package totalled same percentage increase
Illinois Bell offer August	14.50	6.00	7.00	Rearrangement of package. IBEW rejected this offer August 31, accepted it September 21

Footnote

1. The long-term contract had rapidly become a favorite in American industry since it was first introduced in 1948, when General Motors and the United Auto Workers negotiated a two-year contract, following that in 1950 with a five-year agreement. In 1951, the Bureau of Labor Statistics reported that 70 percent of the union contracts it examined were of one year's duration. But five years later, the Bureau reported that only 35 percent of the contracts were for one year.

Discussion Questions

1. Illinois Bell's president called a strike "legalized extortion." What is the basis for the claim?

2. Should public policy require use of impasse procedures to avert strikes? If yes, under what conditions?

3. Should public policy require a union membership to vote on the company's last proposal before a strike is started?

4. Is it an unfair labor practice to bargain from a pre-determined position? Did either or both sides bargain from a pre-determined position in this case?

5. Negotiator Nickey at one point argued that the men did not like long-term agreements. With other unions agreeing to three-year contracts, speculate on Nickey's reasons for wanting annual negotiations.

6. What role did public opinion play in this case?

7. Arbitration was proposed. Speculate on what might have been the outcome of the case if the parties had been subject to compulsory arbitration? To public fact-finding?

8. The company, in rejecting arbitration, said "Arbitration in a wage dispute is still a one-way street." Does this seem a valid objection? What seems to underlie this rejection of an important method of impasse resolution?

9. The New York Times commented editorially that, "This reluctance (of Bell) is understandable, but it cannot be controlling. No public utility can legitimately place its private preference above the needs of the public it exists to serve . . ." Apply this reasoning to the steel industry, the Atomic Energy Commission, a city school board.

10. Based on the information in the case, formulate a strategy involving impasse procedures for a public utility and for a governmental unit.

11. Assess the company's ability or inability to pay a wage increase.

THE WAUKEGAN POLICE STRIKE III

Introduction

The case of the Waukegan Police Strike focuses on union recognition. This was a major issue in the private sector prior to the Wagner Act and is an issue decades later in many governmental units. Resolution of the recognition problem is complicated in this case by absence of legislation and procedures to provide for an orderly settling of this issue.

The case concerns the right of public employees to representation of their own choosing and the right to strike in order to gain recognition, a procedure that placed the police on a collision course with Civil Service requirements that they report to work when ordered to do so. It deals, too, with aspects of the employee-employer relationship which led to the organization of a union and the demand for bargaining rights.

In the background is another question, one that is of increasing importance in public sector collective bargaining: If it is granted that public employees have a right to some say over terms and conditions of employment, at what point do the public and its governmental officials draw a line and say: "Thus far and no farther. This is the basis upon which we will deal."

Chronology

1968   Cook County Police Association was organized by Sgt. John Flood of the Sheriff's Police.

1969   Police in several Chicago suburbs joined the new association and sought recognition for collective bargaining. There were five job actions of some kind, from "sick-ins" to full-fledged strikes.

Spring 1970   Discontent was building in the Waukegan police department. The city council's labor relations committee turned down all police demands for salary increases and other changes, including a grievance procedure. The police chief, unpopular with the men, accused some of them of taking money from a drawer and subjected most officers to lie detector tests.

June 1970   Sixty-eight policemen signed a petition to Mayor Robert Sabonjian, protesting the police chief's actions. The mayor viewed the petition as a demand that he fire the chief; he refused, but did hold a meeting with the chief and the men.

July 1970   Leaders of the Waukegan Police Association sought membership in the Cook County Police Association for help with bargaining. CCPA officials explained the procedure and sought a meeting with Mayor Sabonjian, who refused to meet.

July 7, 1970   Seventy Waukegan police signed cards authorizing CCPA to represent them.
     Later in the month city officials met with police bargainers and made some concessions, including a grievance procedure and a wage increase, but refused recognition of CCPA as bargaining agent.

July 24, 1970   Police in Waukegan and in four other communities near Chicago, all CCPA members, called in sick with the "blue flu." They refused orders to return to work.

July 27, 1970   Mayor Sabonjian issued an ultimatum to police: return to work by 10 a.m. the following day or face immediate suspension.

July 28,   The men did not return to work and were suspended. Dis-
1970   missal procedure was started.

July 30,   A circuit judge sought to conciliate the dispute but failed.
1970   Other offers of mediation were refused by the mayor.

August   The Waukegan Civil Service Commission fired 54 police-
10, 1970   men for insubordination. Later court efforts to regain
           their jobs and settle the labor dispute failed.

Discontent Builds Toward a Strike

1

The first phone call came about 9:30 p.m. from Police Lieutenant William Moore. He was sick, the lieutenant said, and he wouldn't be in for his 10:30 shift.

Then Patrolman John Malloy called, then Patrolman Richard Kovach, then others. Acting Police Chief George Pasenelli took some of the calls, a police dispatcher and a typist took some others. It was "a hectic night," Pasenelli recalled later.

The scene was the police department in Waukegan, Illinois, a medium-sized industrial city about 50 miles north of Chicago. The date was July 24, 1970, the start of Waukegan's blue flu epidemic, later a full-fledged strike. Blue flu is a fiction police have used where they have no legal right to strike.

Nineteen police officers were scheduled to work that night in Waukegan. Only two arrived and for a couple of hours they were the entire police force. "On a Friday night in July in Waukegan, Illinois, that's serious," the city attorney was to comment later. So serious, in fact, that Waukegan's mayor, the dominant political power in Waukegan and Lake County, was never to recover from his sense of frustrated anger that the police — he always had called them "my boys" — would leave the city unprotected. The gap was filled later that night when Lake County deputy sheriffs were called out to patrol the city.

The blue flu action was rather sudden, only definitely decided upon earlier that same evening, when a majority of the city's 78 policemen met in the American Legion Hall and voted not to report to work, that night, or the next day, or until city officials began to act on some of their demands. But the fact that some kind of job action was imminent was no great surprise. Friday morning newspapers in Chicago had listed Waukegan as one of five suburban police departments likely to be engulfed by the blue flu that day. Tension in the Waukegan police department had been brewing — over an unpopular police chief whom many of the men thought insulting and demeaning, over the lack of any grievance system, over stalemated salary negotiations, over refusal of city officials to meet with officials of a police union the men had just joined. That refusal was particularly galling

to the men because Waukegan has a city ordinance designed to give
city employees the right to bargaining representation of their choice,
a right very few Illinois public employees have as a matter of law.

The matter of union recognition was to become a key issue in the
struggle that was to build during the rest of the summer in Waukegan
and to end with the firing of 54 patrolmen, lieutenants and sergeants.
The men contend they were fired because they joined the union and
the city refused to deal with it, in violation of the policemen's rights.
City officials contend they were fired because they repeatedly refused
to report for duty, thus violating nine Civil Service Commission rules
and their oaths of office.

On that tense July night in Waukegan — Friday, July 24 — the acting
police chief, George Pasenelli, working with a typist and a sergeant
who had reported to work, called all the rest of the men listed on the
duty roster for the night shift. Each replied that he was sick.

"Prior to reporting for duty," the acting chief recalled telling each
of them, "You'll bring in a doctor's certificate stating that you were
examined, and for what ailment."

Pasenelli was a 16-year veteran of the department and had been
assistant chief for just over a year. The men he was calling were friends,
long-time associates, many with years of service equal to or greater than
his own. It was, as he said, a "hectic night." The burden was his alone
because the police chief, John Della Valle, was away on vacation. He
came back the next day.

That first night Pasenelli sent a telegram to every member of the
police department: "All days off and vacations are herewith cancelled
effective immediately. You are ordered to report to the Waukegan
police station at one p.m. on Saturday, July 25, 1970."

The telegrams were ignored. The men did not report on Saturday.
Nor Sunday. Nor Monday. Nor, many of them, ever again.

The blue flu was barely launched in Waukegan before the dispute
began to center around two colorful, powerful persons. One was the
mayor of Waukegan, Robert Sabonjian, who's proud of his nickname,
"the Rock," and who was operating from one of the firmest political
bases in the nation. The other was a great bear of a young man named
John Flood, a sergeant in the Cook County sheriff's police and the
founder and president of the Cook County Police Association, which
had in the year and a half since its birth moved into 20 suburban
Chicago police departments, conducting strikes (or sick-ins) in some
of them before beginning to make some gains. Apparently each of the
two instantly recognized the other as an appropriate antagonist.

They were the major adversaries, although they met face to face
only once. In some ways the two men are remarkably similar, although

neither would like the characterization and it is, indeed, only true in part. Both are self-made men, with little formal education but with quick, shrewd minds. They are fiercely proud of their achievements. They are strong, stubborn men, quick to anger but well able, too, to exert considerable charm. Each has proved an ability to lead people. Each has the politician's grasp of where power lies and how to use it. But there are many differences.

Mayor Robert Sabonjian and Waukegan

Sabonjian was 53 years old and in his fourth term as mayor at the time of the police strike, the only mayor in the city's history to have served more than two terms (he'd be pleased if that reminded you of F.D.R.) He considers himself an independent in politics, and was elected first, as an independent Democrat in 1957 (the story goes that when he filed for office that year, he borrowed a key to City Hall and arrived at 4 a.m. to assure his position at the top of the ballot). By the time of his third election, in 1969, he called himself an independent Republican. Actually, he's claimed rather wide support by people in both parties, many of whom feel that he's been good for Waukegan. An ardent booster for his city, he's brought in many new industries - offering some favors and demanding some in return. Here's an example: when the Dexter Corporation was talking of moving its Midland Paint Division out of Waukegan, the mayor arranged for the city to vacate a street and sell the land to Dexter for five cents a square foot (he said he really wanted to give it to them). In the years since, the city has openly solicited free paint from the company and its president now heads Waukegan's Civil Service Commission, which makes him a part of this story.

The city government makes a point of using local products and businesses are under considerable pressure to buy locally, too.

"We tell contractors they'd better hire local subcontractors and buy cement locally," Sabonjian once explained. " 'This town has been good to you,' we tell them. 'Keep the money and the jobs here and we'll all grow together.' It all comes back to the city, to the people. But not one penny comes back to Robert Sabonjian."

Sabonjian has fostered a building boom in Waukegan. There's a trim new municipal building, with the police and fire departments housed at one end. There's a trim new library and a glamorous new county building, towering near Lake Michigan in the heart of downtown and wrapped around a vast plaza with fountains, flowers and sculpture.

Old-timers claim he's cleaned up the city and Sabonjian proudly agrees. The son of an Armenian immigrant who worked in the steel mill, Sabonjian grew up in the mill area in the south of the city and says he saw all sorts of crime, gambling and prostitution there.

"I saw all this as I grew up here," he recalled, "and I promised myself that if I ever became important, I'd clean up this town. When I became mayor I let everyone know that the good ol' days were over. The slots, the wire rooms and gambling and the crumbs who ran 'em - they all got the word. I was determined that this was going to be a town where men can get work, honest work, and where kids can grow up, get an education, and come back here to work and raise families."

He presides over it all with a kind of fierce ardor; he is the city and the city is him. No detail is too small. He'll worry, for example, about the width of the parking spaces in a new city lot, fretting that the yellow lines are so close together that the women will have trouble getting their car doors open if they're carrying packages, fretting until he finally calls his public works superintendent and tells him to repaint the lines, providing wider spaces.

For the most part, the city's people have been with him and the city council has been made up of his supporters. Only one alderman opposed him in his tough stand against the police. But there have been rumblings of dissent, too, with some saying he's so entrenched politically that he's become arrogant and autocratic. "I run the City Council," he once said, "by Robert's rules of order. My name is Robert."

From time to time, usually during election campaigns, there are charges that gambling still thrives in Waukegan, with official protection from the city. There are charges of government by crony and of potent black lists for those out of favor.

Part of the controversy over Sabonjian centered around the nature of his tough stand during 1966 rioting in Waukegan's black ghetto. He called the rioters "scum, hoodlums, bums and animals." Some people applauded but others did not, including the leadership of the black people who make up about 15 percent of Waukegan's population. Later he suggested to a legislative commission that unwed mothers be jailed and their children placed in orphanages: there were more then who called him racist. Apparently he was encouraged by the kind of backlash support he was getting and ran for the senate in 1966, as a write-in candidate against Charles Percy. He drew 41,965 votes, Percy more than 2 million.

Sabonjian feels, probably rightly, that the police appreciated his strong law and order stand, backing them up, at the end of the riots. During most of his terms, Waukegan police have been among his supporters and he was theirs.

"I was damned good to our policemen," he said. "We got them a color squad and the best quality nickel-plated revolvers so they could be in competition. They had very high morale. Sometimes, when I had

no business making more rank, I did it anyway, because there were
boys on the list (the civil service eligibility list) that was expiring and
they might not make the next list. I made four lieutenants in one
night - seven officers in one night, three sergeants and four lieutenants.
Is that a curmudgeon mayor? I loved these guys. They had the finest
equipment money could buy."

Waukegan people close to Sabonjian are amazed that the mayor,
whose ear is usually so close to the ground, had so little inkling of the
discontent that was brewing in the department in the months before
the strike. It's possible that one factor in the bitter strike was Mayor
Sabonjian's own hurt feelings at his political failure to judge the extent
of the trouble.

Sgt. John Flood and the Cook County Police Association

John Flood was 31 years old at the time of the Waukegan strike, a
huge, burly man with 10 years of police experience in the Chicago
area. His father was a long-time New York City policeman, and the
son, the third oldest of eight children, grew up in New York, attending
parochial schools and studying for the priesthood before entering the
army for three years. He finished his service at a guided missile site in
Arlington Heights, Illinois, a Cook County suburb of Chicago, then
stayed in the area, joining the police department of Wheeling, another
suburb. He moved to the Cook County sheriff's police in December,
1962. Still in his early 20's, he was given responsible assignments under
Sheriff Richard B. Ogilvie, who had gone on to become governor
of Illinois by the time of the trouble in Waukegan.

Flood has always read a lot, incorporating many people's thinking
into his own (he's particularly impressed with Ramsey Clark), and he
kept his eyes open. He says he learned, for example, that "most local
police service stinks," that most municipal governments with their
part-time aldermen "have no knowledge of sound managerial techniques,"
that there are many inequities in police departments, that politics
dominates every action, and that the ordinary policeman gets a pretty
raw deal.

"Police departments are administered with the top sergeant philosophy," he says, "a philosophy that says 'you do what I say because
I have these stripes on my arm.' The individual officer was always
sacrificed for political reasons. He had to do what the politicians
wanted, then take the rap when there was a complaint. Local police
are constantly used by the politicians to put down social causes. I
could see we could get power with organization - no other way. We
want power, not for power's sake, but to effectuate change. I don't
like police departments as we see them now. Law enforcement agencies

are the backbone of democracy; to work they need better personnel, better policies, more professionalization. They should be responsible to the community they serve."

He toyed with the idea of organization for a long time, he recalls, rejecting the idea of a traditional police association, which he claims "gets by by selling associate memberships, magazine subscriptions, or psychologically strong-arming businessmen for donations." He was thinking of a more professional kind of organization, something that would give police more of a say in the operation of local departments and back them up if they stood up to the politicians.

In 1968 he began to put together his organization in the Cook County Sheriff's department. One of the men knew a labor lawyer, Arthur Loevy, counsel for the Amalgamated Clothing Workers in Chicago, a young and thoroughly dedicated unionist. Loevy told Flood how unions worked, helped draw up a constitution, and agreed to work with the new Cook County Police Association on a volunteer basis. It was the start of a partnership - and of a mutual admiration - that continues.

The new union gained recognition from Sheriff Joe Woods, who apparently wasn't quite sure what he was getting into but knew he didn't want a strike. Flood says he didn't quite know what he was getting into either and that he had plenty to learn, about organizing, about bargaining, about sensing where the power lies in a community and how to get a share of it.

The new union won its salary demands from the Cook County Board of Commissioners and then began to think about branching into other police departments in the county. There are about 120 of them, most of them, Flood claims, "with chaotic administration."

Flood, who has incredible energy, works about 16 hours a day, half of them at his paid job as a deputy, and half of them at his unpaid job as union president.

"We'd go out and talk to the men," he explained. "Every police department lives in fear of the politicians. We'd tell them, 'You go out on the street and you can do anything. You're up against toughs, all kinds of trouble. You have no fear. But you go in to the politicians, hat in hand, scared as hell. You'll only be able to act like men when you've got an organization to help you, an organization to offer you professional help, expertise.' And they'd agree. We'd help organize, but would only bring the organization in when 75 to 80 percent of the men signed up."

There were five strikes (some of them sick-ins) that first year, 1969, caused, Flood says, because "we went to the political officials of the municipalities whose departments voted the CCPA as their representative and used every sort of logic and reason to obtain our basic requests and for the most part they absolutely refused. We had no choice but to fight them. They'd give something one day, then take it away the next. It was completely frustrating. They had to see that they have to deal with us."

It wasn't just more money the men wanted, Flood insists, although that was part of it; most of the local chapters were seeking parity salaries with the Chicago police, who start at $12,000 a year. Mostly, he said, they wanted union recognition and, through it, the right to have some voice on how departments are run, about transfers, promotions, recognition of work done, the internal investigation systems. They wanted grievance procedures and dues checkoff.

Municipal officials tended to greet Flood as they would the arrival of the plague. He is almost frighteningly big and he had a habit of bringing along some more very big policemen. The men were armed and stubborn and municipal officials found the confrontation unnerving if not downright threatening. Flood is also rather quick on the trigger. "I'm kind of a gut guy," he says, "but I'm watching Art Loevy and trying to learn from him. I'm trying to learn how to relax, not to get heated up and stomp out, to learn to work toward agreement. But it is frustrating."

Many of the municipal officials said they had no legal authority to recognize a police union (an issue still before the Illinois courts) and many more simply didn't want the union, legal authority or not. But the men were interested and about 20 departments had come into the association by the summer of 1970. Not all those departments were in Cook County; some were in Lake County. Lake County deputy sheriffs joined the association and that probably influenced the Waukegan police, who are closely associated with the Lake County deputies.

The Discontent in Waukegan

One center of controversy in Waukegan was the chief of police, John Della Valle, a 19-year veteran of the force promoted to chief by Mayor Sabonjian in October, 1968, less than two years before the strike. He was extremely unpopular with the men in the department.

One of them, Lt. Charles Fletcher, said, "The chief just doesn't get along with people. He came up through the ranks and is an old-time cop, a politician's policeman. It was a sloppy operation. There was no chain of command, no communication between the command and the men."

Dick Maier, an earnest, quiet young officer who had made detective in four years, unusually quickly, said the chief kept calling him, "Meathead."

"He had names like that for most of us," Fletcher said, "He was insulting. There was a lot of discontent."

Murray Conzelman, the Waukegan city attorney (corporation coun-sel) and probably the mayor's most influential adviser, in looking back, added another angle: "Our present chief is technically the best man we've ever had. But he's a book man - if it's in the book, you do it, no questions asked. Apparently that rankled. The previous police chief was a really nice guy that everybody liked. So they'd gone from a nice guy to a tough guy."

Mayor Sabonjian added a comment, too: "Maybe it was a problem of familiarity breeds contempt. They worked with him all those years and knew him as just another guy, and then all of a sudden they had to call him chief. He used to smoke in the patrol cars, but then, when he got to be chief, he told the men they couldn't, that it was against the rules. That kind of thing. I could have gone outside and brought in someone else, but I don't believe in that. I believe in promoting up from the ranks."

Early in June, 1970, Conzelman, the city attorney, recalls, "the chief came to me to tell me some bond money had been stolen from the front desk. I asked him if he knew who did it and he said he thought it was one of three men in the department. I suggested that he give them lie tests. Unfortunately, instead, the chief asked a whole group to take lie tests and they all refused."

The "whole group" that the chief called in for lie tests consisted of eight command officers ("all gold braid" as Fletcher puts it); two captains, all the lieutenants, two sergeants, and only one patrolman. The group included officers who had not been on duty at the time the money disappeared.

"Some said they wouldn't take the tests - why should they?" Fletch-er recalled. "The chief said, 'Because you're going to do what I tell you to do.' It was really a power play; he knew those men weren't responsi-ble. The chief had been using lie tests before, too. The men didn't like it. It was humiliating. He'd never even tell the results."

The stolen funds, a $50 bond and a $25 bond, were in a small envelope within a larger envelope containing about $2,000 in all.

"Here's the thing about that bond money, " Fletcher continued, "If you're going to steal money, you'd have to cover it up by stealing the bond report and the accident report, too. The police would all know that. But the reports weren't taken, only one of the small envelopes. We say it was a set-up. Anyway, it brought everything to a head."

Sixty-eight of the 78 men in the department signed a petition to take to Mayor Sabonjian. It read:

"We, the undersigned, officers and patrolmen of the Waukegan Police Department, because of the threat and the shadow of suspicion directed at eight of our ranking officers and one patrolman, feel that we can no longer effectively work for Chief of Police John Della Valle."

The officers took the petition to the mayor and Lt. Fletcher made a bitter speech, starting, "Mayor, assembled before you are the highest ranking line officers of the Waukegan Police Department. We represent 149 years of police work for the city of Waukegan. Until now, these have been 149 years of loyal, honest police work. With one blow, Chief of Police John Della Valle has destroyed all of this, and turned these years into a nightmare for all of us. He has indiscriminately used his powers as a chief of police. We are all now suspected thieves. Our reputations have been smeared. Our men eye us with suspicion. Our names have been dragged through the mud. Our families are hurt and disgusted."

He went on to complain that, in the 20 months since the chief took over, 11 other men had been given lie tests, although all were found not guilty, and "during these 20 months, we have been harassed, shouted at, threatened and treated like a bunch of school children."

Fletcher went on to assure the mayor that "we have no quarrel with you," but that they were turning to him because, "As you may or may not know, Chief Della Valle is not a man one can sit down with and discuss a situation with."

Neither the petition nor Fletcher's prepared speech said so, but it was the mayor's clear understanding that he was being asked to fire the chief. He refused.

"I can't deal this way," he recalls telling the officers. "Tomorrow who'll you tell me to fire? I'm mayor. Nobody's going to tell me who to fire and hire. But why hadn't they come in to talk about their problems? My door is open to them. It's always open to anyone.

"I asked for a meeting, with the chief present, and asked them to repeat the charges. I told them, I promise you there will be communication between the chief and the officers, there'll be some changes made. They did have some legitimate complaints - but they had never told me. . . We had the meeting with the chief. It was a good meeting, with good discussion. The guys said they had confidence in me and they'd tell that to the men. They kept saying, 'we have faith in you.' They said they would recommend to the men that they go along with the mayor, that he'd work things out and get better conditions."

Fletcher agrees that the meeting with the chief was held but he doesn't recall that much was accomplished. "We all just sat there," he said. It was not the end of the affair.

There are other strands to the Waukegan story in early June, too. The police were getting nowhere in their efforts to get a salary increase, a grievance system that would work, and some other changes they wanted.

Collective bargaining for Waukegan police was not a new venture as it is in many police departments. The Waukegan Police Association

for many years had met with city officials to discuss salary and benefits and the city considered the police association the recognized bargaining agent under terms of the city's ordinance which guarantees such
recognition.

"Waukegan is essentially a union town," Murray Conzelman, the city
attorney, explained. "During the 1930's there was tremendous labor
strife here. The first sit-down strike took place here. A lot of our city
labor legislation dates from those days."

One such ordinance established a city council Labor Relations Committee to deal with employee organizations. One section of the ordinance is titled "Union Participation" and reads:

The city recognizes the right of its employees to organize, join a
union, and to be heard on matters affecting their employment
through their duly authorized representatives. A union shall be
recognized as the bargaining agent for the employees who are members of that union, subject to the following conditions:
1. There shall be no discrimination against any employee because
   of his connection or non-connection with a union.
2. Any union which negotiates with the Labor Relations Committee
   will use its influence to protect the property of the city and to
   improve the many municipal services to the public.
3. No request for a check-off shall be made.
4. Grievances for which redress is sought from the Labor Relations
   Committee shall be reduced to writing and delivered to the Mayor.

Conzelman contends that the police association has bargained "successfully" with the committee, made up of three aldermen, in much the
same way as firemen have, even though the police group was strictly
local and the firemen have been members of the International Association of Firefighters for "as long as anyone can remember." In 1969,
the year before the strike, there had been some talk among the men of
joining the police union but the talk ended when Waukegan offered
substantial salary increases, which were accepted.

Captain William Kennedy was heading the police association's bargaining in 1970 but negotiations weren't going well. The aldermen met
the police negotiators in June, who asked for a salary increase and
seven other items, including an increase in the clothing allowance, and
the right to live out of the city.

"The aldermen just said no," Lt. Fletcher said. "They said there
isn't any money this year. They wouldn't even discuss it. That's when
we began to think we needed help and began thinking about the CCPA
(Cook County Police Association.) It's a strictly professional outfit,
by police, for police. It's all business. We didn't think we'd get any
help from the Illinois Police Association, which is strictly social."

After the negotiations stalemate early in June, the police launched a slowdown in ticket-writing for traffic enforcement, as a method to put pressure on the city. Usually about 1200 tickets a month are issued; the level dropped to 50. The move irked Sabonjian and was one of the issues he talked to the police about at the time they were protesting to him about the police chief.

"They had just quit writing tickets," Sabonjian said. "They said they should be spending more time solving crimes, instead of placing so much emphasis on traffic enforcement. I told them that wasn't for them to decide. There were 13 fatalities here in a year; that's reason enough to think traffic enforcement is important. I told them to go back to writing tickets, not to play games with the security of this city."

Conzelman, the city attorney, has suggested since that the police might have been more successful in their demands had they stuck to the slowdown instead of turning to the blue flu. "The slowdown was a highly successful tactic," he said. "Or they could have stuck with that and picketed during off-hours. Four or five years ago the firemen picketed in off-duty time, then put on their uniforms and went to work. They were very successful. They won. The community was with them." At no point, he contends, was the community with the police after they left their jobs. "People generally feel that policemen and firemen shouldn't strike and it's hard to get that feeling to change. The public was very unclear about what was going on here. There was real chaos for a while and you surely don't get public support that way. It was incredible mass psychology."

But the unhappy police did not see that the slowdown was accomplishing anything. Despite repeated meetings with the mayor, the attorney and other officials, they thought they were getting nowhere, in their complaints against the chief, in their negotiations, even in getting a grievance system that would work.

Dick Maier, the young detective that the chief called "Meathead," explained one of the grievances, "We were supposed to have seven paid holidays a year but instead of getting them at the time of the holidays, the chief would just tack one week onto our two-week vacations. But that meant that we were only getting five days off instead of seven holidays. We were short two days, but we couldn't make him understand that."

Maier proposed at one police association meeting a new five-step grievance procedure that would lead to action.

"The next day," he said, "the chief came down to the detective bureau and said, 'If you have any grievance, you can quit.' "

With all the stalemates, the leaders of the police association, including Capt. Kennedy, its head, decided to turn to the CCPA. They were ready to strike, and they had heard about John Flood and his toughness.

Lt. Fletcher called Flood at 2 a.m. one morning early in July. Flood and Art Loevy, the union attorney, went to Waukegan the next day to meet with about a dozen of the police leaders there, to explain the union and the way it operates, and to bring a stack of authorization cards for the men to sign. A signature means that the man has joined the association and authorizes it to represent him in collective bargaining.

One of the things they had to do, too, both Flood and Loevy recalled, was to cool the situation a bit and see what could be accomplished without a strike.

"The issues were not clearly formulated," Loevy said. "The men just knew they were being cheated. We said we couldn't help them with setting up grievance procedures unless they cooled down."

The first step, the CCPA men explained, would be for Loevy to call Mayor Sabonjian and ask for a meeting to explain the purposes of the union. The next step would be for the Waukegan leaders to proceed to get signatures on the authorization cards.

Loevy called Sabonjian the next day; it was the first of a series of calls.

"I asked for a meeting to discuss representation," Loevy went on. "He was very friendly to me, but he was very demeaning to his police. He called them all miserable so-and-sos . . . . he uses very strong language. He said to me, 'Well, I suppose I'll have to deal with you, but those blankety-blanks . . . . After all I've done for them.' He viewed it as a personal affront. We did set a meeting date. But the meeting was never held."

Sabonjian turned for advice to Murray Conzelman, who was vacationing with his family at Georgian Bay. Conzelman, an important figure in the Waukegan business and political community, conducts an extensive private law practice in addition to his work as the city's chief legal officer. But, despite his active role in city politics, he says he prefers a quiet, contemplative kind of existence. He lives in a rural area outside Waukegan and treasures his Georgian Bay summer home; he speaks ruefully of the installation of a telephone there. Conzelman said he was on the beach reading (a favored occupation for him) when the telephone call came. The mayor reported the conversation with Loevy.

"I asked the mayor," Conzelman said," 'Are you going to recognize the CCPA?' I told him he had to decide that before he met, because the meeting would mean that he is recognizing it."

The mayor called Loevy back and said, Loevy recalls, that "on the advice of his attorney, he could not hold a meeting with me. If we met, it would amount to recognition, which he refused. I asked him to reserve judgment, that we would just be talking about the idea. I tried to soft pedal our differences. He seemed amenable, but then Conzelman again advised him not to meet with us. There was one last phone call in which he said he absolutely would not meet with us. I told him I thought the men would take job action. It's odd, but we never even mentioned wages. I never lost my temper in these calls and he was always rather polite to me, even when he was being hard on the men. Only later did he claim that I had been rude on the telephone."

(At the time the blue flu started, Sabonjian stated publicly that Loevy had tried to blackmail him and he told Loevy, "If you're looking for a fight, you're knocking on the right door." In an interview later, Sabonjian said Loevy had been abusive and threatened Sabonjian, "From now on, we're going to get you, destroy you politically. Sabonjian is the issue now. We'll blacken your name from one end of the state to the other." The two men simply do not agree about the nature of their private telephone conversations.)

Meanwhile, Waukegan police leaders were meeting almost nightly, said Fletcher, the Waukegan police lieutenant who increasingly played a leadership role. They called a mass meeting for the policemen for July 7, in the American Legion hall. It was at that meeting that most of the authorization cards were signed, although a few were signed the day before and the day after. Fletcher said 70 men signed up to have the CCPA represent them, including some who never did go out on strike and some who returned to work before the strike was over. Fletcher was elected president of the Waukegan chapter at the July 7 meeting.

Fletcher, 43 years old, is a frank and candid man who gradually moved into the leadership role out of conviction rather than out of political ambition. He'd been a Waukegan policeman for 16 years, working his way up to important police responsibilities. "I always loved being a policeman," he said quietly, looking back on the Waukegan turmoil after a year. "I used to be a real hard-nosed, conservative cop. I'm much more liberal now than I used to be." He is quick to admit that nothing in his background had prepared him for leading a bitter strike. "We were amateurs," he repeated several times. "We did what the experts told us, what had worked in other cities." It is likely that he did not particularly relish his new adversary relationship with Sabonjian.

Angered by the July 7 meeting and the new link with the CCPA, Mayor Sabonjian called his entire police force to a session in the council chambers on Thursday, July 9. He said the city would no longer favor the police and he threatened "a little austerity" in the running of the department, mentioning the possibility of cutting out all overtime.

He complained about their lack of gratitude. A Waukegan newspaper reporter was there and wrote about the tirade, under the headline, "Sabonjian 'Chews Out' Cops."

"Maybe I assumed too much from our friendship, our camaraderie," he told the officers. "You used to be my boys, but from now on its business as business."

Lt. Fletcher commented after the "chewing out:" "We were ordered to that meeting today. We were a complete captive audience. He said his things. I said 'yes, sir' three times. These are the types of things we are trying to get away from. We don't want to be a captive audience. We want something to say in what goes on in the department." The men had joined the CCPA, he said, "so we can negotiate. We have never been able to negotiate in a proper manner." '

There were more meetings, too, with the mayor and sometimes other city officials. But there was no agreement. Conzelman recalled that he thought one of those sessions had been successful, and he was surprised to find that the process hadn't worked.

"On the Monday before the sick-in (Monday, July 20), we had a meeting , the mayor, the clerk and I, with representatives of the police association. The problem with some of these meetings was that we never really knew what the issues were; every time we met, the issues were different. This time they wanted the mayor to fire the chief. We tried to explain that the mayor couldn't fire the chief just because the men wanted it, that you don't have a referendum in the department on who should be chief - or who shouldn't be chief. We convinced them that the mayor wasn't going to fire the chief.

"Then they presented a list of demands that I had never seen before. I guess they had presented them to the Labor Relations Committee of the city council and the committee had turned them all down. I looked down the list and frankly I don't know why the committee didn't grant some of the demands. There were things there that would have been possible without too great expense. One, for example, was to increase the uniform allowance from $200 to $300 a year. It's surely true that a man can't keep himself clothed for $200 a year, and, with a 78-man force, that would only have been $7,800. I thought we should agree to that. Another demand was to waive the residency requirement; that wouldn't have cost us anything. But the first demand was for a huge salary increase, to a starting rate of $12,000. Probably the committee saw that and just stopped looking at the rest of the list.

"We said okay on the uniform allowance and residency requirement, and offered a $1,000 increase, starting on November 1. We had authority, as of May 1, 1971, to increase the police levy and we thought we could somehow come up with money for the increase for the six months starting November 1, 1970. I proposed a grievance procedure: the police should select a grievance committee and bring grievances to the chief. If the chief did nothing, then they should go to the Labor Relations Committee, then to the mayor.

"I thought the offer fell on willing ears. I believed it was all settled.

"I don't think the subject of the CCPA even came up at that meeting. I had never heard about it from the men, and didn't think it was a very serious thing. There were six to eight of the men at the meeting, including Quilty, Fletcher, and Moore. Fletcher said he'd been elected bargaining representative.

"Well, that meeting was on Monday before the council meeting. When the men left, they said they would talk to the men in the department and let the mayor know by Wednesday. But they didn't wait that long. They came in before the end of the council meeting the same night and they talked to the mayor afterwards. They reported no deal. Apparently they never checked with the men, just the union, and the union said they had to get recognition."

From that point on, the question of recognition became the key issue in Waukegan, as it had in many of the other CCPA disputes the year before. Conzelman had been right about the issues changing. They changed as the situation changed. The first issue was wages and the second issue was the chief and his lie tests. After that, the men joined Flood's tough union and the issue became recognition. A week later, after the start of the blue flu, the mayor was to announce that he would "negotiate any question . . . . with the exception of recognition of the Cook County Police Association."

But none of the parties knew then just how far the dispute would be carried, or that each side would become increasingly locked into a position from which it felt no change was possible. The police certainly felt that tactics which had proved effective in other Chicago-area communities would work in Waukegan, too. They reckoned without Mayor Sabonjian, who has said, "If they had the flu, I had the prescription for it. I would charge them with insubordination for being absent without leave."

Discussion Questions

1. What events precipitated the blue flu action?
2. What other strategies or tactics were open to the Waukegan police in seeking redress of their grievances? Do you think any of them would have been more effective than the blue flu?
3. Should police officers have a right to organize for collective bargaining? What are the implications of your answer?
4. If police should have the right to organize, should the employer be obligated to recognize the organization for bargaining purposes?

The Legal Background of the Police Dispute

2

At the time of the Waukegan police strike, in the summer of 1970, there was no legislation in Illinois regarding the right of public employees to organize for collective bargaining, the necessity of a governmental unit to recognize and bargain with an agent chosen by the employees, or the right of public employees to strike in support of their aims. These rights were neither given nor prohibited. The law was simply silent, even though public employee unionization was growing rapidly, modeled on patterns long established in the private sector but not necessarily transferable to the public sector.

One basic legal question was: Do public employees have the right to organize, bargain and strike unless these rights are specifically denied them by legislation or do they not have these rights until they are specifically granted them by legislation? There was no answer upon which everyone agreed.

In the absence of legislative determination of the answers, these bargaining relationships were determined by case law, by court decisions on whatever of these issues have been taken to court. But case law didn't answer all of the questions either. Some court precedents had been established, but the body of case law was only then developing. And even the case law that existed was not final; some of it was still being appealed through the state's court structure. Thus neither system of formulating law had provided solid answers to the legal issues that were to be posed in Waukegan.

But some Illinois cases, decided during the decade of the 1960s, have at least some bearing on the Waukegan dispute. They will be briefly considered here.

Board of Education of Community Unit District No. 2 versus Doris Redding, et al. 31 Ill 2d 567

School custodial workers in the Greenville, Illinois, area organized and sought a collective bargaining agreement with the school board in 1964. When the board refused to enter into any kind of agreement, the employees struck and picketed the school buildings. The school board sought an injunction against the strikers but the trial court refused to issue an injunction, saying that no irreparable injury had been shown and that the picketing was peaceful. The decision was appealed to the Illinois Supreme Court, which ruled on May 20, 1965, that there is no inherent right in municipal employees to strike against their government employer and that a strike of municipal employees for any purpose is illegal because it impedes or obstructs a government function.

In answer to the union's claims that picketing was an expression of free speech, protected by federal and state constitutions, the court said picketing is "more than free speech because (it is) designed to exert influence which produces action. Picketing may be subjected to restrictive regulations, without abridging free speech, to protect the public interest and property rights and where picketing is for a purpose unlawful under state laws or policies . . ."

This 1965 Supreme Court decision has not been reversed, so Illinois law, established in this decision, states that strikes by public employees are illegal and that picketing in support of such illegal strikes is also illegal.

Chicago Division of Illinois Education Association versus Board of Education of Chicago and John M. Fewkes, et al., as officers of the Chicago Teachers Union 76 Ill Ap 2d 456

This case grew out of a representation struggle between an education association and a teachers union. After a rather complex legal battle, an appellate court ruled that:

1. Without state legislation to the contrary, a governmental unit such as the Chicago Board of Education has the power to recognize and bargain with an exclusive collective bargaining agent.

2. The board has the power to require certain bargaining provisions, and any agreement "shall contain specific provisions whereby the employee organization shall agree not to strike, not to picket in any manner which would tend to disrupt the operation of any public school."

The court order was signed November 9, 1966, and has not been further appealed. Thus, at least in the first appellate district of Illinois, a governmental unit has the power to recognize a bargaining agent chosen by its employees. Undecided was the question of whether a governmental unit *must* recognize such a union.

Peoria County versus Harold L. Benedict et al. Illinois Supreme Court, Docket No. 42160, September Term, 1970

In support of wage demands, employees of a county-operated nursing home struck and picketed the home. County officials got an injunction against the strike, but union employees, who continued the

strike anyway, appealed to the Illinois Supreme Court, arguing that
the injunction "constituted a prior restraint on speech and imposed
servitude in violation of the first, thirteenth, and fourteenth amendments to the Federal Constitution, and section 14 of Article II of the
Illinois Constitution."

The court did not rule on the constitutional issue but referred instead
to an anti-injunction act passed by the Illinois legislature in 1967,
which provides: "No restraining order or injunction shall be granted
by any court of this state . . . in any case involving or growing
out of a dispute concerning terms or conditions of employment . . ."
It noted that a previous decision had held that the anti-injunction
law was applicable to employees of a non-profit hospital and said it
should apply in this case too.

The decision was announced December 4, 1970, after the Waukegan strike, and it does not specifically apply to the Waukegan situation
in which no injunction was sought by city officials. But labor lawyers
in Illinois — or some of them at least — are wondering whether this
decision in some way alters the Redding decision, which said public
employees have no right to strike. If a governmental unit no longer
has the power to enjoin a strike by public employees, does the public
employee strike thus have greater legality than in the past?

Cook County Police Association versus City of Harvey (Case No. 55670 in Appellate Court of Illinois, First Judicial District)

In November, 1969, Sergeant Flood's very young CCPA sent a telegram to Mayor James Haines of Harvey, a Chicago suburb: "Please be
advised that the CCPA presently represents over 90 percent of the
uniformed patrolmen in Harvey. We request recognition of our organization as a duly authorized, collective bargaining representative of
our members."

Harvey employs 44 policemen, 29 of them uniformed patrolmen.

The mayor took the request to the city council, which refused to
deal with the association. The minutes say, "Inasmuch as this Association does not represent 100 percent of the Harvey policemen that it
not be recognized."

The policemen then began a "job action" to gain recognition. They
began calling in sick on November 28 and 29. Twenty-one of them
stayed away from their jobs. Police Chief Leroy Knapp sent notices
to all of them, then fired them December 10 because they had abandoned their jobs, which is cause for firing under the city's civil service
regulations. He set December 16 for new civil service examinations
to fill the police jobs.

The CCPA filed a complaint in circuit court on December 11, seeking a court order for recognition of the union and bargaining in good

faith. The city, in its answer, replied that there is no legal authority to require the city to recognize the union and that refusal to do so is not illegal or wrongful. The city also said there was no cause for action because the CCPA did not represent any patrolmen in Harvey, since they had all been discharged.

On December 18, the court ordered that the 21 patrolmen be reinstated. It prohibited the union from seeking recognition for six months and the city from recognizing any other bargaining agent for six months. The judge was thus providing a cooling off period and leaving the door open for continuing efforts later at collective bargaining.

In September, 1970, the CCPA sent a new petition to the city, seeking recognition and listing its 33 members. The city council took no action, so the CCPA went back to court. On October 29, 1970, the court issued a permanent order enjoining the city from refusing to recognize CCPA as the duly authorized bargaining agent, and directing both parties to bargain in good faith. The city of Harvey appealed the order, however, and the appellate court reversed the lower court's ruling. Thus there is no requirement that the city recognize the police bargaining agent.

The Meaning of the Decisions

Taken together, the decisions in the cases say, at least tentatively, that public employees in Illinois do have a right to organize for collective bargaining purposes and to request recognition and that a governmental unit has the power to recognize such a union. But there is no requirement that a governmental unit recognize such a union. With or without recognition, the union has no right to strike but the government employer has no right to seek court action to prevent a strike.

It is in this rather confusing context that the Cook County Police Association came into being and began to push against the limits of the court decisions, even going to court itself (in the Harvey case) to alter the limits. It was plagued with such fundamental organizational questions as:

— What good is a union if no one will bargain with it?
— What good is the right to bargain if you have no weapon, such as the strike — an entirely acceptable, legitimate and effective weapon in the private sector   to lend force to your demands?
— In the absence of law, how can rights basic to employees throughout the state be denied to employees of public agencies?

The denial of the right to strike, combined with the need for some method of bringing pressure on public employers, gave birth to the fiction of the blue flu, a way of withholding services for a period of

time without actually calling the "job action" a "strike." In some
ways it is comparable to private sector union practices such as slowdowns or informal work restrictions. But the blue flu is a fiction with
some built-in defects. Under most civil service regulations, if an employee is sick, he must prove he is sick. If he is not sick, and still stays away
from work, he is violating civil service rules and can be dismissed.

But, despite the built-in defects, the blue flu fiction worked effectively for the Cook County Police Association in a number of instances. When persuasion failed in 1969, the first full year of CCPA
operation, the CCPA chapters in five Chicago suburbs conducted some
form of job action, or blue flu, or strike. They won some of their
demands, even though they did not always gain formal recognition
or achieve a formal written contract. The CCPA was trying techniques,
like picketing, which had never been tried by police before, and it was
finding that some of them worked. In that first year, the job actions
came one at a time. Each local chapter elected its own officers to
bargain, then had the help of Loevy or Flood in actual negotiations;
they brought with them ideas about techniques that had been working in other communities and Loevy brought bargaining table experience. (It is an interesting sidelight that most of these negotiations
were conducted on weekends, early in the morning or in the evening.
Loevy was a volunteer negotiator for CCPA and still put in his regular
office hours in his job as counsel for the Amalgamated Clothing
Workers.)

But by the summer of 1970, when the situation was heating up
in Waukegan, some of the CCPA local chapters were planning a concerted job action, and thinking about July 24.

In Wheeling, where Sergeant Flood had started his police career a
decade before, the issue was recognition. The village attorney there
believed strongly that Illinois law provided no possible authority for
union recognition by a governmental unit. In Skokie, where the
chapter had gained a measure of recognition the year before, the issue
was a salary increase. Police in Harwood Heights and the sheriff's
deputies in Lake County (Waukegan) were thinking of a job action,
too. And then there was Waukegan. Perhaps joining the union early
in July when there was no much talk of job actions (and job actions
had won the year before) added a certain element of strike contagion
to an already volatile situation.

On July 24, when Waukegan police started calling in sick, police
switchboards in Wheeling and Skokie were lighting up with sick calls,
too. Lake County deputies went out a few days later. Some form of
agreement was reached in Wheeling and Skokie after a while. But the
Lake County deputies didn't fare very well. And there was never agreement of any kind in Waukegan.

Discussion Questions

1. Would the existence of a state law governing collective bargaining for public employees have solved the problems in Waukegan? Why or why not?

2. If a law seems justified, what elements should it include?

3. If a law requires a public agency to bargain with its employees, how does this affect the agency's responsibility and accountablity to the public? Is the public interest sacrificed if the agency's decision-making powers are thus curtailed?

During that first hectic weekend of the blue flu in Waukegan, when most of the police were not reporting to work and when the city was being patrolled by sheriff's deputies, there was a flurry of informal meetings aimed at getting the men back to work. Some of the aldermen volunteered to talk to policemen they'd known for years, since school days. None of the informal contacts paid off. Mayor Sabonjian asked for time on the local radio station and pleaded with the men to return. They didn't. Anger and tension mounted.

The mayor reported that on Sunday night he received a threatening phone call. The anonymous caller told him, he said, that political corruption, including 1,500 traffic ticket fixes, would be revealed if he didn't cooperate. The phone call infuriated Sabonjian. He told the press about it the next morning; "I've been in office for 13 years," he fumed. "And if these people think they're dealing with a country boy, they'll find that I won't back off."

That phone call, which no one admits making, seems, in retrospect, to have been a crucial turning point in the Waukegan conflict. It was the point at which the mayor became personally involved, not as an official but as an individual, a prideful and scrappy man, who had been personally challenged. He apparently felt, thereafter, that to deal with the Cook County Police Association would be an admission that the anonymous charges were correct.

Sabonjian's memory of the phone call continued to infuriate him long after the strike was a dead issue. He talked about it, getting angrier as he spoke, almost a year later in an interview in his office, a memento-crammed room in which his desk faces a large, brightly-colored, brightly-lit, smiling picture of himself.

"Somebody called me one night and threatened to go to the FBI, to the Illinois Bureau of Investigation, to other agencies," he recalled in the interview. "They said, 'We have enough to send you to prison, so you'd better back off.' I said, 'Fuck you. Go to any damn agency you want. I stand on my record. In every election, there've been accusations, attempts at shakedowns. I stand on my record. I'm the first four-term mayor in this city. No one can call me a crook.' "

On Monday morning, July 27, when Sabonjian fumed to the press about the phone call, he said he felt the men were being misled by John Flood. He said he had offered the police $1,000 a year raises above the $9,400 top base salary for patrolmen. He said he'd made other concessions, too, and that he would "negotiate any question . . . with the exception of recognition of the Cook County Police Association."

And that morning he issued an ultimatum to the police: Return to work by 10 a.m. the following morning or face immediate suspension.

It was on that same day, Monday, after the Waukegan city council met in a hectic session in the evening, that Sabonjian and Flood met face to face for their only encounter. Their versions of what happened in the private meeting do not really agree, except in the fact that the meeting took place.

The council session was packed, with perhaps 350 people jammed into a room that normally holds about 150. Besides the local police, Flood was there with a busload of policemen from other communities. He said many of them were from Skokie, one of the suburban Chicago communities hit by the same blue flu epidemic that had engulfed Waukegan. The city attorney believes many police had come, too, from Berwyn and Cicero, tough westside Chicago suburbs with reputations for considerable lawlessness. He said the police had guns. During the meeting, the city attorney pointed out Flood to the mayor and the mayor allowed Flood to speak. He urged that the city recognize the union and was loudly cheered by a noisy audience. During the meeting, too, a local man, angered over continuing sewer problems in Waukegan, stood up and yelled at the mayor that he was a "son of a bitch." The city attorney recalls thinking conditions were ripe for riot.

The attorney says Flood approached the mayor to ask for a private meeting. Flood says he was summoned into an anteroom by the mayor.

"We got together and really talked," Flood said in an interview, recalling the session. "It was man-to-man. I gave him a way out. I've learned you have to do that; you can't just have a showdown. I said, 'We'll back off. We'll leave for six months. We just want recognition and checkoff. You can do that through a judge.' (What Flood was suggesting was the solution that had worked in Harvey a few months before. A circuit judge, involved in the dispute when the police went to court to appeal their firings, reversed the firings and ordered a six-months cooling off period. It didn't work in Waukegan.) The mayor said he'd think about it and he'd call me in the morning. He called about 6 a.m. and said, 'No deal, my aldermen wouldn't go for that.' Well, that's ridiculous. The aldermen would do what he wanted. It was his decision."

In Sabonjian's recollection of the meeting, Flood was much less reasonable. He says, "Flood told me, 'You're our toughest nut to crack. If we can crack you, every other mayor will fall in line. Can't we make a deal?' I told him if I made a deal with him — the way he was behaving — my council would spit in my face."

It is quite possible that both men's recollections of the meeting are correct, that both themes were explored, and that the failure to reach any kind of agreement explains why each feels that he was in some way wronged. At any rate, that single meeting between the two most volatile figures in the dispute was one of the few times when a settlement might have been possible. There was none. Perhaps the anonymous phone call of the night before was the major reason.

Sabonjian had already made his ultimatum: Return to work by 10 a.m. Tuesday or face suspension. He repeated it the following morning, asking, about 6 a.m., for air time on the local station and being granted a time slot at 7:40. As he recalled it later, this is about what he said:

"This is your mayor. Search your souls and your consciences. This city has been good to you and you have obligations to it. Think of your families. You're being led down the primrose path by this John Flood. Come back by 10 a.m. today, and there'll be amnesty, no reduction in rank. All of you will be restored to your jobs. This is my last offer. Don't make me do what I'm afraid I'll have to do."

He had decided, he recalled, what he would have to do. He said he'd spent four sleepless nights worrying about it, worrying because "I didn't want to hurt these men. I don't want to sound corny, but I prayed for guidance. There was just no way to compromise with these tactics."

When 10 a.m. came, none of the missing police had returned. "That's the end of amnesty," Sabonjian says he told his city hall colleagues. "We'll file formal charges for dismissal."

Dismissal Procedure Started

Police Chief John Della Valle prepared a formal notice to send to each of the 55 officers still away from their posts: three lieutenants, five sergeants, the rest patrolmen. It read:

> You and each of you are hereby suspended without pay for thirty (30) days from the Police Department of the City of Waukegan, Illinois, for failure to report to duty in violation of Section 12; Rule XIII of the Civil Service Commission Rules.

On the same day, Tuesday, July 28, the chief sent his list of charges against each man to the Civil Service Commission, launching the procedure for dismissal. The secretary of the Commission notified each officer that a hearing would be held on the charges on August 4.

Under civil service regulations, the 30-day suspension is the most serious punishment the police chief can mete out. Any more punishment, such as dismissal, must be acted upon by the Civil Service Commission. The Commission consists of three members, appointed by the mayor. The mayor said publicly that he would recommend to the Commission that all of the men be fired. He added, at least once, that he would see to it they were fired, no matter what the Commission did. (Later, when the hearing was held, the Commission chairman would not allow that statement to be entered in the record, despite repeated attempts by attorneys for the policemen.)

Meanwhile, John Flood told reporters there was a "strong possibility" that the CCPA would take legal action against Waukegan officials for their refusal to bargain with the police union. "Waukegan has an ordinance that requires the city to recognize the right of city employees to be represented by a union or organization of their choice as a bargaining agent. The mayor has violated the law by denying the police representation by the association."

But the CCPA did not immediately launch the legal action, perhaps because it thought it might not really be necessary, and perhaps because of the utter confusion of the week. Strikes were proceeding in Wheeling and Skokie, too, and meetings there — with Flood and Loevy trying to get to as many as possible — were just as tense as they were in Waukegan. In each, the issue was a bit different, but just as knotty; these issues required attention, too, from a hard-pressed union leadership.

Thursday, July 30, almost a week after the start of the blue flu, found an angry swarm of people in downtown Waukegan. Police were demonstrating on the streets around the city hall and the elegant new county building across the street. They were frustrated over events that seemed to allow them no course of action and angry over the threatened dismissals; many were accompanied by their wives, who tended to be even angrier than the men. "Blow your horns if you're with us," they urged motorists, sometimes blocking their way in the streets until the horns were blown. Mayor Sabonjian claims policemen's cars were parked in no parking zones, or driven the wrong way on one-way streets. The confusion in the streets brought many curiosity seekers downtown, among them members of juvenile gangs, traditional police enemies who tended to side with the police in this dispute and came to help picket. Fletcher, the lieutenant who headed the local CCPA unit, recalled that one gang carried signs reading, "With guys like us on the streets, you need your police back."

Assessing the situation afterward, Murray Conzelman, the city attorney, guessed that the street scenes did the police no good, that if public opinion had ever been with the police — as it might have been in a labor town -- it was lost at this point.

"The average Waukegan citizen — really Mrs. Citizen — goes downtown to shop, is harassed with all that noise, blocked in the streets, sees all these local weirdos," he said. "Well, it was real chaos. You surely you don't get public support that way. It was incredible mass psychology."

But it was essentially unplanned, the result of a strike that wasn't quite a strike. The police were new to organized union activity and, in day-to-day dealings, had no skilled leadership. Because of the blue flu fiction, there were no organized picket line duties, no regular strike bulletins to keep up morale, no real way to direct the activities of frustrated, unhappy people.

"We would have been better off if we'd just called it a strike from the beginning," Lt. Fletcher guessed later. "Or, better yet, if we'd stayed on the job longer and tried to work from within."

An Attempt at Conciliation

It was in this chaotic setting, on Thursday, July 30, that Circuit Judge LaVerne Dixon, chief judge of the Lake County Circuit Court, called the mayor, city officials, and representatives of the CCPA into his chambers for a conciliation session. To members of the police union, his was a hopeful move. In other communities, when negotiations were rough — or nonexistent — individuals or groups had often come forward, impartial third parties who could help mediate differences and hold the community together, in the public interest. In Harvey, the strong man mediator had been a circuit judge. So the police leaders were hopeful about Judge Dixon.

"It was the first time we had been able to talk about our organization," said Arthur Loevy, the Amalgamated Clothing Workers lawyer who was the only one in negotiations who had really had this kind of experience before. "It was our only chance to talk about the things we wanted: the right to raise grievances and have them processed, the right to negotiate economics — and we were willing to include a no-strike provision — and the right to checkoff of dues. We did get a chance to talk about these things. Outside the men were picketing city hall and there was a lot of horn blowing. Sabonjian was angry about it. We told the judge we'd stop all demonstrations, that we only wanted another date for a meeting and no publicity. The meeting was set. I thought we were close to working out an agreement."

Judge Dixon was hopeful, too. After his two and a half hour session, he told reporters, "I feel we made some progress. Sabonjian and the CCPA are going to talk to each other and report back to me next Thursday. We're trying to work things out without agitating any more on either side."

But the next week's meeting was never held; Loevy says Sabonjian called the judge and said the deal was off. The two sides never got together again.

Flood said later, "Sabonjian violated every part of our agreement with Judge Dixon. We never got back together. Judge Dixon did really try to bring something together, but he couldn't really use his influence. He's so bound to Sabonjian. We were hoping he would take the initiative. We wanted someone to lead to a solution."

The next day the Waukegan city council met in executive session for two hours. Afterwards, Sabonjian refused comment, except to say that the city would make no new offers, beyond the week-old offer of a $1,000 increase without recognition of the Cook County Police Association as bargaining agent.

There was some further urging that help be sought in reaching a solution. The Illinois division of the American Civil Liberties Union asked Sabonjian to recognize the men's right to organize and bargain collectively. "Effective grievance machinery with arbitration as a terminal step" would be an alternative to the police strike, the ACLU director said. City Attorney Conzelman, the mayor's closest advisor, also thought the mayor should deal with the men, perhaps through arbitration, saying that otherwise the city would be harmed by the bitter cleavage. Later a group of Waukegan attorneys offered to help mediate. They were all refused. Sabonjian had issued his ultimatum; he was going to stick with it. And he was convinced that the people of Waukegan were with him.

The chances at settlement were slipping away and the date for the Civil Service Commission hearing was approaching. The face-to-face meeting between the mayor and Flood had produced nothing. The session with Judge Dixon had led nowhere. The efforts at conciliation were refused.

At this point, the police began to escalate their pressure. A week after the start of the blue flu, they turned their job action into a full-fledged strike, picketing city hall on an organized basis. The picketing was to go on for two full months, until long after they had been fired and their young successors hired and launched on a training program.

There was one more event that might have helped bring about a settlement. A Waukegan attorney named Louis Brydges filed suit in circuit court, seeking a court order to force the city to follow its own labor relations ordinance and recognize the CCPA as bargaining agent. Brydges contended in his complaint that he was being deprived of police protection because of the dispute and the city's refusal to deal with the representatives chosen by the police. But the suit was dismissed by Circuit Judge Harry Strouse, who ruled that Brydges did not have a cause of action, that he was not being deprived of police protection because the sheriff's deputies and later the state police were patrolling Waukegan. The judge said he would reconsider the suit if it were filed on the behalf of a third party, such as the CCPA, instead of by an individual citizen. As events turned out, perhaps the union should have joined the suit at that moment. It did seek to do so later, but the ruling went against it then.

Feelings run high and bitter words are spoken in most strikes but the tension and bitterness was greater in Waukegan than usual, perhaps because the strike experience there was new to most of the participants. Sabonjian claims that strikers followed his car wherever his family went, "hollering 'crook' and threatening us." Flood says Sabonjian was behind a wave of anonymous letters in the community, stating Flood was a "New York Communist sent out here to infiltrate the police department."

Civil Service Commission Acts

The Waukegan Civil Service Commission met the morning of August 4 to consider the dismissal of the strikers. Police and their supporters disrupted the meeting, calling it a "Kangaroo Court" and charging that they wouldn't get fair treatment because the Commission, composed of Sabonjian friends, was biased in favor of the mayor. Angry, Flood and the police walked out. The chairman continued the hearing until the following Monday, after Loevy argued that none of the 55 men had received proper notice of the hearing and needed time to retain lawyers.

On Monday, August 10, when the hearing was resumed, attorneys for the policemen again raised a series of protests. They contended that the city had not complied with state regulations in serving notice of the hearing. They contended that the chairman of the Commission should disqualify himself because he was an officer of a company that does business with the city and thus could not be impartial. They contended that the Commission did not really have jurisdiction in the case because it was a labor dispute. "Charges have been filed in this matter," the lawyers contended, "not because of the alleged misconduct of certain city employees . . . but rather because these employees desire to negotiate with their employer, the City of Waukegan, with respect to matters affecting their employment pursuant to the provisions of subsection c of Section 4.34 of the General Ordinances of the City of Waukegan. The Constitutional rights of the people to petition government for the redress of grievances is provided in the

Illinois Constitution, Article II, Section 17 and in the United States Constitution, in the First Amendment and the Fourteenth Amendment. The state and federal constitutions provide support for the argument and the right of public employees to discuss the terms and conditions of their employment with their employer. This right of consultation serves the public interest by permitting informed government action."

On each point, the lawyers' motions were denied. The chairman ruled that proper notice had been shown and he refused to disqualify himself as chairman. He ruled that the Commission did have jurisdiction over the charges brought against each of the policemen, all of which stemmed from failure to report for duty.

As the hearing proceeded, only the case against the policemen was presented. The 54 policemen, on the advice of the lawyers, chose not to testify.

"As you gentlemen on the Commission saw last week, as I am sure that you sensed this morning," Attorney Loevy explained, "the patrolmen, the sergeants, the lieutenants of the police department of the City of Waukegan do not have complete confidence in this Commission."

The Commission made public its decision two and a half weeks later, on August 28. It reviewed the evidence presented and reaffirmed its jurisdiction, answering the labor dispute argument this way:

"This argument is irrelevant, at best, and is not supported by evidence in the record. If the conduct of the respondents in failing to report for duty was in fact motivated by some feeling that the withholding of services would improve their position in negotiating with the city, then, such conduct is not only inconsistent with any suggestion of illness on their part but is also in violation of the policy of the state. We therefore cannot accept the . . . argument in defense of the charges filed herein."

The Commission ended its order with the statement:

"The Commission is well aware of the fact that many of the police officers named in these charges have served the City of Waukegan for many years. We are saddened by the conduct of these men which necessitated the charges and regret we are compelled to announce that the decision of this Commission is that 'cause' for removal or discharge has been established. The Commission orders the City of Waukegan and/or Chief of Police John Della Valle to remove or discharge each and every individual so named."

"This may be the end of the Cook County Police Association," commented Mayor Sabonjian. "I hope other mayors have as much guts."

Charges of Corruption

The announcement of the mass firings came in the midst of a political maelstrom. On August 10, the day of the Civil Service Commission hearing, the striking policemen had let loose the threatened barrage of charges that Waukegan politicians were corrupt. Nine policemen talked to reporters of gambling and prostitution protection and massive ticket fixing. They turned over to reporters more than 1,500 traffic citations issued since 1963 which they say were ordered voided by the mayor, judges, aldermen, and the state's attorney's office. They claimed excessive ticket writing had been encouraged to allow political fixing of the tickets. They took reporters on a tour to point out gambling and prostitution establishments which they said were protected.

Sabonjian, absolutely infuriated, said all the charges against him were lies and that he had opened his own investigation "of the personal activities of these striking policemen . . . Let's see how clean they were."

Both state and federal law enforcement officials promised to look into the charges and State's Attorney Jack Hoogasian said he would present the charges to the county grand jury. State officials said they would ask Hoogasian to step aside so a special grand jury, with a special prosecutor not related to Waukegan politics, could lead the investigation, but that effort came to naught.

Whether the striking police made a tactical error in unleashing charges of political corruption, an error that absolutely guaranteed they would be fired, will be long debated. One who calls it an error is Murray Conzelman, the city attorney.

"I just don't understand why they did that," he said. "We're human beings. No human being is going to stand for something like that. The mayor told Judge Dixon, 'If we make an agreement with them now, everybody in Waukegan will think the charges are right.' I just can't understand why they did it. It would have made life impossible if they came back to work and we had to all go on working together."

The mayor will be forever furious about the charges and about what the police thought they might accomplish through them.

"My men knew I wouldn't give in to threats," he said a year later. "Or surely they should have known. I had backed them to the hilt in the riots. I told them to take any action necessary to preserve peace in the community — kill the bastards. I told them, if they throw rocks at you, don't wait to tell them about their constitutional rights. Why did they think they could push me around?"

John Flood, the CCPA president, views the matter differently, as a kind of gut issue that shows why policemen have to begin to speak out and seek a louder voice in the management of police departments. He said his organization has given police a new solidarity that enables them to speak out against corruption. He said Waukegan was a "glaring example" of the type of community where police had "to keep their mouths shut and their eyes closed."

Charles Fletcher, the 16-year police veteran who headed the Waukegan police unit — and who might one day have been chief of police himself — wonders. He says the feelings that led to the charges of corruption were very real.

"There were a lot of sore spots," he said, "like the gambling we couldn't do anything about. Johnny Huey runs a million dollar game, but he's protected by the mayor and the chief. Huey used to be a narcotics pusher — he did seven years in the penitentiary. His place is in a high-tension area; there are 11 or 12 murders a year around there. We'd be pursuing a man in connection with a crime and he'd duck into Huey's. Then we couldn't do anything about it. We weren't supposed to go in there. There was a no-raid policy. How did I know that? I flat asked. I was shift commander when I asked.

"Everybody kind of got backed against the wall. I guess neither side realized how tough the other side would be. The major would have taken most of the men back, I think, except for maybe the hard core, if we'd never made the charges of corruption. Maybe that was wrong, but it wasn't just a tactic. It was something we cared about, part of the whole problem."

On part of Fletcher's statement, at least, everyone involved in the Waukegan dispute can agree; "everybody kind of got backed against the wall." Whatever action anyone took, and whatever reaction it brought on, seemed to lead inevitably to the firing of the 54 policemen, men who really believed what the Waukegan ordinance said, that they had a right to representation of their choice. The two main challengers in the fight, Flood and Sabonjian, each tend to view the other's inflexibility as the major cause of the drastic outcome.

"In Waukegan it was politics all the way," said Flood. "Sabonjian likes his tough guy political image. The thing that brought about the strike was his administration. He simply would not recognize the men's needs."

Scoffs Sabonjian, "Flood was the major problem. In normal labor relations, you don't go in and close down three cities and a sheriff's office and then say you're bargaining in good faith. He wasn't the spokesman for our men. I wouldn't recognize him. The men followed the big John Flood and they all drowned."

Discussion Questions

1. Who was chiefly responsible for the Waukegan police strike?

2. Which element — personalities or issues — was most important in bringing on the strike?

3. What events caused a change in the quality of the relationship between the mayor and the police?

4. Was a strike inevitable, given the circumstances and the people involved? If not, and assuming the goal of the union was a pay increase and a grievance procedure, construct a scenario for the parties which would have led to that achievement without the resort to strike.

5. Lt. Fletcher is quoted as saying, "Everybody kind of got backed against the wall." Assuming you agree, what alternative actions, by all parties, might have been possible? How do you account for the inability of the parties to recognize the inevitability of the outcome?

6. How is public opinion involved in this case?

7. If the mayor and the police were competing for public support, how would you evaluate the impact of these tactics on the outcome of the case:
> the ticket slowdown
> the traffic tie-ups
> the mayor's radio appeals to police
> police charges of corruption against city officials
> the mayor's offer to negotiate any issue except recognition of
> > CCPA

How did these events alter the bargaining strength of the parties?

8. If public opinion is a significant factor in this case, what alternate tactics might the police have pursued to bring more public support to their side?

9. The mayor is quoted as saying, after all the striking police were fired, "I hope other mayors have as much guts." Can you make a case for the mayor's handling of the situation?

10. Is there a point in a public bargaining relationship at which the political structure should draw a line and say, "Thus far and no farther; this is the basis on which we will deal."? Where should that line be

drawn in regard to economic demands? The scope of bargaining? The quality of the relationship between the employees and the employing institution?

11. Speculate as to the possibly different outcomes had the parties accepted third party intervention? Under what conditions do parties agree to intervention? Were these conditions present? Would the public interest have been better served had there been successful intervention?

12. Illinois Circuit Judges played very different roles in similar police bargaining cases in Harvey and in Waukegan. How were the cases similar and how were they different? How do the judges' roles illustrate the complexities of public collective bargaining?

Days in Court 4

The Waukegan police dispute did not end with the firing of the policemen. A number of legal actions followed the dismissal order.

The matter of the Waukegan ordinance, guaranteeing recognition of a bargaining agent chosen by city employees, is one of the most puzzling parts of this complex dispute. The existence of the ordinance seems to make public employees in Waukegan a rather privileged group; other public employees in Illinois do not have this right as a matter of law. It seems an irony, then, that the Waukegan police, who had the right of recognition, should be the only public employees in Illinois who were fired after they sought to claim the right.

Did the police, perhaps, not follow the rules in seeking recognition of their union? There is no answer to the question because there are no rules. The ordinance that presumably guarantees recognition provides no procedure; it merely says "a union shall be recognized as the bargaining agent for the employees who are members of that union . . ." When there is no procedure, how do you follow it? What do you do when the mayor, who is the undisputed power in your town, both legally and politically, says he will negotiate any issue except recognition of the union the employees have chosen? In private enterprise, where bargaining is governed by the National Labor Relations Act, the procedures for achieving recognition are spelled out and there is an agency to supervise the process and enforce the rules; the same is true for public employees in those states which have labor legislation, but Illinois is not among them. In the Waukegan ordinance, there is not only no procedure but there is also no method of enforcement, no penalty for failure to carry it out. Who, then, is the referee? The courts? Can the courts, part of the established political structure of a community, really act as referee, particularly where there are no written rules to enforce?

Waukegan officials, in discussions long after the dispute in the summer of 1970, have hinted that had the police proceeded in a different fashion, the result might have been different.

Conzelman, the city attorney, said, and Lt. Fletcher agrees, that

Judge Dixon, in his effort to bring both sides together, suggested that the men, both the Waukegan police and the sheriff's deputies who joined the strike, form a Lake County Police Association instead of joining the Cook County Police Association.

"We would have recognized that," Conzelman said. "You have to know Lake County to understand this, but this union, the Cook County Police Association, just has a bad name here. To come up with the name, Cook County, just doesn't work."

The police rejected the suggestion. They wanted to be part of a going organization, one with a history of some victories that could provide support. They didn't want to form a new group, one that might be weaker, one that might be, in essence, a company union. In addition, what happens to the element of free choice of representation when your employer tells you what choice you may make?

Conzelman raised some further questions about the process of seeking recognition. "Loevy told me," he said, "that the union had authorization cards from 50-some of the men, but I never saw them. And we never got a written demand for recognition — until later, after I had said to the press that we'd never gotten such a demand. The process was the problem. If they'd picketed with off-duty men, and not struck, and made a demand for recognition, obviously we would have recognized the union. We might have objected a bit along the way. But they put us in an impossible spot; if we recognized the union at that point, it would seem all the charges were true."

Mayor Sabonjian, in interviews during and after the strike, raised other issues regarding the procedure his unhappy police chose to follow. He has said, for example, that he didn't know the men had joined the Cook County Police Association. It is a statement that has been received with considerable skepticism. The mayor had had a series of phone calls with Art Loevy on the subject and the July 7 meeting at which the police signed the union authorization cards surely was no secret. Sabonjian knew enough about it to call his police together two days later for the tongue-lashing reported in the press. Actually, he said at that meeting, according to the Waukegan News-Sun of July 10, 1970, that he would deal with the police negotiators from then on, but that is a statement that was never repeated, and was not acted upon.

Sabonjian has also made mild objection to the fact that the police group is called an "association" rather than a "union," intimating that the name is deliberately misleading, designed to pull the wool over the eyes of public officials. Perhaps there is a semantic misunderstanding, but there has been a long tradition among groups that consider themselves professional to choose the name association even

though a major aim is collective bargaining. Education associations
and nurses associations, to name two examples, have long behaved
as unions behave and certainly must be considered to be unions.

"At no time did anyone say we've joined the union and things are
different this year," Sabonjian continued. "They never told the
Labor Relations Commitee (of the city council). Why didn't they tell
us they wanted CCPA to negotiate for them? But they didn't bring a
business agent in here. They came in themselves. Fletcher said he was
bargaining agent."

Some of the answers in the series of questions Sabonjian raised lie
in the time sequence of events leading up to the strike. At the time
the police were talking to the Labor Relations Committee — and
getting nowhere — they had not joined the CCPA; that came later,
after the group had given up dealing with the aldermen and was seeking the help of the mayor. The police involved give no credence to the
mayor's contention that he didn't know they had joined the CCPA.

They explain further that they "didn't bring a business agent in here"
because the CCPA has no business agent. It has, in fact, only volunteer officers, who are working policemen. When a unit is formed in
a community, that unit's officers are chosen from among the membership, a negotiating committee is chosen to bargain for themselves with,
when possible, some assistance from Loevy, the lawyer, or from John
Flood. When Fletcher told the mayor he had been chosen bargaining
agent for the officers, he was speaking the truth.

But it is apparent that Waukegan city officials do have strong points
on their side of the argument. They cannot be charged with refusing
to bargain with police spokesmen because they had long bargained
with the Waukegan Police Association and did, indeed, do so at the
beginning of the 1970 negotiations. And it is true that no official
notification was sent to Waukegan before the strike, informing officials
that the men who formerly were represented by the Waukegan Police
Association now wished to be represented by the CCPA. Such notification from the CCPA had been a routine order of business in other communities where policemen had joined the union and sought bargaining
rights. But it was not sent to Waukegan until after the strike began,
after the city could contend that the men were guilty of insubordination
because they refused to report for duty when ordered. Sabonjian,
for example, repeatedly insisted that the issue was not union recognition but insubordination.

On the other hand there is a nagging rumor in Waukegan. Newspaper
reporters there widely believe that long before the trouble started,
Mayor Sabonjian told a News-Sun columnist that "The police are going to join the CCPA and they're going to go on strike and I'm going
to fire them all."

Loevy and Edward J. Copeland, a Chicago attorney who lives in Lake County, filed a series of court cases on behalf of the CCPA. Two of them have particular bearing on the case.

A Suit to Require Waukegan to Follow Its Labor Ordinance

On August 21, after the Civil Service Commission hearing but a week before the Commission issued its order to fire 54 striking policemen, CCPA began a legal action seeking a court order requiring the city to recognize CCPA as a bargaining agent, in line with its own ordinance. The firings took place before there was a court hearing in the case and CCPA later, on September 9, amended its original complaint.

The amended complaint claimed that the police "were unlawfully discharged from their employment." It said that the CCPA had sought recognition from city officials as bargaining representative but the city had refused the request and had failed to negotiate. It asked three kinds of action from the court:

1. An injunction restraining the city from these unlawful acts — refusal of recognition and refusal to bargain — and directing officials to recognize the Association, to bargain, and to reinstate the fired policemen.
2. A writ of mandamus requiring recognition and bargaining.
3. An award of $5,500,000 in damages to the fired policemen who "have been hindered and prevented from following their occupation as policemen and have thereby lost their usual wages and earnings; the policemen have suffered great mental anguish, fear and intimidation which have contributed to injure and impair their health."

The city officials named as defendants sought dismissal of the complaint on all counts. Circuit Court Judge L. Eric Carey heard the case and on December 9 ruled in favor of the city officials. He presented this reasoning:

On Count I, the request for an injunction, he said that remedy is "entirely unsuited to this case. It would require a mandatory injunction continuous in nature and which might well compel this court to pursue the case and the effects in the future of its order granting the injunction to make certain that certain or many of the defendants were indeed obeying the injunction order." He cited other cases pointing up the difficulties of an injunction "continuous in nature."

On Count II, the request for a writ of mandamus to require recognition and bargaining, he said that this remedy too "would require a continuous course of action on the part of the court to insure that its order would continue to be activated and obeyed in the future by the defendants." Another sufficient reason for denying the writ, he said,

was the fact that the firing of the policemen by the Civil Service
Commission was at that time being reviewed by the court under the
state's Administrative Review Act and "that cause of action is the
only remedy available to challenge the ruling of said commission."

Count III, he ruled, was in violation of Illinois statutes.

(Judge Carey's order has been difficult for the fired policemen to
understand. One reason is that it is opposite to the ruling made by
another circuit judge a year earlier in Harvey. The case was in many
ways exactly comparable to the Waukegan case and the judge in the
Harvey case did issue an order to the city, telling it to stop refusing
to recognize the CCPA and to start bargaining. Another reason is that
in the Harvey case there was no local ordinance involved as there was
in Waukegan. As Fletcher put it, "Judge Carey said he didn't have
time to make the city obey its own ordinance.")

A Suit for Court Review of the Civil Service Dismissal Order

Copeland and Loevy filed the complaint on September 29, noting
that they had petitioned the Civil Service Commission for rehearing
and review, ahd been denied that, and had "exhausted every administrative remedy." The complaint listed 10 reasons why the fired police-
ment believed the commission's order was "erroneous and illegal,"
among them:

— The Commission did not have jurisdiction over a labor dispute
  and the police were not allowed to present that aspect of their
  case;
— Notice of the hearing was faulty;
— The Commission chairman was "prejudiced and personally
  hostile" to the police but refused to disqualify himself;
— The action was in violation of the Waukegan ordinance and was
  "in fact an act of discrimination against the plaintiffs because
  of their exercise of their legal rights."
— The plaintiffs were discharged "not because of their alleged misconduct but rather because they charged the Defendants City of
  Waukegan and Robert Sabonjian with condoning ticket fixing,
  gambling and prostitution."

In later arguments before the court, Attorney Copeland claimed the
acts of the police were an "exercise of constitutional rights, coinci-
dent with a labor dispute," over which the Commission had no jurisdiction.

Circuit Judge James H. Cooney heard the case and issued his decision
in April, 1971, upholding the Commission in its dismissal order. He
pointed out that under the Administrative Review Act, the court is
limited to the record of proceedings before the administrative agency

and "if there is competent evidence to support the finding the decision will be affirmed." (The police did not testify at the hearing so there was no evidence presented beyond the city's charges.)

On some of the specific points raised by the CCPA attorneys, Judge Cooney ruled:

— That proper notice of the hearing had been given;

— That the Commission did have jurisdiction even though the phrase "valid labor dispute" was the "appropriate characterization for the initial circumstances leading to the controversy." He continued, "However, plaintiffs for varying lengths of time had accepted and functioned under the terms and conditions of their employment, including the rules of the Commission. Verily it was under these rules that the appointment of many of them was made possible and effected. Involvement in a labor dispute is not an exception to the sanctions that the Commission rules impose. One cannot accept the benefits while escaping the responsibilities." He also referred to the Illinois Supreme Court decision in the Redding case that "there is no inherent right in municipal employees to strike against their government employer;"

— The record fails to show prejudice on the part of the Commission chairman and even if he were prejudiced it would not have mattered since the three-man decision was unanimous and the "vote of the (other) two would have effected the same decision;"

— The claim of the plaintiffs that they had not been given reasonable opportunity to be heard could not be taken seriously since they had chosen not to testify;

— The record showed that, whether the men were sick or thought they were sick or feigned illness, they had clearly failed to report for duty. "It is not the city's obligation," said Judge Cooney, "to prove that the man was not sick. The psychological comfort that may come from being a fellow among others in a cause may well be something else when tested by the light of the law."

The police attorneys' next step was to begin work on a court appeal of Judge Cooney's decision upholding the Civil Service Commission. They filed their 31-page brief in September, 1971, and they filed it directly with the state Supreme Court rather than with an appellate court because they claimed consititutional issues were involved. They raised two constitutional issues, both involved in interpretation of the 14th amendment to the United States Constitution: "All persons born or naturalized in the United States, and subject to the jurisdiction thereof, are citizens of the United States, and of the State wherein they reside. No State shall make or enforce any law which shall abridge the privileges or immunities of citizens of the United States; nor shall

any State deprive any person of life, liberty, or property, without due
process of law; nor deny to any person within its jurisdiction the equal
protection of the laws."

This second aspect of the case tackles head-on the 1965 ruling
by the Illinois Supreme Court that public employees have no inherent right to strike. The argument includes these sections:

> There is no real and substantial difference between public and
> private agencies with respect to the general question of employer-
> employee relations and the specific question of strikes. To argue
> that the mere fact that one employer is public and another pri-
> vate is a sufficient basis for making a distinction between their
> employees, as groups, is to presume that there are fundamental
> and far-reaching differences between public and private employ-
> ment. There is no basis in logic or in law for making this pre-
> sumption.

> . . . Both categories of employment contain the same potential
> for a clash of interests as employers and employees seek to
> realize their goals. Regardless of whether the employment is
> public or private, there exists the opportunity for arbitrary and
> discriminatory practices against employees. In both cases, the
> employer is under pressure to pay as little as possible and still re-
> retain his personnel . . . It is precisely this similarity in result
> that is significant here.

> . . . This lack of basis for distinguishing between private and
> public employees has long been recognized by the State of
> Ilinois in its approach to employment problems. The courts have
> not, for example, distinguished between private and public
> employees in the application of statutes regulating working
> conditions. Though Illinois' eight-hour-day law is silent on the
> subject, the courts have consistently applied it with no sugges-
> tion that its application be limited to private employers . . . The
> same is true of legislation protecting female employees . . . and
> of legislation regulating the safety of scaffolds . . . The important
> thing to note here is the court's recognition of the fact that there
> is nothing about the nature of the two kinds of employment which
> suggests that the two groups of employees should be treated dif-
> ferently. Thus, a difference in treatment would violate the
> Fourteenth Amendment.

> There is, moreover, nothing about the nature of public employ -
> ment which creates a 'real and substantial difference' between a
> strike against a government employer and a strike against a pri-
> vate one . . . It cannot be argued realistically that a strike by
> municipal employees is a challenge to the authority of the state.

It is, as in the private sector, a means of compelling an
employer to grant the thing he is empowered to grant. It is not
a strike against the state, a political action, but a strike by employees against their employer, an economic action, which is
identical to its counterpart in the sphere of private employment.

. . . A strike by public employees cannot be distinguished, as
some have suggested, as an attempt to usurp the power of the
government. Striking public employees seek not to subvert the
will of the people by dictating policy of the legislature; rather
they seek to exercise a voice in the allocation of resources bud-
geted to a specific agency. The Waukegan Police Department has
the discretion to make a wide variety of decisions about the terms
and conditions of the employment of police officers. The plaintiff-
police officers assert only the same right granted to private employees — the right to use the strike as a means of pressuring the
employer to grant those things he is empowered to grant . . .
Like a strike by private employees, a strike by public employees
is an effort by those who are affected by decisions to gain a voice
in the making of those decisions. Again, strikes in the private
and public sectors are essentially the same and there is no constitutionally permissible basis for distinguishing them.

The final argument which is sometimes advanced in favor of
denying public employees the right to strike is the proposition
that a strike by public employees contravenes the public welfare
and results in paralysis of society. It is clear, however, that the
disruptive potential of a strike by private employees has not been
a sufficient basis for a general denial of the right to strike in the
private sector . . . Because the threat of social damages is not
grounds for denying private employees the right to strike, it cannot constitutionally be the basis for denying public employees
a similar right in the absence of a showing of real and substantial
difference.

The constitutional arguments were not all dealt with directly in
the brief prepared by Murray Conzelman on behalf of the Waukegan
city officials. He contended, instead, that no constitutional issues were
raised in the trial court and, therefore, no such issues can be raised
on appeal. Conzelman's motion that the case be transferred to the
Appellate Court in the second judicial district was granted.

"This case is brought under the Administrative Review Act to review a decision of the Civil Service Commission of the City of Waukegan discharging the plantiffs as police officers," the Conzelman brief
continues. ". . . The law is clear that we are restricted to the record . . .

The Court does not reweigh the evidence or rehear the case on the record. The decision of the Administrative Agency is presumed to be correct and must be affirmed if there is competent evidence in support . . . None of the plaintiffs took the stand to testify in the case. There is no denial that they were absent from duty, that they failed to exercise their duties, that they failed to respond as ordered and there is no suggestion in the record that they had any excuse for these failures."

Referring to a claim by the police attorneys that issues stated in their brief were, indeed, raised in the trial court, Conzelman wrote, "It is true that four of the issues were raised in trial, but not in the way they are being raised now. They were raised simply as factual issues and, of course, there was no evidence in the record to support them. Now they are raised as constitutional issues and the trial court never heard arguments on these questions raised in this fashion.

"The first issue raised in this court that police officers have full constitutional rights has never been raised before and it is really not an issue in this case. We have no quarrel with the proposition, but it is only half the story. In addition to their rights, they also have responsibilities. The plaintiffs took an oath to uphold the Constitution and to faithfully discharge their duties. If they are to receive the benefits of the Civil Service, then surely they must accept its burdens and comply with the Civil Service laws and rules of the Commission. Among those rules is the obligation to appear when assigned to duty, to exercise and discharge their duties and to obey proper orders. The record does not show any excuse for these failures. If a defense was available then the plaintiffs were required to provide it and their failure to testify should not be used by them now as an excuse or defense."

Conzelman's brief also restated that adequate written notice had been given the officers and that the record shows complete fairness rather than prejudice.

It went on to say that, "There is no evidence in this record that a labor dispute was involved. No plaintiff testified and we have only the unsworn statement of counsel for that. Even if it were true it would not be a defense because the Supreme Court in the case of Board of Education v. Redding, adopted 'the universal view that there is no inherent right in municipal employees to strike against their government employer . . .'

". . . The simple answer to plaintiffs' suggestion that they were denied 'the right to strike,'" the brief continues, "is that they have no such right. The law of the case of Board of Education v. Redding binds them and all other public employees . . .

"None of the cases cited . . . (in) plaintiffs' brief have to do with public employees and their so-called 'right to strike.' The only case that comes close to this proposition is the case of County of Peoria v. Benedict. In that case the Supreme Court held that the Illinois Anti-Injunction Act applied and an injunction could not issue to restrain a strike by public employees . . . The Anti-Injunction Act does not repeal or affect the Civil Service Act regarding discharges of Civil Service employees . . . The Anti-Injunction Act is not intended to do anything more than remove one remedy, namely the remedy of injunction. That is not an issue in this case because no injunction was ever sought. The case of County of Peoria v. Benedict does not purport to overrule the case of Board of Education v. Redding.

"We no longer burn murderers at the stake, but this does not mean that murder is no longer an illegal act. The crime remains, only the remedy is changed. Here a strike by public employees cannot be enjoined, but this does not relieve them of the other burdens of the law, including the burdens and benefits of the Civil Service laws.

"If the legislature had intended that the Anti-Injunction Act overrule the Civil Service Act, then they would have said so. In fact, if the Civil Service Act is overruled, then the plaintiffs have no right to any public employment at all because it is only under that Act that they obtain public employment and its protections."

The Illinois Supreme Court did not hear the case. Instead, agreeing with Conzelman that constitutional issues were not involved, it sent the case back to the appellate court. That court upheld the lower court and the city officials.

The Grand Jury Hearings

Off and on over a period of months, the Lake County Grand Jury met to hear witnesses, not only regarding the police charges of corruption but also regarding charges against the policemen (for example, the "illegal act" of taking traffic tickets from the police department to back up the charges of political fixing.) Some of the fired policemen were called to testify, but others who said they wanted to testify about gambling were not called. The investigation was conducted by State's Attorney Jack Hoogasian, although Illinois law enforcement officers had originally sought to have him step aside in favor of a special prosecutor.

The jury issued its report, with no indictments of anyone but with some comments and recommendations of its own, in March of 1971. The report noted that "The charges investigated . . . were originally voiced by striking members of the Waukegan Police Department. The strike arose from serious labor-management disputes within the Police Department." It said it would not attempt to resolve the labor-manage-

ment problems or to fix blame for them but that the evidence was
considered "in light of the conditions which gave rise to the allegations."

Sections of the report were devoted to specific charges. Regarding
gambling, it said:

"The Grand Jury finds that gambling in the form of cards, dice,
sports parlay cards and bookmaking existed in the City of Waukegan
throughout the 1960s and during most of 1970. Such gambling may
continue to exist at present. The Grand Jury further finds that, without the statements made by admitted gamblers after receiving im-
munity, there is not sufficient proof of gambling occurring within the
statute of limitations to justify indictments.

"The initial hearings upon the subject of gambling clearly showed
that the dismissed officers could not legally prove that gambling
existed . . . In our view it was more important to discover whether
gambling was aided by official corruption than to indict accused
gamblers on flimsy evidence or to belabor transactions that had occurred
beyond the statute of limitations . . . ."

The jury urged improved training and better methods of handling
vice control by the Waukegan Police Department.

Regarding prostitution, the jury said it found little evidence. The
police had never made much of the charge, either.

The report went on to deplore the long silence by police if their
charges were really serious, to say the bitterness of the accusations
detracted from their credibility, and to state "the conduct of the
accusing witnesses is nearly, if not wholly, as deplorable as the alleged
conduct of those they accuse."

It then recommended that the police department "either implement
a vigorous program of enforcement of existing vice laws or give a
clear and sufficient explanation as to why it is unable to do so."

Regarding ticket fixing, the jury said any suggestion "that traffic
tickets were voided in exchange for money or other valuable consideration the Grand Jury finds . . .to be totally unproven." It said witnesses
produced four large envelopes containing 1,890 traffic tickets with
the word "void" written on them, covering a period from 1963 through
1970, but it said the witnesses could not sustain charges of corrupt
voiding or even show that the names on some tickets had not been
"added recently." It presented a number of reasons why voiding had
occurred, including changes of mind by the issuing officer or because
of insufficient evidence. The jury recommended some reforms in the
handling of tickets, including a new system whereby each ticket
written must be sent to court, to be disposed of there rather than on
the street or at the police station.

In conclusion, the jury stated:

"In the course of its investigation the Grand Jury learned much about the Waukegan Police Department. It is beyond dispute that the Department was torn by discontent. A police 'strike' would not have occurred otherwise. Further the dissatisfaction has existed for some time. Neither the present Chief of Police nor his predecessor has escaped serious opposition within the Department though whether that is the fault of the Chiefs or of their opposition or of both is not clear. On the basis of the nature and quality of the testimony of the officers we heard, we would conclude that the standards of performance in the Department were low. Of the officers we heard testify only a fraction impressed us as knowledgeable and competent. We might hesitate to voice this opinion merely on the basis of what was before us, however, we have the benefit of the study of the Department conducted by the Field Operations Division of the International Association of Chiefs of Police. This study confirms our opinions and much that we have heard confirms the conclusions in the study. We recommend that the study be carefully considered and its recommendations followed to the extent it is practical to do so."

The study referred to, that made by the highly-respected International Association of Chiefs of Police, was paid for by the Illinois Law Enforcement Commission and launched at the request of the Lake County Law Enforcement Committee. The study was started before the strike and completed well after it, in January, 1971. It made broad recommendations for department reorganization, for better record keeping, improved community relations particularly with the black community, for tightening of vice control operations, and for better relations with employees.

"There is unquestionably a need for responsible employee organizations and formal grievance procedures to allow such groups, and all employees, to be heard," the report said. It noted that lack of a grievance procedure was one cause of the strike, not the only reason for the dispute but contributory to "the state of mind."

The LACP report went on to admonish police to choose the right kind of organization so there would be "proper regard for the protection of the community," and it assailed the use of militant tactics, saying "Under no circumstances should excessive militant tactics be employed by or tolerated from police employee groups . . . Police strikes, over or through the guise of feigned sickness, can have no moral justification."

Discussion Questions

1. Should public employees have the right to strike? Why or why not?

2. If some public employees should have the right to strike, should some be exempted? Why or why not?

3. If some public employees do not have the right to strike, what methods can be provided to assure just treatment? Will they work?

4. How can the public interest best be represented in relationships between a public employer and the employees?

AURORA TEACHERS AND MANAGEMENT RIGHTS

Introduction

The dispute between the Aurora teachers union and the school administration is a clash of the legitimate rights of employees and the legitimate rights of the superintendent and the school board.

Deeply involved in this question is the issue of the scope of bargaining, or what issues can or should be submitted to the collective bargaining process. At what point do the interests of teachers as workers conflict with the responsibilities of the school board to the community? How does one distinguish between bargaining over working conditions and bargaining on the management of the schools?

This case in microcosm represents the dilemmas of the public and its employees over justice and fairness to employees, the opportunity for them to have a say about the conditions under which they work, and over the matters which involve the cost and quality of education which citizens and their representatives can and do decide through their willingness or unwillingness to levy taxes upon themselves to achieve their objectives.

Although the words "good faith bargaining" are not highlighted in the case, the issue they represent seems important throughout. It is a difficult issue because the meaning and intent of bargaining in good faith as established through private sector experience leaves wide latitude of behavior to the parties. But there are guidelines in private sector experience. The case of the National Labor Relations Board v. American National Insurance Company, 343 U.S. 395 (1952), regards a management functions clause which listed matters such as promotions, discipline, and work scheduling as the responsibility of management and excluded them from arbitration. The union took the position that it could not agree to such a clause since it covered matters subject to the duty to bargain collectively under the National Labor Relations Act. The controversy in turn raised the issue of good faith bargaining.

The NLRB in this case made four points:

1. . . . the making of voluntary labor agreements is encouraged by protecting employees' rights to organize for collective bargaining and

by imposing on labor and management the mutual obligation to bargain collectively.

2. . . . . it was held that the duty of an employer to bargain collectively required the employer to negotiate in good faith with his employees' representatives, to match their proposals, if unacceptable, with counterproposals, to make every reasonable effort to reach an agreement.

3. . . . . that the fifth employer unfair labor practice in the Wagner Act which concerns refusal to bargain was accompanied when introduced in Congress by an explanation of "good faith" as meaning to bargain collectively in good faith *to reach an agreement*. This understanding of the duty has been accepted and applied throughout the administration of the Wagner Act.

4. . . . . Section 8 (d) of the Act does not compel either party to agree to a proposal or require the making of a concession.

Chronology

1965	Beginning of yearly Professional Negotiation Agreements with Aurora Education Association East.
February 1968	AEAE presented big package of demands. School administration decided a collective bargaining policy was needed.
March 1968	School board adopted policy 1.30, an adaptation of President Kennedy's executive order 10988. The policy included a strong management rights clause that was to become a subject of controversy with the association.
April 1968	School board unilaterally adopted a salary schedule for the next school year.
May to July 1968	School administrators and teachers' negotiating committee continued dispute over the policy statement. In July, agreement was reached to begin bargaining under the new policy in the fall.
Fall 1968	Bargaining began on the big package of demands presented the previous February.
December 1968	Agreement reached on the first five articles of a formal contract: recognition, grievance procedure, negotiation procedure, responsibilities and rights of the teachers association, responsibilities and rights of the board.
February 1970	Agreement reached on second formal contract, including an "improvement of instruction" clause which management wanted.
November 1970	AEAE brought in its "modest proposal" for the next year's contract, including more than 800 demands. Board policy 1.30 came under a renewed attack.
March 1971	The management negotiating team presented its "response in kind," including more than 800 demands. It also presented an "alternate counterproposal" to abolish collective bargaining of any kind for four years.
Spring 1971	Impasse declared in negotiations.

June 9,
1971

AEAE members voted to "withhold services" in Septemtember if no satisfactory agreement had been reached by that time. At a negotiating session that night, teachers were asked repeatedly whether a strike vote had been taken. When they finally announced the result of the vote, the management team walked out on the grounds that the board policy does not allow negotiations with an organization that "asserts the right to strike."

June 21,
1971

School board agreed that AEAE had lost recognition and was no longer the bargaining agent for the teachers. The board approved issuance of individual contracts to all teachers, indicating that those who refused to sign would be considered resigned from their positions.

The Right to Bargain 1

Members of the Aurora Education Association East gathered in the auditorium of East High School after classes on June 9, 1971, to hear a report from their negotiating team.

The Aurora East School District, No. 131, operates 14 schools staffed by about 450 teachers in Aurora, Illinois, an industrial community 40 miles west of Chicago. There are other public schools in Aurora, operated by another school district.

There was tension in the high school auditorium on that June afternoon. Negotiations on the district's third formal contract with teachers had been going on since school started the fall before. Ten bargaining sessions had been held and no tentative agreements had been reached on any part of the contract that would govern teacher employment during the next school term, starting in September 1971. There were other problems too. The teachers and the school administration were locked in a bone-deep philosophical division over a school board management rights policy, a division of opinion that seemed to mean there might be no new contract at all. And the teachers were worried about their medical insurance. The contract under which they were working was to expire at the end of June, only 21 days away, and the teachers feared all their insurance might expire with it. When the teachers association had inquired about the status of insurance coverage, it had been told that the school board's obligation to provide insurance would end on June 30, with the end of the contract.

Robert H. Davis, vice president of the association and the teachers' chief spokesman in negotiations, rose to make this report. A tall, young high school math teacher, Davis is a quiet, intent kind of person who had come to have an idealistic commitment to the idea of collective bargaining. He had studied it thoughtfully, had gone to a National Education Association summer training session on the techniques of bargaining, and had worked uncounted hours on the fat package of demands the teachers had delivered to the Aurora East school board the fall before. He was viewed as a tough bargainer, tougher than the spokesmen of the past two years.

Davis' report to the teachers was discouraging. Progress was slow, he said. The last meeting, the week before, had been non-productive.

School board negotiators had offered no concessions but had instead talked of the costs of some of the teachers' proposals. The proposal for unlimited sick leave would cost the board $6 million, they had said.[1] The proposal for severance pay would cost $32 million. Raising the salary schedule to meet the teachers' demands would cost $1,856,000; providing individual desks and files for each teacher would cost $129,000; allowing a 10-minute break each day for elementary school teachers would cost $86,000; allowing teachers to leave school at 3:15 on Friday afternoons would cost $27,000, and providing dictionaries for each classroom would cost $4,300.

Davis reported that the teachers' team had, at that last negotiating session, lowered its salary demands and dropped its efforts for unlimited sick leave, severance pay and dictionaries. They hadn't had a school board answer yet, but another negotiating session was scheduled for later on the day of the teachers' meeting, June 9.

The president of the teachers' association, AEAE, told the teachers he was disturbed, too. He said he had pleaded and begged with the board team for progress in negotiations. He said board negotiators had asked if Aurora East had been singled out as a "target district" by the National Education Association and the Illinois Education Association, a district that would get special attention and bargaining help in order to set a good pattern for bargaining elsewhere. He said he'd told the board, "No, we're a local organization and we're only attempting to win some rights. As a last resort we have called on outside help."

Some of the "outside help" was in the auditorium with the AEAE teachers that afternoon. Don Rogers was there, the northeast division field service representative for the Illinois Education Association. He gave the teachers a brief pep talk, saying their problems were no different and no worse than those of teachers in neighboring school districts, and asking, "Are you going to stand up or lie down and take it?" Richard Croll was there, the office manager for the nearby regional office of the Illinois Education Association. He gave a pep talk too and told the meeting that the board's inaction on the health insurance coverage was an example of "terror tactic." And Leo Wotan was there, an attorney from Elgin, Illinois, a city similar to Aurora and north of it along the Fox River. Wotan reminded the Aurora East teachers that teachers in neighboring Carpentersville "withdrew their services for a day last year" before they got a signed contract. He added, "You have a right to bargain in good faith. Collective bargaining is a democratic process." And he tried to reassure any teachers who might fear they'd be fired if they pressed harder for a contract. The school code provides that tenured teachers have a right to their jobs, he said, unless they are notified of dismissal by a certain time. "That time has passed," he added.

An elementary school teacher then stood up to read a carefully-worded resolution:

Be it resolved that the teachers of District 131 will not return to the classroom in the fall if there is at that time no satisfactory settlement of the contract between the Board of Education and Aurora Education Association East and further that an open meeting be held on September 2 for all teachers to assess the position of the Aurora Education Association East at that time.

The language was similar or identical to that other teachers in other districts were using in attempts to reach contract agreement. Such resolutions had, in fact, become rather standard practice in Illinois school negotiations during the preceding few years. Each September a dozen or more Illinois school districts have been unable to open schools as scheduled, until concentrated negotiations have produced settlements.

The teachers called for a standing vote on the resolution and the vote was counted: 201 in favor, 24 opposed.

Another motion was passed, too, before the meeting adjourned at 6:02 p.m. The teachers, by voice vote, approved a motion that no agreement entered into with the Board of Education could be subject to the board's policy statement on bargaining and management rights, so disliked by the teachers.

That policy statement, long an issue between the school board and the teachers' association, AEAE, was "Policy 1.30: Board Policy Establishing Regulatory Guidelines for Collective Negotiations with Employee Groups," a rather lengthy document modeled after President John Kennedy's Executive Order 10988, governing collective bargaining for employees of federal agencies. The board's policy will be considered further later in this case, but there is a need here for an understanding of the disputed section of Policy 1.30. Part of Article VII, which deals with management rights, reads:

In the administration of all matters governed by the agreement, officials and employees are governed by the provisions of any existing or future laws and regulations, including policies set forth in the Board of Education Policy Manual and other board regulations which may be applicable, and the agreement shall at all times be applied subject to such laws, regulations and policies.

The effect of the clause had been disputed from the beginning of formal collective bargaining in Aurora East, in 1968. Although the same language had been incorporated into each of the negotiated contracts with the teachers, the Aurora Education Association East was increasingly determined to get rid of it. The teachers believe that clause says that any provisions of a negotiated contract can subsequently be changed by a new regulation of the board of education, wiping out the contract guarantees and rendering the contract meaningless, "not worth the paper it's written on." The board contends the clause is a reasonable assertion of its right and responsibility to govern in conformance with state law and with its own regulations and policies. Board spokesmen insist that they have not used this management power capriciously and never intended to so use it; they contend that courts would protect the teachers' contract rights if the board ever asserted its power unfairly.

The board was absolutely adamant, during the 1971 negotiations, that the clause would stay in the negotiated contract and in its own policy manual. In fact, board spokesmen said, every aspect of the negotiations was being carried on under the policy, which must be recognized and accepted by the teachers' association. The association was equally adamant that any agreement reached was not to be "subject to board of education policy" and that it would sign no agreement requiring its recognition. That is why that matter was the last order of business at the teachers' association meeting on June 9.

The Final Negotiating Session

Less than two hours later a negotiating session started between the AEAE team and a bargaining team of Aurora East administrators headed by Dr. Roy J. O'Neil, the coordinator of research and development for the school district. It was O'Neil's research that led to the adoption of the disputed Policy 1.30 in 1968 and he had headed negotiations for the district ever since. His reputation for rigorous bargaining and some innovative approaches to bargaining have placed him in some demand as a bargaining consultant to other school districts.

The Aurora district keeps a transcript of negotiating sessions and the record shows that O'Neil opened the June 9 session at 8:01 p.m. He told the teachers' team that he had some responses to make to their demands, and said, "Prior to enumerating these responses, I must point out that . . . the concessions we are about to offer are conditional upon your withdrawal of your objection to negotiating under terms of Policy 1.30, which, of course, is the matter at impasse . . ."

O'Neil then proceeded to outline a salary offer, increased insurance benefits, 10 dictionaries for every classroom, and offered to reduce a long list of the board's counterproposals, which had been developed to match the teachers' long list of demands.

The teachers' team caucused for about half an hour then returned to say, "We receive your reductions in the counterproposal but not your conditions." In other words, the impasse over acceptance of the board's policy continued.

Before there was opportunity for any further discussion O'Neil was called out of the meeting to answer a telephone call. When he returned, the following conversation took place:

O'Neil: Would you care to make any comments about the purposes and the results of your meeting tonight? (He was referring to the teachers' association meeting that started after school and ran until 6 p.m.)

Davis: In what way, and for what —

O'Neil: What were the purposes of the meeting?

Davis: What bearing does that have on what we are doing here?

O'Neil: That's what I'm asking.

Davis: I don't understand your question.

O'Neil: What were the purposes of the meeting tonight? Why was the meeting called?

Rogers: (The Illinois Education Association field representative) Let me talk about it a little bit.

O'Neil: I'm sorry. I have a question for Mr. Davis.

Rogers: And I'll try to answer it.

Davis: He's a member of our team — he can speak.

O'Neil: All right.

Rogers: I don't think it's any secret that the negotiating team has been negotiating (with the school administration) for some time. There are no tentative agreements, which would indicate there must be some problems. The teachers merely took a stand —

O'Neil: Was a strike vote taken at the meeting tonight?

Rogers: I didn't hear anything that said strike.

O'Neil: Was there a vote on any matter like that?

Rogers: There sure was.

O'Neil: Can we (the administration negotiating team) have a caucus? (Caucus from 9:03 to 9:07 p.m.)

O'Neil: Can you tell us the results, Mr. Rogers, of the strike vote? Was it —

Rogers: Counted? No, I didn't happen to be at that part of the meeting.

O'Neil: Were you at that part of the meeting, Mr. Davis?

Davis: Strike vote?

O'Neil: Yes — withholding of services, concerted, whatever —

Davis: All right.

O'Neil: Were you present at that part? Were votes counted?

Rogers: You know, I really don't think that's going to help negotiations at all —

O'Neil: That's quite — you may be very right — let me finish, please.

Rogers: What I'm here for —

O'Neil: Let me finish, please. I think you are right, and maybe I can speed things up a little bit. What were the results of the vote?

Rogers: The point is, I really don't think that's any of your business, you know —

O'Neil: Well, okay. I appreciate that concern, but I do believe that it is.

Rogers: The point here at this table is, let's try to get some work done.

O'Neil: Excuse us, please.

(Caucus 9:08 to 9:09 p.m.)

O'Neil: I ask you again, Mr. Davis, were the results of that vote affirmative?

Rogers: I'lll answer for him. The results were affirmative, yes.

O'Neil: All right, now, that's the information that we have received and since, as a spokesman for this organization you have affirmed that, let me read Board Policy to you. We are talking about Board Policy 1.30 — I think you have become somewhat acquainted with that.

(Reading from Article II) "When used in this policy statement, the term 'employee organization' means any lawful association, labor organization, professional organization, federation, council, or brotherhood having as a primary purpose the improvement of working conditions among school employees, or any craft, trade or industrial union whose membership includes both school employees and employees of private organizations; but such term shall not include any organization (1) which asserts the right to strike against any local, state or federal agency of the government, or to assist or to participate in any such strike, or which imposes a duty or obligation to conduct, assist or participate in any such strike, work stoppage, or interference with the conduct of official business . . ."

You have, as a spokesman for this organization, in my opinion asserted that the organization has asserted the right to strike, and therefore it appears to us that you have violated Board Policy, and if so I am sure that you are aware that for any employee to do it — perhaps not you, Sir — but for any employee to violate Board Policy is a matter which has been and could be held to be — well, let me put it this way — it appears to disqualify the AEAE from recognition and to exclude it from the perimeters of the kinds of an organization with which we are permitted to bargain, and therefore, we feel at this time that we must withdraw and seek the counsel of the Board of Education. So thank you for coming.

AEAE Spokesman: May I ask just a question before we —

O'Neil: Not now, we're done.

AEAE spokesman: Well then, I'm going to make a statement that you can hear on the way out.

O'Neil: We're finished.

AEAE Spokesman: You're saying that you're walking out tonight, right now — right? You are leaving, you are walking out?

O'Neil: You heard what I said.

AEAE Spokesman: I just wanted to make sure — you're going to walk away from the table.

O'Neil: We're finished now.

Thus, less than four hours after the teachers voted not to go to work in September without a settlement, bargaining ended for Aurora Education Association East. But the withdrawal of recognition of the Association as a bargaining agent did not end the controversy.

Footnote

1. No explanation was offered as to how this figure was reached. The teachers had asked for unlimited sick leave. If 400 teachers, each earning $15,000 a year, took sick leave every day and never worked at all during the school year, the cost for sick leave would be $6 million.

Discussion Questions

1. Is it legitimate for a local teachers association to seek bargaining help from the state or national association? Is it legitimate for a state teachers association to pick target districts for concentrated bargaining efforts?

2. Was the association's vote a strike vote? Is there any significance in the fact that the vote was taken in a private meeting and not officially transmitted to school board negotiators? An IEA spokesman said the vote was not "any of your business." Do you agree or disagree?

3. Does the school board have the unilateral power to adopt a policy governing collective bargaining?

4. Is the board's management rights clause a legitimate statement of management's right to manage?

5. Does the wording of the board's management rights clause mean that negotiated contracts can be abrogated by management? Does the clause negate collective bargaining?

6. If you had the power to do so, how would you resolve the difference of opinion over the management rights clause?

7. Is "asserting the right to strike" comparable to striking? If striking is illegal for public employees, is asserting the right to strike also illegal?

The Aurora Education Association East, like other teacher associations in other cities, got into collective bargaining as much by drift
as by design. The education associations were not organized for bargaining purposes and, until the 1960s, had never played that role. They
worked, in a variety of ways, for the improvement of education, chiefly
through lobbying activities in the state legislatures and in Washington.
Local chapters would meet occasionally to consider problems common to school people, whether they were classroom teachers, principals,
or superintendents, all of whom were represented in the same organizations. Usually the associations were dominated by school administrators and not by classroom teachers.

Some pervasive trends in the 1960s changed all that. One of them
was the political activism of the period. Perhaps influenced heavily
by the civil rights movement, many other kinds of groups, including
teachers, were seeking ways to play a part in making decisions that
affected their own lives.

"Teachers are more aggressive and want to participate more in
decisions about their schools," said the president of the Illinois Education Association in 1972. "Traditionally, teachers went to schools
where administrators set their pay, hours and curriculum. Now they
want changes. Materials aren't adequate and classes are too big. We
tried for years to talk to principals, but saw many of our proposals
just filed away. The only alternative was to organize and achieve
through formal negotiations."

A continuing shortage of teachers in the years following World
War II tended to give teachers a bargaining power advantage they had
never had when teaching jobs were harder to find. The competition
for teachers led to relatively higher salaries, too, which in turn attracted
new kinds of students to the profession.

Another apparent trend was a general upgrading in the status of
teachers, related to efforts of the colleges of education to attract
better students during the years after World War II and to the improvement of teachers' salaries during a period when much public attention
was devoted to the schools, their successes and failures. The graduates

who were attracted to the profession found much to criticize in the public schools and were determined to do something about it. The education associations offered one vehicle for change, for a voice by classroom teachers in the determination of educational policy.

Among the things that teachers criticized, problems that eventually found their way to the bargaining table, were top-heavy administrative bureaucracies that stifled teacher initiative in the classroom, crowded classes, increasing disciplinary problems with academically uninspired students, and the system of priorities that failed to take into account the extra work needed in the poorest schools.

These problems surfaced against the backdrop of continuing inflation and the pressure on taxes, both state and local, that left school boards scrambling for money to meet the spiralling costs. At the same time enrollment was booming, the result of the baby boom that followed World War II. Not only were costs per pupil mounting rapidly, but the number of pupils was mounting at the same time. The demand for money was exceeding the tax supply and taxpayers were beginning to become increasingly stingy about passing referenda that would mean higher taxes. State legislatures, fearing a tax revolt and pressed by growing welfare and public health costs as well as other state needs, were not producing greatly increased funds for schools either. The trend fed classroom discontent.

Another significant change was in the number of men who chose teaching as a profession. Male teachers accounted for only 17 percent of all classroom teachers in the middle 1920s, but by 1965, their proportion had increased to more than 30 percent. From 1954 to 1964, the number of male teachers increased 93 percent, compared with with a 38 percent increase in the number of female teachers.[1] These men teachers play leadership roles in many local teacher associations and most of the pressure for bargaining comes from junior and senior high school staffs, where men serve in greater numbers than in the elementary schools. The increase in the number of men teachers has led to a change in salary expectations. Women teachers have long been considered secondary earners in families, not in need of as much pay as the heads of families.

Coupled with these trends was the success model of the American Federation of Teachers, which is affiliated with the AFL-CIO. The Federation was formed in 1919, but was not a particularly significant factor until 1961 when the United Federation of Teachers, the New York City affiliate, was elected bargaining agent of the 44,000 teachers in that system. The UFT negotiated its first contract in 1962, won substantial improvements in working conditions, and thus started real efforts by other Federation locals to win bargaining rights in other cities. A Chicago local won exclusive bargaining rights in 1966, beating out an affiliate of the Illinois Education Association in a historic contest that first established, in Illinois, the right of a local school board to grant exclusive bargaining rights and to bargain collectively if it chose to.[2] Although most of the American Federation of Teachers activity was in large cities, the AFT successes spurred the teacher associations into more strenuous bargaining activities. It was clear to teachers, even in small and placid communities, that by using traditional trade union methods, AFT locals were winning, not only higher salaries and better benefits, but also more voice in the management of schools.

The New York teachers' strike in 1967 — that was a new and novel idea then — had another kind of impact. In New York, the rallying cry of that 1967 strike was "More Effective Schools" and the union won, not only higher salaries but also some important school policy changes, including vast sums of money for schools in impoverished areas where the pupils were doing poorly. The idea of a teachers' strike, or some sort of collective action to bring pressure on school boards, has been around ever since.

In 1962, the year of the New York City teachers' first contract, the convention of the National Education Association approved a dramatic change and formulated policy for what it termed "professional negotiation." It provided for several levels of bargaining activity, ranging from mere recognition that an association chapter represents its members to full-fledged bargaining agreements that include outside mediation for the settlement of disputes. Five years later, the NEA convention took the next step and voted to support local affiliates who had gone on strike.

And so throughout the country, even in communities where the idea of teacher bargaining was almost as alien as the thought of teachers carrying picket signs, local teacher associations began to turn to bargaining, slowly at first but with growing momentum all through the 1960s.

"We have gotten out of the tea-party syndrome where teachers would simply meet and break bread," said an Illinois Education Association spokesman in 1972. "We're an activist organization now, and those that prefer tea parties will have to look somewhere else."

One other factor, a rather ironic one, probably contributed to the growth of collective bargaining for teachers: the passage, in some states, of legislation establishing procedures for collective bargaining by public employees.[3]

Illinois was not one of the states that passed public employee bargaining legislation; bills introduced have repeatedly been defeated. But

organizing and bargaining activities have proceeded rapidly
in Illinois anyway, in a sometimes chaotic pattern in which pragmatic
realism takes the place of legal sanction. Whatever the status of bargaining rights in Illinois, the state supreme court has held that public
employee strikes are illegal.[4] They take place anyway, as they do in
other states, in most of which public employee strikes are also
illegal.

Bargaining in Aurora East

The idea of collective bargaining came gradually in Aurora East
schools as it did in other communities. It wasn't formal bargaining
at first, just some teacher committees that met with the superintendent
under a professional negotiation agreement reached in 1965. That was
the first year that Andrew Hook, who had taught in the district for
five previous years, served as superintendent.

Hook, a tall, slim man, rather soft-spoken, appointed teachers to
committees to consult with him on salary and school year affairs.
Some of the Aurora Education Association East spokesmen have since
said that the committees were a "rubber stamp" designed by the
administration to "stave off negotiations." But Hook feels that he
did not seek to prevent negotiations and that he has never been "anti-
union."

Hook says he has come to feel strongly, though, that bargaining is
a "two-way street," that most school districts haven't shown that
they understand that and that the Aurora teachers never showed that
they understood it either.

"We have had formal negotiations for many years with the janitors
union, the Building Service Employees Union," he said. "They're experienced union people. They understand what negotiations are about."

The following school year, starting in the fall of 1966, AEAE members decided they were not satisfied with the professional negotiations
agreement and that they wanted formal negotiations. The efforts
proceeded methodically. Don Ireland, president of the association that
year, appointed committees to draft a package of demands. The committees studied the problem for a whole year. They rounded up all the
information they could find on bargaining elsewhere. They wrote to
other school districts, got copies of sample agreements, and hashed
them over, provision by provision, in a series of meetings before
developing the package of proposals they finally presented to Superintendent Hook on February 8, 1968.

The package came as something of a blockbuster. Roy O'Neil, chosen
by the superintendent to be the school district's chief negotiator, recalled, "The demands we received from the teachers that winter covered

51 or 52 pages and included not only what they had a legitimate right to seek but also, we thought, tried to usurp the rights of the people. There were a couple of extra eager activists among the teachers that year. Don Ireland was one of them. They really plunged in headlong without great concern for long-range consequences. We didn't feel they really understood the implications of some of their demands. Perhaps they had gotten a message from the National Education Association."

Superintendent Hook recalls, too, "They got in every demand anybody's ever heard of."

O'Neil adds that the "real problem" in that first set of demands was in the association's article IV, "which spelled out what they wanted in the scope of bargaining — terms and conditions of employment 'including but not limited to specialists, class size, teacher loads, performance of nonteaching duties, teacher facilities, teaching assignments, transfers, promotions, in-service training, summer school, summer recreational programs, protection of teachers, all kinds of leaves, substitute teachers, salaries, fringe benefits, professional development and educational improvements.' We felt they didn't really perceive the implication of all they were asking. They really included all decision-making. They didn't develop all those points, but the issue was the scope of bargaining."

The Aurora East administration was, at that point, as poorly prepared for formal bargaining of this kind as most other administrations have been in other cities. There was simply nothing within their training and experience to prepare them for formal bargaining. And the process was usually alien for most school board members, too. Rather than to move directly into negotiations anyway, Hook and O'Neil took an action that was unusual and one that has given the Aurora East story a wider circulation than is accorded to negotiations in similiar communities. They decided to back off and work out a policy covering collective bargaining.

"Many districts laughed at us when we talked about it," Hook said later. "But we feel that many districts have bargained away so much that they are almost immobilized."

O'Neil added, "The concept evolved from the fact that we have made a pretty good effort to maintain complete written policies. We saw this as an extension of state law. The board has a quasi-legislative function. It follows the state code but the state code was silent in this area. There were no guidelines at all, no base line data. We were operating in shifting sands."

O'Neil began researching public collective bargaining and his research led him to President John F. Kennedy's Executive Order 10988, issued in 1962 to govern negotiations with employees of federal agencies, the first of its kind.

"I adapted that to our local school setting and the board adopted the policy, Policy 1.30, in March 1968," O'Neil said. "It was only after that that we began to negotiate."

President Kennedy's executive order, signed January 17, 1962, established the ground rules under which federal employees could organize, seek recognition, negotiate conditions of employment and seek redress of grievances. It included a strong management rights clause, guaranteeing that the management of any federal agency would retain the basic rights of management to direct employees, hire and fire and assign workers, determine methods of operation and take whatever actions may be necessary to carry out the mission of the agency in an emergency. It denied the right to strike.

O'Neil, in his adaptation of the federal policy to the Aurora East school district, exactly followed the format of the executive order, leaving out only inapplicable parts such as references to the federal civil service, and used almost all of the language exactly, substituting "the board of education" for "the agency" wherever management was referred to.

Board Policy 1.30

The overriding importance of the Aurora East district's policy in the progress of negotiations and its novelty in school negotiations seems to require a fuller consideration of the policy document.

Board Policy 1.30 is titled "Board Policy Establishing Regulatory Guidelines for Collective Negotiations with Employee Groups" and begins with a preamble:

Recognizing that participation of employees in the formulation and implementation of personnel policies affecting them contributes to the educational program; and

That the efficient administration of the school system and the well-being of employees require that orderly and constructive relationships be maintained between employee organizations, the administrative staff, and the Board of Education; and

That, *subject to law and the paramount requirements of the public school system,* (emphasis in the original) employee-employer relations within the school district may be improved by providing employees an opportunity for greater participation in the formulation and implementation of policies and procedures affecting the conditions of their employment; and

That effective employee-employer cooperation in the public interest requires a clear statement of the respective rights and obligations of employee organizations and school management;

By virtue of the authority vested in the Board of Education, School District 131, Kane County, Illinois, by the laws of the State of Illinois, it is hereby established that the following policy shall govern subsequent actions of the Board of Education, its administrative staff, teaching staff, and all employee organizations subsequently to be recognized as official representatives of employee groups by this Board.

Article I protects the right of any employee to "form, join, and assist any employee organization or to refrain from any such activity." It further protects the right of any employee to act in a leadership capacity in the organization unless such action, in the judgment of the superintendent of schools, represents a conflict of interests. (For example, supervisors could join the organization but not serve as officials of the group.)

Article II is one of definition and is the article that was referred to when school administration officials ended negotiations in June of 1971, claiming that the AEAE had violated the article. It reads:

When used in this policy statement, the term 'employee organization' means any lawful association, labor organization, professional organization, federation, council, or brotherhood having as a primary purpose the improvement of working conditions among school employees, or any craft, trade or industrial union whose membership includes both school employees and employees of private organizations; but such term shall not include any organization (1) which asserts the right to strike against any local, state or federal agency of the government, or to assist or to participate in any such strike, work stoppage, or interference with the conduct of official business, or (2) which advocates the overthrow of the constitutional form of government of the United States, or (3) which discriminates with regard to the terms or conditions of membership because of race, color, creed or national origin.[5]

Articles III, IV, V, and VI deal with levels of recognition. The Aurora East school district proceeded under the exclusive recognition provisions which meant that an employee organization recognized as the representative of the majority of the employees was entitled and charged to act for all the employees in the bargaining unit. The final part of Article VI, again in language like the federal order, refers to management rights. It states:

In exercising authority to make rules and regulations relating to personnel policy, the Board shall have due regard for the obligations imposed by this document, but such obligations shall not be construed to extend to such areas of discretion and policy as the public mission of the Board of Education, its budget, its organization and the assignment of its personnel, or the technology of performing its work.

Article VII is a further statement of management rights. It was the article that led to the greatest controversy between the school administration and the teacher association in Aurora East. But, again, it follows the language of the original federal order almost exactly. The Aurora East article reads:

Any basic or initial agreement entered into with an employee organization as the exclusive representative of employees in a unit must be approved by the Board. All agreements with such employee organizations shall also be subject to the following requirements, which shall be expressly stated in the initial or basic agreement and shall be applicable to all supplemental, implementing, subsidiary or informal agreements between the Board and the organization:

(1)   In the administration of all matters covered by the agreement, officials and employees are governed by the provisions of any existing or future laws and regulations, including policies set forth in the Board of Education Policy Manual and other board regulations which may be applicable, and the agreement shall at all times by applied subject to such laws, regulations and policies;[6]

(2)   Officials of the school district will retain the right, in accordance with applicable laws, regulations and policies: (a) to direct employees of the Board; (b) to hire, promote, transfer, assign and retain employees in positions within the school district, and to suspend, demote, discharge, or take other disciplinary action against employees; (c) to relieve employees from duties because of lack of work or for other legitimate reasons; (d) to maintain the efficiency of the school district operations entrusted to them; (e) to determine the methods, means, and personnel by which such operations are to be conducted; and (f) to take whatever actions may be necessary to carry out the responsibilities of the Board in situations of emergency.

Article VIII provides that agreements negotiated may contain grievance procedures for employees in the covered unit, that there may be arbitration of grievances — advisory only — that arise from the agreement or board policy, but there is no provision for arbitration concerning proposed changes in the agreement or policy.

Article IX provides that employee organization business shall be conducted during non-duty hours of the employees, but that officially requested or approved consultations between the organization and the school admistration may be conducted on official time. It states, however, that the superintendent may require that contract negotiations take place during non-duty hours.

Article X gives the superintendent the power to implement the policy. Article XI says the board is responsible for determining the appropriate bargaining unit and may require an election to determine whether the employee organization represents a majority. Article XII, the last, says, "The superintendent shall establish and maintain a program to assist in carrying out the objectives of this policy."

Controversy over the Policy

The policy itself rapidly became the central issue of negotiations between the school administration and the AEAE. O'Neil, the school's negotiater, recalls, "The teachers balked on some of the terms of the policy. They said they were too restrictive." The teachers emphatically agree with that recollection.

Article VII, the management rights clause, was at the heart of the dispute. That is the article which states that any agreement reached must be subject to present and future laws and must also be subject to present and future policies and regulations of the board of education.

Robert Davis, the math teacher who was later to head the negotiating team for the AEAE, claims that "board policy 1.30 gives the board and the superintendent the unilateral right to alter the agreement any time they choose." The teachers believe, Davis says, that such power means that any negotiated agreement is worthless. In a phrase that became commonly used, such an agreement — if it can be changed unilaterally — "is not worth the paper it's written on."

O'Neil says the management rights clause "really means the right of the district to stay open or closed. This public right takes precedence. The teachers said the clause makes meaningless any collective agreement. They said the clause was indicative of our arrogance. But that language was from Kennedy's executive order, which says the public interest is paramount. This is the major manifestation of that principle."

Superintendent Hook believes, "The AEAE spokesmen oversimplified the matter in talking to the teachers. They said, 'This means they can sign anything and then renege on it.' "

O'Neil adds, "There is judicial relief if capricious use is made of that clause, but they couldn't seem to see that."

The controversy over the new policy continued from March 1968, when the board of education adopted it, into the summer. In the meantime, on April 1, the board of education unilaterally adopted a salary schedule for the coming school year; the association wasn't consulted on it because it had refused to agree that the new policy governed all negotiations. There was a timing problem, too; the school administration felt it would be impossible to wait for protracted negotiations before it began to recruit teachers for the next school year.

Superintendent Hook explained, "We were still in the midst of a teacher shortage then. We were desperate for teachers. It was obvious that if we waited until summer to adopt the salary schedule we would not have enough time to recruit teachers for the next year. Spring is the season to do that. So I recommended arbitrarily setting salaries, so I could get recruiting teams out.

"The teachers, at that time, had been conditioned to know early in the year what their salaries would be the next year," Hook continued, "so the reception I got from the teachers was pretty good. In other words, the rank and file was pleased — but not the negotiators. It was a problem because the negotiators had not even made salary demands and were refusing to talk about salary until other matters were negotiated."

O'Neil commented then, "Holding off on salary bargaining is a teacher association tactic, a way to keep members interested in negotiations. Otherwise, once salaries are set, the membership doesn't follow what's going on. As a consequence of the board action adopting the salary schedule, the organization lost the interest of much of the membership. So the organization turned to the policy and that controversy went on until July 1968. On July 15, at a regular school board meeting, there was an open discussion between the board and the AEAE representatives concerning the terms and intent of the board policy. At the conclusion it was agreed that the controversy had been satisfactorily resolved and that negotiations would resume in the fall of 1968."

The First Negotiated Agreement

Negotiations did resume in the fall of 1968 to arrive at an agreement that would cover the following school year, 1969-70. O'Neil and Hook recall that they were "productive, fairly cooperative negotiations." On the table was the teacher association's big package of proposals from the year before, plus the school board's policy 1.30, which the school negotiating team insisted that the teachers accept before any other bargaining took place.

Davis was not on the teachers' negotiating team that year but he says it was his understanding that neither side got anywhere until both teams agreed to put the teachers' proposals aside and "start from scratch."

Agreement was reached on the first part of the contract (called "Professional Negotiation Agreement") on December 9, 1968. This first part was to be effective upon ratification by the board of education and the membership of the Aurora Education Association East. It was ratified shortly.

Article I provided recognition of AEAE as exclusive representative of the teachers in negotiations "upon certain matters," provided the AEAE demonstrated that it represented a majority and each fall showed again that it still represented a majority.[7]

Article II set up a four-step grievance procedure and defined a grievance as "a complaint by a teacher or group of teachers concerning an alleged violation or misrepresentation of professional rights or an alleged inequitable application of any policies, rules, or regulations of the school district, or of the provisions of this agreement." The last step in the grievance procedure would be advisory arbitration if arbitration was sought by the AEAE; it called for a three-member panel whose sole power would be "to determine whether policy or terms of agreement were misinterpreted or inequitably applied."

Article III established negotiation procedures, to start in September each year and terminate by January 15. In case of failure to agree on terms, the procedure calls for a three-member outside mediation board to gather information and recommend solutions within 15 days. It states, "The Board and association may agree to abide by the recommendations, but recommendations are not binding."

Article IV is titled "Responsibilities and Rights of AEAE," and they include: the association may discipline members of the profession; teachers are free to join the association or not; the association may use school buildings at reasonable hours and may use equipment not otherwise in use.

Article V is entitled "Rights and Responsibilities of the Board of Education" and includes all of the wording of the disputed management rights article VII of the school policy 1.30, including the reference to "any existing or future laws and regulations."

The teacher negotiators signed the agreement despite the inclusion of the management rights clause.

"Our people signed it," Davis said later, "but we just didn't recognize the full impact of what we were signing. I think most teachers were unaware that the board policy was written into the agreement."

A subsequent attachment, a couple of months later, included a new salary schedule (not a major issue that year).

The Second Negotiated Agreement

The following fall, 1969, Robert Davis was a member of the AEAE negotiating team for the first time. He was bothered by the inclusion of the disputed article in the agreement and urged that the team "negotiate it out." But the head of the team, Fred LaChance (who was made an assistant principal during negotiations) and the other teacher members "felt that would not be wise," Davis said.

Agreement was reached on Feb. 9, 1970, on the contract that would cover the following school year, 1970-71. The first five articles were basically unchanged. The salary schedule set the base salary, for an inexperienced teacher with a bachelor's degree at $7,800 and provided increments for advanced degrees and for additional years of experience; it was a traditional sort of salary schedule for the teaching profession. The teachers won one new concession; they would be allowed one day a year of personal emergency leave, to be deducted from their sick leave days.

The second agreement also included two concessions the school administration wanted, both dealing with experimental educational ideas not usually found in school collective bargaining agreements. O'Neil was grappling, in these new provisions, with two significant issues in the profession, both related to the quality of teaching: How to reward particularly effective teachers and how to make individual teachers accountable for improving the instruction they offer to students?

One of the new articles in the negotiated agreement, a concession the administration won, set up an "advisory committee on salary differentiation," with four members appointed by the board of education and four from the executive committee of the teacher association. The article set out an agenda for the committee that included defining instruction positions, establishing criteria and evaluation methods for each, placement in positions and the method of reimbursement in each. The committee did meet and act; the results will be considered below.

The other new article, the second concession, was titled "Improvement of Instruction" and it read:

> Each teacher shall be required to submit annually to his principal or designated supervisor evidence of a substantial effort to improve the quality of his instruction. A plan for improved instruction developed by the teacher is to be discussed and approved in advance by the principal or his designee. The outline of a major plan should be presented with suggested procedures and techniques of evaluation. The summary submitted at the conclusion of the plan must include an evaluation in terms of teacher growth and satisfaction, student attitude and response, or student achievement.

Superintendent Hook pointed out that that clause was "different from any other district" and that it was an example of what he means when he insists that "collective bargaining is a two-way street." Too many school boards, he contends, have made no effort to make bargaining accomplish some of their own aims, too, and have merely been pushed further and further against the wall in granting teacher demands.

"This article was our quid pro quo," O'Neil said. "It was what we were getting out of the bargaining. The district's administrative council devised the idea. The teachers were bargaining in their own interests, and we decided upon what we could ask in the interests of the schools. It was this article that began to draw the attention of association members in other districts. Probably this led to the Illinois Education Association's attempt to make this a target district. Some of the teachers told us that."

Hook said, "I made a point to the association at that time that if they were really viewing themselves as a professional organization they could hold their heads high. This was a positive way to improve the profession."

"They looked on it as a weakness though," O'Neil added. "Their chief negotiator thought it was."

Davis, in an interview, said of the improvement of instruction clause, "It was a pet project of O'Neil's and I thought it was a good idea, a valid way to provide accountability. But almost everyone else was upset with the clause during the year. Practically everyone disliked it — teachers and administrators alike. It imposed such a burden. Principals don't really do a good job of evaluation and they saw this just as extra work. Every one seemed to regard it as busy work for the teachers, without any consideration of the real intent. Since almost no one wanted it to work, it didn't. I haven't heard of one improvement of instruction effort that has received any significant response from any member of the administration. The idea just died a quiet death."

The Plan for Salary Differentiation

The other innovation in that second contract didn't really fare any better. But it seems likely that its failure had some bearing on the troubles that were to come in Aurora East. In Davis' view, "it underlay much of the disagreement."

O'Neil and other educators have long sought a way to provide extra financial reward to the teachers who do the most effective jobs. Although the idea seems sound it is difficult to put into effect because of the lack of adequate evaluative tools to determine just who the most effective teachers are. It is an idea often discussed in education circles.

O'Neil, whose job in Aurora East involves research, had been thinking of a merit pay plan which he called a "quality decimal factor" plan. This plan was among those to be considered by the Committee on Salary Differentiation, the joint committee established in the negotiated agreement.

The quality decimal factor plan is based on the idea of peer review, or peer evaluation. It assumes that those best able to choose the most effective teachers are the other teachers and supervisors in the school, those who know the teachers in their day-to-day work. The plan called for each teacher and principal to list their choice of the top ten teachers in that school. Multipliers would be applied and eventually a rank order would be established of teachers according to their effectiveness, from the top to the bottom. Then, under this merit plan, the top 10 percent would receive a 10 percent salary increase and the bottom 10 percent would lose 10 percent of their salaries.

A plan was worked out to be presented at a teachers' meeting late in the spring of 1970. It was presented and it was Robert Davis who was instrumental in shooting it down.

"The hatred of that proposal by the teachers was unimaginable," Davis said. "They saw it as a popularity poll, much too political to be effective. Some of the administration favored it, some opposed it, some were neutral. But most of the teachers didn't like it. The teachers had been told they would have a chance to vote on the proposal, but, shortly before the meeting, we heard the administration had scrapped the idea of taking a vote. The teachers were furious about that; they wanted a chance to express themselves.

"The meeting was held," Davis continued. "The administration laid out the proposal. Some teachers spoke in favor of it, too. After the meeting, as a representative of the teachers in my school, I read my teachers as totally negative to the plan. So I asked for a special meeting of the AEAE board of directors. At the board meeting, a resolution I drafted was passed, saying that the AEAE had studied the quality decimal factor plan and opposed it, that the AEAE would not enter into any agreement involving the plan.

"O'Neil had repeatedly said the plan would not be imposed unilaterally, so it couldn't be implemented. O'Neil was furious with us and I do think that anger carried over into the negotiations."

Negotiations in 1970-71

Roy O'Neil has himself written a brief summary of the abrupt end of collective bargaining in East Aurora and the events that led to it. In his article, "Showdown in Aurora,"[8] he wrote that in the summer of 1970 "Aurora East administrators detected murmurings from various quarters that theirs would be a 'target' district for the IEA (Illinois Education Association) during negotiations in the 1970-71 year."

Davis, who headed the AEAE negotiating team during that year, scoffs at the claim that East Aurora was a "target,":

If IEA were going to pick a target district, they would have picked one with better potential than this one. Of course, we asked IEA for help. We didn't know what we were doing; we proved that with the contracts we had written. The board negotiators didn't know what they were doing either; their attorney told the board it was impossible to determine what was meant by some of the clauses.

Of course, we turned to the IEA. The IEA supplies research, assistance, advice, counsel and funds. We needed all the help we could get because none of our team had even been negotiators before. Four of the five on the team went to the National Education Association negotiating school in Lincoln, Nebraska, during the summer, just to learn the basics. We got a good deal of information. But the administration here read that as a school of subversion — almost a Communist plot.

With some outside help and advice, then, the AEAE bargainers drew up their proposals for the new round of bargaining. They sent questionnaires to members, asking what they'd like to see in the agreement, held a series of meetings for discussion, and put it all together. Proposals for changes were not listed separately but were incorporated into a draft of a whole new agreement covering 54 typed pages. The document was presented at a negotiating session in November, 1970.

O'Neil later said the draft, which he claims the AEAE called "our modest proposal," contained 863 separate and distinct demands. The draft was, indeed, a rather encyclopedic listing of bargaining ideas, including many that had been bargained elsewhere and others that have often been sought but seldom won. The draft greatly expanded the scope of bargaining, increased the rights sought by teachers and the association, and increased the areas in which the AEAE said it should be consulted by the board before the board takes action.

Where the previous contract included 10 articles, the new proposal included 21, with some articles including up to two dozen clauses and the article on "Responsibilities and Rights" (which referred mostly to board responsibilities for teacher rights) including 33 separate clauses.

Among some of the demands were many that pertained strictly to employer-employee relations and board relations with the bargaining agent. These include:

— Final and binding arbitration of grievances instead of the advisory arbitration included in the previous contract.

— Fact-finding to help resolve an impasse, if mediation has failed. (Arbitration was not proposed for dispute settlement.)

— Abandonment of the disputed management rights clause and the adoption of this wording, "The Association agrees that the Board retains all powers conferred by statutes, as long as they are exercised in conformity with this agreement."

— An agency shop.

— A liberal transfer policy, no involuntary transfers and considerable association involvement in the process of filling vacancies.

— Negotiations with the association over reductions in personnel.

— Fourteen different kinds of leaves, including unlimited sick leave days with sick leave interpreted to mean "personal illness, quarantine at home, or serious illness or death in the immediate family or household" and "immediate family" interpreted to mean, "parents, spouse, brothers, sisters, children, grandparents, parents-in-law, brothers-in-law, sisters-in-law, and legal guardians."

— A 35 percent boost in the base salary, to $10,500, plus increases in the amount of increments paid in yearly steps for experience and additional educational preparation.

In addition, some of the AEAE proposals sought changed educational policies and school improvements and a voice in establishing educational plans. Among these proposals were:

— The right of the association to "confer" with the board on textbooks, testing materials and other tools of teaching.

— The right of the association to be consulted and to make recommendations to the board of education "on any fiscal, budgeting or tax programs, construction programs, . . . annexation of consolidation plans, or revisions of educational policy."

— Professional librarires for each school building.

— One nurse for each 1,500 students.

— Special teachers for elementary school physical education, and extension of the art education program downward to kindergarten children.

— Establishment of a joint instructional council and other joint committees, including one to improve reading instruction.

O'Neil and his team, with the school district's administrative council, studied the AEAE proposals for four months before returning with what O'Neil called "a response in kind." The management team's counterproposals were presented late in March, 1971, and were also couched in the form of a complete new agreement, numbering 58 pages plus some attachments. The counterproposals amounted to a sweeping negation, not only of the new AEAE proposals but of previously-negotiated teacher rights as well. But the counterproposals were more than just a negation of the demands; they reached into entirely new areas and placed upon the association many new kinds of obligations unusual in employee-employer relationships.

Among the counterproposals were these:

— A complete reversal of the grievance procedure, in which grievances would be charged against teachers by the administration or parent or pupil.

— Reimbursement by the association to the school board for all expenses incurred in conducting negotiations and in implementing the agreement.

— An end to negotiations if either side fails to ratify an agreement within 15 days. And a termination of the existing agreement if any teacher association tries to force continuation of negotiations when there has been a failure to agree.

— Agreement to a check-off of dues but, instead of paying the dues over to the association, paying them "to the educational fund of the district . . . in order that the educational interests of children may be protected from undue costs arising from the association's demands to negotiate."

— A new clause: "Association renounces the strike and agrees not to join or cooperate in any way with any individuals or organizations which may have among their goals a conspiracy which may lead to a strike, slowdown, or picketing or other public or private act which could affect the public schools, or their pupils, or which may tend to limit the abilities of the board with respect to control of the normal operations of the schools, or which may tend to control the teachers' salaries in a manner inconsistent with the concept of the free market place and the laws of supply and demand."

— A requirement that teachers improve their professional qualifications annually at their own expense, presenting evidence of completing, with a grade of B or better, a minimum of three semester hours of graduate credit.

— Time clocks to be installed to assure an eight-hour work day each day.

— A requirement that the association recommend to the board "an objective and workable plan whereby each teacher can be paid precisely in relation to the value of services rendered . . . to include not only a precise scale of pay, based upon current anticipated revenue, which would fairly reward teachers most valuable in terms of what children have learned, but must also include a plan for retrieval of public funds paid to any teacher whose services may have had negative effects upon the learning opportunities of the children."

— A new form of compensation in which teachers would be paid for the time spent in three different classifications: $8.75 an hour for regular teaching duties, $4.39 an hour for supervision of school activities outside the classroom, $2.19 an hour for preparation of materials. Each teacher may request the number of hours he wishes to devote to each classification.

A study of the proposals and counterproposals shows that often the board's reply was a parody of the association's demand, reversing the meaning. The following examples are illustrative:

Association Document	School Board Document

Article VIII
Teacher Protection

B.	B.
The Board shall provide legal counsel which is mutually acceptable to the Board and the teacher and shall render all necessary assistance to the teacher in his defense as a result of any action taken by the teacher while in pursuit of his employment.	The Association shall provide legal counsel which is mutually acceptable to the Board and teacher and shall render all necessary assistance to the teacher in his defense as a result of any action taken by a teacher while in pursuit of his employment.

Article XX
Effect of Agreement

A.	A.
All conditions of employment, including teaching hours, extra compensation for duties outside regular teaching hours, relief periods, leaves, and general teaching conditions shall be maintained at not less than the highest minimum standards in effect in the district at the time this agreement is signed, provided that such conditions shall be improved for the benefit of teachers as required by the express provivions of this agreement. This agreement shall not be interpreted or applied to deprive teachers of professional advantages heretofore enjoyed unless expressly stated herein.	All conditions of employment, including but not limited to, teaching hours, extra compensation for duties outside regular teaching hours, relief periods, leaves, and general teaching conditions in effect in the district prior to and at the time this agreement is signed are null and void. This agreement terminates and supersedes all past practices, agreements, procedures, traditions, and rules or regulations concerning the matters covered herein. This agreement shall not be interpreted or applied to provide teachers of professional or other advantages heretofore enjoyed unless expressly stated herein.

How did the AEAE view the board's package of proposals? Explaining the reaction, Davis said:

First you have to understand O'Neil's views of negotiations. You place demands on the board. Then he places equal demands. To the extent that you want to make a gain, you must make a concession. So he finds out what the association wants, reverses it and puts it back to them. Then you knock out 50 pages of your proposals, he knocks out 50, you knock out two more, then he knocks out two more. Then you get down to salary and let all the rest blow over.

In a way, we took the board's proposal as a joke. Obviously these were not proposals they wanted to see enacted. But we knew it was serious trading material — a deadly serious move on their part. They wanted us to throw our package away, then they would throw theirs away. Then we'd pick up three or four issues — school year, home visitation, salary — and settle. They wanted to do that early because East Aurora has usually set the pattern for this part of the Fox River Valley. O'Neil likes to do that early.

The School Board's "Alternate Counterproposal"

At the same March, 1971, bargaining session in which the board's "response in kind" was given to the AEAE, the school board negotiators presented an alternate suggestion, a joint resolution by the board and the association to dissolve all current contracts and discontinue any collective bargaining for four years. The alternate suggestion was never seriously considered by the teacher association, but it is presented here because it seems clearly to represent the administration's views on collective bargaining:

A JOINT RESOLUTION

The Board of Education, District 131, Kane County, Illinois, hereinafter the Board, and the Aurora Education Association East, hereinafter the Association, upon due consideration of the advantages and disadvantages of the processes of professional negotiations or collective bargaining; and

WHEREAS, it has been the experience that negotiations inevitably develops an adversarial relationship between teachers and their school boards and administrators, and this relationship fosters polarization and divisiveness in working relationships between the two; and

WHEREAS such negative relationships are deleterious to the common and highest interest of all parties in the educational opportunities for the children; and

WHEREAS the scope of negotiations broadens each year, consuming valuable teacher and administrative time away from the children we serve; and

WHEREAS severe conflicts of interests between teacher's aspirations for pupils and for their own self-interests can occur when they attempt to represent both interests at the bargaining table; and

WHEREAS the negotiations process demands collectivism — not professionalism — and creates a negative public image of teachers and of education; and

WHEREAS the creation of adversarial conditions between teachers and administrators is destroying the unity so urgently needed in the profession; and

WHEREAS the costs of negotiations to teachers increases steadily, and their organizations become dominated by paid executive directors and negotiators; and

WHEREAS costs of negotiations to the Board (i.e., the public) increases proportionately; and . . .

WHEREAS the gains made by teachers in salaries and other benefits in this district in recent years may in fact have been less via collective negotiation than they would have been via professional cooperation:

NOW THEREFORE BE IT RESOLVED that the Board and the Association agree to renounce collective bargaining or negotiations as a means of achieving beneficial change in public education; and agree to sever all relationships with any and all organizations which advocate collective negotiations between them; and agree to restore traditional relationships between the Board and its teaching staff through the professional leadership of the Superintendent and the professional cooperation of his administrative and teaching staff.

BE IT FURTHER RESOLVED that this agreement constitutes the revocation of any and all Board and Association covenants, agreements, contracts, constitutions, policies, bylaws, or other articles relating in any way to collective bargaining or professional negotiations; and that this Joint Resolution shall be effective from this date through June 30, 1975.

Negotiations in the Spring of 1971

The two negotiating teams met seven times after the Board's counterproposals were placed on the table, once in April, four times in May, and twice in June. Board policy 1.30 continued to be a major issue. Davis and the AEAE team were determined not to negotiate within its framework; the administration negotiators were just as insistent that it was the controlling document. Davis said:

Actually, we never did negotiate. We talked a good deal. We were trying desperately to reach some agreement. But they wouldn't agree to anything — even whether to put a title page on the proposals — until we once again recognized the board as the sole decisionmaker.

Asked how he himself viewed the responsibility for educational decision-making, Davis answered:

I assume I was hired as a professional, for expertise in my area, which is math. I am held responsible for knowing my area and I believed that when it came to math education my expertise would be involved in what the school did. I didn't personally meet with much difficulty, except that I continually advised the district that there had to be some articulation between schools. The administration held that every building ought to be autonomous. There were never any serious curriculum discussions between the junior high schools and the high school. The two junior highs used different texts and wouldn't agree on tracking. It seemed to me committees ought to be formed, made up of the teachers involved, to make recommendations.

The right to make the final decisions was not at issue. What was at issue was the right of teachers to a voice, to some input. Previously the superintendent had thought input meant his selecting pet teachers to serve on his advisory committee. This was not my view.

Whether or not the parties were really very far apart on the basic responsibility for decision-making, the section of the management rights clause referring to "existing or future laws and regulations" continued to be the sticking point, with the association continuing to believe this could be used to make any agreement void.

It was in this climate that the association declared, in May, that negotiations were at an impasse and sought mediation. The association named a mediator, but the mediation process was never carried out.

There were no agreements, then, or even tentative agreements on any part of the contract as June arrived and, with it, the end of the school year. The contract would end in July and the teachers were worried about what would happen to their insurance. That was the status of bargaining when the AEAE met and passed its resolution not to report to work in September unless agreement had been reached.

Footnotes

1. Michael H. Moskow and Robert E. Doherty, *Teacher Unions and Associations: A Comparative Study*. Albert A. Blum, editor. University of Illinois Press. Urbana. 1969.

2. Chicago Division of Illinois Education Association v. Board of Education, 76 Ill Ap 2d 456.

3. Moskow and Doherty, in their chapter on the United States in *Teacher Unions and Associations*, put it this way:
  . . . The pressure for bilateral determination of employment conditions has in several states been happily coupled with opportunity. Indeed, the statutes providing teachers with collective bargaining rights, most of which were enacted initially in response to public employee demands for such legislation, had in several states become a very important *cause* for bargaining activity. Once these laws were passed, a great many teacher organizations which had not sought a change in the informal method of dealing with boards of education began to bargain vigorously with their employers. It is probably fair to say that in some instances legislation created dissatisfaction . . . Opportunity stimulated a need which a great many teachers barely knew existed.

4. Board of Education v. Redding, 32 Ill 2d 567

5. Most of the language, with very few changes and additions, is exactly that of the federal executive order, including the prohibition of any organization "which asserts the right to strike against the government . . ."
  There have since been rather considerable changes in the federal guidelines covering bargaining by federal employees. President Richard M. Nixon issued Executive Order 11491 on October 29, 1969, retaining some of the old provisions, altering others, and adding new provisions. President Nixon's order was further amended on August 26, 1971. This newest version of the federal guidelines retains the prohibitions of the earlier order but leaves out the words "which asserts the right to strike . . ." It keeps only that part of the clause which reads "assists or participates in a strike against the government . . ." Thus assertion of the right to strike is no longer an issue in federal employment; only actual assistance or participation in a strike would allow a denial of continued recognition.
  The Nixon changes, of course, were written after the adoption of the Aurora East policy statement. But the Aurora East board of education had apparently not revised its policy to match the new federal

guidelines. If it had so revised its policy, the vote by the AEAE to "not return to the classroom in the fall" without a contract apparently could not have led to withdrawal of recognition.

6. President Nixon's revision of the original federal order made a significant change in the wording of this provision, too. The present executive order reads:

> In the administration of all matters covered by the agreement, officials and employees are governed by existing or future laws and the regulations of appropriate authorities, including policies set forth in the Federal Personnel Manual; *by published agency policies and regulations in existence at the time the agreement was approved* (emphasis added); and by subsequently published agency policies and regulations required by law or by the regulations of appropriate authorities, or authorized by the terms of a controlling agreement at a higher agency level.

7. This relationship, in which recognition must be granted anew each year and expires with the contract's expiration, is unusual. In any negotiations covered by the National Labor Relations Board, recognition of a bargaining unit, once granted, continues until it is formally disestablished, either through withdrawal by the union or by a decertification procedure which calls for a majority vote of the membership.

8. Illinois School Board Journal, September-October 1971

Discussion Questions

1. Should strikes by teachers be illegal? Why or why not? Should public employees who are represented by a recognized bargaining agent be required to work, even if there is no contract governing terms of employment? Is that involuntary servitude?

2. Can legislation prevent strikes? If not, how can the public interest in operations of governmental units be protected?

3. Scope of bargaining means the range of issues that will be submitted to joint decision-making rather than unilateral decision-making by the employer. From the point of view of management, what school issues should be included within the scope of bargaining? From the point of view of the employees, what issues should be included? How do you distinguish between bargaining on working conditions and bargaining on the management of schools?

4. If some issues are not included within the scope of bargaining, how can they be dealt with?

5. In the board's "alternate counterproposal" to end bargaining in the school district, are the points listed in the "whereas" section valid objections to public employee collective bargaining? How can they be reconciled with an employee's theoretical right to representation in decision-making?

6. The argument is made that the union went too far. What is too far? How does a union know at the time what is too far? And for whom is it too far; the membership of the union? the school administrators? the general public? the pupils?

7. Much is made in the case of the intervention of "outsiders." To what extent was this intervention a critical determinant of the strategies of the parties and the outcome of the negotiations?

8. How would you evaluate the tactics of the Aurora Education Association East? The very extensive package of demands? The refusal to bargain under Policy 1.30? The vote to withhold services?

9. How would you evaluate the tactics of the Aurora school management? The insistence of adherence to policy 1.30? The alternate counterproposal to end bargaining? The nature of the "in-kind" counterproposals? The curtailment of bargaining?

10. Does collective bargaining for public employees lead inevitably to an antagonistic split among teachers, administrators, and citizens? Can it be used to the advantage of all these groups?

11. How in collective bargaining can commonality of concern for the children be preserved at the same time the parties try to further their own interests?

If there was ever any doubt that O'Neil and his management negotiating team meant what they said when they declared collective bargaining had come to an end in East Aurora on June 9, 1971, the doubt was soon resolved. They meant it.

By the time of the next school board meeting, on June 21, school administrators had prepared for school board approval a whole new course of action, based on no bargaining rights at all. The plan was presented by the school board's attorney, Lambert Ochsenschlager of Aurora. Ochsenschlager had never actually taken part in the contract negotiations, but had been kept informed and consulted at each step. During the summer, he was to play an increasingly active role in the developing drama.

In a statement to the board's June 21 meeting, Ochsenschlager:

1. Agreed with O'Neil that the teacher association, by its vote to withhold services in the fall (he referred to it as a "strike vote"), had violated school board policy and "no longer remains qualified as the bargaining agent for the teachers";
2. Offered the opinion that the vote by the teachers in the association "amounts to a resignation from their employment in the school system";
3. And recommended that the school board go into court to seek a declaratory judgment that the teachers had indeed resigned and the board's course of action was legal.

A resolution, prepared ahead of time, was presented by one of the board members and approved. The resolution stated:

Resolved, that inasmuch as this Board of Education considers that Aurora Education Association East has breached its agreement with the Board by noncompliance with Board Policy 1.30, by reason of its vote at an AEAE meeting on June 9 to strike at the commencement of the next school year, this Board no longer recognizes the AEAE as a bargaining agent of the teachers of School District 131, Kane County.

Resolved further, that inasmuch as this Board has been advised by counsel that said vote of the teachers to withhold services or strike amounts to a voluntary resignation on their part, that this Board hereby authorizes the president and secretary to tender to each teacher in the district a contract in the form attached to this resolution and subject to all the terms and conditions therein, including the salary schedule herewith adopted for the 1971-72 school year.

Resolved further, that this Board hereby authorizes the law firm of Reed, Ochsenschlager, Murphy and Hupp, counsel for the district, to institute immediate court action to determine the issues now existing between the teachers of the district and the Board of Education.

Resolved further, that the superintendent and staff charged with personnel procurement immediately embark on a recruitment program to employ whatever teachers may be necessary as a result of the failure of teachers to sign and return the contracts which are being submitted to them.

The individual contracts prepared for each teacher to sign included a long first section which restated this opinion that the AEAE had taken a strike vote and thus forfeited its right to bargain and that the teachers, in their vote, had resigned their teaching jobs. Signing the individual contract thus meant that each teacher agreed with this interpretation. Other parts of the contract listed the base salary offered to the teacher for the coming year, granted the hospital and medical benefits increase that had been discussed in negotiations, stated that the teacher would retain his tenure rights upon signing (which was to be done by noon on July 1), stated that all were bound by the provisions of the Illinois school code and by East Aurora school policies, and included a very strong no-strike pledge:

The teacher will not participate in, condone or encourage a work stoppage, sit-in, strike or any activity similar thereto that would, or tend to, interfere with the operation of the school system based upon the established and approved school calendar. (A sub-paragraph in the contract added that any breach of this no-strike pledge would terminate the tenure rights of the teacher "at the option of the school board.")

The salary schedule adopted at the June 21 board meeting provided increases of about 5 percent, with the base starting salary for a beginning teacher going from $7,800 to $8,150.

Superintendent Hook had letters ready the same day to mail to each teacher with the individual contract. In the letter, he repeated the board's contention that the teachers had resigned. The letter continued:

. . . However, it is not the Board's desire, nor my own, to relieve any teacher of his duties should he choose to remain a teacher in District 131. Therefore individual contracts are being extended to each teacher of the district giving him the right to return to District 131 at an increased salary and additional insurance benefits, without losing his tenure rights . . . If by chance you feel you could not function effectively in School District 131 you may choose not to sign the contract . . ."

The school board's June 21 action brought a series of prompt reactions: consternation among the teachers about the meaning of the individual contracts and the apparent threat to their jobs if they refused to sign, a flurry of legal actions, efforts by AEAE leaders to resume bargaining on some basis, and a battle for public opinion waged by both sides through a series of press releases to the local newspaper. Although these actions and reactions proceeded concurrently throughout the summer months, they will, for the sake of clarity, be presented separately in this case.

Consternation Among the Teachers

The letter and the individual contracts seemed absolutely clear to many of the teachers in the district. They seemed to say that if the teachers did not sign and return the individual contracts promptly, they would have no jobs when school opened in September. It was a frightening prospect and some of the teachers signed immediately.

The question of the legality of the school board's action was promptly raised by the Illinois Education Association, which cited the job tenure rights of teachers under the Illinois school code. The code provides, in section 24-11, that ". . . any teacher who has been employed in any district as a full-time teacher for a probationary period of two consecutive school terms shall enter upon contractual continued service unless given written notice of dismissal stating the specific reasons therefore, by registered mail by the employing board at least 60 days before the end of such period . . ."

But the code applies to dismissal and the school board's resolution did not dismiss the teachers. It said, instead, that by voting to withhold services the teachers had all resigned. Ochsenschlager, in his legal opinion to the school board, claimed the teachers were thus giving up their tenure rights under the school code. No one among the organized teachers ever agreed that there had been any resignations, however, and their lawyers insisted that the school code protected the teachers' jobs.

An attorney who does considerable work for the Illinois Education Association, Robert W. Deffenbaugh of Springfield, Illinois, called to tell Ochsenschlager, "You can't require tenured teachers to sign those contracts." He claims that Ochsenschlager replied, "I know. We just want to see how many will sign them."

Deffenbaugh wrote letters to AEAE members, stating his opinion that the school board's action was improper and that the board had "violated the school code by proposing a scheme by which a tenure teacher must either execute a new contract or subject himself to the possible loss of his teaching position." He stated further in his letter that the June 9 teacher vote was, in his opinion, "entirely an internal matter of the association and . . . cannot logically nor legally be deemed capable of constituting the resignation of one or more particular teachers."

Both Deffenbaugh and Dr. Curtis Plott, executive secretary of the Illinois Education Association, went to Aurora on June 24 to speak to a meeting of the teachers and urge them to stand together. Plott charged the East Aurora board with "obstinate refusal to address itself to resolving the problems through the channel of good faith bargaining and with an attempt to destroy the organization."

But the teachers' fears were not answered. Robert Davis and Thomas Osborne, the newly-elected president of AEAE, worked ceaselessly, urging the teachers not to sign the individual contracts and claiming that their jobs were protected. But their efforts failed. A big majority of the teachers signed and returned the contracts. So disheartened was Davis by the failure of the teachers to present a united front that he later resigned as vice president of the association and remains bitterly disillusioned.

Legal Actions

Both sides took their cases to court on June 24. The AEAE filed suit in Circuit Court in Geneva, Illinois, asking an injunction to block the board from replacing tenured teachers who refused to sign the individual contracts. Ochsenschlager, acting for the school board, filed suit for a declaratory judgment, in effect a court approval of the legality of the school board's actions.

The AEAE suit was heard first by Circuit Judge Charles G. Seidel. On June 30 he denied the request for an injunction and also denied the teachers' request for an order requiring the school board to continue the teachers' insurance. He said both requests were guaranteed under the law and a court order to follow the law was not necessary. "The board has no right, and I have no right, to make teachers sign the contract," he stated, but added that the court could not stop the board from negotiating contracts with tenure teachers. Because the ruling did not answer all the questions, in the minds of the AEAE attorneys, they gave notice that they would file an amended complaint. After they did so, Judge Seidel ruled on July 21 that a class action such as this suit was not a suitable action. The judge's rulings thus left the board's actions in effect without really ruling whether they were proper.

The school board's suit for a declaratory judgment was never heard by the court. Instead it was withdrawn by Ochsenschlager because so many teachers had signed and returned the contracts that, he said, the decision was not needed.

There was other action during the summer regarding the individual contracts. Late in July, school officials did recognize the right of tenured teachers to keep their jobs even though they did not sign the individual contracts, but they added a new dimension: those who did not sign would not get a salary increase. The new provision was included in a letter from Superintendent Hook to the teachers who had not returned the contracts. The letter stated:

The present controversy over your teaching contract has been as unpleasant to me as it has been to you. I definitely respect your right to sign or not to sign the contract sent to you. I trust that you are aware of my obligation when the more than 10,000 students return to school in September.

Both the school board and I regret that since you have voluntarily elected not to sign a new contract and eliminate any question about your tenure, it will be necessary for us to employ a new teacher to replace you. However, before we tender a contract for your replacement, we desire you to be certain that we would like to have you continue teaching in District 131. We are offering you, and all other tenured teachers who have not signed the new contract, either of the following options:

A.   The right to sign the contract dated June 21 previously sent to you by the Board of Education;

B.   The right to return to the district in accordance with Sec. 24-11 of the school code. The insurance benefits and salary terms would be the same as last year.

I am sure you are aware that Option A contains increased benefits. However, if you prefer you may still choose Option B.

If you have found more desirable employment or for other reasons you do not want either of the above options, the Board and I respect your decision. Having twice offered you the new contract, and now adding to it the option for you to select your statutory right under tenure, we feel that there is no reason why you should have any personal financial loss during the coming school year especially in view of the fact that litigation proceedings are often very lengthy. Whether you are able to find other work or

not, you do know that you are offered this opportunity for employment.

I hope that you will be with us and the more than 400 of your
colleagues who have now signed an individual contract (sufficient
to assure the opening of school on the first day). Unless we receive
the signed individual contract within five days, we shall assume
that you are returning to work under Option B unless you notify
us to the contrary.

This offer is made to resolve a difference that now exists and in
no way is meant to indicate a change in our position as expressed
to you in previous correspondence or by resolution of the Board.

(Despite the disclaimer at the end, the letter from the Superintendent
did represent a change. The letter was an admission that the school
officials could not assume the teachers had resigned unless they took
specific action to do so, as provided in the Illinois school code.)

The legality of the board's requirement that teachers sign an
individual contract in order to receive a salary increase is still, at the end
of 1972, being challenged in court action. Included in the material
now before the courts is a statement from Dr. Michael Bakalis, State
Superintendent of Public Instruction:

It has long been the opinion of the legal division, Office of the
Superintendent of Public Instruction, that school boards may not
condition the return of tenure teachers to a teaching position upon
the return of an employment contract. N.E. Hatson, the legal
officer, in an opinion on March 16, 1967, stated, "No new contract
with a tenure teacher is either necessary or legally enforceable. Such
proposed contracts and requirements of the board simply confuse
the teachers, the board members and the general public. You are,
therefore, advised that boards of education may not and shall not
issue new contracts to tenure teachers or may not or shall not take
any action in effect requiring teachers to execute and return such
contracts."

Efforts to Continue Bargaining

The AEAE made a series of attempts to bypass the school board's
June 21 resolution, which confirmed an end to bargaining. Responding
to the salary schedule adopted unilaterally by the board at the June 21
meeting, Thomas Osborne, AEAE president, issued a statement that the
association was "satisfied with the board's offer for salaries and fringe
benefits. The real issue is an article in the contract which empowers
the board to arbitrarily create policy which could eliminate provisions
negotiated between the two groups . . . Beyond that, we want to maintain a decent grievance procedure and the same index structure in the

pay schedule that existed last fall." The AEAE was thus givin̶ ''o
most of its big package of demands. Osborne announced the A
was ready to go to the bargaining table at any time.

A week later, in another statement, Osborne said the AEAE was
willing to submit all issues to final and binding arbitration. The basic
issues, he said, were:
- the right to a contract binding on both parties for its duration,
  instead of a contract binding on the AEAE but not on the
  board.
- the right of the professional staff to use their expertise for the
  benefit of students in planning curriculum, and to be consulted
  before drastic changes such as dropping the remedial reading
  program.
- an adequate grievance procedure.
- the failure of the Board to negotiate in good faith.

On July 9, Osborne and Davis issued a joint statement, saying, in
part, "Our proposals were viewed as negotiable. Some of them were
never seen as a final position from which we would not compromise
or even totally relinquish. Rather, they were issues on which we hoped
to begin discussion and eventually reach a mutual agreement that would
be reasonable for the district to adopt in view of its available finances.
Unfortunately, negotiations never progressed to this desirable level.
Negotiation is a process to determine the conditions of employment
between employer and employee. These conditions in the field of education include items designed to better the educational process for students as well as establish rights of teachers and improve financial conditions. This is what we hoped would take place in the give and take of
negotiations. For the board's representatives to picture our proposals
for discussion as final and unrelenting is a distortion of the facts . . .
We feel that the majority of people in the community would agree that
teachers should have the right to sit down with their employers and
negotiate benefits for themselves and the students. This is what we are
interested in doing . . .''

Davis then sought to appear before the July 19 meeting of the Board
of Education. Following board policy regarding statements by citizens
to be placed on the agenda, he wrote in advance and requested time.
A letter from the board secretary refused permission, saying it was
"not being granted due to the fact that the AEAE is no longer recognized as the bargaining agent for the teachers." At the meeting, Davis
asked to present his statement as a private citizen. The board voted
not to hear the statement but told Davis he could hand it to the
secretary. Davis began reading the statement aloud as he walked slowly
up the aisle. As he was reading, the board passed a motion to adjourn

and filed out. The Davis statement said:

> The AEAE does not accept the decision of the board to rescind
> recognition of the association, thus preventing further negotiations.
> The association did *not* vote to strike. The resolution . . . was to
> withhold services on September 3, a workshop day, in the event
> a mutually acceptable agreement had not been reached with the
> board . . . and this action was subject to review and reassessment on
> September 2. We did not then and do not now consider this a strike
> vote . . .
>
> The AEAE now offers to reduce its bargaining proposal to approx-
> imately 15 items. The original proposal represented an "ideal" edu-
> cational program for the children and teachers in Aurora. The associa-
> tion still stands for that ideal and regrets that it will not be im-
> plemented for the 1971- 72 school year.
>
> In addition, the AEAE is willing to change personnel on its bar-
> gaining team in an effort to insure meaningful dialogue between
> the two parties. This in no way reflects any discredit or lack of
> faith in our prior team; it merely reflects a sincere desire to reach
> settlement.
>
> Since all teachers will have a position when school opens, the
> problem of job security has been solved, but the district's educa-
> tional problems have not. Negotiations can provide the machinery
> for solution of present and future difficulties. The AEAE would
> like to move toward progress and settlement rather than conflict.
> We are certain that the community concurs. Knowing that the
> board recognizes the importance of an early solution, we are confi-
> dent that it will respond in the affirmative with all possible speed.

None of the efforts to resume negotiations succeeded.

The Battle for Public Opinion

Throughout the summer of 1971, along with the court suits and the
efforts to resume negotiations and the many letters exchanged over
the status of the teachers who had not signed the individual contracts,
both sides carried on an unusual publicity campaign. Long statements
from each party were printed in the local paper, the *Aurora Beacon-
News*, giving the readers an extraordinary view of the kinds of issues
involved and the differences in points of view and in interpretation.

One of the opening guns in the public opinion campaign was a
statement attributed in the July 11 edition to Mrs. Bonnie Schoeppel,
the board president:

> . . . We understand that there is great pressure being placed upon
> the local teacher association by organizations outside Aurora to take
> the control of schools away from local boards.

. . . Of the 863 seperate demands . . . at least 15, if incorporated into a contract, could severely limit the ability of the people to control their schools:

— No one may limit what any teacher says or does in a classroom.
— AEAE must have free use of public address systems
— All public school equipment and property must be available for free use of teachers
— All school buildings must be available to AEAE use free of charge
— Calendar for school children must be approved by AEAE
— Board must provide any services teachers need for their "information"
— Board must consult AEAE before every action or considered action
— Teachers may not be disciplined or discharged according to law alone
— "Right" to strike
— State law must be subject to terms of teacher contract
— National Education Association "Code of Ethics," subject to change only by teachers, must become part of board policies (Teachers would write their own laws)
— Final decision on any matter in bargaining or grievances, including financial expenditures, to be made by private "fact-finders" or "arbitrators" instead of publicly elected representatives
— Permit teachers to represent principals and supervisors in bargaining
— Permit anything, including the aims and purposes of public schools, to be bargainable

A statement from Lambert Ochsenschlager, the board's attorney, followed the AEAE's request to resume bargaining or to go to arbitration. Ochsenschlager said the whole dispute developed because AEAE was "ill-advised" by the Illinois Education Association. He continued:

. . . IEA's poor judgment in advising AEAE to adopt a strike resolution has resulted in such professional embarrassment that it has to keep up some semblance of a fight to cloud the issue.

Further, it is a well-known fact, later borne out, that the IEA never intended to reach a negotiated settlement. Its real purpose was to delay the negotiations during the summer and then use strike tactics to gouge the taxpayer by seeking higher wages than the economy of the district would permit.

. . . It was AEAE that refused to bargain in good faith. The evidence of this is seen in the fact that now the teacher's union admits that it made an abundance of demands it never expected to obtain and actually was not serious in requesting. To negotiate in this manner and not to withdraw its ridiculous requests before the termination of its contract on June 30 is in my opinion the evidence of a lack of good faith.

A statement from Davis printed on July 13, stressed that teachers do not want to get into the business end of school affairs. He continued:

That's the role of the board and administration. It is the teacher's obligation, however, to be concerned and have great input along with parents, into how and what children are taught. This is really all we're asking for.

. . . What we want is the best education for East Aurora children. Our proposal reflects the ideal. By aiming for it, we might at least achieve progress in the district. So far, the board has refused to even consider how we might collectively improve the program. Instead it continues to hide behind a smoke screen of distortion and pressure. The kids are going to be shortchanged as long as the board continues to refuse to join the community's educational team.

. . . it is clear that the board's attorney is pulling the strings.

A July 14 statement was attributed to the board of education.

. . . We will do everything within our power to keep control of the schools in the hands of the citizens and parents . . . We personally deplore some of the recent activities and statements made by several members of the teaching profession and from organizations outside of Aurora who are aiding and supporting these individuals in their attempt to control the schools . . .

Four days later, on July 18, a long statement from Attorney Ochsenschlager appeared:

The AEAE-IEA wants just one thing. That is to control how much money the publicly elected board spends and who it spends the money on — school children or teachers.

The school board is determined to not turn over that control to the IEA instead of retaining legal authority for the citizens of the district to run their schools as they see fit through their elected representatives.

It is confusing that IEA is asking to resume negotiations with the board . . . That would be illegal, as the AEAE and IEA disqualified themselves as representatives of our teachers by their strike vote. This vote was a breach of the teachers contract and a violation of state law.

. . . After the presentation of the AEAE-IEA-NEA proposal to the school board last fall, the superintendent on two separate occa-

sions asked the president of AEAE if he would reconsider this extensive document . . . The superintendent informed that it would
certainly impair meaningful negotiations when the proposal was
so long and full of so many demands. He was assured both times
that the organization was extremely sincere about the proposed
package, which was referred to as "modest" in scope.

Because of this refusal to reconsider . . . the board's team prepared a counterproposal as an in-kind response . . . The record
shows that the AEAE negotiations went to impasse over board
policy 1.30 and stopped all official negotiations at that point.

We know that the overall strategy of the IEA was to stall negotiations until fall and then, by using kids as a shield, to try to force a
negotiated settlement to their extreme favor upon the board . . .
If the AEAE had wanted to negotiate just a few key items as they
now claim, why in the name of the children of the East Side of
Aurora, wouldn't they agree to do this last fall?

Several leaders of the AEAE are stating now that they are willing to let the board of education build schools and the physical
plant. However, they feel that teachers should have control over
salaries, curriculum, fringe benefits, leaves, school calendar, and
all other areas of this nature.

The question before the citizens of the East Side is very basic. Do
the East Side residents want to control their public schools or do
they want the teachers to do so through the AEAE and IEA? The
public will have to make the ultimate decision.

On the same day, July 18, the AEAE paid for a full page ad in the
Beacon-News. It headlined:
> The District 131 School Board
> has built an empire at the
> expense of the children
> That's WRONG.
> East Aurora's teachers want you
> to help us build the best education
> system in Illinois for
> the benefit of the children.
> That's RIGHT.

Part of the ad continued:

Let's face it. Parents and citizens of East Aurora have no voice in
what kind of education their children receive. Control rests in the
hands of a flamboyant lawyer and a few tight-lipped individuals
who claim to represent the public in school affairs. The lawyer is
paid taxpayers' money while leading the board by the nose. You
have been squeezed out of the picture.

Now this "power structure" has turned its sights on teachers to make domination complete. This year we proposed a program of educational progress for District 131. We were tired of seeing our schools slipping into a "second-class" category. We were rebuffed, intimidated and openly humiliated for even thinking we had a right to be part of the educational team.

The ad then listed some of the association's proposals and the board's action in response, and urged citizens to call school board members (it listed the telephone numbers) to "demand that they consider the teacher's proposal immediately in a 'good faith' series of negotiations. Tell them you're tired of the circus-like actions of their expensive lawyer. Tell them to start representing your interests or you'll get someone who will . . ."

A statement from Superintendent Hook was printed on August 1, accusing the teachers of conducting a "typical IEA publicity campaign" and trying "to divide administrators, board members and citizens . . .," a "technique that has been used in other communities to try to convince citizens that the negotiation demands are made solely on behalf of students and parents." He said the school board could not possibly resume negotiations with the AEAE because that "would be in violation of its own policy."

In the same release was another statement from Ochsenschlager defending the board's proposal for a reversed grievance system. "The board is deeply concerned about the rights of all individuals," he said. "The board feels that if teachers should have the right to file grievances, why shouldn't students, parents, administration and board members have the same right? Why shouldn't a parent have the right to file a grievance against a teacher on behalf of his child?"

Within a week, Osborne, the AEAE president, again asked for new negotiations and stated, "Public education is facing its greatest challenge during the decade of the 1970's. Teachers around the country have redefined professionalism. Teachers are beginning to call for educational change and improvements. We feel that negotiation is the means through which these improvements can be accomplished . . . The day of autocratic school boards making unilateral decisions is almost past. The future of school districts will be determined by a negotiated agreement which will create a partnership of citizens, school boards, administrators, and teachers."

Osborne repeated his appeal for renewed negotiations in September, just before school opened, but was again turned down.

Thus, at the start of school in September, 1971, the bargaining picture in East Aurora was just where it had been when school closed for the summer in June. The summer of activity had not led to a resumption of recognition or of negotiations.

It was only in East Aurora that negotiations ended thus. Agreement was reached in all other negotiations with IEA units, although strikes loomed as possibilities in 22 school districts by the end of the summer and actually took place in 13 of them.

When school opened in East Aurora, there were 70 teachers in their classrooms who had not signed the individual contracts issued by the board. Those 70 teachers were not paid the salary increases that were paid to the contract-signers and did not get the step increase for the additional year of experience, an increase that had been negotiated in the previous contract. They thus lost about $700 pay apiece. It is pay that they still hope to recover through the courts.

The IEA filed suit on behalf of Robert Davis and Jerry Lubshina, as representatives of the 70 non-signers, seeking pay at the same salary schedule as the other teachers. In April, 1972, Judge Seidel ruled that Davis and Lubshina had elected to "continue under their rights of tenure" and "are not entitled to the increase in salary that was offered to the other of the teachers who during the controversy entered into new contracts of employment for the present year." The judge further stated:

> It also occurs to me that the sovereign people who elect members to the school board by their vote and the school laws mean and intend that such elected people should manage and operate the school system and have some latitude of authority in exercising discretion. If I were to accept a contrary view, it would be indicative that the teachers had the right to operate a school system rather than the Board.

The case is being appealed and both sides say they will take it to the Illinois Supreme Court.

Another suit has been filed in U.S. District Court for Northern Illinois, contending that the civil rights of the teachers have been violated by the board's discriminatory salary procedure. The suit was dismissed but an appeal is pending.

Discussion Questions

1. At what point do wages, hours of work and conditions of work become a matter of rules and policies reserved to the management of the schools? Where is the dividing line? How can it be determined?

2. Should teachers have the right "to negotiate benefits for the students" as well as for themselves? Are they serious in attempting to do so, in your opinion? Is there an inherent conflict between a teachers' union bargaining for the students and a sound management rights position?

3. How do you grant workers an effective role in the decision-making process, which affects their lives, while at the same time preserving the fundamental concept of representative government, which includes the power of the individual citizen to participate in allocating the community's resources?

4. Who has the better claim to representing the public interest, the welfare of the children — teachers? school board? administration? How, in collective bargaining, can the public interests be properly represented?

5. Is there a need for legislation covering collective bargaining by public employees? If so, what basic provisions should be included? What prohibitions should there be?

6. If there is a prohibition on strikes, what machinery should exist for the settlement of disputes that have reached an impasse?

7. If arbitration is suggested, could that be considered illegal delegation of a school board's ultimate financial responsibility to the taxpayers? Besides arbitration, what other impasse procedures might be effective?

8. The Illinois Association of School Boards contends there is a conflict between "professionalism" and "collectivism" (which it apparently uses as a synonym for collective bargaining). Do you agree or disagree? Why?

9. What role do you think public opinion plays, or should play, in the collective bargaining process for public employees? How can this role be exercised?

10. There have been proposals for holding open meetings (open to the public and press) for bargaining between public employees and their

employing institutions. What would be the advantages and disadvantages? What other methods might be used to inform the public of demands by both sides and what is happening in the negotiating process? Would such information be useful to the public?

11. Does an education association's efforts to bargain teacher contracts represent an effort "to take the control of schools away from local boards?"

12. Do you consider the conclusion of collective bargaining in East Aurora a pattern for other schools boards to follow?

13. What effect will the changed labor market for teachers have on collective bargaining in education?

OCEAN HILL-BROWNSVILLE: V
A MODERN GREEK TRAGEDY

Introduction

This case involves multilateral bargaining among teachers and their union, the school board, and the citizens of a local community. It introduces new complexity into the relation of public employees to their institutions because of its setting, at the heart of political and social controversy over the rights of black people to help determine the course of their own lives.

In contrast to the previous case, about schools in Aurora, the community people did not automatically assume that the school board represented their interests either well or properly. In fact, they seemed to see both the union and the school board as operating more in the union's and board's interest than in the interest of the citizens of the local community.

The case broadens out to include consideration of efforts to change the status quo respecting the school board, the teachers union, and, to some extent, the political structure of New York City and the state. The change concerned an experiment in local governance of schools to improve the quality of education for the children of the area. This involved the consideration of societal centralization and decentralization, accountability for the quality of education, responsibility for the operation of schools, selection and supervision of faculty, and the capacity of people — in this case black people — to reorganize their society to make it more responsive to their needs and aspirations.

The role of the union in the case is examined with respect to these changes and conflicts, including the rights of teachers to preserve their union position and tenure and to have due process.

The teachers, as public employees, were covered by state law which prohibits public strikes. When they struck, they were punished. The judge, in assessing fines and sending the union president to jail, said, "Law means nothing unless it is the same for all. This strike against the public is a rebellion against the government; if permitted to succeed, it would eventually destroy government with resultant anarchy and chaos." Yet that did not seem to answer the question of what remedies are available to public employees against employer actions they consider are unjust, arbitrary, or a violation of a collective bargaining agreement.

Chronology

February 1967	Ocean Hill planning board organized.
April 1967	McGeorge Bundy appointed head of a panel to plan decentralization.
June 1967	Ford Foundation gives Ocean Hill a grant.
August 1967	Ocean Hill elects a governing board, hires a project administrator and prepares to open its schools in December.
September 1967	United Federation of Teachers strikes against the Board of Education . It lasts two weeks.
Fall and Winter 1967-1968	Tension grows between Ocean Hill people and union teachers.
November 1967	Bundy's panel submits decentralization plan.
May 1968	Ocean Hill board seeks to get rid of "uncooperative" teachers.
May 1968	New York legislature passes Marchi Bill, which really just postpones the decision on decentralization.
August 1968	Judge Rivers rules that Ocean Hill cannot transfer out any of its teachers. Ocean Hill votes not to accept findings.
Sept. 9, 1968	Scheduled opening day of school; first day of 2-day strike.
Sept. 11, 1968	Teachers return to work and are terrorized in Ocean Hill.
Sept. 13, 1968	Second strike begins.
Sept. 30, 1968	Schools open again, with 1000 policemen in Ocean Hill.
October 14, 1968	The long strike starts.

Nov. 17,
1968

Settlement is reached.

April
1969

State legislature passes weak decentralization bill.

Ocean Hill-Brownsville:
A Modern Greek Tragedy

Frederick Nauman's copy of a fateful letter was mailed to him just as school was closing for the afternoon. Nauman had been teaching in Brooklyn schools for nearly a decade and was working in one of the eight schools that made up a controversial and experimental special school district.

Opening the registered letter, Nauman, a guidance teacher with a background of science teaching, read that the governing board of the experimental district "has voted to end your employment in the schools of this district" and that "this termination of employment is to take effect immediately." He was not to report to his school the next morning.

Identical copies of the letter were sent to twelve other teachers, to one principal and to five assistant principals. The date was May 9, 1968. The letters were history-shaping; they were to become the focal point of long and bitter teachers' strikes that would convulse the entire New York City school system and heat racial tensions to a danger point.

Each of the nineteen letters went on to tell the staff member where he might appear the following day if he wished to "question this action" and told him, too, that he should report the next morning to New York's central board of education headquarters "for reassignment" to schools somewhere else in the city. The letters were signed by the chairman of the governing board and the superintendent of the experimental district.

No reasons were given in the letters for the governing board's action, but spokesmen said the board and the community it represented had "lost confidence" in these teachers and suspected them of trying to "sabotage" the special experimental school district. The district was one of three set up with the half-hearted blessing of the board of education to experiment with methods of decentralizing school administration, of breaking up a huge and sometimes stultifying city bureaucracy into units more answerable to local communities.

The powerful teachers' union, the United Federation of Teachers (AFL-CIO), reacted to the letters in horror; its president called them "a kind of vigilante activity." The central board of education reacted in horror, too, and promptly termed the letters illegal. The central board and the superintendent of schools sent telegrams to the 19 staff members, telling them to ignore the letters and report to work.

Trouble built. In the next few days, people—mostly black and Puerto Rican— in the dingy Brooklyn neighborhood around the experimental schools barricaded the buildings to keep out the disputed teachers — mostly white. Then massive police details arrived to escort the teachers into the schools. Some of the schools were closed and there was anger in the community.

The issue was a head-on conflict over who was to run the schools: local communities, who felt they had the most at stake and who had some powers to act, or the central board, which had powers that seemed to conflict and had, too, complex contract agreements with the potent teachers union.

At stake, from the community's point of view, was the right it thought it had to choose what teachers should teach in its experimental district. To the people of the district, the aim of the decentralization plan was to give communities, including poor and black communities, more real control over their own schools. Many in these communities believe schools have been a prime part of the whole dismal poverty picture and believe their children cannot be helped until the local folks have a stronger voice.

At stake, from the union's point of view, was the safety of its teachers to work unthreatened and unmolested, and the security of the teachers' jobs, protected under hard-won union contract provisions.

At stake, for the vast metropolis of New York, was the very fabric of its life, the ability of its diverse people to live together without fear and with justice.

The central board of education was caught in the middle, with commitments to both sides and no clear way to resolve the conflict. There was right on both sides, and there were passionate convictions on both sides. The letters to the teachers brought the issue to an angry impasse and brought into focus many of the great divisions and fears in American society.

Origin of the Dispute: Change

Where did it all begin? What problems and what tensions led to the ousting of the nineteen teachers and the bitterness that boiled over into a vast, illegal teachers' strike?

One might contend that the story started with World War II and the massive shifts it launched in the country's population. Many Negroes came North in the years following the war, seeking economic opportunities and a greater sense of individual dignity. During the same years and for many of the same reasons, large numbers of Puerto Ricans came to the mainland. New York was a magnet for many of both groups.

Since the end of the War, New York City has absorbed a migration of about two million Negroes and Puerto Ricans. The number is so vast that it bears repeating: two million new migrants in one city since 1945. By 1966, the majority of the city's public school children were black or Puerto Rican.

For many migrants, the city turned out to be less than paradise, usually because it takes a better education than they'd had to be able to make one's way in today's world.

In New York, as in other northern cities, the pattern of segregated housing kept the newcomers confined to certain areas. The areas spread under the pressure of population, but the spread followed the segregated pattern. And wherever the ghetto existed, it seemed to blight its citizens with a whole range of social problems. Poor schools were only part of the treatment meted out to those in the ghettos but, because everyone knows a child who goes to school—or is supposed to go to school—the schools seemed near at hand and tremendously vulnerable to complaint.

There had been clear warnings of growing crises in city schools for more than ten years. The suburbs were attracting more and more of the affluent middle class and those who stayed behind in the cities were more and more likely to enroll their children in private schools. In 1961, Dr. James B. Conant, the former Harvard president who has become a significant education leader, warned in the book, *Slums and Suburbs*, of the widening abyss between decay and affluence.

The schools seemed to be failing in the ghettos and that seemed increasingly clear to those who lived there. The youngsters fell farther and farther behind; many simply dropped out—or were pushed out by a system that often looked on them as misfits. It's probably unreasonable to expect a school, or any single social institution, to offset the stultifying effect of growing up in a ghetto and growing up in poverty. Experts know that even the food a small child eats will permanently effect his ability to learn later on when he starts school. But Americans have an abiding kind of faith in education. Even those parents hopelessly bound into poverty look on schools with hope, as a way out for their children.

For a decade after the Supreme Court's desegregation decision of 1954, many Americans believed that integration would solve the problem of the ghetto schools. It is still the policy of the nation and the abiding hope of the majority of black people. But there's not been much integration, partly because so many whites still fight it so bitterly, partly because of the physical impossibilities of moving so many thousands or hundreds of thousands of youngsters out of their neighborhoods to go to school.

New York did make some efforts to face up to integration. Fred M. Hechinger, the *New York Times'* education editor, outlined some of them in a background study.

"Open enrollment," he wrote, "a plan that permitted Negro parents to ask that their children be sent by bus to schools outside predominantly Negro sectors, was introduced in 1960. Some efforts at rezoning districts on the fringe of Negro slums were made, and after much argument and heat, a few schools were 'paired,' which meant that all the White and Negro children from two adjoining neighborhoods attended one school together for the first two or three years and then moved together to the second school for the remaining elementary school years.

"But the demands for city-wide integration according to a fixed time schedule were in excess of what the realities of the ethnic composition of the population permitted. Moreover, there was considerable opposition to what some parents considered extreme proposals, along with a combination of lethargy and outright hostility to drastic changes in the school organization among much of the professional education staff.

"Some opposition was based on fear that the exodus of whites and even Negro, middle-class parents would defeat integration. There was also concern that, by traditional standards, the influx of disadvantaged children into middle-class schools would depress academic standards.

Other efforts in integration met heavy opposition or delaying tactics in some parts of the school bureaucracy, even when the efforts were in the form of directives from the State Foundation Commissioner.

Many New York teachers were in the forefront of the integration movement then. Some of them staged a city-wide school boycott in 1964 and their union, the United Federation of Teachers, said it would support any member who might be punished for taking part in the boycott. Many of those who boycotted worked in "freedom schools" set up in community buildings outside the schools.

But not in many places, and certainly not in New York City, could there be claims of successful integration of schools. Compensatory education was the next idea: massive extra aid for services in poor schools, to give extra help to the youngsters in the worst schools, so handicapped already by poverty and by exhausted families in depressing surroundings. Many union teachers fought hard for these ideas too. A 1967 strike by New York teachers had as one major aim a union plan for "more effective schools." It called for almost doubling expenditures in some slum schools, to provide the boost the teachers thought the youngsters needed.

Like integration, compensatory education still has many adherents and some practitioners. But it can be very expensive and school systems in the late 1960s were increasingly hard-pressed for sufficient money to keep up with inflation. It is inevitable, too, that there will be some opposition to spending lots more in some schools, opposition from the parents in schools that aren't getting the extra benefits. Further, there have been some educational studies which indicate that extra funds for smaller classes, more supplies and new techniques are far from the whole answer. The studies suggest that what really counts is pupil attitude, what the child believes about himself and his abilities to learn.

If that is true, it puts a premium on a certain kind of teacher, one who is truly innovative and responsive, one not burdened with the belief that poor kids, particularly poor black kids, really are not able to learn very well.

One of the educators who understood the problem most clearly was Bernard J. Donovan, the New York school superintendent who had been associated with the city's schools since 1930, through all these changes.

"Our school system has not really responded effectively enough to changed conditions and different children," he once philosophized.[1] "Neither has anybody else's school system . . . that I know of . . .You have teachers who are used to a child coming from a middle-class home with a certain amount of educational background and a certain amount of acceptance of the middle-class mores. Now we have an influx of children who have not had the middle-class background and the middle-class mores. I'm not saying they're good, either, but they just haven't had them. They come to a kind of artificial classroom which is teaching about things and about people and about events and about concepts that don't fit these children. We have not learned to adjust to it . . . They bring with them the deprivation that society has put on their families, and that deprivation creates a different feeling in that child. It creates a problem that we have not yet solved . . .

"I think we need a complete change of attitude in our system . . . on the part of a large number of teachers. I still think that after all the efforts we've made, a sizeable number of our teachers still have the impression that there are some children that cannot be taught. There is no such thing as a child that can't be taught, but it is mighty difficult to reach some. . ."

Another idea was being born of the failure of integration plans and of the desperate problems of the ghetto: the idea of black control of black schools and of other city services in black areas. Many black people, increasingly determined to have a say in their own lives, began to say that the school system was part of a conspiracy to keep their children ignorant and thus keep them subservient, powerless to change their lot or alter the system. The solution, they began to claim, was more blackness—black teachers and black principals, attuned to the problems of black kids and thus able to help them climb out of the troubled ghetto. Too often, they observed, as Donovan did, that some teachers (both black and white) are convinced that black children can't learn and treat them in such a manner that they convince the children of their belief and thus fulfill the prophesy.[2] Their reasoning made a nagging kind of sense to many good teachers, black and white. There began to be calls for new methods, new teaching techniques, and above all, new attitudes, with less adherence to the traditional teaching methods that seemed to be floundering. One way to bring about the essential changes, growing numbers of people felt, was to give local communities more voice in running the schools in their area, to answer the needs of the children as their parents saw them, not as some remote and gigantic bureaucracy saw them.

That's not really a very radical idea. It's a current of the 20th century, in white areas as well as black. People, poor ones as well as rich, simply want to have some control over their lives; they are refusing to accept the fact that nothing they say will ever be heard. The Kerner Commission report on civil disorders took note of the fact in studying the root causes of ghetto distress. Regarding the schools, the commission's report said:

". . .the isolation of ghetto residents from the policy-making institutions of local government is adding to the polarization of the community and depriving the system of its self-rectifying potential . . . Expansion of opportunities for community and parental participation in the school system is essential to the successful functioning of the inner-city school."

Local control was an idea that was taking strong hold in the dingy square mile of Brooklyn that was to become so excruciatingly important to New Yorkers in 1968. There's a neighborhood there called Ocean Hill.

Ocean Hill lies between the slum districts of Brownsville and Bedford-Stuyvesant. Census figures show that four-fifths of its adults had moved to New York from somewhere else. More than two-thirds had never finished high school and more than half the families had less than $5,000 a year to live on. Almost three-quarters of the population was black, the other quarter Puerto Rican. Martin Mayer, who has written extensively about the New York school strike, had this to say about the neighborhood:

"Though there are some blocks of pleasant, owner-occupied private homes, most people live in deteriorating rooming houses and tenements, and much of the area's housing is simply abandoned by its owners. All the well-known social problems are present. It is a highly discouraging place in which to live and to bring up one's children."[3]

But Ocean Hill was not a place with no potential for action. There were tenants' groups and block clubs, parents' organization in the schools and other community-wide organizations, some of them militant and some much milder. The point is there was communication. And there were leaders. And there was a grievance: the schools run by a bureaucracy that seemed a long way off. Small board of education efforts at school reform had not paid off in Ocean Hill.

Black people in Ocean Hill and in other New York neighborhoods found a rallying point in the fall of 1966, with the opening of a new school in Harlem, Intermediate School 201 (similar to a junior high school).

"Many community spokesmen opposed locating the super-modern windowless, air-conditioned school on its present site," Hechinger wrote in the *Times*, "because, they said, it would be segregated. The Board promised to persuade white pupils to enroll voluntarily, but could not make good its pledge. It was this incident that led to the demand for local control, with community leaders saying that if they could not be offered integration they wanted to run their own schools . . ."

Talk of community control spread rapidly; it was a new dream. In November of 1966, Ocean Hill people began to try to make it real. All the local groups that had dealings with the Board of Education, such as the parents' associations in the schools, cut off all dealings with the District 17 board and the central board of education. Local chapters of the United Federation of Teachers joined them in support—then. A month later, black parents marched on the school board's headquarters in Brooklyn and occupied its office for three days, calling themselves "the people's board of education." There was to be a new intermediate school in the Ocean Hill district soon and the "people's board" wanted to have something to say about it; specifically, they wanted to choose its principal. They were to be an important nucleus in the growing drama over control.

The Idea of Community Control Spreads

The stage was set for one of the big figures in the drama, McGeorge Bundy, who arrived in New York in 1966 as the new president of the Ford Foundation, the nation's richest foundation. Bundy, descended from the Lowells of Boston, seemed destined always for places of power. Brilliant and determined, Bundy had been a dean at Harvard (almost its president) and a key adviser to President John F. Kennedy. He was an action man, one who knew how to get things done, right away. He and the Ford Foundation were to give the community control idea big help in two ways: by promoting the idea at every level of political life and by spending money to subsidize some experimental local districts. One of them would be Ocean Hill-Brownsville.

"I often wondered why he moved so quickly," a Bundy friend said later.[4] "I know he felt Ford should move into areas of significant political change, move and move quickly. So he has this Kennedy style. He arrives in New York. What's the worst problem? Answer, race. What's the head of the dragon? Answer, the schools. What's the worst problem with education? Answer, the bureaucracy. How do you break up the bureaucracy? . . . click, click, click."

Bundy found a ready partner in Mayor John V. Lindsay, once the exuberant young mayor who set out to make New York "Fun City" but who was becoming increasingly bedeviled by urban enigmas of tremendous proportions, enigmas for which there seemed to be no solution. New York, like most cities, hasn't the legal power to find its own solutions and is often dangled like a yo-yo by the legislators in Albany and Washington. New York can't even raise the price of a dog license without lobbying for a law in Albany. The city was, at this point in history, engaged in a legislative controversy over more state aid from Albany for the city's schools.

One of Lindsay's qualities is a genuine streak of idealism. He really believes, for example, that all New Yorkers should put the interests of the whole city first (his speeches on the subject in labor negotiations produced looks of incredulity among leaders of, say, the sanitation workers, or the teachers, or the subway workers, or the police, or the firemen).

He really believes, too, in the idea of community people participating in the affairs that directly concern them. He is absolutely committed to the position of the National Advisory Commission on Civil Disorders, (the Kerner Commission), which he served as vice chairman. The commission warned of increasing separatism, a path toward violence and apartheid, and concluded that the only hope for a happy ending was a massive and immediate commitment to improving the life of urban Negroes. It placed much of the responsibility on the cities themselves and stated:

"This is now the decisive role for the urban mayor. As leader and mediator, he must involve all these groups—employers, news media, unions, financial institutions and others—which only together can bridge the chasm now separating the racial ghetto from the community. His goal, in effect, must be to develop a new working concept of democracy within the city."[5]

Despite complaints from some that Lindsay was trying to turn the city over to the Negroes, the mayor was trying to divide up the city's governmental structures into "little city halls," closer to the people, more responsive to their needs. He felt the same way about the sprawling school bureaucracy; it was too far from the people, too cumbersome to adapt to changing needs, too bound up in its old commitments to permit any real innovation.

It was the community control aspect that put Lindsay at odds with New York's central board of education at that time. The board favored decentralization and had been working to bring it about, but there's a big gap between administrative decentralization and real community control. The board of education had another problem too. Under state law, it couldn't delegate very many of its duties to smaller districts within the city, even had it wanted to (and it wasn't sure what it wanted to delegate). Through the turbulent months to come, there was real semantic confusion about decentralization. The board of education, when it used the word "decentralization," simply did not mean the same thing by it that the people in Ocean Hill meant by the word. The difference was to become the heart of the conflict.

It was April, 1969, when Mayor Lindsay appointed McGeorge Bundy chairman of an Advisory Panel on Decentralization of the New York City Schools. The panel was charged with drawing up a decentralization plan to present to the state legislature the following year; the legislature had requested such a plan, tying it in with a promise to increase state aid to city schools. Bundy and his panel developed a plan in great detail. He himself, often working 18 hours a day, wrote much of the report and its strong argument for local control. The Bundy panel included a representative of the board of education but no representative of the teachers, the school supervisors, the trade union movement or the organized parent movement.

While the panel was deliberating and writing, and several months before it made its report, the Ford Foundation began to provide financial help for three experimental school districts that would test some of decentralization ideas. One of them was Ocean Hill-Brownsville, where the "people's board" and its supporting teachers seemed to offer a nucleus for effective community action.

Ocean Hill Launches Its Experiment

A grant of $44,000 to Ocean Hill-Brownsville, to begin setting up its "demonstration district," was made in July, 1967, and was followed in the fall by another $15,000 and a promise of more if all went well.

Eight schools were to be in the Ocean Hill-Brownsville district; one of them a not-yet-completed intermediate school, plus junior high school 271 and six elementary schools. The local planning council for the new district was charged with having its project ready to start in the fall of 1967, just a few weeks away, a truly prodigious task when the new local board did not yet even exist and its duties and powers were as yet unknown.

The demonstration district was set up, of course, with approval by the central board of education. The board had adopted a policy statement in the spring of 1967. It read, in part:

"All members of our board are committed to the principle of decentralization of operations. In a city as large and varied as New York, we believe it is essential to have as much flexibility and authority at the local level as is consistent with our need for centralized standards. Two years ago, the board of education and the superintendent of schools took the first steps in a decentralization program based on the principle of strengthening and enlarging the responsibilities of the various districts; their boundaries were adjusted to equalize their burdens, and their number was increased to thirty.

". . . Now the board proposes to further facilitate decentralization in the districts, in two major directions. The first. . . confers increased responsibilities, especially in administrative matters, on the district superintendents and the local school boards. The second embodies the superintendent's recommendations, requested and approved by the board, regarding various demonstration projects that would permit experimentation to determine more effective methods for achieving greater community involvement within different types and sizes of districts. . .

"Through one or more of these demonstration projects, we hope that new techniques and new approaches will be developed for teacher training and instruction and for increasing parental and community involvement and will thus strengthen our educational program."

But what did "community involvement" mean? How much control goes with involvement? Who would decide what? With guidelines still to be worked out—and that process was destined to take many, many months—what kind of powers would the new local board in Ocean Hill-Brownsville have in running its demonstration project? There wasn't much time in which to find out.

The Ford grant to Ocean Hill-Brownsville, in July, provided a 26-day timetable for planning. The plan was to be completed by July 29. It was. The local planning council submitted a set of proposals, covering its role, to the central board of education early in August. But the board did not act on the proposals then; it saw a need for further negotiation and clarification, and there was no clear delineation of power at that time.

The proposals called for election of a local governing board which would be responsible and answerable to the New York City superintendent of schools and the State Commissioner of Education; they did not call for complete independence from the school system. Although there was no formal adoption of a plan of procedures, it was clearly understood that the local governing board would choose a district superintendent (or project administrator—the terms were used interchangeably) and that the central board of education and superintendent would try to go along with local plans as far as they were legally able to do so.

And so there was an election in Ocean Hill in August, 1967, an unusual sort of election by conventional political standards, and one that came as a total surprise to the New York Superintendent, Bernard Donovan , and the central board of education. The central board had assumed that the Ford-sponsored plan would be presented to it for an okay and then an election would be held. In Ocean Hill, the under-standing was that the plan, once made, was to go into effect. Superintendent Donovan came back from vacation to find an announcement that the local governing board had been chosen.

"They had the election before we ever got a plan, before we ever got an outline or framework," Donovan said later.[7] "And once you do that, it's pretty hard to back off." The central board, he said, never officially recognized the local board but dealt with it "on an off-and-on basis" anyway.

The board was made up this way: The parents in each of the seven schools then in the area elected seven representatives. The seven then named to the board five "community representatives," among them the Reverend C. Herbert Oliver, a Presbyterian minister with a solid background in the southern civil rights movement; he was elected chairman of the board. The community representatives got together and chose a college representative, a Brooklyn College professor who had served as consultant to the local planning council. Teachers in the district chose four representatives and the supervisors, two. It added up to nineteen members.

"You wound up with a governing board rather non-kosher by any kind of traditional criteria for how you put a board together," a state education official commented later.[8] "They had poor people, people on welfare, Catholics and Protestants, a Jew. (I'm pretty sure of that. At least one of the principals who was a Negro was also a Jew.) It's a body more representative than an average board in terms of having some members who can identify with about every segment of the population. I think a regular election would have produced a different

kind of board and yet this board, in some respects, is more representative of the people who actually live in the district and whose kids
go to school there."

The local governing board promptly selected Rhody A. McCoy as
the project administrator; he had been serving as consultant during the
planning period. McCoy, a compact, pipe-smoking, tennis-playing
schoolman with a habit of getting to work at 7 a.m., was no radical.
He'd been working his way up in the New York education establishment for 18 years ("I knew which doorknobs to put my hand on and
which ones to rap on," he once said) and was a highly-regarded black
educator.

No one really opposed McCoy, but it is apparent that the teachers in
the district were beginning to get edgy. Although they had been in on
the start of the project, most of the planning had taken place without
them—during July (stipulated in the Ford grant and its 26 day timetable) while teachers were on vacation. Teacher representatives on the
planning group felt the new board had been elected and McCoy appointed too quickly, without time to consider other possible candidates.

High on the local governing board's agenda was the need to choose
five new principals for the district, four of them for schools where
there were vacancies and a fifth for the new Intermediate School 55,
which was to open the following February.

The planning council, in the proposals it wrote, claimed the right
to pick principals if they met the New York State requirements for
the position of principal. It wanted to disregard the civil service
list drawn up by the city school system. Only four Negroes were
on that civil service list of several hundred, and the list
was not due to expire until 1972.

In a time of rising demand for "black power" and for "local control,"
it is easy to see how the civil service list looked like just one more way
to keep black people out of the top jobs and to keep in those jobs the
very educators the black community felt had been doing a poor job
with their children.

It is true that civil service can be a brake on change. That is, in fact,
its intent. Civil service reform throughout the nation had long been
aimed at protecting career government people, like teachers, from
being swept in and out of jobs along with switches in political office
holders. It does protect incumbents. But Ocean Hill people felt deeply
that the incumbents were a part of the problem.

The city board of education supported the local board's reasoning
and applied to the state commissioner of education, James E. Allen,
Jr., for permission to hire principals for Ocean Hill who met state
requirements but were not on the city's civil service list. Allen
gave a legal "no" but provided an alternative; he said the city could
create a special category of "demonstration elementary school principal" and name persons not on the list. (Later, the courts were to rule
that Allen's plan was illegal, and the ruling was to come at a time that
greatly complicated the strike picture. Later still a higher court upheld the original procedure, too late to help. It was only one of sever

instances in which timing spelt disaster in New York City.)

The Ocean Hill board's efforts to select its principals without regard to the civil service lists—entirely reasonable from the community's point of view—rang a warning bell to many of the professionals, both teachers and supervisors, in the school system. It seemed to hint of more to come, perhaps of future abandonment of the complex system of job protection originally designed to save the schools from political whim. It was unnerving to people who had spent their lives in teaching and regarded civil service—and union contract regulations—as protection of their careers. Many saw the Ocean Hill move as ominous change. It's true at the same time that many teachers were ardently for change, really supported the need for decentralization and even supported the idea of community control. But there's a big difference in supporting reform in general and supporting reform when it may affect your own job. These worries were stirring and were to grow.

The chief spokesman for the New York teachers was Albert Shanker, a bespectacled former math teacher who was president of the United Federation of Teachers, the largest local union in the nation. The union had been one of the leaders in the drive toward unionization of public employees during the 1960s; it had increased tenfold in membership since 1960, and it had increased correspondingly in power. Shanker, like many of his teachers, had been a long-time civil rights supporter and was committed to the idea of better education for youngsters in the sprawling slums.

He was committed to decentralization, too, because the school system was so big and impersonal that neither teachers nor parents had enough voice to be adequately heard. But Shanker, again and again, emphasized the differences between decentralization and community control; of the latter he said, "it is a new name for what the southern Senators used to call states' rights, that is, the right of any local group to decide that the broader society can go to hell because they've got the right to mistreat individuals as they see fit."[10] There should be local powers, he thought, but there should be strong central powers, too, to oversee the use of local power and, above all, to protect the rights the teachers had fought so hard to gain.

Shanker represented almost 60,000 teachers in 900 schools with more than one million pupils. More than 90 percent of the teachers were white, and most of them were native New Yorkers.

New York City school teachers usually came from the city colleges, and the city colleges restricted enrollment to top students in the New York high schools. Full-time black and Puerto Rican students in the city colleges numbered fewer than five percent of the total. In addition to this education-employment pattern, the city had its own teacher licensing system, based on a series of examinations, that was more complex and demanding than the New York State requirements for a teacher's license. Partly for these reasons, fewer than ten percent of the New York City teachers were black or Puerto Rican, compared with about 30 percent in many large cities. Very few blacks and Puerto Ricans had reached the level of school administrators.

A large proportion of the teachers were Jewish, themselves children of families that had been trying to make good in a big and often hostile city, with education as their key. It was a fact that was to become increasingly important as the school tragedy unfolded and vague fears began to seem more real.

The teachers' jobs were protected in many ways, both by civil service and by union contract with the board of education. The contract even includes twelve pages covering the transfer of teachers from school to school (with part of that complexity aimed at not allowing a mass exodus from hard luck slum schools.)

Fred Hechinger of the *Times* has noted that the school system's "strong commitment to civil service procedures, with special examinations and eligibility lists, designed at an earlier era to eliminate patronage and graft, today largely reinforces conservative personnel policies. It makes the selection process too standardized to feed into the system rapidly enough the kind of unconventional talent needed to cope with the urban slum school."

Hechinger's comments are rather gentle compared with those of other writers who have studied the bureaucracy and the Board of Examiners. Only New York City and Buffalo, of all the school systems in the state, use their own more-stringent local rules; all the others rely on state certification of teachers, based on courses taken in accredited colleges. In New York City, the examiners, although technically responsible to the board of education, have considerable independent authority over the tests they give to candidates for school positions and in other matters related to the merit system. Critics say the examiners' written tests and interviews and (for supervisors) simulated on-the-job evaluations are restrictive, unproved, discouraging to many outstanding candidates, often irrelevant and favor insiders and in-groups.

That kind of rigidity posed a problem in Ocean Hill, where the people and their educational leader, Rhody McCoy, were indeed looking for something different. They wanted new methods, new ways to challenge kids, to give them a sense of excitement about their own ability to learn.

"We're trying to get teachers to teach," McCoy explained at one point, "to get involved with kids in a one-to-one relationship, not simply stand up in front of a class and dispense facts. Out here we tell them to jump in. Go beyond the printed page and the blackboard. We want them to think of themselves as coordinators." Too often, he said, the teachers "have been losing sight of what the kids need. What's relevant . What they relate to. We've got to motivate kids. And teachers."

The first step, in Ocean Hill, was naming the new principals, some of them black, one Puerto Rican, one Chinese. One of the blacks chosen was a supermilitant, Herman Ferguson, who was particular anathema to white teachers in the district. He was never approved by the central board of education, but the others were.

(Almost every time Ferguson is referred to by any observer, he is called a "militant." But Rhody McCoy makes an interesting point about militancy: "There're all kinds and forms of militancy, but the definition of who is a militant comes from the white community. It's the guy they don't want to deal with. The moment a person speaks up for his community—Well, for example, Reverend Oliver is a 'militant'.[12])

The week after the choice of principals, in September 1967, the United Federation of Teachers called a city-wide strike. Its aim, the union said, was pay raises and smaller classes, plus more funds for its "More Effective Schools" program. The pickets' signs read, "Teachers Want What Children Need."

The Ocean Hill governing board felt strongly that what its children needed was to have their schools open and operating. And the local board had a feeling that one purpose of the strike was a show of power against the new experimental district. Its feeling was fed by one of the teachers' demands, that teachers be permitted to eject "disruptive pupils" from class. Black parents felt certain it was black children the teachers were talking about and many opposed the strike for that reason.

Ocean Hill tried to keep its schools open despite the strike and there were bitter words outside its schools, bitter words spoken by both sides: the picketing teachers, on one side, and parents and teachers who opposed the strike on the other. After the two-week strike, the UFT forbade its teachers to serve any longer on the Ocean Hill governing board. In a statement doubtless made more bitter by the hard feelings of the strike, the teachers complained they had been bypassed in the planning phase and were seldom listened to. They described the atmosphere of the planning meetings as "extremely hostile and negative. There was a constant stream of remarks to teachers which stated that teachers were bigoted, incompetent, disinterested, obstructive, and were attempting to sabotage the plan."[13]

The teachers' union also supported a lawsuit filed by the Council of Supervisory Associations demanding the ouster of the new principals on the claim that they were illegally appointed. The Council of Supervisory Associations is made up of principals, assistant principals, and bureau chiefs employed by the central board of education. They felt particularly threatened by the different method of choosing principals.

The United Federation of Teachers strike in 1967, whatever its underlying motivations, was illegal under the state's Taylor Act, which had gone into effect just 10 days earlier. (See Appendix I). The law, considered a model for labor-management relations in the public sector, bans strikes by any public employees and provides other methods to help reach agreement. Because of the strike, the state board that enforces the new law deprived the union of its dues checkoff privileges for a year, the harshest penalty it could impose. And, for violating a restraining order prohibiting the strike under the law, the courts fined the union $150,000 and sentenced its president, Albert Shanker, to 15 days in jail. He served the time. Ironically, the process probably strengthened the union, gained it support from other members of organized labor, and made Shanker a martyr.

Different observers provide differing accounts of what happened in Ocean Hill that fall of 1967 after the striking teachers came back to work, but they all agree that the tensions which had been stirring were intensified. Ocean Hill people, sometimes egged on by real militants, increasingly distrusted the union's actions . Teachers claimed they were being harassed in the community and subjected increasingly to anti-Semitic insults. But the New York Civil Liberties Union charged that the union itself "began to fan the flames of racial fears as it increasingly harped on 'extremism,' 'the militants' and 'black power.' "[14]

It seems fair to say that there was some truth on all sides. There was some racism, both black and white, but perhaps it's been exaggerated because feelings breed on feelings. It is true, on the one hand, that some black people are so embittered that they see all whites as enemies, particularly those close at hand; in this case those close at hand were teachers, many of them Jewish and many of them active union members. Some Ocean Hill people did oppose them on all three bases, but these opponents apparently were not in the majority and they certainly did not dominate the local governing board, which never expressed any of these feelings. The board wanted responsive teachers and hoped to have more black ones to meet its special needs, but the vast majority of the teachers in its schools were white and many of them were enthusiastic supporters of the Ocean Hill project and its aims. It is true, on the other hand, that among many Americans, there is a deep fear of rising black aspirations and demands and the fear increases with the feeling of insecurity; some incidents and a lot of the language used feed the fear directly.

There was certainly consternation among some of the teachers about Herman Ferguson, the super-militant. Ferguson had been fired earlier as an assistant principal after he was indicted on a charge of conspiring to murder the moderate leaders of the National Urban League and the National Association for the Advancement of Colored People. Ferguson was to be a continuing issue.

Inside the schools, the four new principals who had been confirmed by the central board were trying to get the project going. Three of them were inexperienced and their insecurity probably was heightened by the lawsuit that claimed their positions were illegal; the principals' top aides in each school, through their association, were parties to the lawsuit. Perhaps the most worrisome part of the growing tragedy was that no one really knew who had what powers. The Ocean Hill governing board and the central board had not yet reached any agreement on the extent of the local board's authority to operate its schools.

In November, 1967, Mayer relates, "all 18 of the district's assistant principals applied for transfer out, leaving the new principals without experienced administrative help in the day-to-day operations of the schools. The local governing board, which never had thought about the role of assistant principals before, now asked the board of education for the right to choose its own assistants, as it had chosen its own principals. ('The very best principal in the world,' a memo from Ocean Hill pleaded a few months later, 'cannot operate a school with assistant principals who are not cooperating.') But the board and Commissioner Allen refused, and new assistant principals—some of them totally inexperienced—were simply assigned in from the civil service list."

Some of the teachers wanted to leave, too, for many reasons: some probably from fear, others because of old loyalties to traditional methods or to former principals. Despite the fact that the union contract makes such transfers difficult, the central board and the Ocean Hill board agreed to gradually transfer out about one-fifth of the district's 550 teachers. Some local people thought the requests for transfers were a union tactic to torpedo the district.

Despite its troubles, the Ocean Hill district was operating, sometimes well, sometimes stumblingly, but with considerable enthusiasm. The community cared. Rhody McCoy, the unit administrator, told an education conference at Harvard:

". . . In Ocean Hill-Brownsville, there are people groping in the dark; they are people who for a long time have felt themselves outside the mainstream of public concern. The city takes no notice of them. These people are obscure, unnoticed—as though they did not exist. They are not censured or reproached; they simply are not seen. They are the invisible residents of a demoralized, poverty-ridden inner city. To be ignored or overlooked is a denial of one's right to dignity, respect, and membership in the human race. These residents have been frustrated at every turn in their attempt to reverse the process.

". . .The parents of Ocean Hill-Brownsville are determined to have a permanent voice in matters pertaining to their schools and to have it now . . .The community, generally acknowledged by the various social and political forces as, in every respect, the most disadvantaged in the city, has finally risen to demand a change - to make history. And it is demanding not only change but also a share in bringing about that change."[15]

The Bundy Report on Decentralization

During that fall of 1967, with its strike, the mounting tensions, and Ocean Hill's struggle to get going, McGeorge Bundy and the other members of the panel on decentralization were working hundreds of hours on discussion and on developing their plan. Presented to Mayor Lindsay on November 9, 1967, the hefty report[16] proposed a sweeping reorganization of the city's school system to put much more power—

but not all the power—into the hands of just such local people as Rhody McCoy talked of.

The Bundy plan called for dividing the system into 30 to 60 districts, with partly-appointed, partly-elected local boards empowered to hire, fire and transfer teachers within their districts, and to plan educational programs and their own budgets, all in line with state requirements. It also called for a central education agency, which would be in charge of some citywide functions and would run the schools in any district that didn't want to run its own.

"The first premise of this report is that the test of a school is what it does for the children in it," Bundy and the panel wrote in a covering letter to Lindsay. "Decentralization is not attractive to us merely as an end in itself; if we believed that a tightly centralized school system could work well in New York today, we would favor it. Nor is decentralization to be judged, in our view, primarily by what it does or does not do for the state of mind, still less the 'power' of various interested parties. We have met men and women in every interest group whose spoken or unspoken center of concern was their own power—teacher power, parent power, supervisor power, community power, board power. We believe in the instrumental value of all these forms of power but in the final value of none. We think each of them has to be judged, in the end, by what it does for public school pupils.

"Neglect of this principle, in our judgment, is responsible for much of what is wrong in the New York City schools today. We find that the school system is heavily encumbered with constraints and limitations which are the result of efforts by one group to assert a negative and a self-serving power against someone else. Historically these efforts have had ample justification, each in its time. To fend off the spoils system, to protect teachers from autocratic superiors, to ensure professional standards, or for dozens of other reasons, interest groups have naturally fought for protective rules. But as they operate today these constraints bid fair to strangle the system in its own checks and balances so that New Yorkers will find themselves in the next decade, as in the last, paying more and more for less and less effective public education."

The Bundy plan went to considerable pains to reassure the teachers of their rights under the new plan. It stated that the United Federation of Teachers has made "real efforts toward constructive change within the system," and assured the teachers that "a master contract covering all teachers in the city would still be negotiated centrally."

"Only duly constituted Community School Boards or their authorized agents would have the right to make any official determination of a teacher's fitness, and even then teachers would retain the same strong tenure rights they now have," the report continued. "Tenured teachers could be dismissed only for cause after standard hearings and appeals procedures had been followed . . . Moreover, the Community School District would be required to adhere to salary and other provisions of any contract negotiated between the United Federation of Teachers and the central education agency."

It dealt directly with some of the teachers' other concerns:

"Some of the concerns the panel heard about local election of community school board members reflected a deep-rooted fear of provincial interests — black power or white power, left wing or right wing. The present central board and other citywide agencies, the argument goes, at least can embody pluralistic interests. The panel does not agree . . . parents can be trusted to care more than anyone else for the quality of education their children get. There may be errors and excesses, especially at the start. But we do not hesitate to put our trust in the collective good sense of the public school parents of New York.

". . . Underlying many of the concerns over the abandonment of the present system of examinations and lists is a fear of antiwhite racism. That some antipathy toward white educators exists in predominantly non-white neighborhoods is plain. What its causes are and how pervasive it is are not so clear. Extreme racist sentiments are undoubtedly reflected in some antagonism toward white teachers. The imbalance in the system between white and nonwhite is one cause. But perhaps the real issue is the dissatisfaction of Negro and Puerto Rican parents with the failure of their children to learn in the school system as it is now organized.

"Whatever the causes, it is certain that once they have a voice in their schools some predominantly Negro or Puerto Rican districts will seek to staff them with more teachers and administrators of their own groups. It is not unreasonable, nor is it educationally unsound, to include knowledge of, and sensitivity to, the environment of pupils as a criteria for appointment and advancement. If a district board believes that otherwise qualified Negro or Puerto Rican candidates are especially likely to meet these criteria, it would be justified in staffing accordingly. The panel is unable to escape the conclusion that the New York school system will be a much healthier place when there has been a substantial increase in the number of qualified Negro and Puerto Rican teachers and supervisors. But we emphasize again that all appointments at all levels would be subject to restraints.

". . . White teachers would be protected not only by law and contracts but also by the predominant concern for educational quality. Under a fully reorganized system, teachers would be in a particular school district because they chose it and the district board chose them. As a result, the parents and other community residents would be likely to view its teachers more responsively than under circumstances where teachers are assigned to a district reluctantly and without any community choice."

The teachers union was not impressed with the panel's arguments. The executive board of the union promptly adopted a critical statement, disputing almost every major recommendation. It said the panel "ignores the new power and integrity of the professional teacher who will not continue to teach in any school or district where professional decisions are made by laymen." It also stated:

"Tenure is a precious right. Tenure gives teachers the security they need to teach honestly, free from community pressures. Under the tenure concept, a teacher can be dismissed only for cause after a hearing on the basis of charges brought against him by other professionals who are competent to evaluate professional performance.

"Under the Bundy report, charges could be brought against a tenured faculty member by a community board of laymen with no professional expertise. This proposal is anti-professional. It could encourage local vigilantes to constantly harass teachers. No teacher with professional integrity could teach in such a district. UFT urges that this proposal be rejected."

The New York Board of Rabbis soon opposed the plan, too, calling it a "potential breeder of local apartheid" and a possible destroyer of quality education and the merit system in the teaching profession.

The rabbis doubtless were reflecting the current of racial and religious tensions stirring in many parts of the city. Tensions that often reached back to Ocean Hill.

For example, one Brooklyn black militant, who was often on the Ocean Hill scene, claimed that Negro and Puerto Rican pupils were being struck and beaten by teachers, increasingly since the September strike. A teacher in the Brooklyn-Stuyvesant area was dismissed when he was charged with striking a black pupil, a charge he denied. That aroused Shanker's wrath; he claimed the board of education was playing into the hands of extremists working against teachers. And he sounded a warning note that was to be often repeated in the coming months: he threatened to close all public schools in any district where a teacher was dismissed or transferred punitively without outside arbitration of the case.

Another example: Newspapers reported widespread consternation in the city over a Malcolm X Memorial Service held by a community group in a Harlem school, part of one of the experimental districts. The speaker was Herman Ferguson, the same Ferguson the Ocean Hill board had sought to name a principal and who later was convicted of conspiring to murder civil rights moderates. At the meeting in Harlem, Ferguson urged Negroes to arm themselves against whites and to practice for "hunting season." He called Superintendent of Schools Bernard J. Donovan a "honkie." Two black teachers who took pupils to the meeting were removed from their schools and one of them was transferred to Ocean Hill. The Ford Foundation, shaken by the meet-

ing and the furor it caused, announced that future grants to the experimental districts would depend upon safeguards against racist
activities. Ferguson was finally severed from both the experimental
districts in which he had played a role.

Trends far removed from the city's schools were contributing to
what seemed a growing rift between Negroes and Jews, groups that
had been long-time allies in struggles against prejudice and had often
seemed to be a clear example of how black and white could work together in common cause. The partnership, at least of some blacks
and some Jews, had weakened by the mid-60's. One of the reasons was
the growth of blacks' pride and determination to deal with their own
destiny; in the process some past white supporters, often Jews, were
excluded or excluded themselves. Another reason was the spread of
black population into more and more neighborhoods in New York
which had been closely-knit Jewish communities; the growing density
and impoverishment of these older areas brought increasing crimes
against slum property or against shops still owned by Jews. The entry
of more Negroes into such fields as teaching and social work contributed
to economic and professional conflict because these jobholders who
were Jewish were fiercely protective of the merit system that had
allowed them to get and hold the jobs they themselves used to be deprived of. Another irritant was the adoption by some black militants
of the Muslim faith, including the traditional antagonism between
Arab and Jew; it seemed particularly ominous to Jews that many of
these militants sided with the Arabs against the Jews in the seven-day
war of 1967.

Into this growing era of unease came a devastating fact of spring,
1968. Dr. Martin Luther King, Jr., was murdered in Memphis, a murder that brought fear and fury across the country. In the ghettos,
angry people looted, in New York and elsewhere. Police in many cities,
following Kerner Commission guidelines, tried to avoid inflammatory
actions. Ghetto shopkeepers in some areas — often Jews who'd stayed
behind in their old neighborhoods — felt that they'd had not much
help from the police. They feared. The black-white confrontation
across the country led to a hardening of lines, on both sides.

(It is important to realize that we speak here of large groups of black
people and large groups of Jews. Not all. In New York City, for example,
some leading black figures, notably Bayard Rustin, continue to vigorously oppose any notions of black separatism, emphasizing that the
only hope for improvement of the black condition lies in the mainstream of American life; with the teachers, Rustin opposed the Bundy
report and worried about apartheid. And on the other side, many Jews
along with other often-maligned "old liberals," still ardently support
black efforts at self determination and have continued working vigor-

ously for local control of schools. When we try to speak of the temper of the times, we know that many individuals will never fit into pigeon-holes.)

It was in this milieu that the central board of education and the governing boards of the experimental districts still struggled to define just what the local powers were. No agreement seemed to be in sight, partly because a hassle continued in Albany, too, over the merits of several different decentralization proposals that had been submitted.

The snail's pace of negotiations with the central board irritated the experimental districts. Parents in all three districts early in April 1968 threatened to boycott the schools unless the board acted to transfer control to the local boards. Then Ocean Hill-Brownsville parents did just that; they kept their youngsters out of school for three days to back up their demands for local control over budgets, hiring and firing, construction and curriculum.

Superintendent Donovan explained that the central board could not delegate all that power, no matter what it wanted to do, because of state law complications. Changes in the law would have to be made under whatever decentralization plan the state legislature adopted before some of the powers could be transferred.

In Albany, there was contention. Lindsay had submitted the Bundy plan, with some modifications. The New York board of regents charged with overall state administration of the schools, had its own plan. Shanker's UFT was lobbying against them all, but still claiming to be for decentralization, as long as all teacher rights were adequately protected.

These were the currents swirling in the background when May 1968 arrived and the Ocean Hill-Brownsville governing board voted to transfer the nineteen teachers and supervisors. Many accounts have been written about that fateful move. Some say the Ocean Hill people were deliberately seeking a showdown with the teachers' union, hoping for stronger legislative support. Some say the union was deliberately seeking a showdown with Ocean Hill, to dramatize to the legislators in Albany the horrors of too much community control. It's likely that there is some truth on both sides. Confrontations were in season; the sit-ins and the growing violence at Columbia University were just beginning and they were indeed a barometer of the times.

May in Ocean Hill-Brownsville

The Ocean Hill-Brownsville governing board met on Tuesday, May 7. It heard a report that its personnel committee had been working on for several weeks. Mrs. Clara Marshall, the committee chairman, said that many teachers, both black and white, were cooperating with the project but there existed "a small, militant group of teachers who continue to oppose this project." The report recommended their removal and the recommendation was approved by the majority — but not all — of the board members.

The letters were written, telling the teachers of "the termination of employment" and directing them to go to the board of education "for reassignment." The wording meant different things to different people. The United Federation of Teachers promptly interpreted the words as meaning the teachers were fired. The Ocean Hill board contended the teachers were transferred. The distinction does make a difference. The process is different. The safeguards are different. The legal issue is different.

To fire a teacher for cause, under New York board of education procedures,[17] requires formal charges and a hearing, with all due process rights guaranteed: the right to counsel, to know the charges ahead of time, to cross examine witnesses and call your own witnesses, to receive a transcript of the hearing, and to appeal. It is a procedure that is rarely used, perhaps only a dozen times over the preceding decade. Most teachers in trouble, confronted with that kind of headache, would prefer to resign and keep all that detail out of their records.

Transfers are quite different. There are two kinds: those initiated by the teachers themselves and those initiated by the school system. Many pages of rules govern transfers by teachers at their own request; the rules are designed to protect schools in poor areas from too great a staff turnover. You can't transfer, for example, unless you've taught in a school for five years. And even then, not more than five percent of the teachers can leave a school within one year. (It is this procedure that was very loosely interpreted by the central board and by Ocean Hill earlier in the year when almost 20 percent of the teachers were allowed to gradually transfer out of the new experimental district.)

Transfers initiated by the school system usually are rather easily accomplished. The regulations give the superintendent of schools the power to transfer staff from one school to another at his discretion, requiring only that he report such changes to the board of education.[18] He may have many reasons for switching staff around and it is generally understood that the right to a job does not include the right to choose your assignment within the system. Probably several hundred such transfers take place during a school year in New York, without complications.

In the case of transfers, unlike that of dismissals, there is no need to present charges and no requirement of due process. It is this kind of transfer which the Ocean Hill board claimed it was trying to bring about, either because it thought it had the power to do so or was seeking to show that without such power it could not control the destiny of its schools.

Thousands of words of conjecture have been written about this point. The by-laws clearly give the superintendent of schools the power to transfer personnel; why didn't the Ocean Hill board ask the superintendent to take the action it wished? The superintendent, Donovan, had long assured Ocean Hill he would try to cooperate with reasonable requests. Some writers say McCoy asked for the transfers and Donovan refused them. Apparently at least some of the Ocean Hill board believed that McCoy had been turned down. Other writers contend that Ocean Hill didn't want to ask Donovan's help because it sought to build an issue over community control. Still others contend there was a great deal of duplicity, and that the more militant members of the local governing board really wanted a direct confrontation with the union and, to assure that they'd get it, named Fred Nauman, the union's chapter chairman at J.H.S. 271, as one of the "uncooperative" teachers.

Perhaps the most dispassionate analysis has come from the board of education's own Advisory and Evaluation Committee on Decentralization. The report, generally called the Niemeyer Report, after its chairman, John H. Niemeyer, states:[19]

"This move was interpreted by the professional staff, the community at large, and the press as dismissal. The project board has steadfastly denied these allegations, arguing that they simply requested that the staff members be transferred out of the district. This request was rejected by the superintendent; the Federation of Teachers demanded written charges, thus placing the request for transfers (for which no charges are required) into the realm of dismissal. Initially, no formal charges were filed against the 19 professionals. The project administrator stated that school safety was a factor in the 'ouster,' charging that those involved had allowed 'hazardous conditions' to exist, which set an 'unhealthy tone' for the schools.

". . . The project administrator regards the strict interpretation of his action by the board of education as an attempt to diminish his authority as district superintendent. He claims that, as the administrative head of a school district, he has the power to reassign personnel. Although this is true to the extent that a district superintendent operates within his own jurisdiction, the lines of authority are not formally delineated nor do they extend when a district superintendent attempts to reassign personnel, via central headquarters, to another area.

"The direct confrontation in Ocean Hill-Brownsville made it a focal point of controversy. Under normal circumstances, the demonstration project might have been able to accomplish the transfer of 'unsatisfactory' personnel informally, but a larger struggle was being waged in the New York State Legislature over a general proposal to decentralize the entire school system. Thus, the events in Ocean Hill-Brownsville became a precursor of what could happen under community control of the schools. The project became a looking glass, and any likelihood of working out informal arrangements in such a sensitive area as professional performance and transfer became most difficult."

So the issue was drawn. Whether called "transfers" or "firings," such a move from a community-run district was a serious concern for the United Federation of Teachers, a threat that Shanker was duty-bound to fight. In the union's view, the Ocean Hill move clearly conflicted with the principles of collective bargaining and job security on which not only the United Federation of Teachers but unionism itself depends. So the union talked about firings and demanded that charges be filed and due process guaranteed. The board of education told the teachers to ignore the letters and report to work.

When eleven of the teachers tried to go to work the next day, McCoy accused them of insubordination and asked Superintendent Donovan to suspend them. Donovan said McCoy had acted improperly, that he could not dismiss or suspend any personnel but that he could have asked for suspension and transfer, accompanying each individual request to the board with specific charges. The governing board issued a statement, repeating that it was only asking for transfer.

Black people from the neighborhood were in the entryway of Junior High 271 on Monday morning May 13. To some of the teachers, they said, "Welcome, brother," or "Peace." But they told the five "ousted" teachers from that school they could not enter. After the lunch break, about 100 junior high school youngsters jammed into the entryway to help keep the five teachers out. Donovan closed the school for the day. At a nearby elementary school, many mothers called their children out of school after the disputed teachers entered. That school was closed too.

That night Albert Shanker met with union chapter chairmen. Shanker said no union members would serve in the rest of the district until the governing board allowed the "dismissed" teachers to return. He accused Mayor Lindsay of failing to uphold law and order and added, "He had better see to it that they are in their schools tomorrow or he better get out of office himself. This particular action on the part of the governing board was not accidental. It was well planned and representatives of the Lindsay administration were present throughout. What the city wanted was a teachers' strike today. Decentralization is dead and the only way to revive it is to get massive hostility against teachers."

The following morning, Tuesday, black people from the neighborhood arrived early at Junior High School 271 and barricaded doors to prevent the entry of the five teachers. About 85 other teachers followed union instructions and stayed out of the school, but about 40 reported for work. More than 600 people from the community met in the building that night to support the Ocean Hill board's transfers.

Lindsay, caught in the middle as he often has been in New York turmoil, issued a statement:

"No city can survive without laws that govern all of us. Tenure for teachers and administrators in our schools is protected by law. An effective education program requires this safeguard for the professional staff. Teachers can be removed only under present and orderly procedures . . .

"Because the community group . . . has taken an action that is beyond the law, I will, of course, support the board of education and superintendent if they ask for police assistance. In doing so, however, I must request greater understanding by them and by all of the causes of the deep community frustrations that have led to the present situation.

". . . Unfortunately there was no definition of the powers and duties of the local board and there has been such mutual distrust between the local and central officials that the entire history of the project has been one of bitter and frustrating struggle to define the powers of the local board. So long as there was no clear line of authority, loyalty within the professional staff of the schools was divided and friction was inevitable . . .

" "Both the state board of regents and I have recommended to the state legislature a decentralization plan which would alleviate this kind of problem by providing for responsible community participation based on cleanly cut ground rules which would spell out both the rights and responsiblities of local boards. The board of education opposed this plan.

". . . the legislature must not evade its responsibility . . . Our children should not pay the price of any further delay in restructuring and reforming our outmoded school system. Meanwhile, it must be understood that under no circumstances will we achieve anything worthwhile through anarchy and lawlessness . . ."

Lindsay's strong stand didn't help him with the UFT, which had prepared scathing advertisements for the New York papers. "Mr. Mayor," said the headline over Lindsay's picture, "When Will You Act?" The ads spelled out the union's complaints:

"19 teachers were denied democratic due process in the Ocean Hill-Brownsville experimental district.

"They were illegally fired by telegram. No charges. No hearing. No due process. In contravention of law and board of education regulations.

"But you, Mr. Mayor, did nothing.

"On Monday, these teachers were physically barred by outsiders from entering their schools, despite the superintendent's order that they report to work.

"But you, Mr. Mayor, did nothing — except tell the people if they passed YOUR School-Take-Over Bill there would not be any trouble.

"Mr. Mayor, do you or don't you stand for DUE PROCESS? Do you or don't you believe that people should be allowed to work at their profession without being barred at the door?

"Will you 'walk' with these teachers in Ocean Hill-Brownsville to assure their right to work without fear or intimidation? When will you act?"

The morning after Lindsay's statement, Wednesday, 300 city policemen arrived early at Junior High School 271, earlier than the demonstrators, thus breaking the two-day community blockade. They cordoned off the building, letting through only pupils and teachers, including the five disputed teachers. Particularly upsetting to the community was the fact that the person assigned by an assistant superintendent to aid police in the screening process was Fred Nauman, one of the five teachers the community did not want.

Schools were closed in Ocean Hill for most of the rest of that spring of 1968; the union teachers followed instructions to stay out. Albert Shanker, the union president, kept demanding hearings for the disputed teachers, with formal charges presented against them.

There were meetings and many attempts to mediate. Lindsay, anxious to preserve the local governing board's role, tried to get the teachers to accept removal from the district. Nothing worked.

On May 15, 1968, the Board of Education appointed Judge Francis E. Rivers, a retired Negro judge (in 1943 he had been elected a city court justice; at that time he reached the highest-ranking judicial post ever held by an American Negro), to be trial examiner on whatever charges McCoy might bring. And McCoy finally did bring charges, after he was directly ordered to do so by Superintendent Donovan.

Some of the charges dealt with what Judge Rivers was later to call "sins of omission" — failure to perform certain duties required of a teacher — and some with "sins of commission . . . the intentional doing of a wrongful act, such as opposing openly the demonstration project." Fred Nauman, for example, who was one of the union chapter chairmen at J.H.S. 271, was in the latter group.

The furor in Ocean Hill was, of course, reflected in the state legislature. Shanker took hundreds of teachers and parents to Albany to lobby against the strong decentralization bills that had been introduced, spending almost a quarter of a million dollars on the lobby effort. The legislature listened and passed what was called the Marchi Bill, which really wasn't a decentralization bill at all, but a postponement of the decision. The Marchi bill did three things:

1. It provided for the expansion of the New York City board of education from nine to thirteen members. The expansion, with new members to be appointed by Lindsay, would make possible the choice of board members more sympathetic to the mayor's decentralization ideas than the "old board" had been.

2. It charged the board with devising a quickie "interim" decentralization plan to take effect in the fall of 1968.

3. And it charged the board with preparing a more comprehensive long-range decentralization plan to submit to the 1969 legislature.

Summer of 1968: A Lull

The end of the school year brought a lessening of outward tension but not an end to actions that affected Ocean Hill. Among the things that were happening were these:

1. Rhody McCoy was assembling a teaching staff with some remarkable characteristics. Many were young, many had not been trained specifically as teachers and had not had teaching experience, many came from other parts of the country, full of enthusiasm for the Ocean Hill project (and cynics say many came because working in a deprived area gave them a way to avoid the draft). McCoy was seeking to replace the union teachers who had stayed out of the Ocean Hill schools for the last six weeks of the spring term.

2. Some new members were added by Lindsay to the board of education and, by the end of the summer, power was shifting to those sympathetic to fairly strong decentralization. The board was working on the interim plan, to be ready for September, but they didn't always work in peace. A public hearing late in August, for example, was noisily discordant — one observer called it a "shambles" — and dragged on for twelve hours. Mrs. Rose Shapiro, the board president, charged that the Reverend Milton A. Galamison, one of the new board members, had to share in the blame for the public discord; he had "encouraged and condoned" disruptions of the hearing, she said, by "self-appointed community groups." (Read "black.") Reverend Galamison was an outspoken civil rights activist and had been the chief mover behind the first pro-integration school boycott a few years earlier. He was a consistent, vociferous and able spokesman for the black perspective. He was also sometimes abrasive.

3. Able mediators sought quietly to resolve the differences between the Ocean Hill board and the central board but did not succeed.

4. Judge Rivers conducted his careful hearing into the charges McCoy had reluctantly brought against ten Ocean Hill teachers (the number

had been reduced to ten after the others agreed to accept assignment elsewhere.) He finished his long report at the end of August, although it was not made public immediately. He detailed the laws and regulations involved and the charges and evidence against each of the teachers; he concluded that McCoy had failed to show that any of the teachers were not performing their duties properly and thus had not substantiated his charges of misconduct.

The judge's report noted that the charges against Fred Nauman and two others, "that they had expressed opposition to the project and contributed to the growing hostility between the Negro and white teachers," had been dismissed because no witnesses were present to give evidence.

The irony of the Rivers report lies in a section which read:[20]

"Perhaps if the unit administrator had sent to the superintendent of schools a simple request to transfer the teachers, without assigning any supporting charges, he (the superintendent) may have been able to do so without a hearing by virtue of Article II, paragraph 101.1 of the by-laws of the board of education. But here the unit administrator of the board requests that transfer be made by the superintendent upon the ground that the respondent, in each instance, has rendered unsatisfactory services as a teacher."

Ocean Hill people had consistently claimed that transfer was all they were seeking and that formal charges were not needed under the regulations. McCoy had only filed the charges, later, when Superintendent Donovan ordered him to do so.

Once the charges of misconduct had been filed, the judge explained, then the due process guarantees had to go into effect. He used these words:

"If it is held that wrongful conduct by the teacher is so serious as to justify his involuntary transfer, then the decision would be potentially effective to deprive him of his property rights (a lowering of his rating as a teacher and consequent lessening of salary or other benefits, or injury to his reputation as a teacher or otherwise) and hence could not be upheld unless it was arrived at in accordance with due process of law. This conformity to due process is required not only by the Constitution of New York State, but also by the Fourteenth Amendment . . ."

When Superintendent Donovan accepted the Rivers report, on September 5, he directed McCoy and Ocean Hill to reinstate the ten teachers. The Ocean Hill board voted not to accept the Rivers report.

The Disastrous Month of September 1968

The month opened with clear evidence that the United Federation of Teachers did not like what it had been hearing about the board of education's interim decentralization plan. The plan had not been adopted yet, but many of the board's ideas had been presented in public hearings. The board had tentatively decided to give local boards the power to pick district superintendents immediately and was considering delegating to the local boards the same authority to hire and fire teachers that the central board had.

The UFT administrative committee and executive board both met at union headquarters on August 31 and both voted to recommend a strike to members because the proposed board of education plan would violate collective bargaining understandings in the present contract, in effect until June 30, 1969. Giving local boards control of hiring and firing, President Shanker told both groups, would "open up a field day for bigots and racists" and would result in a critical shortage of teachers in some areas.

It seems significant that the *New York Times* report of the strike recommendation does not include any mention of the ten Ocean Hill teachers. Ocean Hill doubtless was in people's minds but the Rivers report had not yet been released. The strike recommendation at this point was solely on the basis of the board of education's proposals.

Over the next few days Shanker further explained the union's grievances and seemed to be escalating its demands. Referring to Ocean Hill, he said the local board should be removed from office if it did not take back the ten disputed teachers. And he called for these modifications in the board of education's tentative plan:

*Disciplining of teachers only for cause, with a final decision by an "outside impartial third party," a proposal that had first surfaced in a UFT ad the previous winter.

*A supplementary agreement to the union contract with the board of education to guarantee that certain "understandings" would not be changed as a result of the transfer of powers to local boards. The understandings involved class sizes, sabbatical and short-term leaves by teachers, lunch privileges and other items. (McCoy was among many who complained that Shanker was trying to negotiate contract items out of season. Shanker felt if the union did not take a stand in the initial stages of decentralization, it would be unable to do so later.)

*Prevention of "union-busting," through some kind of assurances from the board of education that union members would not be harassed by local districts and would be free to execute their union membership. "Decentralization is fine but not at the expense of the rights we have won and not with the smashing of the union," Shanker said. This was a sore point, not much discussed in public at the time, but the proportion of union members among the teachers in two experimental districts had dropped from 95 percent to 50 percent under local governing board control. It was a fact that seemed ominous to union leaders.

   *Guarantees that children would be taught and supervised only by "properly licensed teachers." (He meant city-licensed teachers, under all the old protective rules, which would keep out some of the new blood sought by Ocean Hill and other localities, who sought to meet the less-stringent state certification of teachers.)

If these modifications weren't agreed to by the board and if Ocean Hill didn't reinstate the ten, Shanker said, the chances were only "fifty-fifty" that the schools would open on schedule on Monday, September 9.

A board of education committee had been working to reach an agreement with Ocean Hill, but it met failure. The ten teachers were just unacceptable to the local community, McCoy repeated. And he added that the local district was proceeding to replace 200 teachers who had opposed its action in May and had stayed out of their classrooms.

With the strike threat dangling ominously and McCoy's words echoing just as ominously, the board met Wednesday, September 4, and adopted its city-wide interim plan for decentralization. Incredibly, the public meeting lasted just four minutes, long enough for a vote of seven for, one against, and one abstention. The vote taken, the meeting was abruptly adjourned, to avoid public controversy or dissension. The plan gave to local boards the power to:

* Replace superintendents;
* Recruit and hire teachers who pass required examinations;
* Dismiss and discipline teachers according to law;
* Modify curriculum;
* Select texts and prepare budget requests;
* Manage expenditures;
* Recommend creation of new types of licensing and teaching positions (an attempt to compromise with the union's hard line on licensing);
* Carry out plans after consultation with parents, staff, and community groups (perhaps an attempt to assure teachers they would have a chance to be heard).

The plan did not give the UFT all the job protections it said it required. Strike talk continued, and it was bolstered by the 4,000 member Council of Supervisory Associations, which voted to shut the schools — for "safety," it said — if the UFT went on strike. (In the strike the year before, the supervisor had played no active role and had tried to keep the schools open wherever teachers were willing to report to work.)

On Friday, September 6, the delegate assembly of the UFT met and voted overwhelmingly to recommend a strike the following Monday;

the rest of the membership was to ballot on Sunday. The recommendation was overwhelming, but not unanimous. Some delegates did speak
up against the strike. One warned:

"Our union is facing the most difficult time in its history . . . The
rightful demands of the black and Puerto Rican communities to control the education of their children cannot in good conscience be
opposed . . . A strike at this time will inevitably be interpreted as a
strike against the black, Puerto Rican and even the white communities
of our city."

But that was a sentiment that could not prevail in the UFT in the
fall of 1968, when its president was talking about the Ocean Hill impasse as a "sink or swim" matter involving survival of the union and all
it stood for.

"The issues are deep and rigid and not susceptible to compromise,"
President Shanker told the delegate assembly. "This is a strike that
will protect black teachers against white racists and white teachers
against black racists." He insisted that all job protections had to be
written into the decentralization plan, or some of them, particularly
those not written into the contract, would be lost with the transfer
of power to local boards.

The weekend was full of tension, with the public caught in the
middle, wondering whether to send their kids to school on Monday
morning. The board of education spent many weekend hours in negotiations — separate negotiations with the UFT and with the Ocean
Hill governing board. They met almost all night Friday and then met
again on Saturday. The board warned that a strike by the UFT would
be "in clear violation of its contract" and that it would seek a court
injunction. Shanker said the union would defy a court injunction as it
had the year before. On Saturday night the board gave Ocean Hill an
"ultimatum" to restore the ten teachers to their jobs. McCoy again
refused and said, "This is about the fifth ultimatum we've gotten so
far. We are now using ultimatums for souvenirs."

Meanwhile, away from the center of negotiations, the teachers were
getting ready for their Sunday strike vote and preparing picket signs
that read, "Justice for Teachers."

On Sunday, the day of the strike vote, Mayor Lindsay entered the
dispute calling all parties to city hall. They didn't all meet together,
but stayed in separate rooms, with Lindsay going back and forth between them. At 6:00 p.m., he made a triumphant announcement. There
would be no strike, he said; agreement had been reached. Ocean Hill
did not agree to the return of the ten but would not seek to prevent
their return, and there would be continuing discussion of the security
issues that plagued the union. Then he left city hall.

Lindsay's optimism was not shared by those who remained behind in city hall. McCoy explained that the ten would be brought back to the district but would not be assigned to classrooms. Shanker said there was no agreement at all, that the union was not a party to any agreement and had seen no proposal in writing. He said the ten would have to return to classroom duties or the strike was still on. Referring bitterly to Lindsay, Shanker added, "I think he's told different people different things in different rooms. Obviously he hasn't settled it at all — he's bungled it."

Later Shanker announced the results of the strike vote: 12,021 for the strike, 1,716 against.

So there was a strike on the first day of school and closed doors greeted most of the city's children. But not those in Ocean Hill, where schools were open and operating, guarded by a big contingent of city police.

True to predictions, city officials got a court order restraining the union from continuing the strike and prohibiting any strike participation by the Council of Supervisory Associations. A court official sent to serve the order on Albert Shanker found the lanky union leader in a restaurant near his office, having a late supper of chicken soup and beer.

"I didn't enjoy the fifteen days I spent in jail for last year's strike," Shanker mused, "and I'm sure I won't enjoy it next time. But we have a union policy of 'no contract, no work' and we feel that our contract has been broken."

Shanker had been working on a newspaper ad, an "open letter" to parents, that explained that claim:

". . .Teachers, like any other jobholder, must be assured of job security and union rights, whether the board of education is central or local. You and the members of your family may be employed on jobs protected by union contracts or by civil service regulations. How would you react if you could be fired or removed from your job and forced to transfer to another section without any charges or any procedures for hearing your objections? I think you will agree that a union is worth nothing if it fails to defend the rights of its members to their jobs and to a fair procedure for dismissal.

"Last year, the teachers won an agreement with provisions designed to improve the schools, including limitation of class size and a special fund for a more effective schools program. This agreement is in effect until September 1969. The UFT is asking simply that the board of education guarantee the provisions of this contract under the decentralization plan. We are *not* striking against decentralization . . . We cannot have successful education in a system where teachers can be fired for no reason after ten years of satisfactory service."

That first teachers' strike of the fall of 1968 lasted only two days. The board of education and the UFT negotiated for seven hours on Tuesday, September 10, and reached a "memorandum of understanding". It called for the return to Ocean Hill of all teachers who wished to return; it extended the grievance procedure of the union contract with the board to bind all local school boards and their administrative staffs. In cases where local boards might want to dismiss teachers, the agreement required that charges be placed before a panel of arbitrators, whose decision would be binding. The memorandum gave the union something else, too: authority for the union's executive board to close the city's schools on forty-eight hours' notice without further action by the UFT membership "in the event the agreements with respect to Ocean Hill-Brownsville are broken." The UFT voted Tuesday night, 5515 to 218 (only about 10 percent of the teachers) to accept the agreement and return to school the next morning, Wednesday.

No one seemed to pay much attention to the fact that no representative from Ocean Hill-Brownsville was present while that agreement was reached. The board of education just issued a statement:

"The board of education believes that the Ocean Hill-Brownsville board will act in good faith and that their public assurance to the Mayor on Sunday will be honored. To the board of education, this means that each teacher who wishes to return to his former school and to his professional assignment will not be prevented from doing so and that these actions will be carried out in good faith and without reprisal."

The view was different in Ocean Hill.

The Ocean Hill-Brownsville board felt the challenge was basic. It felt it had the power--or ought to have the power--to determine the quality of education in its schools and that it couldn't do so without the power to determine who would teach, within the restrictions laid down by the state. It was convinced that the union, no less than the board of education, was seeking to impose restrictions that were incompatible with true decentralization. To some extent, it saw the union and the board as part of the same establishment. The local people had no intention of welcoming back the unwelcome teachers, no matter what agreement was reached between the board of education and the union.

Community people tried to block the doors at some of the schools on Wednesday morning, and police had to force their way through to enable the union teachers to enter. Finally, the union teachers were assembled for a meeting in the auditorium at one of the schools, but community people joined them there and, teachers complained to the union, subjected them to a "reign of terror."

"You're dead! We know your faces. We'll get you, your families, your children," the community people threatened, according to the teachers' report to the union. "We'll be where you live."

That afternoon, the union executive board announced a new strike, to start Friday morning, September 13, because none of the teachers was allowed to resume teaching. That second strike was to last more than two weeks.

Efforts by the Ocean Hill-Brownsville governing board to demonstrate that there was no reign of terror against white teachers were largely unheard. The governing board announcement that 70 percent of replacement teachers it had hired were white and that many of them were Jewish did nothing to alter the feelings of fear in the city.

Frustrations on all sides deepened during the two weeks of the second strike and solutions daily seemed farther away. The union made new demands: get rid of McCoy and the Ocean Hill-Brownsville board and send back to the district not only the ten teachers but the 200 or so who had supported them and been replaced during the summer. The local board repeated, "We refuse to sell out."

Among the developments of those bitter two weeks in mid-September were these:

*Mayor Lindsay, trying hard to be a bridge between the widening factions, was shunned by both sides. He was picketed and jeered by union teachers at a rally outside City Hall, with teachers chanting, "Lindsay must go." The Ocean Hill governing board walked out on one scheduled meeting with him and its chairman charged the mayor was trying to help the union "rape" the Ocean Hill community. And a white parents' group who thought that Ocean Hill was clearly out of line in preventing the return of the teachers, booed him roundly when he tried to say a good word for the Ocean Hill experiment and its leaders. Lindsay, truly in the middle but with no real authority to resolve anything, continued to defend the "legitimate" rights of both sides. "The teachers have a right to due process and to appropriate safeguards for tenure where they work," he stated. "The community also has a right to a meaningful voice in their community schools and to seek to establish conditions which will give them a sense of pride in their schools and a chance to achieve quality education for their children. Neither side has a right to break the law to deliberately provoke violence."

*The central board of education, feeling that it had exhausted all means of resolving the controversy, turned for help to State Education Commissioner James E. Allen, Jr., the hard-working and highly-respected educator who was firmly committed both to the orderly operation of the state's school system and to the idea of decentralization. Allen, with the aid of Theodore Kheel, one of New York's most successful mediators, suggested trying to remove the source of trouble on both sides: suspend the Ocean Hill board temporarily and transfer the ten teachers to headquarters duty temporarily, so that negotiations could proceed in a calmer atmosphere. The Allen truce pleased no one. A howl of rage came from Ocean Hill and from Kenneth Clark, noted Negro psychologist and the only Negro ever to serve on the state board of regents; it seemed to them that the proposal was balancing the rights of ten teachers against the whole idea of community control of schools.

*The central board of education tried to act on the Allen plan, but did not succeed in bringing an end to the strike. It did suspend the Ocean Hill board and temporarily transferred the ten teachers. But the United Federation of Teachers added some new conditions before it would accept the Allen Plan. Shanker said the union demanded:

1. A pledge that the suspension of the local board would not be lifted before the ten were reinstated;

2. That all the teachers who backed the ten be allowed to return to their jobs (the number was now about 100, since the others had accepted transfers to other schools);

3. That neutral observers be stationed in the schools to check on cases of intimidation, with the understanding that the mayor would close any such school.

Superintendent Donovan tried to reassure the union that the issues would be resolved and the teachers' rights would be protected, but Shanker said Donovan's wording was "fishy."

In Ocean Hill, Rhody McCoy defied the board's order and said he could not take back any of the teachers. "Since I am responsible to the governing board and the community, I cannot in conscience accept any dictated terms reached by the collusion of Shanker and Donovan even if, as reported, it means my job . . . The collusion between Shanker and Donovan strips black and Puerto Rican men of dignity and self-respect. They jointly make a decision to determine the action of a third party. It's indecent."

*The Ocean Hill board and its lawyer, William Kuntsler, began preparing a federal court suit challenging the local board's suspension on the grounds that it had been denied due process of law. And, on one occasion, the local board rejected an invitation to meet with the central board because, since it had been suspended, it had no power to negotiate and the meeting would be a waste of time.

*A New York judge, who had been holding hearings on the UFT walkout, ruled that it was an illegal strike under the Taylor act and ordered the strikers back to work.

*Thousands of New Yorkers joined in the dispute, some by picketing and rallying (teachers and supporters, for example, picketed the

Ford Foundation, claiming it was supporting racism and union-busting), some by signing newspaper advertisements, setting out conflicting claims about the problem. Many old-line liberals, together in past days, split over the issue. Support for the teachers came, for example, from Michael Harrington, Socialist leader, and from Bayard Rustin, the black executive director of the A. Phillip Randolph Institute, who has been insisting more and more that black separatism is folly.

Setting forth the issues of the strike as he saw them, Rustin stated in his ad, signed by other black union leaders:

"It is the right of every worker not to be transferred or fired at the whim of his employer. It is the right of every worker to be judged on his merits--not his color or creed. It is the right of every worker to job security. These are the rights that black workers have struggled and sacrificed to win for generations. They are not abstractions. They are the black workers' safeguards against being 'the last hired and the first fired.' These rights have been denied to teachers in the Ocean Hill-Brownsville district by the local governing board . . .(the action) suggests other boards could fire teachers because they're black."

Ocean Hill people and their supporters prepared an ad, too, under the headline: "Why don't they want our children to learn?" It claimed the suspension of the local governing board had "left the United Federation of Teachers in full command . . . The Ocean Hill-Brownsville community has lost faith in the willingness of these teachers to accept and to teach their children. . . It has been fashionable for the educational bureaucracy to complain that ghetto parents were 'apathetic' about the education of their children. This alleged apathy was given as an excuse for the failure to teach these children. Now that these parents are aroused with a concern for the education of their children, the educational establishment now threatens to defeat them . . . To suspend the local governing board is not to quiet the community; it is to further enrage it."

All these swirling pressures made September of 1968 chaotic. All the animosities were expressed with great freedom. But negotiations were continuing and, toward the end of the month, there seemed to be some progress.

By that time, one of the remaining divisive issues was the union's demand for "neutral" observers in the Ocean Hill schools, empowered to call a halt to operations if they found threats of intimidation. There was trouble about defining "neutral" and how to guarantee it.

The issue was finally resolved, or so people hoped, in a bruising, 16-hour negotiating session in Gracie Mansion, the mayor's residence, on the last weekend in September. Lindsay appeared on the steps of the mansion at 2:20 p.m. Sunday, September 29, with Superintendent Donovan, Albert Shanker of the UFT and Walter J. Degnan of the

Council of Supervisory Associations, to announce the agreement. They were unshaven and weary. Lindsay had had no sleep at all during the night. Shanker, during the night, had stretched his lanky frame out on the floor for a 20-minute nap, his only sleep in 36. hours. But they all managed a big smile for the photographers and their pictures appeared the next morning under the headlines, "Schools Reopening Today."

"The board of education and the UFT have signed a written agreement to reopen tomorrow," Lindsay announced from the steps of his home. The agreement (subsequently agreed to by the teachers by a vote of 5,825 to 592) called for a return to Ocean Hill teaching duties of the 110 teachers currently under dispute, with large numbers of police on duty to protect the teachers and maintain order. Teams of observers would be present in each of the schools, with each team made up of one representative from the superintendent's staff, one named by the union, and one impartial observer named by the mayor. The observers would not have the power to close schools themselves in the event of disorder, but would report recommendations to a special board of education committee, which could then act and could close the schools if necessary.

No one paid much attention to the fact that, in the jubilant announcement that agreement had been reached, there were again no representatives on hand from Ocean Hill. They had no part in the settlement. Practical men might assume that they would just have to go along with it. But that's what the black community calls colonialism. It is the very heart of the problem.

The Schools Reopen—Again

On Monday, September 30, New York youngsters trooped off to school to meet their teachers, again. In Ocean Hill, where the kids had been going to school all along, there really were no major incidents that day. Hundreds of police were on hand there, including more than 300 at Junior High School 271, which had become the focal point of the dispute. A police helicopter flew overhead. Barricades were up to keep demonstrators away. The disputed teachers were escorted safely into the buildings; there were 83 of them, the number reduced from 110 when some of the group quietly transferred to other areas and a few just didn't show up. There were police inside the schools, too, and that earned the vocal opposition of many of the teachers.

An angry community met that night in the auditorium of J.H.S. 271. They heard speakers charge that Lindsay was giving in completely to the UFT and that the community was being humiliated in two ways, by being forced to take back the teachers and by "occupation by the police."

"We have taken directive after directive and have tried to accept them," said the Reverend Oliver, chairman of the local governing board. "We have bent over backward to comply, but it didn't work. We plan to issue a directive to Mr. McCoy and the principals not to assign a single one of those teachers tomorrow morning." The board had met, he said, with eleven members present, and the majority of them voted to issue the directive.

Some of the schools' teachers reported to the meeting that they had prepared a statement to give to the union teachers at 8 a.m. the next morning. "Ocean Hill-Brownsville does not want teachers who are apathetic," it said. "Our position is perfectly clear. We don't want the police who must escort you into the schools; we do not want the so-called impartial observers; we do not want the union and we do not want you . . . We appeal to you to leave."

Wooden police barricades surrounded the eight Ocean Hill schools the next morning, October 1. More than 1,000 policemen were on hand, with a particularly strong contingent around the troubled J.H.S. 271, on Herkimer Street. Teachers and pupils were allowed to pass the barricades; no one else was allowed to pass.

There was a growing crowd of community people outside the barricades. Some had come to accompany their children. Some had come to express their support of the local board. Some were there simply out of curiosity.

"We don't need all these police around here," one aging woman complained. "We're talking about education and they got enough cops around here to fight a war."

Inside J.H.S. 271, the teachers met, angry, and decided to call a one-day walkout to protest the return of the unwanted staff and to demonstrate support for the local board. Shortly after 9 a.m., the teachers walked out, led by Albert Vann, acting assistant principal and president of the African-American Teachers Association, and Leslie Campbell, the teacher who had been disciplined for taking youngsters to the Malcolm X. memorial meeting in Harlem a few months earlier. Hundreds of youngsters, told that school was out for the day, poured out after them.

The teachers began a march to nearby I.S. 55, to ask teachers there to join the walkout. Some of the youngsters and some of the neighborhood people outside the barricades went along. Police, using walkie-talkies, called for reinforcements at I.S. 55.

"As the groups of teachers, parents and students merged," the *New York Times* reported, "violence erupted. Bottles were hurled at the police massed in front of the school. As the crowd moved toward the police barricades, other objects were thrown. The police tried to shove back the surging crowd and some in the crowd tried to knock down the barricades. Finally, one of the wooden railings was picked up and heaved into the group of policemen . . .Some of the officers used their clubs and were confronted by teachers who charged them with overreacting."

The clashes went on for 90 tense minutes, the *Times* continued, leaving 10 officers injured and leading to the arrest of at least nine persons.

Bands of young people, with the police, shifted to other schools in the district, and there were more fights, more arrests, and a considerable amount of name-calling, on both sides. Caught up in the struggle were many people not really a part of it, parents, for example, frightened and trying without success to get to the schools to find their children. Many were crying.

Four of the Ocean Hill schools were closed down. And the mayor, who had been so smilingly hopeful two days earlier, told the city, "I want to make it absolutely clear that no further disturbance of this sort will be tolerated. The stakes are too high. If we do not retain education under the law, we will have neither education nor law."

Shanker began talking of a new strike, because the agreement wasn't being kept, and went to meetings with the mayor, the board of education subcommittee and the police commissioner.

In Ocean Hill, the Reverend Oliver said, "If the mayor wants order in the schools, then let him get those 83 teachers out."

Thusday and Friday were quiet in Ocean Hill, but there was new feeling stirring in other parts of the city, with other groups beginning to think about their own brand of community control. A rump board took over a central office in another district.

The executive board of the UFT authorized a new strike and the city leaders began to worry about reaction in Albany, where a new legislature was going to be asked soon to act on the long-postponed decentralization proposals.

Rhody McCoy and the eight Ocean Hill principals wrote a new recommendation to the central board of education:

"In the twelfth hour of crisis, we, the professional staff, having observed the consequences of four days of imposition and show of uniformed force by the city administration, are of the opinion that no education of quality is taking place nor will it take place as long as the siege is in effect." Their letter asked the board, "in accordance with its bylaws," to transfer the 83 teachers. They referred to the bylaw provision that gives the superintendent the authority to transfer teachers at the request of a district superintendent.

The board of education received the letter right after hearing from Shanker that there would be a "long, huge strike" if the board didn't assure reassignment of the 83 teachers in their Ocean Hill jobs.

Then the board acted. It suspended the Ocean Hill governing board, for 30 days this time, and directed the superintendent to take over direction of the Ocean Hill schools, suspending anyone found to be blocking their operation.

The next day, Monday, October 7, most of the 83 teachers were assigned to classrooms, but they had no pupils assigned to the classrooms. McCoy met with his teachers after school and asked them, whatever happened, even if principals were removed forcibly, to stay with the children.

UFT chapter chairmen met with Shanker that day, too. John O'Neill, a union vice president, spoke up at the meeting, urging the teachers not to strike again.

"The conflict is political and social," O'Neill told his colleagues, "arising out of a very complex set of conditions—the thrust of the black and Puerto Rican peoples against the white establishment; the struggle of the outs against the ins; the struggle of the poor to get into the middle class—all the while President Shanker tries to sell the incredibly simplistic notion that this is a simple labor-management dispute in eight shops." He went on to accuse Shanker of turning "a brush fire into a conflagration that is sweeping across the city."

Shanker attacked the "dubious morality" of a union official— O'Neill—who runs for office on a platform and "betrays the trust of the members who voted for him." (The next meeting of the executive board ousted O'Neill from his paid position on the union staff.)

The following morning, Tuesday, October 8, McCoy assigned the 83 teachers to non-teaching jobs, then was informed he was removed from his job. "They'll have to carry me out of here," he said. Seven of the eight principals were ousted, too; the eighth requested reassignment, saying he would follow the central board's order but, by doing so, he would lose his effectiveness in the community. The Reverend Oliver announced a court suit against the board of education for removing the board and top staff without due process.

The beleaguered Lindsay went on the radio, with a long statement about "what happened today." McCoy and the principals had been relieved of their duties, he explained first. Then he went on:

"The governing board, the administrators and the principals have refused to adhere to the law. They have insisted on defying lawful directives of the board of education and superintendent of schools, directives issued to protect the legal rights and personal safety of teachers, and to assure the orderly operation of the schools.

"We have also had illegal acts by the union, specifically the shutdown of our public schools. That illegal condition will be dealt with by the courts."

Lindsay said the city had had enough of "illegal pressures on our schools," from both sides, and urged changed attitudes to bring about the needed changes in the schools. Step by step, he went through his ideas again: increased local responsibility for communities in running their schools; protection of teachers against arbitrary dismissal and a-gainst harassment, "placing the teachers and the communities on the same side of the fight for better schools."

"Community spokesmen have to understand," he said, "that it is simply not acceptable to turn grievances against our schools into racial and religious epithets. Nor do we gain a better system by threat-ening economic and physical reprisals against our teachers.

" . . . Teachers must recognize that these communities have a right to participate in the schools, a right to accountability . . . Further, it is time the union recognized that they must stop turning every local dispute which is going to occur" into a spark for the "illegal shutdown of the city's schools."

Lindsay's was an anguished statement, and heartfelt. It put him right where he's always been, in the middle, damned by both sides and in-creasingly in trouble with the voters, too, who were tired of the terrible wrangle. He hadn't made the wrangle and he had no power to end it, except the stature of his office and the dimming force of his charm. But he was blamed.

Lindsay was immersed in other labor troubles, too, involving thou-sands of city employees and keeping the city's residents distraught. Police, firemen and sanitation workers were about to turn down all wage settlements and start a chaotic period of slowdowns. To the people of the city, government seemed to be coming apart at the seams.

The following day, Wednesday, October 9, brought a new agony to J.H.S. 271. Police, acting on board of education orders, kept the prin-cipal from entering. Inside 271, the superintendent's aides were in charge, presumably, but one complained that the teachers were "in rebellion" and would not follow orders. Vann said the charge was "ridiculous" but there was, at the least, confusion.

The acting principal announced over the public address system that school would be closed, and some youngsters started to leave. Her voice was then followed by, "This is Mr. Vann. Classes will be held today." Teachers followed the youngsters outside, telling them to "Come on back." Police let that group back in, but would not admit other young-sters who had not yet passed the checkpoint at the barricades. Protesters there grew angry. Finally, an order came to let all the youngsters in, but by then there were 200 protesters, and the old, familiar insults began. The police beat one Negro man severely, according to the New York Times account.

After that, the superintendent announced that J.H.S. 271 would be closed for the next two days. "There had been animosity between teachers of different points of view," he said. "And people have been coming in from outside the community disrupting classes. Instruction just cannot proceed."

Later, there were conflicting accounts about the extent of disorder in 271 that day. Superintendent Donovan told the board of education that "reports from the observers indicate to me the building up of an intense racial antagonism not only among the staff members, but among the pupils of the school. Bulletin boards, auditorium activities and pictures indicate a racist approach not suitable for public schools. There was also a threat to the safety and life of at least one of my observers in the school." Reports from the observers, never made public officially, went further. It said that union teachers were barred from the time card room and told, "You are the enemy of my people." It said union teachers were surrounded in the teachers room, told "We don't want you in this school," and called "white racist pigs." It said children in the auditorium were chanting, "We will die for Rhody McCoy;" they were being led by teen-agers in the presence of teachers. It said the acting principal had been threatened, but was fuzzy about the details. It said an observer and a union teacher were told by two teachers loyal to the governing board, "You are going to die, and they are going to put you six feet under."

The UFT and Shanker made much of this "death threat" in the days to come but others claimed it was greatly exaggerated. The city's Human Relations Commission chairman said the "only disorder" was caused when the police tried to bar the children from going into the school. And Charles Issacs, who was there as a teacher—young, white, Jewish, and very pro-community—said there was some harassment on both sides but it was "petty." Then he added, "The entire issue of harassment was best summed up by the Reverend C. Herbert Oliver, the chairman of the governing board, when he said, 'I wish people wouldn't interpret an exclamation of 'drop dead!' as a threat on their lives.' "

What happened in 271 that day, and the way the union teachers felt about what happened, is important because it led directly to the really crippling teachers' strike, the long one that dragged on for five weeks.

At the other Ocean Hill schools there had been no trouble that day, mostly due to Rhody McCoy. When McCoy was relieved of his assignment, and he responded, "They'll have to carry me out," he was not, in fact, carried out.

"His government in exile remained a key command post for both sides," Fred Hechinger wrote in the *Times*. "His authority in the district kept the rebellion down to one school . . . and his credentials with the establishment kept communication open with Donovan. They 'speak the same language.' " (McCoy never was very radical. After all, he'd been working in the educational establishment, and moving up the ladder, for almost twenty years. Sometimes Ocean Hill people thought he wasn't really on their side. But when the community crisis came and he had to choose among loyalties, he chose the local board, even though it meant a break with the system.)

On Thursday and Friday, J.H.S. 271 was closed and its teachers were meeting with the superintendent, the sixteen "unwanted" teachers along with the rest. The teachers wanted another chance to resolve their differences, Donovan said. He was working out a compromise about teaching assignments, too.

While Donovan was meeting with the J.H.S. 271 teachers to work on on these details, Shanker arrived. The superintendent asked him to leave, saying, "I called the meeting for the faculty and you weren't invited." Shanker replied, "I have as much right to be here as you do." Donovan said, "I don't think our positions are comparable." When Shanker again refused to leave, Donovan walked out of the meeting. He later announced that J.H.S. 271 would reopen the following Monday and the principals would be returned to their schools.

Shanker charged that the superintendent had betrayed the teachers and called for another strike vote.

"You do not have the right to take a single school in a single district and use it to cripple this city," Lindsay criticized. Donovan asked again for "one day's trial to see whether this staff can work together;" he pledged no one would be harassed or threatened. But no one seemed ready to trust anyone else. The union teachers voted 6,042 to 2,128 on Sunday, October 13, to strike the next morning. And if the teachers did go on strike, Shanker announced, the union would not call it off until the board of education declared the Ocean Hill experiment a failure, terminated it, dismissed the local governing board, and returned Ocean Hill-Brownsville to the "regular school system."

And so the third strike started, on Monday, October 14, and no observers have ever had any good words to say for it. Even Martin Mayer, the writer who tended to be most sympathetic with the union's position, said the third strike turned "nihilist."

For five weeks, no efforts to settle the strike succeeded. Skilled negotiators were called in and they gave up. The state commissioner proposed the state should intervene and run the disputed district; Shanker said no. Lindsay suggested closing J.H.S. 271 and the board said no. Donovan proposed moving out the whole faculty and converting the school to a high school and everybody said no. The Ocean Hill board even made its first offer to take back the disputed teachers, but Shanker wouldn't listen; he said the offer could not have been made in good faith.

John Doar, a man who displayed great skill in past civil rights
battles, was elected president of the board of education, but he didn't
have any luck either. ("I'm a reformer at heart," Doar told an inter-
viewer. "I like to run against the dragon." Doar had been head of the civil
civil rights division in the justice department during part of the 1960s
and was the man who shepherded James Meredith through the early
weeks of his riot-torn admission to the University of Mississippi.)

Parents were furious. Doar ordered the schools open if "only one
teacher" was there, but many principals would not open the schools.
Some parents and nonstriking teachers smashed windows and forced
locks to get into the buildings. The custodians changed the locks.

The UFT organized mass picketing at some schools to keep out
the non-striking teachers and the children who wanted to enter the
buildings. And vicious names were called back and forth.

Lindsay warned of "intolerable racial and religious tension." For
many, that was the most distressing aspect of the whole dismal fall.
Two educators close to the events have tried to deal with the topic
without hysteria. Maurice R. Berube and Marilyn Gittell wrote:[21]

". . . Most studies indicate less anti-Semitism among blacks than
among whites, but the strike significantly increased black hostility
to the Jewish community. It did not create black anti-Semitism but
crystallized it in New York . . .

"In part, the racial tension can be viewed merely as the result of an
out-group's resentment of those in power. In New York, both the
teaching and the supervisory staffs are predominantly Jewish. Their
interest in maintaining the status quo was seized upon by black extremists who produced leaflets attacking not the staff or teachers but
the Jews. In turn, the UFT and the CSA distributed copies of those
leaflets in an attempt to gather support for their own positions. At
this point, the leadership of the Jewish community overreacted.

"Black anti-Semitism was not the product of community control.
The Ocean Hill board and unit administrator clearly disavowed anti-
Semitism, and the board pointedly noted that it had hired a predominantly white, predominantly Jewish teaching staff to fill the classrooms
of striking teachers. These new teachers, estranged from the union because of the decentralization issue, eventually took a newspaper advertisement in order to deny publicly the existence of anti-Semitism
in the district's schools."

Looking back, there is a tendency to believe that the issue was
exaggerated, but to the people who lived through those days the fears
were very real. Hitler's Germany will live long in Jewish memories,
and it was often mentioned in 1968.

There was potent anti-Semitic literature circulated by some black
militants in the Ocean Hill community and elsewhere. One anonymous

tract distributed in the fall of 1968 said, "It is impossible for the Middle East murderers of colored people to possibly bring to this important task (education) the insight, the concern, the exposing of the truth that is a must if the years of brainwashing and self-hatred that have been taught to our black children by those blood-sucking exploiters and murderers is to be overcome."

Another said, "Get off our backs, or your relatives in the Middle East will find themselves giving benefits to raise money to help you out from under the terrible weight of an enraged Black community."

The teachers' union reprinted the inflammatory handbills and gave them far wider circulation. The union's aim, Shanker said, was to make the threat clear. "You don't mobilize the conscience of the community by making believe that racism doesn't exist," Shanker said,[22] "and you don't mobilize the conscience of the city or the state of New York by making believe that this kind of garbage doesn't exist."

The Strike Winds Down

Eventually, of course, there was a solution to the strike, or at least a sort of solution that allowed the kids to get back to school after missing 36 days of classroom time. Many forces had to converge before the time for a solution could come. Among the forces were these:

*John Doar, the school board president, kept stressing the need for both sides to show some faith in the board's abilities and skills. And he kept pointing out the illegalities on both sides. "It is unacceptable in a civilized society for a teacher to be driven from his post by threats, intimidation or violence," he said. But he was just as critical of the teachers' union: "How can the board gain compliance with the law when one powerful group threatens and condemns each action it takes?"

*James E. Allen, the state education commissioner, remained remarkably flexible, patiently pursuing first one idea and then another, to find an acceptable combination. The idea of a state committee to oversee the Ocean Hill experiment began to grow in importance. It was a way to take the heat out of the direct conflict with the New York City board of education.

*Governor Nelson Rockefeller resisted strong pressure to call a special session of the legislature, which would have spelled the doom of any decentralization efforts. When that possibility was removed, the union was forced back to the bargaining table.

*The union gained a face-saving device with a court decision in November that three of the Ocean Hill principals had been illegally appointed. (The decision was later reversed again.)

*Superintendent Donovan announced the start of disciplinary procedures against some of the J.H.S. 271 teachers accused by the union of threatening behavior on the chaotic day of October 9, the day when the acting principal said the teachers were in rebellion. That turned out to be a face-saving device for the union, too. (The teachers were later cleared of the charges.)

*Important New York labor leaders, ardent supporters of Shanker and the teachers' union during most of the strike, switched their position and began pressuring for settlement. The labor leaders had first tended to view the strike as a contract compliance issue and had believed City Hall was engaged in union-busting. But the same racial tensions involved in the strike finally enmeshed the other labor leaders too.

According to A.H. Raskin, *New York Times* labor editor, Negro and Puerto Rican union officials, who supported the strike at first along with white union leaders, grew more hostile as they came to believe that Shanker really was trying to wipe out the Ocean Hill experiment and cripple decentralization. They put increasing pressure on Harry Van Arsdale, head of the Central Labor Council, who had earned a reputation for fairness to minority groups. In early November, Negro and Puerto Rican union officials conducted a five-hour sit-in at Van Arsdale's headquarters. About the same time, three white members of Van Arsdale's executive board arranged a meeting between Van Arsdale and Shanker and Bayard Rustin, the black leader who had publicly supported the teachers' strike but had grown increasingly horrified at what it was leading to.

"Shanker and Van Arsdale listened attentively," Raskin wrote, "as Bayard Rustin made a poetic and passionate plea for the United Federation of Teachers not to insist on a punitive settlement and not to hold out for a legislative solution in Albany . . . He pleaded for reconciliation of the UFT and ghetto parents."

All the pieces of the puzzle were beginning to fit together; a negotiating session was set for 10 a.m. Saturday, November 16, at Gracie Mansion, Mayor Lindsay's residence. It was not to end for almost 28 hours.

So many groups were involved that they were spaced out in different areas of the mansion. Shanker and his aides were in the main floor ballroom. With him were Degnan, president of the supervisors' group; David Selden, president of the American Federation of Teachers, and, significantly, Van Arsdale, president of the Central Labor Council.

In a basement conference room were city and state education officials, among them Superintendent Donovan, John Doar and the Reverend Galamison of the board of education and two of Commissioner Allen's aides.

Across the hall, Lindsay waited with two deputy mayors.

Theodore Kheel, crack arbitrator, and Kenneth Clark, the black psychologist who served on the state board of regents, called Lindsay that morning with some new suggestions for settlement, and they were invited to the mansion. Whitney Young of the National Urban League was invited to join the group, and then Rhody McCoy and some of the Ocean Hill governing board. The Ocean Hill group met with Young and Clark in a room of the mansion's residence wing.

Kheel and Harold G. Israelson, the labor lawyer who had been instrumental in settling the 1967 teachers' strike, served as go-betweens, shuttling back and forth from group to group, carrying messages and encouragement, and, as the session dragged on and on, stepping over the bodies of nappers on the floor.

"There's a kind of a second sense you develop after having been around negotiations for years," Israelson said later. "You can sense when the parties have finally decided to make an agreement, and then you keep working at it until at a particular point you reach language that everybody can accept." Israelson's second sense helped hold the session together.

Mrs. Lindsay shuttled back and forth, too, serving hamburgers, ice cream and coffee.

These were some of the pieces of the agreement, hammered out in those long hours:

1. Ocean Hill was to be put under state trusteeship, with a representative of Commissioner Allen.

2. A special panel, responsible to the state, was named to investigate charges of violation of teachers' rights in all the city schools, not just Ocean Hill.

3. In Ocean Hill, the trustee was to see that all striking teachers were reinstated in their jobs, with teachers paired in classrooms where necessary, so that all teachers hired — the strikers and replacements — would have assignments.

4. The Ocean Hill-chosen principals, those the court had just ruled were appointed illegally, were to be removed, at least temporarily.

5. The Ocean Hill governing board, suspended October 6 when it refused to reassign the union teachers, was to continue under suspension until the commissioner was convinced it would comply with the agreement. Rhody McCoy and the remaining principals — also under suspension since October — were not to reassume their duties until they agreed to comply with the directives of the trustee.

6. No one in Ocean Hill would be admitted to any school there unless he had a child in that school or received the permission of the trustee.

7. Any dispute involving the involuntary transfer of an employee would be subject to the grievance procedure, including arbitration.

8. Staff meetings by either group of Ocean Hill teachers by themselves would not be permitted.

9. Longer school days would be scheduled and extra days added during vacation so striking teachers would lose no pay for the 36 days of the strikes.

Ocean Hill people, again, were not represented by the time agreement was finally announced. Oliver, McCoy and the others from Ocean Hill had left in bitterness about 7 a.m., Sunday morning, the second day of negotiations. The walkout came when they got the word that their three highly-regarded principals would be removed.

"It is obvious that the black and Puerto Rican people of the city are not going to be allowed to determine the future of their children," the Reverend Oliver said on the way out. "It is equally obvious that this may be the beginning of the end of Ocean Hill-Brownsville."

Gloom was deep in Ocean Hill. There was a community meeting there that Sunday night. Kenneth Clark and Whitney Young went to explain the agreement. They were accused of being "sell-outs" and "Uncle Toms," but Ocean Hill was powerless to affect the terms of the agreement.

It was the teachers who almost upset the settlement. At a union delegate assembly meeting, called for Sunday night after the long negotiating session, Shanker urged acceptance, but he too was greeted with cries of "sell-out." There were demands from the assembly for more time to consider the agreement. Shanker called the hecklers' behavior an "atrocity" and a "disgrace" and adjourned the session, postponing the balloting until the following day in the apparent belief that the agreement would be rejected if the voting were conducted that night.

In the process of reporting to the teachers, Shanker charged that Lindsay had "created racial welfare in this city." "Impeach Lindsay," came cries from the crowd.

Balloting was concluded the next day and Shanker reported the vote was 6 to 1 to call off the strike. Schools were to open the next day, November 19.

"I know some people blame Al Shanker for all this," one of Lindsay's advisers mused. "But it's not a matter of the very militant head of a union pulling the membership along with him. There are people on his side who are in on the negotiations because they're afraid he'll be too soft. The fear among some of the teachers and supervisors is really something. They say they're trying to protect the future of the union and the future of the system that got the supervisors where they are. But it's the past they're trying to protect, and you can do that only so long. What you see here, and what you're going to see in other institutions in this city, is the beginning of a shift of power. It won't happen peacefully. It never has. There'll be more tensions, more arrests, just plain more trouble. Those now in control will put up obstacles. The state legislature will. But in time the blacks and Puerto Ricnas will get their share of power, as others have before them."

There was "just plain more trouble" in Ocean Hill, the same kind of trouble there had been before, but it did not again lead to a teacher walkout. Some despondent residents and a large group of teachers, protesting the settlement, ran a sit-in in two of the schools overnight, but the trustee, representing the state commissioner, just kept the schools closed the next day until the people finally left.

The union teachers were reassigned. Fred Nauman, the UFT chapter chairman who had incurred such local wrath, was assigned to classes in J.H.S. 271. But the kids were hostile and they badgered him; they blamed him for the suspension of the school's principal and the popular teachers who were facing disciplinary charges. By afternoon of his first day back, Nauman, tense with frustration, was trying to make a seating chart for yet another noisy class. He asked one small boy his name, and the boy responded, "I'm not going to listen to you. Don't talk to me."

Nauman leaned over the boy's desk and saw, he said, that the boy's fist was doubled up, ready, Nauman thought, to hit him. He pushed the fist roughly against the desk, injuring the boy's thumb and almost bringing on a new showdown with the community.

Talking to a reporter, Nauman, who'd been born in Germany but was brought to New York in 1937 to escape the Nazi horror, talked of his pleasure in teaching in the Ocean Hill area.

"I think it's a lot more rewarding," he said, "to teach children that you have a lot to offer than to teach children that don't particularly need a teacher anyhow. They're going to get it by themselves."

Footnotes

1. Bernard Donovan interview in *Why Teachers Strike*, edited by Melvin Urofsky. Doubleday. New York. 1970.

2. This cycle and its devasting effect on white children as well as black is one of the recurring themes presented by Charles E. Silberman in his vast study of United States schools, *Crisis in the Classroom*. Random House. New York. 1970.

3. Martin Mayer, "The Full and Sometimes Very Surprising Story of Ocean Hill, the Teachers' Union and the Teacher Strikes of 1968," New York Times Magazine, Feb. 2, 1969.

4. Quoted in "The Very Expensive Education of McGeorge Bundy," by David Halberstam. Harper's, July, 1969.

5. Report of the National Advisory Commission on Civil Disorders. Bantam Books. March, 1969.

6. Board of Education Policy statement on decentralization, adopted in public session, April 19, 1967, quoted in *Confrontation at Ocean Hill-Brownsville*, edited by Maurice R. Berube and Marilyn Gittell. Praeger. New York, 1969.

7. Donovan interview in *Why Teachers Strike*.

8. Wilbur Nordos interview in *Why Teachers Strike*.

9. Mayer, *Op. cit.*

10. Albert Shanker interview in *Why Teachers Strike*.

11. Mayer, *Op cit.*

12. Rhody McCoy interview in *Why Teachers Strike*.

13. The statement is quoted from a report made on July 30, 1968, to the New York board of education by the board's advisory and evaluation committee on decentralization. Excerpts are reprinted in *Confrontation at Ocean Hill-Brownsville*.

14. The Burden of the Blame: NYCLU Report on the Ocean Hill-Brownsville School Controversy. Reprinted in *Confrontation at Ocean Hill-Brownsville*.

15. Speech by Rhody McCoy, January, 1968, reprinted in *Confrontation at Ocean Hill-Brownsville.*

16. Reconnection for Learning, the report of the Advisory Panel on Decentralization of the New York City Schools.

17. By-laws of the New York board of education, Section 105 a-1.

18. By-laws, Article II, Section 101.1

19. Report filed with board of education, July 3, 1968.

20. The Rivers report, dated August 26, 1968, is reprinted in full in *Confrontation at Ocean Hill-Brownsville.*

21. Berube and Gittell, *Op. Cit.*

22. Albert Shanker interview in *Why Teachers Strike.*

Discussion Questions

1. Many writers in the field of labor-management relatations have discussed multilateral bargaining. Is this present in this case? If so, what is its shape or form? How does it operate?

2. Differentiate between decentralization and community control; define their purposes. Are they compatible with each other? What part did they play in this case?

3. Examine the effect of local control of schools, or community services, upon union-management relations and upon the union members.

4. The New York teachers' strikes led to profound changes in the politics of New York City, the state of New York, and may have contributed to changes in national politics culminating in the 1972 presidential election. Examine these assumptions for their validity.

5. How can the public best be represented in the determination of school policy? How can public aims be reconciled with aims of the teachers and their unions?

6. Examine the proposition that a teachers' union — or for that matter any union — institutionalizes the conservatism of its membership and cannot therefore be expected to respond to changes, especially social changes, in any other way than outright resistance.

7. What are the critical issues involved between the United Federation of Teachers and the community school boards? How did they affect the case?

8. Everyone in the case, especially the parents, seemed to agree that achievement scores of New York pupils were declining. What does research suggest as the causes of this decline? How would the causes espoused in the case alter the decline?

9. What are the relationships between racial composition of schools and the issues in collective bargaining?

10. How can the public be protected against strikes by teachers or other public employees? If public employees are prohibited from striking, what forms of impasse interventions are feasible? If the public employees are prohibited from striking, what recourse do they have against acts of public employers to provoke a strike? What sanctions are available to impose on the public manager?

11. Could a strike, illegal under the law, gain legitimacy because of extreme provocation?

12. Acting on certain assumptions, the parents in this case brought about a chain of actions. Some of these assumptions were:
   a. White teachers are ruining black kids.
   b. The school bureaucracy doesn't listen to us and we are powerless to affect the education of our children.
   c. The union is hand-in-glove with the bureaucracy and is our enemy.
   d. The school system is racist.
In what ways did these assumptions determine the strategies of the parents, their demands, and their perceptions of the union, the central school board, and their own situation?

EPILOGUE

The Ocean Hill-Brownsville experimental district is gone, the victim of politics among the powerful.

The 1969 New York legislature fought a bitter battle over decentralization and finally passed a patchwork plan more pleasing to Albert Shanker than to John Lindsay. It abolished the appointed central school board, through which Lindsay had sought some degree of local control and called instead for a seven-member board, with one member elected from each of the city's five boroughs and two appointed by the mayor. The city was to be divided into between 30 and 33 local community school districts, with a minimum of 20,000 pupils (Ocean Hill-Brownsville was not big enough to qualify and was split up among other districts). It gave some powers to the local boards, but retained strong control of hiring, bargaining and other personnel functions in the central board.

Through the law and through subsequent court decisions, these powers have been assigned to the local boards:

*Hiring the district superintendent and the principals plus new teachers for schools with low reading scores:

*Choosing textbooks, subject to approval of the central board;

*Instituting curriculum changes or innovations;

*Sitting in on collective bargaining sessions between the central board and the unions, but contributing to negotiations in an advisory capacity only;

*Hiring school custodians and overseeing school maintenance;

*Presenting budget requests to the City Budget Director.

* * *

When the district school boards were chosen throughout the city in the 32 districts created by the new board, fewer than 15 percent of the parents voted; the winners tended to be white, and many of them were parents who favored public aid to parochial schools. This pattern was largely repeated in the second local board election in 1973. Shanker and the teachers' union played an active role in the local elections.

* * *

Bernard E. Donovan, the superintendent whom McCoy always described as "the sharpest guy in the business," retired from the superintendency in 1969 to become an educational consultant in Albany.

* * *

James E. Allen, Jr., the state commissioner whose plan finally brought peace to the New York schools, served briefly in the Nixon administration as head of the United States Office of Education. He left because of policy disagreements, and has since died.

* * *

New York's Taylor Act, the one that's supposed to forestall public employee strikes, is still on the books and still does not forestall all public employee strikes. The labor movement says the law is unfair, that it's unreasonable to deprive workers of the right to strike, and that the law "contributes to disputes, provokes strikes and penalizes unions for the just performance of their duty to their members."

Under the law, Justice Francis J. Bloustein of the State Supreme Court fined the United Federation of Teachers $220,000 for its illegal 1968 strikes. He also fined Shanker $250 and sentenced him to another 15 days in jail, a sentence that was appealed all the way to the United States Supreme Court before Shanker went to jail again.

The AFL-CIO Council, indignant over the Taylor Act it doesn't like, promptly shipped in $100,000 and launched a labor fund drive to pay the rest of the UFT's $220,000 fine.

Judge Bloustein wrote a 27-page opinion, in which he said he was limited to ruling on the Taylor Act violation and could not explore the issue of "extreme provocation" raised by the UFT in defense. He then explored it anyway, noting there was "uncontroverted evidence that known militants and extremists, strangers to the communities involved, contributed to the unrest and violence . . . There were daily confrontations of a destructive character. Whites against blacks, blacks against whites. Hate-mongering was current and anti-Semitism was practiced by many." He criticized the "appropriate governmental agencies" for failure to forestall the crisis.

* * *

In Ocean Hill, before the final demolition of the experimental project, there was continued unrest over the force applied to prevent local people from governing their schools. The first two trustees sent by Commissioner Allen from Albany didn't last long. The third was a man of remarkable understanding. His name was Wilbur R. Nordos; he and McCoy came to respect each other highly. Nordos once said that he thought often of a quote from a Columbia professor, "One of the greatest obstacles to change is the inability to imagine alternatives to the present situation."

In defending the Ocean Hill governing board before an audience of educators, Nordos said:

"I think that many people who grow up in any society imbibe a whole value system almost without knowing it. The ways we judge people and events reflect certain assumptions that we have taken for granted as being normative in our society, and we don't really question them. It's very difficult to question tenets that you don't know you have; they are so much a part of your habitual ways of evaluating persons and situations that you don't even think they are subject to debate. And one of these habits is that we still tend to judge people mainly on the basis of economic criteria. If a person hasn't made it economically, this is an adverse judgment on him as a total person. He is a second-rate person, a second-rate citizen; because if he were a first-rate person, he wouldn't be poor. A man's economic level is used as a measure of him as a total person. This I personally reject. Being poor does not of itself mean poor quality as a person. I think I knew this intellectually, but I learned it viscerally and operationally. When you get to the point where you get past what I call the 'Adam Smith hangup,' then you encounter a poor person as a real person and see him more totally.

"And when that black man, maybe even with some whiskey in him to keep his courage up, can tell you that the white man is ruining his kids and so on, and still feel your acceptance of him as a person with the right to speak out, then you are making it. Whatever may be the outward appearance, get past that first thing and be patient enough to connect with the man or woman who is trying to tell you something. When you can reach that place, you find that all people, not least the poor, have the full range of human qualities. I found, for example, that when people leveled about the school, about its deficiencies and all the rest, they were able to participate creatively and actively in solving school problems. They had patience, understanding, loyalty, generosity in judging teacher-pupil relationships, teacher-teacher relations, parent-home relationships, and so on. All you could ask for.

"Because there's an awful lot of wisdom that can be learned, or can arise from human experience, which is not taught in schools. Many of these poor people have a wisdom that you haven't got, that I haven't got, forged in the hot crucible of living and raising a family under very difficult circumstances. You find people willing to take a homeless child and, because they feel sorry for him, take him in and raise him

as their own. How many middle-class families do you know like
that? I don't know of any — very few at least. People who share their
poverty or their little temporary affluence, without worrying about
their savings for a rainy day. In our history, it used to be you had to
have certain property qualifications to be worthy of voting and deciding public policy, or be male or free and so on. This harks back to the
economic criteria for full citizenship . . . We still tend to think, you
see, that it's the persons of quality who should decide what's best
for those of less quality. *We* know what's best for them. There are,
of course, some disadvantages and problems with . . . a 'People's
board.' But in this situation and at this place and time they deserve
a chance to develop."

* * *

Out of the racial and religious tensions of the strike period was
born the militant Jewish Defense League.

* * *

Rhody McCoy left New York, where he had worked for two decades. For a while he had a chance to be superintendent of schools
in Washington, D.C., but the board there decided McCoy had been
"too divisive." So, in the late summer of 1970, McCoy went to Massa-
chusetts, where he became a part-time lecturer in the state university's
school of education.

* * *

The new central board of education hired Harvey B. Scribner,
former Vermont education commissioner, to take the new position
of chancellor of the New York schools, similar to superintendent. He'd
been there less than two months, in the fall of 1970, before incurring
the wrath of teachers and supervisors by proposing to scrap the board
of examiners and the traditional licensing system. The system, he said,
was "too impersonal, too inflexible to be responsive, too authoritarian
to allow independence, too single-minded to tolerate non-conformity,
too convinced of the rightness of their course to permit radical experimentation with unorthodox ways."

* * *

In the fall of 1972, Scribner and the central board, seeking both to
promote integration and to lessen overcrowding in a Brooklyn junior
high, transferred 32 black and Puerto Rican children from a Brownsville housing project to a junior high in Brooklyn's School District 18,
composed of largely Jewish and Italian families in the neighborhoods
of Canarsie and East Flatbush.

A familiar drama developed. White pupils and parents greeted the 32 Brownsville youngsters with jeers and epithets, trying to keep them out of the junior high school they viewed as their own. Police barricades were erected and whites and blacks faced each other daily across the barricades, sometimes slinging rocks and eggs along with racial epithets.

The white-dominated local school board sought to send the children to one of their schools that was largely black, but this was in violation of the central board's integration policy. The issue, said the local board, was community control of schools. Canarsie parents and children boycotted the schools for several weeks, while the central board and the local board wrangled over school zoning.

Albert Shanker's union teachers this time stayed in the schools and Shanker himself personally led teachers into one elementary school, condemned the boycott and deplored what he termed "mob rule" in the schools.

Shanker had predicted four years earlier that decentralization might be used by white neighborhood school boards against blacks, just as he maintained the Brownsville blacks were using community control against white teachers.

"We couldn't possibly support this boycott," said one union official, "even though some of our teachers out there are scared. You can't say that abuses of power by community school boards are bad when they're committed by blacks and perfectly understandable when they're commited by whites."

* * *

Dr. Kenneth Clark, the psychologist who was an early and ardent advocate of decentralization and community control, expressed disenchantment with the way the system was working. He said in 1972 that many involved in decentralization "have forgotten what the purpose was. The purpose was not a struggle for power or control. The purpose was to try to find some way in which the quality of education provided children in a particular school could be increased by more direct monitoring, supervision, more effective teaching accountability. I do not see that we have kept — or the local boards have concentrated on — quality and methods for raising quality as much as they have concentrated on power, actions, control of finances."

* * *

In December, 1972, Chancellor Scribner announced that he would not be a candidate for reappointment when his contract ran out the following June. He cited a widening gap of confidence between himself and the central board and added, "the distinction between policy and administration, which admittedly is difficult under the best of conditions, has become, at best, uneven and unpredictable."

His announcement brought mixed reactions. Mayor Lindsay said his departure would be a loss and that "he won the respect of the city for his vigorous style, his independent spirit and his unflagging commitment to justice and fair play." The head of the Civil Liberties Union warned that "if the school system now falls back into the hands of the career bureaucrats, then the cause of racial integration and student rights will be weakened and the future of the schools dim." The head of the Principals Association said his group had been disappointed because Scribner did not consult enough with the professional staff. And Albert Shanker said, "I think the system became further polarized during his administration."

APPENDIX

STATE OF NEW YORK PUBLIC EMPLOYEES' FAIR EMPLOYMENT
ACT (Summary)
(The Taylor Act, signed by Gov. Nelson Rockefeller on April 21,.
1967, to take effect on September 1, 1967)

Article 14

Sec. 200. Statement of policy.

The legislature of the state of New York declares that it is the public
policy of the state and the purpose of this act to promote harmonious
and cooperative relationships between government and its employees
and to protect the public by assuring, at all times, the orderly and uninterrupted operations and functions of government. These policies
are best effectuated by (a) granting to public employees the right of
organization and representation, (b) requiring the state, local governments and other political subdivisions to negotiate with and enter into
written agreements with employee organizations representing public
employees which have been certified or recognized, (c) creating a
public employment relations board to assist in resolving disputes between public employees and public employers, and (d) continuing the
prohibition against strikes by public employees and providing remedies
for violations of such prohibition.

Sec. 201. Definitions

(This section defines the terms used in the law, including a definition of "public employer" as including a school district, and the
meaning of strike as "any strike or other concerted stoppage of work
or slowdown by public employees.")

Sec. 202 Right of organization.

Public employees shall have the right to form, join and participate
in or to refrain from forming, joining, or participating in, any employee organization of their own choosing.

Sec. 203. Right of representation.

Public employees shall have the right to be represented by employee organizations to negotiate collectively with their public employers in the determination of their terms and conditions of employment, and the administration of grievances arising thereunder.

Sec. 204. Recognition and certification of employee organizations.

(This section requires public employers to recognize and negotiate collectively with employee organizations.)

Sec. 205. Public employment relations board.

1. There is hereby created in the state department of civil service a board, to be known as the public employment relations board, which shall consist of three members appointed by the governor, by and with the advice and consent of the senate from persons representative of the public. Not more than two members of the board shall be members of the same political party. Each member shall be appointed for a term of six years, except that of the members first appointed, one shall be appointed for a term to expire on May 31, 1969, one for a term to expire on May 31, 1971, and one for a term to expire on May 31, 1973. The governor shall designate one member as chairman of the board. A member appointed to fill a vacancy shall be appointed for the unexpired term of the member whom he is to succeed.

2. Members of the board shall hold no other public office or public employment in the state. The chairman shall give his whole time to his duties.

3. Members of the board other than the chairman shall, when performing the work of the board, be compensated at the rate of $100 per day, together with an allowance for actual and necessary expenses incurred in the discharge of their duties hereunder. The chairman shall receive an annual salary to be fixed within the amount available therefor by appropriation, in addition to an allowance for expenses actually and necessarily incurred by him in the performance of his duties.

4. The board may appoint an executive director and such other persons, including but not limited to mediators, members of fact-finding boards and representatives of employee organizations and public employers to serve as technical advisers to such fact-finding boards, as it may from time to time deem necessary for the performance of its functions, prescribe their duties, fix their compensation and provide for reimbursement of their expenses within the amounts made available therefor by appropriation.

5. In addition to the powers and functions provided in other

sections of this article, the board shall have the following powers and functions:

(a) To establish procedures consistent with the provisions of section 207 of this article and after consultation with interested parties, to resolve disputes concerning the representation status of employee organizations.

(b) To resolve, pursuant to such procedures, disputes concerning the representation status of employee organizations of employees of the state and state public authorities upon request of any employee organization, state department or agency or state public authority involved.

(c) To resolve, pursuant to such procedures but only in the absence of applicable procedures established pursuant to section 206 of this article, disputes concerning the representation status of other employee organizations, upon request of any employee organization or other government or public employer involved.

(d) To make studies and analyses of, and act as a clearing house of information relating to, conditions of employment of public employees throughout the state.

(e) To request from any government and such governments are authorized to provide such assistance services and data as will enable the board properly to carry out its functions and powers.

(f) To conduct studies of problems involved in representation and negotiation, including, but not limited to (i) whether employee organizations are to be recognized as representatives of their members only or are to have exclusive representation rights for all employees in the negotiating unit, (ii) the problems of unit determination, (iii) those subjects which are open to negotiation in whole or part, (iv) those subjects which require administrative or legislative approval of modifications agreed upon by the parties, and (v) those subjects which are for determination solely by the appropriate legislative body, and make recommendations from time to time for legislation based upon the results of such studies.

(g) To make available to employee organizations, governments, mediators, fact-finding boards and joint study committees established by governments and employee organizations statistical data relating to wages, benefits and employment practices in public and private employment applicable to various localities and occupations to assist them to resolve complex issues in negotiations.

(h) To establish, after consulting representatives of employee organizations and administrators of public services, panels of qualified persons broadly representative of the public to be available to serve as mediators or members of fact-finding boards.

(i) To hold such hearings and make such inquiries as it deems necessary for it properly to carry out its functions and powers.

(j) For the purpose of such hearings and inquiries, to administer oaths and affirmations, examine witnesses and documents, take testimony and receive evidence, compel the attendance of witnesses and the production of documents by the issuance of subpoenas, and delegate such powers to any member of the board or any person appointed by the board for the performance of its functions. Such subpoenas shall be regulated and enforced under the civil service practice law and rules.

(k) To make, amend and rescind, from time to time, such rules and regulations, including but not limited to those governing its internal organization and conduct of its affairs, and to exercise such other powers as may be appropriate to effectuate the purpose and provisions of this article.

6. Notwithstanding any other provisions of law, neither the president of the civil service commission nor the civil service commission nor any other officer, employer, board or agency of the department of civil service shall supervise, direct or control the board in the performance of any of its functions or the exercise of any of its powers under this article; provided, however, that nothing herein shall be construed to exempt employees of the board from the provisions of the civil service law.

Sec. 206. Procedures for determination of representation status of local employees.

(This section empowers local governmental units to establish procedures to resolve disputes concerning representation and provides that, if they do not act, the public employment relations board will do so.)

Sec. 207. Determination of representation status.

For purposes of resolving disputes concerning representation status, pursuant to section or 205 of this article, the board or government, as the case may be, shall

1. define the appropriate employer-employee negotiating unit, taking into account the following standards:

(a) the definition of the unit shall correspond to a community of interest among the employees to be included in the unit;

(b) the officials of government at the level of the unit shall have the power to agree, or to make effective recommendations to other administrative authority or the legislative body with respect to, the terms and conditions of employment upon which the employees desire to negotiate; and

(c) The unit shall be compatible with the joint responsibilities of the public employer and public employees to serve the public.

2. ascertain the public employees' choice of employee organization as their representative (in cases where the parties to a dispute have not agreed on the means to ascertain the choice, if any, of the employees in the unit) on the basis of dues deduction authorization and other evidences, or, if necessary, by conducting an election.

3. certify or recognize an employee organization upon (a) the determination that such organization represents that group of public employees it claims to represent, and (b) the affirmation by such organization that it does not assert the right to strike against any government, to assist or participate in any such strike, or to impose an obligation to conduct, assist or participate in such a strike.

Sec. 208. Rights accompanying certification or recognition.

A public employer shall extend to an employee organization certified or recognized pursuant to this article the following rights:

(a) to represent the employees in negotiations and in the settlement of grievances;

(b) to membership dues deduction, upon presentation of dues deduction authorization cards signed by individual employees; and

(c) to unchallenged representation status until the next succeeding budget submission date and, thereafter, for an additional period of either twelve months or, if the parties so agree, not less than twelve months nor more than twenty-four months, which period shall commence one hundred twenty days prior to such next succeeding budget submission date.

Sec. 209. Resolution of disputes in the course of collective negotiations.

1. For purposes of this section, an impasse may be deemed to exist if the parties fail to achieve agreement at least sixty days prior to the budget submission date of the public employer.

2. Public employers are hereby empowered to enter into written agreements with recognized or certified employee organizations setting forth procedures to be invoked in the event of disputes which reach

an impasse in the course of collective negotiations. In the absence or upon the failure of such procedures, public employers and employee organizations may request the board to render assistance as provided in this section, or the board may render such assistance on its own motion, as provided in subdivision 3 of this section.

3. On request of either party or upon its own motion, as provided in subdivision 2 of this section, and in the event the board determines that an impasse exists in collective negotiations between such employee organization and a public employer as to the conditions of employment of public employees, the board shall render assistance as follows:

(a) to assist the parties to effect a voluntary resolution of the dispute, the board shall appoint a mediator or mediators representative of the public from a list of qualified persons maintained by the board;

(b) if the impasse continues, the board shall appoint a fact-finding board of not more than three members, each representative of the public, from a list of qualified persons maintained by the board which fact-finding board shall have, in addition to the powers delegated to it by the board, the power to make public recommendations for the resolution of the dispute;

(c) if the dispute is not resolved at least fifteen days prior to the budget submission date, the fact-finding board, acting by a majority of its members, shall immediately transmit its findings of fact and recommendations for resolution of the dispute to the chief executive officer of the government involved, and to the employee organization involved, and shall simultaneously make public such findings and recommendations;

(d) in the event that the findings of fact and recommendations are made public by a fact-finding board established pursuant to procedures agreed upon by the parties under subdivision 2 of this section, and the impasse continues, the public employment relations board shall have the power to take whatever steps it deems appropriate to resolve the dispute, including the making of recommendations after giving due consideration to the findings of fact and recommendations of such fact-finding board, but no further fact-finding board shall be appointed;

(e) in the event that either the public employer or the employee organization does not accept in whole or part the recommendations of the fact-finding board, the chief executive officer of the government involved shall, within the five days after receipt of the findings of fact and recommendations of the fact-finding board, submit to the legislative body of the government involved a copy of the findings of fact and recommendations of the fact-finding board, together with his recommendations for settling the dispute; and the employee organization may submit to such legislative body its recommendations for settling the dispute.

Sec. 210. Prohibition of strike.

1. No public employee or employee organization shall engage in a strike, and no employee organization shall cause, instigate, encourage or condone a strike.

2. A public employee who violates the provisions of subdivision 1 of this section shall be subject to the disciplinary penalties provided by law for misconduct, in accordance with procedures established by law.

3.

(a) An employee organization which is determined by the board to have violated the provisions of subdivision 1 of this section shall, in accordance with the provisions of this section, lose the right granted pursuant to the provisions of paragraph (b) of section 208 of this chapter.

(b) In the event of a violation of subdivision 1 of this section, it shall be the duty of the chief executive officer of the public employer involved (i) forthwith to so notify the board and the chief legal officer of the government involved, and (ii) to provide the board and such chief legal officer with such facilities, assistance and data as will enable the board and such chief legal officer to carry out their duties under this section.

(c) In the event of a violation of subdivision 1 of this section, the chief legal officer of the government involved, or the board on its own motion, shall forthwith institute proceedings before the board to determine whether such employee organization has violated the provisions of subdivision 1 of this section.

(d) Proceedings against an employee organization under this section shall be commenced by service upon it of a written notice, together with a copy of the charges. A copy of such notice and charges shall also be served, for their information, upon the appropriate government officials who recognize such employee organization and grant to it the rights accompanying such recognition. The employee organization shall have eight days within which to serve its written answer to such charges. The board's hearing shall be held promptly thereafter and at such hearing, the parties shall be permitted to be represented by counsel and to summon witnesses in their behalf. Compliance with the technical rules of evidence shall not be required.

(e) In determining whether an employee organization has violated subdivision 1 of this section, the board shall consider (i) whether the employee organization called the strike or tried to prevent it, (ii) whether the employee organization made or was making good faith efforts to terminate the strike, and (iii) whether, if so alleged by the employee organization, the public employer or its representatives engaged in such acts of extreme provocation as to detract from the responsibility of the employee organization for the strike.

(f)   If the board determines that an employee organization has violated the provisions of subdivision 1 of this section, the board shall order forfeiture of the rights granted pursuant to the provisions of paragraph (b) of section 208 of this chapter, for a specified period of time, as the board shall determine, but in no event to exceed eighteen months; provided, however, that where a fine imposed on an employee organization pursuant to subdivision 2 of section 751 of the judiciary law remains wholly or partly unpaid, after the exhaustion of the cash and securities of the employee organization, the board shall direct that, notwithstanding such forfeiture, such membership dues deduction shall be continued to the extent necessary to pay such fine and such public employer shall transmit such moneys to the court.

(g)   An employee organization whose rights granted pursuant to the provisions of paragraph (b) of section 208 of this chapter have been ordered forfeited pursuant to this section may be granted such rights after the termination of such forfeiture only after complying with the provisions of clause (b) of subdivision 3 of section 207 of this article.

4.   Orders of the board made pursuant to this article (including, but not limited to, orders made pursuant to subdivision 3 of this section) shall be (a) reviewable under article 78 of the civil practice law and rules, and (b) enforceable, upon petition of such board, by the supreme court, which shall have jurisdiction of the proceeding and the power to grant such temporary relief or affirmative or restraining orders as it deems just and proper.

Sec. 211. Application for injunctive relief.

Notwithstanding the provisions of section 807 of the labor law, where it appears that public employees or an employee organization threaten or are about to do, or are doing, an act in violation of sec. 210 of this article, the chief executive officer of the government involved shall (a) forthwith notify the chief legal officer of the government involved, and (b) provide such chief legal officer with such facilities, assistance and data as will enable the chief legal officer to carry out his duties under this section, and, notwithstanding the failure or refusal of the chief executive officer to act as aforesaid, the chief legal officer of the government involved shall forthwith apply to the supreme court for an injunction against such violation. If an order of the court enjoining or restricting such violation does not receive compliance, such chief legal officer shall forthwith apply to the supreme court to punish such violation under section 750 of the judiciary law.

Sec. 212. Local government procedures.

(This section provides for local procedures to take precedence where they have been approved by the public employment relations board. It further provides that New York City need not submit its local procedure for settling disputes to the board and that such procedures shall be in full force unless a court rules the New York City procedure to be out of line with the state provisions.)

Section 751 of the judiciary law is hereby amended to read as follows: Sec. 751. Punishment for criminal contempts.

(Punishment)

1. Except as provided in subdivision (2), punishment for a contempt, specified in section 750, may be by fine, not exceeding $250, or by imprisonment, not exceeding thirty days, in the jail of the county where the court is sitting, or both, in the discretion of the court. Where a person is committed to jail, for the nonpayment of such a fine, he must be discharged at the expiration of thirty days; but where he is also committed for a definite time, the thirty days must be computed from the expiration of the definite time.

Such a contempt, committed in the immediate view and presence of the court, may be punished summarily; when not so committed, the party charged must be notified of the accusation, and have a reasonable time to make a defense.

2.(a) Where an employee organization, as defined in section 201 of the civil service law, willfully disobeys a lawful mandate of the court of record, or willfully offers resistance to such lawful mandate, in a case involving or growing out of a strike in violation of subdivision 1 of section 210 of the civil service law, the punishment for each day that such contempt persists may be by a fine fixed in the discretion of the court in an amount equal to one fifty-second (1/52) of the total amount of annual membership dues of such employee organization or ten thousand dollars, whichever is the lesser; provided, however, that where an amount equal to one fifty-second part (1/52) of the total amount of annual membership dues of such employee organization is less than one thousand dollars, such fine may be fixed in the sum of $1,000. In the case of a government exempt from certain provisions of article 14 of the civil service law, pursuant to section 212 of such law, the court may, as an additional punishment for such contempt, order forfeiture of the rights granted pursuant to the provisions of paragraph (b) of section 208 of such law, for a specified period of time, as the court shall determine, but in no event to exceed eighteen months; provided, however, that where a fine imposed pursuant to this subdivision remains wholly or partly unpaid, after the exhaustion of the cash and securities of the employee organization, such forfeiture shall be suspended to the extent necessary for the unpaid portion of such fine to be accumulated by the public employer and transmitted to the court. In fixing the amount of the fine and/or duration of the forfeiture, the court shall consider all the facts and circumstances directly related to the contempt, including, but not limited to: (i) the extent of the willful defiance of or resistance to the court's mandate, (ii) the impact of the strike on the public health, safety, or welfare of the community and (iii) the ability of the employee organization to pay the fine imposed; and the court may consider (i) the refusal of the employee organization or the appropriate public employer, as defined in section 201 of the civil service law, or the representatives thereof, to submit to the mediation and fact-finding procedures provided in section 201 of the civil service law and (ii) whether, if so alleged by the employee organization, the appropriate public employer or its representatives engaged in such acts of extreme provocation as to detract from the responsibility of the employee organization for the strike.

(b) In the event membership dues are collected by the public employer as provided in paragraph (b) of section 208 of the civil service law, the books and records of such public employer shall be prima facie evidence of the amount so collected.

(c) The term "total amount of annual membership dues of the employee organization" as used in paragraph (a) of this subdivision, shall include initiation fees, periodic dues, and all assessments collected by such employee organization in the twelve-month period preceding the contempt attributable to the members of such employee organization in that part of the collective negotiation unit actually on strike; provided, however, that if such strike effectively prevents the functioning of the entire collective negotiation unit or units represented by such employee organization, it shall mean such fees,

dues, and assessments attributable to the total number of
members of the employee organization in such unit or units.

(d)   (i) An employee organization appealing an adjudication and
fine for criminal contempt imposed pursuant to subdivision
2 of this section, shall not be required to pay such fine until
such appeal is finally determined.

(ii) The court to which such an appeal is taken shall, on motion
of any party thereto, grant a preference in the hearing thereof.

Taylor Act Revision

The Taylor Act was revised in the 1969 legislative session to provide
tougher penalties on unions or employees striking against government
agencies. Taylor himself has termed the changes "unduly harsh."

The *New York Times* of June 8, 1969, said Taylor "expressed the
opinion that the public employee labor relations in the state had
developed a 'cycle of futility' with some big and powerful unions conducting illegal strikes, followed by legislative action establishing stiffer
penalties.

"The changes in the statute would mandate the loss of two days'
pay for individual strikers for each day they were on strike and also
a year's probation with loss of job tenure. The previous version of the
act contained no such penalties for individual employees.

"The amended version of the law also permits unlimited fines against
striking unions of government employees and for unlimited suspension
of their dues check-off -- a procedure by which the employer takes dues
from an employee's earnings and pays the money directly to the union.

"The original Taylor Law, passed in 1967, limited fines to $10,000
a day and the check-off suspension to 18 months.

"Although Dr. Taylor questioned the toughened penalties, he made
it clear that he was holding firm to the view expressed in his committee's
recommendations to the Governor that strikes by public employees
should not be permitted.

"The real issue now, he said, is the demand of some public employee
unions that they be given the right to strike and the conviction of the
public generally that such strikes should not be allowed.

"Dr. Taylor said that he was concerned by what he called "a run
on the bank" for state and municipal services and for higher wages and
benefits. He emphasized the close relationship between the problems
of the government employee and society's problems in such areas as
education, health, safety and sanitation.

" 'I am concerned with the preservation of representative government,'
he said. 'I do not believe that you can run a society if you always give
the lion's share to the lion.' "

Introduction

Like Ocean Hill-Brownsville, this case arose from the profound social ferment which swept the United States in the 1950's and 1960's. The ferment was fueled by and in turn fueled the efforts to secure changes in the law and conditions of life of the black minorities of the nation.

The Supreme Court decision in Brown v. Board of Education in 1954 had outlawed school segregation. The Montgomery, Alabama, bus boycott the following year catapulted the Rev. Martin Luther King, Jr., into national prominence and brought into being the Southern Christian Leadership Conference and its non-violent attempts to achieve equal rights for blacks.

This was in reality a revolution in the expectations of America's minorities, characterized by their rejection of second class citizenship and the demand that minorities be accorded equal access not only to eating facilities and seats on the bus, but also to jobs, housing, and participation in the political process. But changing large institutions and entrenched ways of living and believing has proved difficult. The provision of job opportunities has proved particularly so.

The March on Washington in 1963 was called to dramatize the need for jobs and to stimulate the federal government to commit itself to action on the job front. The Civil Rights Act of 1964, together with various executive orders to assure equal employment opportunities under all federal contracts, followed.

Although blacks were hired in increasing numbers, mass unemployment and underemployment remained and they played a part in the riots of the late 1960's. As Dr. Vivian Henderson pointed out in his testimony before the National Advisory Committee on Civil Disorders:

> No one can deny that all Negroes have benefited from civil rights laws and desegregation in public life in one way or another. The fact is, however, that the masses of Negroes have not experienced tangible benefits in a significant way. This is so in education and housing. It is critically so in the area of jobs and economic security. Expectations of Negro masses for equal job opportunity programs have fallen far short of fulfillment.

Thus the stage was set for this case, concerning the demands of a minority to equal treatment and equal opportunity in employment, meaning access to all jobs, not merely the menial tasks assigned by the powerful to the weak.

The point of attack is the craft union and construction contractors which had systematically excluded blacks from the crafts and had not responded effectively to the social ferment of the era. The mode of action was confrontation in the streets and the use of street gangs as support troops.

In this case, society began to experiment with changed rules and structures to assure equal opportunity in the crafts, the task being one of achieving equality for one group without jeopardizing the rights possessed by another group.

Public policy and politics are intertwined from the federal to the city levels. Collective bargaining seemed to take new forms and cover new kinds of issues.

Chronology

1963	A federal judge in Chicago ruled that a structural iron-workers union was "invidiously discriminatory" in its apprenticeship program.
1964	Civil Rights Act passed by Congress, outlawing discrimination in many areas of employment, including discrimination by unions.
1965	President Lyndon B. Johnson issued executive order 11246, prohibiting contractors who do business with the federal government from discriminating on the basis of race, creed, color or national origin and requiring employers to take affirmative action to insure equal employment opportunity.
Fall 1965	Mayor Richard J. Daley, prodded by the Labor Department, announced a campaign to bring minorities into the building trades in Chicago and to open up Washburne Trade School, where most apprenticeship programs are conducted, to blacks and other minorities. The program led to some improvements but they were minimal compared to the numbers of persons involved.
June 1969	Federal officials announced the Philadelphia Plan, with specific goals for minority employment by any construction contractors on federally-aided jobs. They said similar plans for other cities would be forthcoming soon.
July 1969	The Coalition for United Community Action, representing many black neighborhood groups in Chicago, launched a dramatic campaign for jobs and training programs for blacks. By picketing and demonstrating, the Coalition closed down more than $80 million worth of big building projects.
August 1969	The construction industry sought an injunction against the Coalition and its leaders. Some Coalition leaders later were jailed for violating the injunction.
September 1969	A series of frustrating negotiating sessions between the Coalition on the one hand and the construction industry and unions on the other failed to produce agreement. The

industry and unions proposed a plan for minority training; the Coalition turned it down because it contained no guarantees; the industry announced it would put the plan into effect without the Coalition.

September 1969 — A team of federal officials concerned with equal opportunity employment enforcement surveyed the situation and agreed with the Coalition's figures on the lack of opportunity for blacks. A federal hearing on the subject led to a near-riot by white construction workers who felt their own jobs were threatened.

Fall 1969 — Mayor Daley, fearing a riot, entered the negotiations for a Chicago Plan that would assure jobs for blacks (without the federal coercion of the Philadelphia Plan). Negotiations broke down a number of times.

January 1970 — Agreement was reached on the Chicago Plan. The federal government, which provided funds, agreed to hold off on official sanctions or on the establishment of firm employment goals, to give the plan a chance to work.

"We're taking over. Get out," one of a group of seventeen black youths told a secretary who had just unlocked the doors to the offices of the Chicago Building Trades Council.

The youths, some of them wearing the berets of different colors that traditionally mark membership in assorted Chicago street gangs, swarmed into the offices and barricaded the doors with furniture so no one else could get in.

The date was July 22, 1969. The moment was the dramatic public launching of a new campaign by black people to get more jobs in the tightly-controlled building trades, a campaign that was to reach a climax within a month with the shutting down of more than $80 million worth of big building projects in Chicago.

Barricaded in the offices of the Chicago Building Trades Council, the black youths refused to admit Thomas J. Murray, the aging president of the Council, and the Council's secretary-treasurer, Thomas J. Nayder.

When police were called, the youths moved the furniture away from the doors and came out quietly to face arrest.

A Demand for Jobs Now

Nearby on that same summer morning about 100 more blacks, many of them also street gang members, were picketing the construction site of the big, new, glass and steel First National Bank building, in the heart of the Chicago loop. At the site they passed out leaflets demanding:

* 10,000 on-the-job training positions for blacks within 90 days;
* Immediate promotion of all blacks with four years' experience to foreman or supervisory positions on present and future construction within the black community;
* No testing programs before entering on-the-job training;
* Union initiation fees to be spread over a period of time;
* Abolition of the union hiring hall system, under which a contractor calls a union hall for workers, and the union selects the men to work (five of the 19 Chicago trades have some variation of this system);

* No future construction in the black community until the community approves the plans;
* Unions that discriminate against blacks to be expelled from the AFL-CIO;
* Union locals confined to a single ethnic group or race to be abolished.

Each of the demands — and they were to shift somewhat as the campaign gathered steam — represented sore points much discussed in the black community but not very widely understood among whites.

At the Building Trades Council office, Murray and Nayder, the officers, assured the press that the black pressure was misdirected when it was used against them.

"The council does not negotiate contracts," Nayder said. "It does not control the apprentice training systems developed between unions, contractors, the Board of Education and the government. It does not recruit workers for any of the trades. It does not have a hiring hall. It does not have any influence at all on the dues structure of any local unions."

Added Lester Asher, legal adviser to the Council, "Building trades workers don't go for this sort of thing. The building trades are making sure blacks get into the apprentice program. I hope this does not make the situation worse because many of the workers who have built these unions won't take kindly to this."

The Shut-Down Process

And indeed they did not take kindly to it, particularly when more than 1,200 construction workers were idled with the shutting down of about 20 big construction projects. The shut-down process worked this way:

The black group would pick targets for the day: a hospital addition, a housing project, a part of a new subway system. Each was a project in which government at some level had a financial stake, so there were public funds involved in the construction. Each was in a black neighborhood, or one with a high proportion of black people. One hundred or more young blacks, including gang members, would arrive at the selected construction site, sometimes on foot, sometimes in bus loads. They would march around the construction site fences, or sometimes cross over the fences into the building area, shouting, telling the workers to "get off our turf," sometimes threatening more than talk. Some carried signs, "How Would You Like a Fire?" or "You Can't Stop Bullets." Some carried baseball clubs or pool cues (they called them "walking sticks") and some picked up pieces of pipe or two-by-fours from the building sites. A spokesman would approach the site superintendent and ask him — or tell him — to shut down the site. "You had better get off the job," he might say, "because we don't know how long we can contain this group."

There was little violence. For the most part, the demonstrations were tightly disciplined. Police were informed in advance of the target sites and were present to observe. In all the projects, only a few white workers were ever touched by anyone in the black groups. But the intimidation was real, perhaps because the projects were in black neighborhoods and some white workers were a shade nervous about being there anyway. The sites were shut down.

The Coalition and Its Leaders

Behind the campaign was a new group called the Coalition for United Community Action, which said it represented 61 community organizations. The chief strategist was a young Drake University graduate named David Reed, who had acquired considerable political know-how as a candidate for congress from a Chicago district and a staff member of Illinois Governor Richard B. Ogilvie's human resources commission. Reed had been needling the United States Justice Department about its lack of action in enforcing provisions of the 1964 Civil Rights Act which outlawed racial discrimination by unions. Reed had joined the Coalition in June, only a few weeks before the picketing started, served as chairman of the strategy committee, and prepared a position paper for the campaign. It was called "Economic Slavery" and stated broad objectives for the campaign, but it was never submitted to contractors or unions in the construction industry.

One paragraph of Reed's paper said the Coalition should "organize mass marches on labor unions and should not relent until labor meets the demands of our times. In addition to mass marches on the various locals, we should and must picket all new construction in Chicago. Unless our men are put to work immediately as trainees in the various trades, without waiting to be put on the list for an apprenticeship program where they have to qualify based on some ridiculous scholastic requirements, we should move to halt all construction in Chicago's downtown area."[1]

Reed was often the leader who approached the site superintendent with the demand for a shut-down. Tall and powerfully built, he's a hard-headed but reasonable activist, intense but not given to shouting. He was very much a part of what young black people call "the movement."

Other top Coalition leaders in the summer of 1969 were the Rev. C. T. Vivian, one-time aide to the Rev. Martin Luther King, Jr., much more flamboyant and dramatic than Reed, and the Rev. Curtis Burrell, president of the Kenwood-Oakland Community Organization (KOCO), a Southside Chicago neighborhood group organized on grass roots lines to grapple with the hard issue of getting power for people who just don't have any.

Another Coalition leader, one around whom much white opposition centered, was Leonard Sengali, an executive organizer for the Rev. Burrell's KOCO and a leader of the Black P Stone Nation, a confederation of about 50 of the much-feared street gangs. (Sengali, who was originally Leonard Dickerson, chose a more African-sounding name, as many other militant blacks have done in the past few years.) Sengali was to become even more controversial as the construction struggle continued. Later he was to be arrested and charged with murder, in what many black people believed was a political frame-up to discredit the Coalition. The whites in the construction industry made no secret of the fact that, all along, they didn't like dealing with Sengali or with any of the street gang members.

The Coalition was armed with the facts that indicated deeply-rooted discrimination in the industry and with the increasingly heady sense of the black liberation movement. Starting with a base of absolutely no power, it rapidly succeeded in tying the city in knots, provoking a confrontation reminiscent of the union organizing drives of the 1930s and opening up a whole new dimension in the collective bargaining process.

A Background of Exclusion

What were the facts? They are complex and there is some right on both sides, a reality that is frequently lost from sight in moments of dramatic public confrontation. But at least some of the facts are not in dispute; no one really denies that for many decades of the nation's history blacks were systematically excluded, with few exceptions, from the lucrative construction jobs tightly controlled by the old line craft unions.

Historical studies of the construction industry are clear about that exclusion. Craft unions in the building trades sometimes had written restrictions against Negro membership; more of them simply kept blacks out by tacit consent. Some international unions set up separate locals for blacks, and they had unequal chance at the good jobs. There was a long tradition in some areas, for example, of allowing black tradesmen to work on construction only in their own neighborhoods, on small jobs the white tradesmen didn't want. Some union locals had black members but wouldn't let them vote. Other unions had many black members and did let them vote, but these were unions established in trades that already had many black workers; the unions needed them in order to organize effectively. Control over the labor supply was often as important a motive for discrimination as racial prejudice was.[2]

About some of the newer facts there was some dispute. The unions contend that their past sins are past and that they are actively working to bring more non-whites into apprenticeship training. Some of them have worked hard at recruiting, not always with great success for a variety of reasons, among them the fact that job patterns are deeply entrenched and the black community has so long been conditioned not to expect a fair shake in the construction business. Recent Chicago figures do show increases in Negro apprentices, significant in percentages but still very small in actual numbers. Black people discount the apprenticeship effort, say the numbers are too small to have any real effect on the industry, and are seeking other ways to enter the trades. They contend that the old overt discrimination has merely gone underground and that many steps which at first seemed to be reform have served instead to institutionalize discriminatory practices.

The struggle against those practices wasn't new to Chicago; the 1969 construction shut-downs made up a new chapter in the story, a very dramatic one, one that seemed loaded with dangerous potential for serious trouble between blacks and whites.

Federal government people, who soon came hustling into the city to help ease the tension, produced a detailed report concluding that of about 90,000 construction trade workers in 19 building trade unions in the Chicago area, only 3.3 percent were black. The Building Trades Council has taken issue with some of the figures, but the government table of union-by-union membership shows a range from no black members in the lathers and sprinkler fitters and only one member each in the glaziers and the architectural ironworkers to 20 percent in the cement masons and 12.5 percent in the plasterers. The groups with the largest percentage of black members are among the lowest paid of these skilled craft workers and do some of the dirtiest work in construction, jobs that throughout the nation have been more apt to be open to blacks.

The government figures, for journeymen tradesmen only and not for apprentices, show:

	1969 Journeymen	Minorities	% Minorities
Asbestos Workers	800	3	0.4
Brick Layers	4400	200	4.5
Carpenters	29300	200	0.7
Cement Masons	2500	500	20.0
Electricians	7831	300	3.8

	1969 Journeymen	*Minorities*	*%Minorities*
Elevator Installers	625	1	0.2
Glaziers	400	1	0.3
Iron Workers:			
Architectural	907	1	0.1
Ornamental	1000	1	0.1
Structural	2300	12	0.5
Metal Lathers	700	0	0
Painters	11000	350	3.2
Pipe Fitters	7800	16	0.2
Plasterers	800	100	12.5
Plumbers	3440	100	2.9
Roofers	1070	74	6.9
Sheet Metal Workers	4668	4	0.1
Sprinkler Fitters	260	0	0
Operating Engineers	8000	486	4.6
Total	87,801	2,349	

Source: Bureau of Labor Statistics, North Central Regional Office, September 10, 1969. The percentage of journeymen who were minority group members was 2.7. When apprentices were included, the total employment figure was 92,095, of which 3.3 percent were minorities.

Union discrimination on the basis of race had been outlawed by the AFL-CIO for at least 10 years and by federal law since the Civil Rights Act of 1964, but the Coalition claimed these policies and the law had made little actual difference in the facts of discrimination, that the trades had merely found newer and subtler ways to keep blacks out.

Many of the unions, particularly those who have had active recruiting programs among blacks, are resentful of the charges and say that if they could find more black apprentices the black share of construction jobs would obviously increase. The blacks reply that apprenticeship isn't as open as it sounds, that many of the standards that have been written into the programs still serve to keep out black youth. They further claim that the whole apprenticeship system is out of tune with the times and that the majority of white construction workers never went through apprenticeship at all but learned their skills on the job. They claim that excessive adherence to the apprenticeship route is a new restriction against blacks.

Apprenticeship at Washburne Trade School

It's a fairly old argument in Chicago, one that has centered in the past around Washburne Trade School, where the majority of the trades have their apprentice programs. The programs are jointly sponsored by the unions, the construction industry, the Chicago Board of Education and the federal government. Because of the public funds involved, Washburne Trade School has long been fair game for attack by civil rights groups. One aspect of the problem is that a prospective student doesn't just go to the school and apply. He must first apply to the union in which he's interested, take the union's tests and answer its interviewers, then wait for an opening in the apprentice program if he is considered to be qualified. The openings are determined in part by the economics of the industry. When it is expanding, more apprenticeships are open. The number of apprentices is a proportion, usually 1 to 4, of the number of journeymen employed.

Past efforts to open up Washburne Trade School and other apprentice programs to more black youths did bear some fruit in Chicago in the last half of the 1960s. The efforts were made by some union and industry representatives, the Chicago Urban League and state, local and national government officials and included recruiting efforts, counseling and special pre-apprenticeship courses. A key role was played by Orvis Wertz, deputy regional director of the United States Department of Labor's Bureau of Apprenticeship and Training; he helped launch the program and his office has kept track of the results.

"Many of the unions were very cooperative," he said. "This doesn't mean there are not still some real staunch bigots out there, but a lot of the union leaders laid their reputations and their jobs on the line to help. They are elected by the membership and it was indeed courageous for some to take the stand they did."

At no time, Wertz continued, were the combined community efforts sufficient to produce enough black youth to fill the slots available for apprentice training. Many of the youth who first seemed interested were unable to meet the qualifications established by the joint apprenticeship committees for entry into the trades.

Among the qualifications for most trades, for example, is a high school diploma or a passing grade on a commonly used test that is supposed to indicate knowledge equivalent to a high school education. More black youth than white are apt to drop out of their discouraging schools and even those who stay frequently find their educations deficient compared to whites. Many groups have suggested that possession of a high school diploma may not be particularly relevant but the apprenticeship committees, made up of industry and union men who are proud of their crafts, feel that it is, that it provides a certain basic level of necessary knowledge and indicates, too, the ability of a young man to stick to his job.

Despite a complex of problems, Wertz's figures do indicate some successes. In 1965, when the special programs were started, only about

2 per cent of the apprentices in Chicago were black, Wertz said. Detailed figures, trade by trade, are available only for 1968 and 1969, but they show that 6.7 per cent of the apprentices were non-whites on June 30, 1968, and 8.8 per cent were non-whites on June 30, 1969, just before the Coalition opened its campaign. They show, too, that for each six-month period in 1968 and 1969, from 10 to 16 per cent of the new recruits to apprenticeship training were non-whites.

Despite the increased percentages of black apprentices, the total picture was discouraging. In June, 1969, in all the trades, there were only 378 black apprentices, a pitifully small figure in a huge city where blacks make up about a third of the population and perhaps 15 percent of the labor force. That's one reason why the Coalition chose to by-pass the whole apprenticeship question, saying it simply does not serve the needs of the time and is never going to bring in enough blacks to provide their fair share of the jobs. The Coalition made it increasingly clear that it was seeking some other kind of on-the-job training, supervised by black people wherever possible, to bring blacks in in greater numbers. The Coalition wanted a training program that the unions did not run.

The industry and the unions, on the other hand, grew increasingly defensive about apprenticeship, emphasizing that the enrollment figures did show progress. Apprenticeship does hold a special place in the hearts of tradesmen; there's a sort of camaraderie involved and it represents the passing on of the skills they're proud of. And through it all runs a basic economic question; keeping large numbers out (not just blacks) helps keep high the price that is paid for their skills, the unions' product in the marketplace.

As one of the Building Trades Council's attorneys, Marvin Gittler, put it, "We tried to explain to the Coalition the difference between discrimination and exclusion. The trades never went out of their way to discriminate against blacks, but as a matter or practice, did try to exclude all so they could control the numbers."[3]

The distinction was not a valid one to members of the Coalition, because it all added up to the same thing for blacks.

Coalition Distrust

The Coalition began to stress more and more that the on-the-job training it was seeking should be training supervised by black people wherever possible, contending that the traditional ways had merely served to train young black people out, not in. It appeared to observers that some of the Coalition's objectives were shifted, altered, and refined somewhat as the movement gathered steam. And it surely did gather steam. Not for years had there been one cause that so rallied

the black community behind it. At one peak of tension, more than
5,000 people jammed Chicago's Civic Center plaza to hear Coalition
leaders and the Rev. Jesse Jackson lambaste the construction industry
and to hear him say to the unions, "You didn't trust us in the 1930s
and we don't trust you now."

Some of the Coalition's changes in emphasis were the result of the
bargaining process it felt it was engaged in. For example, the Coalition
gave up the original demand for 10,000 construction jobs within 90
days, but drew up a list calling for 30 percent participation in each
trade within five years, with one-fifth of those jobs — 5,000 — to be
delivered in the first year. But the shifting demands tended to confuse
the public and the construction industry people at whom the demands
were addressed. There was considerable confusion about just what was
going on. It was confusion compounded by consternation.

"Their first demand was for 10,000 jobs immediately," Gittler
reminisced later. "Well, our first reaction had to be, that's impossible.
We've been told since that that was a bargaining position, asking for
more than they intended to get, but we certainly weren't convinced
about that at the time of the demonstrations. We really just didn't
know. We didn't know who they were and they didn't know who we
were. Actually, the Coalition didn't know what it wanted, or the
entity it was dealing with, or how to achieve its aims."

Gittler recalled that there was much initial confusion among contractors and unions about how to deal with the Coalition, or even
whether to deal with the Coalition

"One position was that we ought not to meet at all," he said. "Others
said we shouldn't meet until they halted the shutdowns. Then we
realized that they were paralleling union activity and the unions
couldn't very well refuse to meet on that ground."

Gittler recalled, too, rather candidly, that "at the beginning, we
were so wrapped up with their methods that we didn't really look
so much at their aims. One of the big stumbling blocks was that we
didn't want to deal with the gangs. Our people thought they were
hooligans and punks."

An Attempt at Negotiation

But there were meetings early in August, while the demonstrations
continued on the streets. Gittler recalls that the groups met first in
a large room with an aisle down the center, trades and employers on
the right, and the Coalition on the left.

"The meeting was very tense," he said. "No one trusted anyone.
There was a dispute about how the table should be placed. Then a dispute about who should move it. Meredith Gilbert[4] announced he was

the spokesman for the Coalition. He sat there with two hat guys —
that's what we'd started calling the gang members, with their berets
— behind him, threatening more shut-downs. That was interesting to
us; it was the first time anyone ever threatened us, the unions, with
shutdowns. That really was a unique feature: employers and unions
on the same side of the aisle, even though there were very real animosities between them over the next round of wage increases. I guess
their rhetoric drew us closer together."

It was not possible at first, Gittler said, even to draw up an agenda
for discussions. Meanwhile, the demonstrations went on.

The Contractors go to Court

The 20 big sites had been shut down — and were still shut down —
by August 12, when the contractors affected and two associations of
building contractors decided to go into court to seek an injunction
against any further disruptive action by the Coalition. Their complaint
listed 23 defendants; among them were Reed, Gilbert, Burrell, Vivian
and Sengali, plus some other individuals, the Coalition itself and nine
organizations that were part of the Coalition, three of them street
gangs: the Black P Stone Nation, the Black Disciples, and the Conservative Vice Lords.

The defendants have "engaged in a combination conspiracy and concerted action by threats, intimidation, coercion and violence" to force
the employers to comply with their demands, the complaint stated.

The demands not only sought work for blacks, the complaint continued, but sought "to force members of the Building Construction
Employers Association . . . to violate, breach and rescind collective
bargaining agreements validly entered into with the various relevant
building trade unions in Cook County," and to breach subcontracts
with white subcontractors in favor of black subcontractors, and "to
cease doing any construction work in the so-called black area of
Chicago."

An injunction was issued, prohibiting harassment of construction
workers and prohibiting demonstrations at the job sites by more than
six persons.

After the judge signed the injunction, the Rev. Burrell called it an
example of "institutions working against the black people. Now you
see collaboration against us by the police department, the Builders
Association, and the courts." He said "our people" would decide
whether the order would be obeyed, and he referred to the judge as
"an oppressive judge in the white courts."

Coalition leaders said the next day they would ignore the court
order, and mass picketing did resume later, but not on such a wide
scale. It became focused chiefly on the University of Illinois construc-

tion site just west of Chicago's loop.

There was more action in meeting rooms, too. O'Neil had told the judge that unions and contractors had met with the Coalition three times, but had failed to reach the point where they could talk about the the real issues. At each meeting, Coalition spokesmen insisted that Building Trades Council and Builders Association representatives must come with the authority to nullify contracts their members held with each trade and be prepared to negotiate new ones. At each meeting, Murray, the Council president, answered that the 19 unions would never give him that power, and O'Neil, representing the contractors, said he was in a similar position. Murray told the blacks that the Council's function is to organize the industry, settle jurisdictional disputes between crafts, and foster good public relations for the unions. It never negotiates contracts, which each union does for itself, he said. He suggested the Coalition should negotiate separately with each union. The Rev. Vivian proposed that any new agreements negotiated by the Council leaders might be subject to ratification by members of each union, but Murray said the unions would not grant him even that much bargaining power. With that stalemate, each of the three meetings had broken up.

(The issue, concerning the power of the Building Trades Council, was one of the intriguing enigmas in the dispute. Doubtless Murray was technically correct about the power of the Council to enter into binding agreement, but technically correct positions don't always fit all the realities of power. The Coalition had some recent history on its side in going to the Council itself rather than to each trade, local by local. Earlier in the 1960s, similar coalitions of black organizations had shut down public construction projects in other cities, but not in Chicago, and had won some commitments from Building Trade Councils.[5] And the effort finally paid off in Chicago, too. The Chicago Plan that was finally neogiated did have the Building Trades Council's president as a signer; the Council also recommended that the individual unions go along with the agreement. But all along the way, that issue of autonomy was troublesome.)

A week after the court hearing in Chicago, on August 21, another, apparently more cordial, meeting was held. The meeting was private; David Reed told the press afterwards that, "We're on the road to finding some solution." Another negotiating meeting was scheduled for the following week, August 28. But that meeting was never held. One cause for its cancellation may have had roots hundreds of miles away, in Pittsburgh, Pa.

In Pittsburgh, another black coalition group had been organizing protest demonstrations much like those in Chicago, but they were

less peaceful. Debris was thrown by workers on projects down onto
the demonstrators and there were some shoving matches with police.
The mayor of Pittsburgh, to prevent violence, himself ordered the
shutdown of controversial building projects and then was besieged in
city hall by workers demanding compensation for their lost pay. The
fight was spreading to other cities, too, and it seems likely that the
growing momentum somewhat altered the position of the Chicago
Coalition. At the very least, there was the feeling that a national climate for action was developing although the demands were different
in different cities. That may have been part of the reason that the
Coalition again shifted the emphasis of its demands. Where it had
talked in the past of 10,000 immediate jobs, it now began to talk of
expanding the industry until blacks made up 30 percent of each craft.

The Coalition's New Demands

On the night before the scheduled August 28 meeting, the Coalition
delivered the new proposal to Thomas Murray of the Building Trades
Council and Arthur O'Neil of the Builders Association of Chicago. The
contractors then postponed the planned meeting for a week, in order
to have time to study the proposal. The Coalition charged them with
foot-dragging and said it would resume mass picketing.

The new demands spelled out how the trades should be made 30
percent black, to coincide with the proportion of the black population
in the city.[6]

The proposal said:

- New training programs (there was no mention of apprenticeship)
  should be started and that trainees would be accepted "until there
  exists an over-all minimum number of blacks as full members in
  each respective craft in the industry at a minimum of 30 percent."
- The cost of training the new workers should be borne by the
  industry.
- But the training program should be "operated and controlled"
  by the Coalition, with the industry providing only technical
  help.
- "Trainees may enter without testing and without prior experience,
  nor shall a police record be a basis for disqualification. A trainee may elect to enter any craft within the industry."
- On the job trainees should be eligible for review to become journeymen after two years of training. (Most of the apprentice programs
  call for three to five years training before a man is eligible to be
  a journeyman.)
- Pay for trainees should be on a scale comparable to apprentice
  pay but in no case less than $3 an hour.

The proposal repeated the claim that only three percent of the skilled building tradesmen were in minority groups and said, "the situation indicates that no material change can be expected to occur on its own initiative."

Some Coalition spokesmen interviewed at the time referred to 40,000 jobs for blacks, which seemed a long, long way from the original demand for 10,000 jobs. They contended later that they were misunderstood and that the 40,000 figure represented a future goal, not an immediate demand. Arriving at the 40,000 figure showed some change in thinking, too, since 40,000 is more than one-third of the construction jobs in the area, which then totalled about 90,000. The Coalition didn't make its ideas entirely clear, but it was beginning to talk not just about sharing existing jobs but of expanding the industry sufficiently to provide more jobs. Government economists had been saying that the existing construction force in Chicago was too small to do the vast building needed in the 1970s and that the force had been artificially restricted by trade agreements that were perpetuating a shortage of workers and forcing the wage rates to staggering levels. The issue was soon to be discussed at length at government hearings in Chicago, but there was talk of a need in the area of 120,000 or more construction workers, and the 40,000 figure was based on that expanded goal.

In a way, the shift in Coalition strategy provided some answers for white construction workers, many of whom strongly opposed the Coalition on the grounds that, "They want our jobs." By talking about a fair share of an expanded number of jobs, the Coalition could begin to take some heat out of that apparent threat, to say, "It's not your jobs we want, but additional jobs." But the case didn't seem clear at the time, the 40,000 figure sounded outlandish, and newspaper editorials, which had been fairly sympathetic to black claims, began to talk about unreasonable demands.

In the following days, the Coalition stuck with the 30 percent figure and prepared a flier, distributed at rallies, that defined its basic aims on a craft-by-craft basis. The fliers gave these figures:

| Trade Union | 1969 Membership | | Coalition Demands | |
	Total	Minority	30%	1st Year
Asbestos Workers	800	3	240	46
Bricklayers	4400	220	1320	264
Carpenters	29300	350*	8790	1758
Cement Masons	2500	500*	750	150
Electricians	7871	300**	2361	472
Elevator Operators	625	1	187	37
Glaziers	400	1	120	24
Architectural Iron Workers	907	1	272	54

	1969 Membership		Coalition Demands	
	Total	Minority	30%	1st Year
Ornamental Iron Workers	1000	1	300	60
Structural Iron Workers	2300	12**	690	138
Lathers	700	0	210	42
Painters	11000	500*	3300	660
Pipefitters	7800	16	2340	468
Plasterers	800	100	240	48
Plumbers	3440	100	1032	206
Roofers	4650	4	1395	279
Sheet Metal Workers	1070	74	321	64
Sprinkler Fitters	260	0	78	5
Operating Engineers	8000	368	2400	480
Totals	87783	2251	25346	5069

*approximations
**not card holders

The Industry-Union Proposal

The meeting that had been postponed because of the Coalition's altered proposals was held on September 4 and the unions and contractors did make specific proposals. They rejected the August 27 Coalition demands which "would in effect take the control of our industry out of our hands and put it in theirs. For every good reason we cannot accede to such preposterous demands which would put hiring, training and construction in inexperienced hands and deprive us of our businesses and our rights as craft unions."

The program the businessmen and unions brought to the September 4 meeting said:

1. "We will endeavor to obtain employment at once for 1,000 qualified journeymen who possess the necessary skills of their respective trades, and look to the Coalition to supply us with such qualified journeymen. Each respective craft union will accept such journeymen into membership within the time period called for in the pertinent collective bargaining agreement, and each craft union will accept its initiation fee or required fees on a partial payment plan to run at least three months. An appeal procedure will be worked out to review the question of qualifications. The appeal board in each particular craft will be composed of two representatives of the employer groups, two representatives of the union involved, and two representatives from the Coalition.

2. "Those persons who possess some of the skills of a particular trade and can furnish proof of employment for two or more years in the particular craft in which they possess some skills will work for a 30-day probationary period, after which they will receive the equivalent

of the apprentice's rate for the applicable year of the particular craft, as determined by its Joint Apprenticeship Committee, and will be enrolled as an apprentice. Or a special training program will be set up in those industries where practicable, and each worker will receive special training in the particular craft involved. We will look to the Coalition to supply us with persons possessing such skills.

3. "With respect to those individuals who have had no prior training and do not possess some of the skills of a particular craft involved, but who are within the age limits of 17 to 23, or the age limits for the particular craft, we propose an information and recruiting program designed to acquaint all applicants with the trades and the requirements of each trade. We will enlarge upon the present facilities and combine the efforts of the Urban League and the Apprentice Information Center to implement this program. We believe such a training program would run about one month and could be funded through the government to provide a modest wage during this month period. There would be no prior tests for coming into this program. The program would prepare each applicant for entering the existing apprenticeship programs for all crafts, would explain what each craft does and would determine the aptitude of the applicant with respect to the particular trade and increase the probability of success of the applicant as well as his adjustment into the construction industry. From this program the applicant who meets the qualifications would go into the existing apprenticeship program for the particular craft. The Coalition would be responsible for the recruitment of applicants into this program. The Administrative Committee would be in charge of the administration of this program to be composed of two representatives of the employers, two representatives of the Building Trades Council and two representatives of the Coalition. We anticipate that at least 1,000 applicants would be accepted into this program.

4. "We propose an on-the-job training program for persons who do not wish to take tests provided for in point 3 above for admission into the respective apprentice programs or who fail in such tests. Provided that the necessary funding can be obtained for such a program for on-the-job training, the wage would be geared to the equivalent apprenticeship rate, and provision would be made for schooling of one day a week or for evening classes as facilities permit. This on-the-job training program would apply in such industries where such trainees could be employed. We believe that at least 1,000 such on-the-job trainees could be placed in those industries which lend themselves to such a training program. The administration of the on-the-job training program in each craft to be under the direction of an Operations Committee for that craft, composed of two representatives from the employer groups, two representatives from the trade union involved, and

one representative from the Coalition.

5. "These recommendations shall be applicable only with respect to persons who have been residents of Chicago for over one year.

6. "We recognize the desirability and the necessity of securing a greater minority group representation into the skilled trades of the building industry of Chicago and will therefore seek to establish further programs in keeping with the demands of the industry, and if general business conditions permit, which will hopefully achieve, over a period of not more than five years, a level of minority group employees at least proportionate to their percentage in the community at large."

The Coalition accepted the idea of 4,000 jobs, but turned down the package proposal, claiming it was "phony." To the proposal to find employment for 1,000 qualified black journeymen, the Coalition responded, "If there are 1,000 qualified black journeymen in Chicago, they are already working. The offer would put them into the union but it wouldn't open a single new job." To the proposal of a probationary period and then apprenticeship for blacks who possess some skills already, the Coalition said, "Any black man partially skilled is also working at his trade and probably making union wages. He is not likely to drop to lower-paying apprenticeship wages. There are no new jobs evident in this offer." To the proposal about preparing applicants for apprenticeship, the Coalition replied, "We reject the union's old apprenticeship program which traditionally works against the black man. We also reject the age limitation that puts a ceiling at 23." To the proposal about on-the-job training, the Coalition said, "There is nothing in this proposal that says these men will ever reach journeyman status."

When the Coalition turned down the industry and union plan at the September 4 meeting, its spokesmen indicated they wanted to go on negotiating. The industry and union representatives said the offer was "non-negotiable," and left the meeting. It was an impasse characteristic of the different views of what was taking place. There was a kind of bargaining going on, but it was new and unusual and construction people didn't like the process. After the meeting broke up, the industry and unions scheduled full-page newspaper advertisements, with the headline:

"We Opened the Doors Wider;
Four Thousand Construction
Industry Jobs and Twenty-five
Million Dollars in Wages Were
Opened to Chicago's Black Workers
Chicago's Minority Workers Were Denied These
Opportunities by the Coalition for United Community Action."

The ads presented the entire text of the proposal and some other comments, among them:

"Our industry — both unions and employers — has been working for years to recruit and prepare black workers for entry into construction employment. A great many construction jobs for qualified workers, regardless of race, creed or color, are going unfilled. But where are the black trainees? Where are the qualified blacks for these openings?"

And, as a final comment of exasperation over the dealings with the Coalition, the ads concluded:

"When responsible leadership in the black community is prepared to discuss these recommendations seriously we will meet with them."

The industry later announced it would proceed with the proposed program on its own, whether or not the Coalition wished to take part. There weren't any more joint negotiating meetings for a while and it was many months before what came to be known as the Chicago Plan was finally agreed upon. It is ironic that the guidelines finally adopted for the Chicago Plan, in January, 1970, contained the exact words, with a few deletions, of those original proposals. It reveals something of the political process needed to reach final agreement to note that more than 100 hours were spent on negotiations in the coming months, negotiations that produced no more job promises and no other real victories for blacks, but did include some small changes in the ways the plan would be implemented. (Those changes will be considered later in the case.) The climate of early September 1969 in Chicago was so tense that no calm and patient negotiations were possible.

Federal Intervention

At about the same time the Coalition was deciding to turn down the proposals, the federal government, alarmed not only by Chicago and Pittsburgh demonstrations but also by the threat of action in other cities, sent a 20-member task force to Chicago.

Included on the federal team were representatives of twelve government departments and agencies, among them Health, Education and Welfare; Labor; and Housing and Urban Development. The team began collecting data, met briefly with both sides and then conducted one — only one — unsuccessful joint meeting before announcing that the situation was hopelessly deadlocked and that the Labor Department would hold open hearings in Chicago on September 24 and 25. The subjects of the hearings were to be discrimination in the industry and whether federal funds for construction in the city, totalling about $100 million, should be cut off.

And in those same early September days, the Coalition heated up the demonstrations, ignored the court injunction against mass picketing, and took hundreds of demonstrators to the University of Illinois' Chicago Circle Campus to try to shut down the construction of the new science and engineering building.

It led to a clash with police, sent to guard the site, on September 8 and to the arrest of five of the demonstrators, including the Rev. Jesse Jackson, dramatic and charismatic young director of Operation Breadbasket, a Martin Luther King lieutenant who had been with King in Memphis when King was assassinated. Jackson, whose base was in Chicago with the economics-oriented Operation Breadbasket, had not originally been active in the Coalition, but by September he was giving it full support. And Jackson's full support is always dramatic.

Coalition Leaders go to Jail

At the main gate to the construction site, Jackson and 19 others from the Coalition asked to be admitted to the site and were allowed to enter. For about 15 minutes, the group spoke to a vice president of the construction company, asking permission to talk to the construction workers. He refused. When most of the group left the site, four remained, refusing to go until they could speak to the workmen. Two of the four were Jackson and Leonard Sengali. Police arrested all four, charging them with criminal trespass. An assistant corporation counsel at the site later said the four were arrested "sort of voluntarily."

The Rev. Jackson refused to post bond and announced he would stay in jail until he was found innocent of the charge or until the dispute with the construction industry was resolved. While he was there, he wrote an eloquent open letter, under the title, "Why We're in Jail." Newsmen had not been allowed to interview him in jail, but his wife was allowed to see him and she gave the letter to a Chicago *Sun-Times* reporter. The letter, printed on the front page on September 11, read:

"We are seeking meaningful participation in the American economy— not just a minimum wage but a livable wage.

"It is significant that a period of despair and hopelessness, characterized by the slogan, 'Burn, baby, burn,' has been transformed into a period of hope with new possibilities characterized by the slogan, 'Build, baby, build, earn while you learn.'

"We do not seek to take white jobs. But neither do we intend to allow whites to keep black jobs while we are passively quiet and docile. There will be no more rest and tranquility until our just pleas are heeded.

"We realize that our protest creates a counterprotest. We seek jobs. The whites seek to maintain their jobs. It is understandable that they would want to remain employed. It should be just as understandable that we seek jobs which offer security, protection, opportunity, food, clothing, shelter, education and the necessities of life. Both groups are frightened that they may be deprived of these necessities.

"White insecurity is expressed by an exclusion of the out-group and a ratio of trained workers to jobs that allows the law of supply and demand to enable them to bargain for higher wages. Black insecurity is expressed by direct challenge to the in-group's exclusive hold upon public policy. Blacks are saying we need to declare a state of emergency because of unemployment and underemployment. We need to create a crisis to deal with the emergency. We need training programs.

"We'll march, protest, break injunctions, boycott and use other forms of creative protest in order to be heard, recognized, respected and allowed to participate.

"Ironically, both groups are right. But each group is hardly able to see beyond achieving security for itself. Both think that the elimination of each other is the solution. The real solution is the expansion of the economy to the extent that it can absorb or employ both whites and blacks.

"Every American deserves a job or an income. A government is responsible for the welfare of its people or it forces its people to say farewell to it. People develop disloyalty and disinterest in a government that will not rise to the occasion of providing basic opportunities for its people to survive."

Mayor Daley's Help is Sought

Jesse Jackson's arrest and his dramatic letter, plus the growing fear that the construction dispute would set off a major black-white battle in Chicago, led directly to action by Mayor Richard J. Daley, who had kept his hands off the dispute in the early weeks. It was a ticklish problem for that politician, whose powerful political position is strongly rooted in an ancient alliance with the building trades. Building trades leaders have been stalwarts in the Daley administration. Chicago's reputation as a good union town (really, a good AFL-type craft union town) is based on many mayoral favors to craft unions. City-employed craftsmen, for example, get the top union rate, but they get it for full-time employment despite the fact that the top rate is high to compensate for the seasonal and cyclical nature of most construction jobs.

Black leaders in Chicago, on the other hand, have never looked on the Mayor as much of a friend. When he deals with blacks, they say, he deals on a plantation basis, doling out jobs and favors only with tight control from City Hall. They say he tends to absorb the opposition, hiring bright young black leaders for city jobs, thus robbing the black community of its best spokesmen. They say he is too tightly locked in with the strong white ethnic groups in Chicago to be able to make needed adjustments in the sharing of power with the black community. And it was, after all, the Daley-appointed Board of Education that had for so long failed to open up the Washburne Trade School apprentice programs to any significant number of black youth.

But it was to the mayor that some blacks turned for help. That's the way it is in Chicago. Daley is a man of action, and even those who don't always like the actions know his power. He is traditionally turned to for mediation and solutions when labor or community controversies get too sticky for agreement. And nothing much of a political nature can be accomplished in Chicago without his blessing.

The day after Jesse Jackson was arrested, his fellow ministers in Operation Breadbasket "challenged" Daley to step into the dispute and settle it. Coalition leaders had been gingerly mentioning the Mayor, too, although they had insisted that they didn't want him to mediate the dispute, but merely wanted him to use his influence to get negotiations going again. They were men with an understandable distrust of officialdom and claimed they really wanted to go it alone in face-to-face negotiations with the building industry.

Daley responded promptly to the ministers' "challenge."

"The mayor's office is open and available to parties involved in the building controversy," he said. "I am willing and anxious to do everything I can to bring them together for discussion and negotiation."

In the months ahead, the mayor's office did become the center of negotiation in the dispute. More than a dozen protracted and often painful meetings were held in his office and he was present at every one of them for every minute, except one brief absence to attend the funeral of an old friend.

In mid-September, negotiations were started again and both sides were making optimistic statements about the possibility of agreement. The optimism didn't extend down, however, to the rank-and-file membership of the building unions. The men were fearful about losing their jobs to blacks, furious about the loss of wages they suffered in the building shut-downs, angry at their belief that blacks were demanding jobs for totally untrained people, and determined to stick with the long-established rules and practices that seemed to be so threatened by the militant blacks.

Those restive union members were going to have their day during the federal government hearings on discrimination in the industry.

The Federal Hearings

The federal team, representing many different government agencies, came to Chicago with two potent but then rarely-used tools. One was Executive Order 11246, issued in 1965 by President Lyndon B. Johnson, one of a series of fair employment executive orders dating back to 1941. The order prohibits contractors doing business with the federal government from discriminating on the basis of race, creed, color or national origin; it requires employers to take "affirmative action" to insure equal employment opportunity; it gives the Department of Labor the power to cancel, terminate or suspend any contract when discrimination is found to exist; it provides for blacklisting a contractor from future federal or federally-assisted contracts, if he is guilty of discrimination. The Labor Department's Office of Federal Contract Compliance was set up to carry out the enforcement of the executive order.

The second federal tool is Title VII of the 1964 Civil Rights Act, which gives the Justice Department the right to file suit if there is "reasonable cause to believe that any person or groups of persons is engaged in a practice or pattern of resistance to the full employment of the right" of equal opportunity to employment.

These two tools thus give the federal government power to act against both contractors and unions who discriminate. But the tools had seldom been used, despite frequent reminders from black organizations and individuals.

A 10-man federal task force began collecting data in Chicago in early September; its findings were to be presented at the federal hearings, scheduled for September 24 and 25 in the LaSalle Hotel in downtown Chicago.

Three federal officials were to preside over the hearings:

Arthur Fletcher, assistant secretary of labor for wage and labor standards, appointed in the preceding May. Fletcher is black, a former football player, school teacher and special assistant to Washington Governor Daniel J. Evans.

John L. Wilks, also black, a public relations man from San Francisco who had been appointed just a month earlier to a new position as deputy assistant secretary of labor, for federal contract compliance.

Horace E. Menasco, the only white member of the group, who also had held federal office for only a month, as deputy assistant secretary of labor for wage and labor standards. He had previously been city manager in Pasco, Washington, and Colby, Kansas.

The first hearing was scheduled to start at 9:30 a.m., September 24. It was never held, because the hotel room was jammed with white construction workers who simply would not let it proceed. Whenever Fletcher tried to speak, he was booed and jeered.

The men had started arriving at the hotel at 7 a.m., and promptly filled the 225 available seats in the hearing room, plus most of the standing room. By 9:30, there were 600 to 800 people wedged into the room. Both entrances to the hotel were being picketed by more union men, perhaps 500 of them. Both outside and in the hearing room, many of the men carried printed signs reading "Concerned Building and Construction Trade Workers Seeking Civil Rights for All." Some of the signs had other messages hand-lettered on the back, among them, "Keep Quality in Jobs" and "Bucks Yes. Gangs No." Many of the signs carried union local numbers, chiefly — that first day — International Brotherhood of Electrical Workers Local 134 and Sheet Metal Workers Local 73. (These two international unions were among six particularly singled out as discriminatory by federal officials who had been working out the Philadelphia Plan to guarantee federal contract compliance.)

Some of the men in the room talked of receiving phone calls telling them to come to the hotel, and others said there had been a union meeting the night before at which everyone was urged to get to the hotel at 7 a.m. Joseph Duffy, one of several Local 134 business agents present, insisted, however, that the packed hearing room was a spontaneous demonstration, that the men had come on their own because they wanted to be heard.

As they waited, they got angrier. They passed around some of the press releases and speech copies that government public relations people had laid out on a table for the press. They were particularly riled by a 12-page statement by Samuel Simmons, assistant secretary of the department of housing and urban development, who was to have been one of the first men to testify at the hearings. It was Simmons who had made the one federal effort to negotiate a settlement between the trades and the Coalition and who, when his effort failed, ordered an investigation of 20 contractors, to see whether they were violating Executive Order 11246. His statement, which did not name the contractors, strongly recommended that existing contracts with 17 of them be cancelled and future ones denied. He also recommended that the government require an alternative to "the present union-controlled apprenticeship training system" and set standards of competence in the building trades, taking the matter out of private hands entirely.

It was a very strong statement, recommending tougher action than had ever before been taken under the executive order, and the union men who were reading it didn't like it. They told each other that they were being prejudged, that the federal officials had already made up their minds and that that proved they never intended to conduct a fair hearing at all, that the hearing was just window-dressing.

When the green-draped table at the front of the room remained empty past the scheduled starting time, the crowd's impatience grew. Someone in the crowd starting to clap in rhythm and many others took it up, adding whistling and stamping.

"Let's go," someone yelled, and that started a rash of yells:

"Bring on the action."

"Come on, government. Let's go."

"We've got jobs to go back to. Let's go."

"Even Nixon's up by now."

"What are you waiting for?"

"C'mon out and hear the truth."

"Tell it like it is, baby." (Loud laughter)

"You can't hide behind that door forever."

Finally Fletcher came out and sat down at his seat at the green-draped table.

"The hotel management is rightly concerned about the size of the audience here . . ." he began. He got a loud chorus of boos, and someone yelled, "What are we — the wrong color?"

"I came here to conduct an orderly hearing and I intend to do just that," Fletcher went on. "Will the union leaders and their lawyers please come forward and discuss the possibility of reducing the size of the audience?"

That brought more boos and calls:

"We're the unions. You deal with us."

"You work for us and you'd better know it."

"We'll take you to our union hall where we can fill it with a lot more people than this."

Fletcher, talking quietly, said ". . . where reason rather than emotion can control . . ."

In the back of the room, somone called out, "Oh, shit."

"Hey, cut that out," someone else demanded.

"A local ordinance is being violated here by overcrowding," said Fletcher.

"How many ordinances are you violating?" someone called.

"How many does the Coalition violate?"

"We'll take you to Circle Campus and then you can talk about ordinances being violated."

"We're the wrong color, huh?"

"Let's see how these geniuses from Washington will get out of this one."

"Let's go - go - go!"

Fletcher then said, "I have made the decision that . . ."

"Who the hell are you?" someone yelled.

"As assistant secretary of labor," Fletcher went on, "and the government official who called this meeting, I have no choice but to postpone this meeting until we can find a larger facility."

To a reporter, Fletcher said, "I think once the emotional atmosphere has subsided and we're able to hear both sides, and people can understand government's role and responsibility, then we can get on with the solutions. This isn't happening just in Chicago. It's going on all over the country. We want to find solutions here because they will be applicable elsewhere too. We're not here to place blame, but to find how all people who want to work can be able to work. There were a slew of people here who wanted to testify, but they were prevented from doing so. This is a tragedy. I came here to get the facts and we're not being allowed to do so."

Fury in the Streets

But the emotional atmosphere was not due to subside. The postponed hearing was scheduled to start the next day, Thursday, September 25, at 10 a.m. And it was not scheduled for a larger hall, but in a small assembly hall in the United States Custom House, across the street from the sprawling Chicago Post Office on the southwest edge of the loop. Long before 10 a.m. the intersection of Canal and Harrison streets was completely jammed with protesting construction workers, many of them carrying the same signs they had carried the day before but this time lettered with the names of many more union locals, locals from the Chicago area but from other places, too. One sign read, "Local 932, Coos Bay, Oregon."

"No Giveaways. No Bums," read the hand lettering on the back of one sign.

"We discriminate against bums, not blacks," said another.

"No school. No jobs. No class. No cash," read a third.

Two yellow-and-black street barricades had been hauled to the front entrance and scores of workers formed a solid wall to keep out anyone who tried to get into the building. Two of the men held a long banner in front of the door. It read, "We like the unions the way they are."

About 200 helmeted Chicago policemen were lined up across the street from the entrance, but they made no effort to clear the doorway. Now and then, they would clear the intersection so traffic could get through, but the crowd kept surging back into the street.

For the most part, in the morning, the street was peaceful. There was a lot of milling around, but a sort of carnival atmosphere prevailed. Cheers would go up as big new groups of construction workers moved into the area, sometimes 100 or more in a group. More cheers would be heard when witnesses, who had come to testify at the hearing, were

turned away at the entrance with a chant of "You Can't Go In!" The
Rev. Vivian, one of the witnesses, was roughed up; that got a cheer.
Jim's Place, a murky little beer hall across the street, did a rushing
business. The crowd moved out of the street readily when a beer truck
arrived with an emergency delivery.

Duffy, the IBEW business agent who had talked the day before of
the "spontaneous demonstration" of the workers, was elated. "You
thought we had a lot of men out yesterday?" he said with a grin. "Well,
how about this? And what do you think of the bigger hall they promised us?"

That was a sentiment often echoed by the men in the crowd. Fletcher
had promised a bigger hall and they felt cheated at the switch. The word
had gone around that only 75 people had been admitted to the hearing; 25 from the industry, 25 from the unions, 25 from the Coalition.

By noon, about 5,000 men ringed the building and jammed the street.
They were eager to tell about their grievances.

They seemed honestly convinced that each one was personally
threatened by the Coalition, that the blacks were after *their* jobs and
they had to fight to protect them. "It's our livelihood," they'd say
again and again. "It's all we know how to do. Why should *they* get
our jobs?"

One sheet metal worker gritted his teeth, shook his fist, and said,
"This is a killing matter! You're talking about the bread on my table.
You try to take that bread off my table — I'll kill you. The last time
I killed it was Nazis. But I'm not afraid to fight here."

They pooh-poohed the idea that the industry can be expanded, providing other jobs — not theirs — for blacks. There might be extra work
in good weather, they'd say, but there wasn't much extra and, come
winter, union men would be looking for jobs, too.

Many of them referred to the halt in federal construction that President Nixon had ordered a few weeks earlier as an anti-inflation move.
One worker with a rich Irish accent said it all proves the Republican
party is out to break the unions. "They cut back on federal construction and at the same time try to bring in a lot more workers. They're
trying to demolish the unions and get us back to $1 an hour wages,"
he insisted.

They seemed to really believe that apprenticeship training is as
open to blacks as it is to whites. "Anybody with the aptitude can
get in," they'd say. "Of course, we can't take in a bunch of dummies."
They readily admitted that apprenticeship wasn't always open to all,
but they insist that has changed. They were furiously angry at any suggestion of any new route up the training ladder. "Let 'em come up the
way we did," they'd say, again and again. One of the Coalition's arguments is that only about one-third of the present construction workers

went through the apprentice system and the rest picked up their skills on the job. But the men outside the U.S. Custom House were strong for the apprentice route.

Many of the workers insisted that there is no race issue involved. "We've got nothing against the colored," they'd say. Then some of them would add comments like, "We're tax payers; they're tax eaters." Or "Nobody gave me nuthin'. Now we have to give them our schools, our homes, our churches, our jobs!" Or, "Nobody here has anything against the colored — when they can act like white men."

Some of the reactions were based on misunderstandings that had been widely circulated. The men were convinced, for example, that the Coalition was demanding two months on-the-job training, then journeymen's wages for all.

"I went to work for 45 cents an hour," said a carpenter. "Now I get $6.20, but it's taken me thirty-five years. Let them work up to it, too."

That set off scores of reminiscences about how rough the old days were and how important it is now to stick with the unions.

Through much of what the men had to say there was a strong under-current of belief that blacks simply aren't able to learn construction jobs, that they lack the aptitude and background. Feeling this way, some expressed fears for their own safety: "You just can't be up there with a man who doesn't know what he's doing. My life is in the hands of the guy who's helping me."

For the older workers, there was another fear, too, that younger, stronger men will be kept on the jobs if jobs get scarce. There is an insecurity inherent in the industry, and it really has nothing to do with blacks, but that issue gets intertwined and seems to compound the threat. Whatever the underlying social issues are, the insecurity is real.

"We don't have any seniority," one said.

"Nobody gives us pensions, or vacations, or even guarantees us a day's pay."

"It sounds like we get high wages and we do — when we work. But it doesn't help much to get $6.50 an hour for a couple of weeks, then spend the next two weeks looking for work."

"We're all here because we feel we have to be. Nobody's doing anything for us. We all have to worry about jobs from day to day."

Another running gripe was the Coalition's demand that black workers with a certain number of years of service be made foremen.

"Twenty years I've got, and never a foreman," said one. Others chimed in, with other yearly totals.

They came back again and again to a defense of the system they say gave them their skills and insisted that no one should follow other routes to training. "Let 'em come up the way we did," was the usual phrase. Sometimes they were inconsistent; one man said he'd been an apprentice for five years and was lauding the system. Then he said, "I didn't learn anything until I was out on the job." "Should everyone learn on the job?" he was asked. "That's the only way," he said, and then he returned to the insistence that "the colored" should come up the way he did.

They were thoroughly angry at the federal government. They believed the government had given them a raw deal in the hearings and they didn't plan to forget it. Many referred to Fletcher's promise to get a bigger hall ("Ye heard him say it. I saw ye there,") and their feeling that the government was giving them a run-around.

By noon the carnival atmosphere was waning; tension had been building up. Jim's Place didn't help. The Rev. Vivian's car, when he returned and tried again to enter the building, was pelted with beer cans. There was a brief but furious battle between white construction workers, a small group of blacks and police who sought to protect them. Shots were fired and two guns were found after the melee; no one was ever sure who they belonged to. Six blacks and two whites were arrested. Four policemen and a construction worker were treated for injuries, but no one was hit by gunfire.

Richard Elrod, the corporation counsel who was present with police as he had been at many of the earlier demonstrations by blacks, called the attacks on police and blacks "at least a near-riot. There was no respect for police out there and those workers damn near lynched us."

After the fracas on Canal Street, many of the construction workers headed downtown toward the Civic Center Plaza, where the Coalition had held its big rally a few days before (where Jackson had said, "The unions didn't trust us in the 1930s and we don't trust them now."). Many drank beer as they marched.

At the Plaza, some of the group clambered up the five-story high Picasso sculpture, and the crowd in the Plaza sang "God Bless America."

Later, some of them marched to the Federal Building, where the conspiracy trial of the Chicago Eight was just getting under way and where political dissenters who objected to the trial were picketing outside. (Many of the construction workers had said earlier in the morning, "I'd really like to get my hands on some of those hippies.") There were scuffling and shouting matches there before the crowd dwindled away toward their homes.

They came back the next day, while the hearings still went on inside the Custom House. They followed the same route to the Civic Center, where some of them shoved and spit on five white women who were picketing in behalf of the Coalition, and to the Federal

Courthouse, where 30 hippies promptly fled. One big group
marched on the Chicago *Daily News* and *Sun-Times* building, shouted,
"We want the truth," pounded on the glass walls, threw newspapers
to the ground, and tore off the lobby walls a display of prize-winning
photographs dealing with integration. Out on the street, they chased
news photographers. (But some of their members stayed behind to
pay for the newspapers that had been destroyed.)

Joe Duffy, the business agent who had been elated at the big Thursday crowd, was despairing on Friday. Walking the street with a bullhorn
he pleaded, "Go home now. There's nothing more you can do here. Go
home. We've had the worst possible press coverage. Just go home."

At the Custom House on that second turbulent day, police had arrived
before the demonstrators and formed a corridor to keep the entrance
open, something they had not tried to do on Thursday. Federal officials
had protested police inaction on Thursday and had threatened to bring
federal marshals to keep the entrance open if police did not act. There
was another clash with police when the Rev. Jesse Jackson arrived with
a body-guard of off-duty black policemen. One of the crowd hurled his
hard hat after Jackson, missing him, and the crowd pressed in against the
police lines. Some of them were arrested.

Inside, there was a hearing going on, uncovering more and more
layers of the complex question of black workers in the Chicago
construction industry.

Footnotes

1. "Economic Slavery," by David Reed. Undated. Unpublished.

2. A landmark study of the historical dimensions of exclusion is *Organized Labor and the Negro*, by Herbert R. Northrup. Harper & Brothers, New York, 1944.

3. Interview, May 25, 1970. Gittler was the attorney who spoke for the Council during the Chicago Plan negotiations.

4. Meredith Gilbert, one of the most hard-line militants in the black group, was later replaced as a member of the Coalition's steering committee. The Coalition apparently felt he never was really seeking a cooperative agreement.

5. Details of the earlier demonstrations, city by city, along with a meticulous analysis of the problem of discrimination in the building trades, are available in *The Negro and Apprenticeship*, by F. Ray Marshall and Vernon M. Briggs, Jr. The Johns Hopkins Press. Baltimore. 1967.

6. Some industry and union spokesmen have consistently contended that this is a "numbers game." They say, for example, that blacks do make up 30 percent of the population of the city of Chicago but not of the Chicago metropolitan area, which is the basis for the construction industry figures. And they say that the age distribution of the black population is such that blacks make up only about 15 percent of the available labor force. On either of these bases, they say, the goals of the "numbers game" would be different.

Discussion Questions

1. What do you feel is the root of the problem presented in this chapter: Exclusionary tactics in the trades? Inadequate preparation of black workers? Collusion between industry and labor to keep blacks out? Black lack of know-how in taking advantage of what's available? The nature of black-white relations in the society? Government indifference? Something else?

2. Was this a bargaining situation? If so, what parties were the bargainers? What were their bases of power? What did each party stand to lose or gain?

3. Jesse Jackson wrote, "We realize that our protest creates a counter-

protest." Do you agree? What other tactics might the Coalition have used in pushing for its objectives? What might have been the results?

4. How is public policy involved in the interactions in this chapter? What public policies? Were the policies effectively implemented? With what results?

5. Was seeking an injunction a wise move on the part of the industry? Why or why not? What were the results?

6. Does any one group in the dispute have a preponderance of right on its side? Which one? Why? Can you make an equally valid case for any of the other groups?

7. Pickets at the hearing displayed a sign, "We like the unions the way they are." What is "the way they are?" Does "the way they are" violate public policy? What actions are possible?

8. Does your analysis of the industry-union proposal to the Coalition indicate that it represents a fair and realistic effort to meet the problems raised by the Coalition? Do you think the Coalition should have accepted it?

The Difficulty of Changing Institutions

The basic problem of the case, that of finding ways to give black workers a greater share in the important construction industry, is the enormous resistance of institutions to any real change. Entrenched interests, entrenched bureaucracies, entrenched beliefs are all just that: entrenched. Efforts at change, even extensive efforts, are blunted, and anything less than extensive efforts are hopeless.

The problem is compounded by the number of institutions that must change in order to produce real participation by blacks in the construction trades.

1. The employers.

Construction is an insecure industry, tremendously affected by the ups and downs of the economy; it is difficult to engage in long-term planning because so many variables are not within the control of the industry (the extent and the timetable of federally-aided construction, for example). The nature of the employers' relationships with the unions has allowed the employers to shift most of the cost of this instability to the workers. As a result, the employers are so bound to the unions for their labor supply that they simply are not free to act on their own in changing employment patterns. To do so, the whole complex fabric of the relationship with the unions would have to be altered.

2. The unions.

In few other industries do the unions wield such power; this position is largely due to union control of entry into the labor market and considerable control over job assignments, a control which the unions have no desire to alter. They believe that the workers' security in this very insecure field is at stake; they see themselves as the defenders of the "integrity of the craft" as well as powerful partners in the control of the wage structure. And they have a long tradition of autonomous power; the international unions do not dictate to the local unions in the construction trades. Those unions which have moved to include more blacks have done so only within the format of their established patterns of control; for example, allowing some more black apprentices. They have tended to insist that only those blacks who are most like the present white workers in background and attitudes will get in. (Interviewees for prospective apprentices often are asked why they want a career in this particular trade and lose points if they just want a job.) Union leaders are not free to move very far away from the position and views of the membership; the fact that union leaders must stand for election cannot be discounted and is a powerful factor in the maintenance of the status quo. Finally, each of these facets of resistance to change must be multiplied by 19 in Chicago, where 19 different construction trades have their own unions.

3. Employment patterns.

The most significant reason behind the exclusion of black people from construction jobs is that historically they have been relegated to inferior occupations. Almost every industry has a hierarchy of jobs, either formal or informal, and blacks are at the bottom of the status ladder. No single institution is responsible for this pattern, nor can it be changed by a single institution. It has been built into our society because black people have never had the political or economic power to force the white decision-makers to share opportunities with them; it is what the scholars call white racism. These employment patterns are deeply entrenched and are perpetuated by many kinds of institutions, both public and private, which operate on the assumption that certain jobs are black jobs and other jobs are white jobs. A simple illustration of the way the system works is the fact that a high school counselor is not apt to steer a black youth toward the kind of jobs which black youths have never had a chance to get.

4. The black community.

The black community, too, is trapped in its own history and many black people tend to accept the job stereotypes that have been developed. In the words of astute scholars of the phenomenon:[1]

"Since Negroes usually live in segregated neighborhoods and go to segregated schools, they rarely learn about occupations with few or no Negroes in them, and they apply for the kind of jobs they know they can get. Since aspirations are conditioned by one's associations, few Negroes are motivated to apply for jobs from which they are excluded."

5. Government.

Even when trying to bring about change in the institutions and job patterns that have discriminated against blacks, government itself is subject to the same problems that it seeks to solve. Government, at each level, is itself an immense institution and is itself resistant to change. Change, when started, often tends to get lost in procedures, altering or at least blunting the end result.

The Federal Hearings

The federal hearings in Chicago in late September 1969, concerning discrimination in the construction industry, revealed many aspects of the difficulty of changing these institutions and unfolded many more levels of meaning, expanding and embroidering some of the issues already touched upon in Section I.

About two dozen witnesses presented testimony and answered questions of the three-man government team during the two-day hearing. Some were from the Coalition, some from industry, some from government, and only a few from labor: the financial secretary of the plasterers' union, two sheet metal workers, and a black bricklayer who claimed he'd been working for years to get the government to take action against union discrimination, without success.

Most of the testimony has never had much public attention. Although there were a few reporters present in the hearing room, most of the press attention went to the action in the streets. But the testimony reveals many significant aspects of the conflict; particularly revealing excerpts will be presented here.

Arthur Fletcher, assistant secretary of labor and chairman of the government team: "It is not the purpose of this hearing to point an accusing finger at anyone or any geographical or occupational group. The panel is present to hear impartially the facts that are relevant to the proper functioning of Executive Order 11246 as it pertains to the construction industry."

Thomas Nayder, secretary-treasurer of Chicago and Cook County Building and Construction Trades Council: "The council is a central labor body for local craft unions whose members are employed under collective bargaining agreements with employers in the Chicago and Cook County area construction industry. Each of our member craft unions are locals of parent International Unions who have affiliated with the Building Trades Department of the AFL-CIO.

"The local council has no control over the actions and day-to-day activities of its affiliates, it does not enter into any collective bargaining, it has no contracts with employer groups, except for the area of adjudicating disputes over jurisdiction or trade lines, and it makes no agreements which would bind a member union to do anything that would take away its right to autonomy.

(Nayder then outlined some of the activities in which the council had participated to bring more blacks into the trades: cosponsorship of the Chicago Apprenticeship Information Center since 1963; assistance to the Chicago Urban League in a pre-training program for blacks who wanted to prepare for apprenticeship; conducting bus tours for high school students to construction sites; participating in career days in schools. He referred to the early September proposals to the Coalition, which had been rejected, and the subsequent opening of a Black Journeyman Recruitment Center without Coalition participation.)

> "We believe and hope that this latest joint effort will encourage greater participation in the building trades by minority groups. It is our further hope that the minorities will respond to our efforts in a sincere desire to learn a skilled trade and earn the benefits that go with union membership."

Fletcher: We are prepared to concede that you are further down the road than where you were, in say, 1960, but we are also prepared to suggest that the present rate of progress is not fast enough. We have studies at the Labor Department which indicate that if we do not accelerate the rate of progress, as it relates to moving non-whites into job opportunities, that by the end of the decade of 1970, the unemployment ratio may move from two to one, to five to one.

Nayder: We really can't speak for the individual who doesn't come forward. We can't speak for the community who is unwilling to respond because perhaps whitey is running the operation. So we, ourselves, are concerned about this lack of interest.

Fletcher: Is the apprenticeship program the only way to become a journeyman? Is there no other way of getting into the union, short of going the apprenticeship route?

Nayder: I can't speak for all unions on that subject, but I do believe there are some who have an experience factor . . . He (the applicant) is permitted an examination to determine his skill. If he has that, he can enter, whether he is black, yellow, or red, or for that matter, it doesn't make any difference.

Fletcher: Who is the judge?

Nayder: Basically, the employer. You make application to the union.

Fletcher: You don't need a recommendation?

Nayder: No . . . We have trades that are begging people to join them: painters, roofers, cement finishers, bricklayers, carpenters. They couldn't get recruits. There are many jobs in the community that are going unfilled.

Herbert E. Menasco, deputy assistant secretary of labor: "Would you care to elaborate on the general economic outlook with respect to construction trade employment?

Nayder: On the day we submitted our proposal to the community, we were also advised by President Nixon of a 75 percent cut-back in the spending of federal funds for construction. In addition, the Governors and Mayors also cut back their spending. On the one hand, we were telling the community we would create job opportunities, but on the other hand, the community was telling us you might be cutting your supply off.

Menasco: (referring to the Coalition's rejection of the proposal) Do you have any concept of why it was rejected as totally unacceptable?

Nayder: In our discussions with some of the leadership of that group, their principal thrust appears to be control. And we don't believe that is something we should give them . . . Our bargaining is with the employer. We don't intend to bargain with a brother or sister union, let's say, of some description. Our technique for labor-management relations is between labor and management. If we are going to enter into any kind of a conflict, it has to be in that posture.

Menasco: Control of what?

Nayder: I would think that the two main items of control were all of training and all of the handling of funds.

Menasco: Is there anything the panel can do to help ease present tensions?

Nayder: I don't know what the panel can do, because I don't think the panel wants to assume responsibility for part of the

pressure, where gang members and other members of that
community are lining up in a military fashion to offer
support to their drive. We think it should be done in a
different fashion and hopefully some of the panel's efforts
might relate to that. Perhaps the panel might help us to
locate or relate to someone in the black community who
is willing to sit down and work out a constructive and
responsible program . . . We are moving ahead with our
proposal and the group that was working at odds with us
had tried to tell the black community not to come into
the recruitment center. Perhaps they don't really speak
for the community . . .

Samuel J. Simmons, assistant secretary for equal opportunity of the
Department of Housing and Urban Development: (This is the statement which had made the white tradesmen so angry the day before;
they claimed it prejudged them and the government had no intention
of conducting a fair hearing. Looked at another way, the Simmons
statement represented the first time ever that a government representative had proposed such strong action under executive order 11246.)

"I have been assigned by Housing and Urban Development Secretary George Romney the responsibility of administering the anti-
discrimination clause included in the Department's federal and federally
assisted construction contracts pursuant to Executive Order 11246.

"At the request of some concerned citizens in Chicago, I came to
this city on September 5 in an attempt to help bring the building
industry, both union and employers, and the Coalition for United
Community Action to the negotiating table to work out a solution
to the serious problem of providing meaningful minority employment
opportunities in the construction industry in this city.

"While we succeeded in bringing the parties to the table, they were
not able to agree on a program for Chicago. Under those circumstances,
it became clear to me that it would be necessary to further carry out
my obligation to see that Executive Order 11246 was enforced in the
construction industry. To achieve that end, on September 9, I directed
that an investigation be conducted concerning compliance with the
Executive Order. It has involved examining the relationship between
some 20 HUD assisted construction contractors and six of the craft
unions in this city who have very few minority group members. These
six unions are Iron Workers Local 1, Sheet Metal Local 73, Operating
Engineers Union 150, Plumbers Local 130, Pipefitters Local 597 and
the Electrical Workers Union 134. In the course of this investigation
we learned much, Mr. Secretary, about the relationship between the

building contractors and the labor unions which goes far to explain why so few minority group persons are employed in the construction industry.

"As a result of these investigations, I recommend to you that enforcement action to impose economic sanctions, in the form of prohibition of future contracts and cancellation of existing contracts, be taken pursuant to Executive Order upon 17 of the contractors whom we investigated and upon other contractors who may, after investigation, be found to have engaged in similar practices.

"Our findings here in Chicago also lead me to the following general conclusions:

1. The federal government's present program to insure equal opportunity . . . is inadequate. It does not adequately or effectively succeed in correcting the effects of the historical patterns of racial exclusion or other practices which have the same effect, nor does it achieve success in establishing a system insuring equal and just participation by minority groups in the future.

2. The present manpower utilization system prevailing in the construction industry makes it next to impossible for even the most creative and just employer to consistently provide equal employment opportunity. There has to be major institutional reform of the system. New methods of recruitment, training and referral have to be developed and implemented.

"My recommendations to correct these problems are as follows:

1. "The Office of Federal Contract Compliance should require each federal agency with compliance responsibilities under construction contracts in the Chicago area to immediately undertake compliance reviews of each contractor, to insist upon immediate compliance . . .

2. The federal government should establish specific goals and performance standards for compliance in all metropolitan areas. Standards should be set for each craft and compliance with these standards should be a precondition for the award of new contracts. In setting the standards consideration should be given to the projected number of jobs needed in the future as well as present opportunities. In those situations where it is obvious that there are few or no available minority group journeymen or persons who can qualify as journeymen, employers should be permitted to be in compliance through the utilization of individuals in legitimate training programs.

3. The obligation to provide equal opportunity must be effectively administered with respect to all work of any contractor who has a government contract and not be limited to federally financed and assisted projects.

4. The federal government should cease to be a passive participant in terms of training or certification of persons in the construction industry. On all direct and federally assisted construction the government must require an alternative to the present union controlled apprenticeship training system and set goals for the number of persons to be trained. In view of the requirements of many federal programs to provide economic opportunities for low income residents of the area and the needs of the industry for greater numbers of trained workers, the government cannot continue to sit idly by and see persons over 27, who are the victims of inferior education, be denied an opportunity to become a skilled worker in the construction industry. Whatever alternative system is developed must contain the following three elements:

a.   Control of the training system cannot be abdicated to the union, or to unions and management. The government must be an active partner. The training program must provide also for the adequate involvement of majority and minority group general and sub-contractors, unions and minority group communities.

b.   The federal government must make a commitment to share the cost of this expanded training. It cannot expect the employers of the sponsors of the construction project to assume this economic burden. Present Labor Department manpower programs must be restructured to provide funds for recruiting trainees, providing counselling and related classroom instruction and cost of on-the-job training for the period it takes to develop a journeyman or an individual who can at least perform most of the functions of a journeyman.

c.   The federal government must develop procedures to insure that once a person is recruited as a trainee, systematic training opportunities will be available on every federally supported construction project. After the successful completion of a certain number of hours of on-the-job training, the trainee would be successively advanced on the pay scale until such time as he receives 100 percent of journeyman pay. The federal government must certify to the competence of an individual completing the training program[2] and require that he be given an opportunity on all construction undertaken by a federal contractor. These standards should apply regardless of whether or not the individual is a member of a union.

"It is only when all of the factors I have outlined are put into effect that minority group individuals can expect to realize equal opportunity in the construction industry.

"Those, in summary, are my conclusions and recommendations.

"Now, with your permission, I should like to explain the background of the problems in the community, the nature and extent of our investigation and the reasoning by which we arrived at the conclusions which I have just stated. I will take as my starting point the year 1962, when GSA contracted for the construction of the United States Court House building in Chicago. The construction contracts specifically included by reference the terms of Executive Order 10925, the immediate predecessor of the Order presently administered by the Labor Department. The whole shoddy story of discrimination by Iron Workers Local 1 was revealed in a law suit which was filed as a result of the alleged discrimination in the building of that court house. Judge Campbell, after reviewing the evidence, concluded as follows:

" 'Based upon rational and reasonable inferences, I find that either Negroes were refused application blanks by the Joint Committee, or if permitted to file such applications, they were never acted upon. I find that the Negro community as such knew of this policy of the Joint Committee and the Union, and that because of the inherent and patent futility of such action, sent few applicants in recent years to the Joint Committee or the Union.

" 'To make my position clear, I should observe that the mere absence of members of the Negro race on the rolls of this specific union or on rolls of that union's apprenticeship list would not in and of itself be proof of discriminatory membership policies.

" 'However, the evidence before me . . . manifests a definite policy and history of discrimination against those of the Negro race. Those facts present a clear picture not of racial segregation, but of racial exclusion. The above cited facts and figures evidence a systematic policy on the part of Union and Joint Committee to exclude Negroes solely on the basis of their race.'

"That is the end of the quote. The Judge also found that the Joint Apprenticeship Committee and the Union discriminated against Negroes who sought admittance to the Union and further found that the facilities and equipment of the Chicago Board of Education (the Washburne Trade School) were utilized to educate classes of all white apprentices.

"And, beyond that, the Judge found both the General Services Administration and the Bureau of Apprenticeship and Training of the Department of Labor 'directly and significantly' made possible and aided in the perpetuation of the Joint Committee and Union's discriminatory policies. The GSA by making it possible for the Union and Joint Committee to function on the government building project, the violent alternative of which, unfortunately, would be to stop construction; the Bureau by extending direct aid and assistance, and recognition and in effect giving its blessing to the practices of the Joint Committee.

"This clear condemnation of the Union and the Joint Apprenticeship Committee, and the inadequate response of those federal agencies charged with the duties of enforcing the executive order should have produced a prompt and widespread response in the construction industry. It should also have produced a vigorous and effective program of governmental supervision and enforcement of the executive order.

"Unfortunately, it produced neither. We investigated three contractors during the week of September 10 of this year who had relations with the same Union, Iron Workers Local 1. That investigation disclosed that the first black employee was taken into the union in 1966, three years after the Chicago Court House decision. These contractors today do not expect to secure meaningful numbers of minority employees from this Union. The state of affairs exists despite the fact that in 1965 the Department of Labor undertook to establish an apprenticeship recruitment program for the building trades in connection with the Washburne Trade School.

"Information available to the department makes it clear that Local 1 remains substantially all white. The compliance review makes it clear the contractors generally obtain their employees through the Union and that the Union refers Union members before it refers non-union members. Under these circumstances, the situation with respect to minority employment in the Iron Workers trade is little changed since 1963.

"I mentioned the Iron Workers Apprenticeship Program because that program has been the subject of searching judicial scrutiny and because the apprentice system has been viewed as a method by which young men could become journeyman craftsmen.

"The evidence with respect to the iron workers established that the apprentice route to the journeyman which was officially closed in 1963 and was opened a trifle in 1966, is still not genuinely available to minority youths. Six years of effort since the Chicago Court House case have brought us only to the point where, of 222 structural iron workers apprentices, 20 are Negro, two American Indians and 11 of Spanish descent, as of June 30 of this year.

"These figures graphically illustrate why it is necessary to develop an alternate route by which interested young men can become journeymen. The apprenticeship program is simply inadequate to provide meaningful equal opportunity under the executive order, taking into consideration the fact that there are only 12 minority journeymen out of a total of 2,300 current members of Local 1. Furthermore, the apprenticeship training program is associated with the Washburne Trade School which has a discriminatory past, and the school's administration standards depend upon the judgment of those who until recent years overtly excluded minorities from the trade.

"Let me turn now to a general summary of the findings of our investigation into the six grades and the contractors who dealt with the six unions involved.

"First, we found that the unions involved had relatively few minority group members. In no case did any union have more than 4.6 percent minority group members.

"Secondly, we found that the unions invariably refer members for work before they refer a non-member. This was stated to us again and again by contractors dealing with each of the trades. It follows from these two factors that to the extent the contractor relies upon the union as a referral device, he will inevitably secure a white labor force.

"All of these unions maintain control over the labor supply through the following techniques: One, direct union referrals and two, union approval of individuals recruited by the employer. The existence of this has made it difficult for employers to secure minority employees because it required them to not only make special recruiting effort to obtain minority employees, but then to send those employees or their names through for approval by the union. In other words, the employers would simply not place a man on the job who had not been approved by the union.

"As a result of the system which I have described, very few employers whom we investigated have made any real or substantial effort to obtain minority employees. They knew that they could not get such employees through the union and few of them actively sought minority employees by recruiting or upgrading their own labor.

"In our investigations we did encounter three cases where it appeared that employers had, in fact, exercised options to recruit and upgrade minority employees.

"As to the other employers, their reliance, whether required or not, on the union referral system has guaranteed that they would secure a substantially all-white labor force. This, in fact, has happened and government contracts are being executed today in Chicago with a substantially all-white labor force in some crafts, which is exclusionary, segregationist and discriminatory against minority employee persons.

"Many of the employers whom we investigated had, as required, submitted affirmative action statements to HUD as a part of an effort to secure compliance with Executive Order 11246. Their performance was in the main in sharp contrast to their affirmative action statements.

With respect to the 17 contractors against whom we are recommending sanctions, the figure shows that these contractors have 1,445 journeyman employees of whom 101 are minority group individuals.

"These facts are well-known in the trade and are known to the contractors. In effect, they enter upon the performance of federally-financed contracts vowing non-discrimination and affirmative action but knowing that their collective bargaining relations and their own recruitment practices will produce a substantially segregated labor force.

"Employers in the construction industry are not immune from the obligations of the executive order. Even if these obligations cannot be fulfilled within the framework of the collective bargaining system operated in the construction industry, the executive order must be obeyed. It is clear that except for three of the employers investigated, these obligations are not being fulfilled.

"In light of all this background and other material which I have been submitting to you, it is clear to me that the time has come for the government itself to take the kind of affirmative action which it has long stated is required of contractors. Court suits, training programs financed by the department of labor, informal efforts at mediation urged on by and supported by government officials at the highest level have all been tried. All have failed to produce meaningful adjustment to the situation.

"The contractors and unions must understand and believe that the federal government now means to implement the powers which Judge Campbell pointed out some six years ago were available to it to assure equality of opportunity. At this late date the credibility of the federal effort can be established only by the application of sanctions. Those sanctions, once applied, should facilitate effective and meaningful action to provide for a rapid increase in minority employment opportunities in the construction trades."

Thomas J. McArdle, regional director of the U.S. Bureau of Labor Statistics, North Central Region:

(McArdle had been working with the federal task force that prepared for the hearings, seeking to collect information about minority group participation in the trades at the time, and projecting the construction industry needs for manpower to 1975, using three different industry growth factors. His table also includes figures no one else had mentioned: the number of jobs that will be available due to "replacement needs," the normal turnover due to deaths and retirements of men currently in the trades. The following table, for the Chicago area, was presented at the hearing by McArdle.)

Projected Growth Rates
Journeymen and Apprentices

	1969 Total Journeymen and Apprentices	1975 Projected Growth Rate Estimates		
		3.3%	6.6%	9.9%
Asbestos Workers	907	937	967	997
Brick Layers	4,593	4,745	4,896	5,048
Carpenters	29,991	30,981	31,970	32,960
Cement Masons	2,620	2,706	2,793	2,879
Electricians	8,623	8,908	9,192	9,477
Elevator Installers	625	646	666	687
Glaziers	400	413	426	440
Iron Workers:				
Architectural	1,014	1,047	1,081	1,114
Ornamental	1,010	1,043	1,077	1,110
Structural	2,522	2,605	2,688	2,772
Metal Lathers	700	723	746	769
Painters	11,303	11,676	12,049	12,422
Pipe Fitters	8,404	8,681	8,959	9,236
Plasterers	823	850	877	904
Plumbers	3,846	3,973	4,100	4,227
Roofers	1,298	1,341	1,384	1,427
Sheet Metal	4,974	5,138	5,302	5,466
Sprinkler Fitters	365	377	389	401
Operating Engineers	8,077	8,344	8,610	8,877
Total	92,095	95,134	98,172	101,213

Current Minority Participation and Replacement Needs
Journeymen and Apprentices

	Journey-men	1969 Minorities No.	%	Apprentices Total 6-30-69	Minority 6-30-69 No.	%	Replacement Needs Deaths & Retirements
Asbestos							
Workers	800	3	0.4	107	2	1.9	100
Brick Layers	4,400	200	4.5	193	42	21.8	550
Carpenters	29,300	200	0.7	691	64	9.3	3,662
Cement Masons	2,500	500	20.0	120	25	20.8	313
Electricians	7,831	300	3.8	792	43	5.4	979
Elevator							
Installers	625	1	0.2	0	0	0	78
Glaziers	400	1	0.3	0	0	0	50
Iron Workers:							
Architectural	907	1	0.1	107	5	4.7	113
Ornamental	1,000	1	0.1	10	4	40.0	125
Structural	2,300	12	0.5	222	33	14.9	288
Metal Lathers	700	0	0	0	0	0	88
Painters	11,000	350	3.2	303	96	31.7	1,250
Pipe Fitters	7,800	16	0.2	604	18	3.0	975
Plasterers	800	100	12.5	23	7	30.4	100
Plumbers	3,440	100	2.9	406	16	3.9	430
Roofers	1,070	74	6.9	228	29	12.7	134
Sheet Metal							
Workers	4,668	4	0.1	306	16	5.2	584
Sprinkler							
Fitters	260	0	0	105	2	1.9	33
Operating							
Engrs.	8,000	486	4.6	77	41	53.2	1,000
Total	87,801	2,349		4,294	443		10,852

(Number of apprentices and number of minority apprentices derived
from BAT reports. Number of journeymen and minority journeymen
derived from EEO reports for referral unions and from information
provided by the Federal Regional Task Force from discussions with
other individual unions.)

Menasco: Let's work with the total for a second. There are 92,000
people in the construction industry in the Chicago standard metropolitan statistical area?

McArdle: Yes.

Menasco: And you are speaking of the fact that there are 10,000
vacancies projected here. Wait a second. 13,000, approximately.

McArdle: Roughly. The economic growth (at the 3.3% rate, which
he had said was conservative) plus the replacement needs.

Menasco: About 13,000 slots in five years is 2,500 a year?

McArdle: Roughly.

Menasco: These are new slots?

McArdle: Yes.

The Rev. C. T. Vivian, chairman of the Coalition for United Community Action:

" . . . In front of this building, a federal building, we found ourselves
surrounded, crowded, overpowered, and dismissed by an unruly mob
of labor people. We found that there was not police protection. The
federal government did not give itself protection even for its own pre-
mises, nor for the witnesses that it called before it. I have seen, in the
last few hours, men beaten who had come on the call of the federal
government. There is no indication that anything was going to be done
about it . . . If you are serious, you will have federal troops tomorrow
outside of this building to insure the black community that there can
be law and order in fact.

"For it is this kind of basic understanding that the black community needs in order to believe that this hearing is anything more than
words . . .And in terms of one of your last witnesses, it's been very
clear that 17 companies in Chicago that are now in the process of
conducting construction have broken the rules and laws and we are
asking that in fact they be turned down; that those projects be closed
down until government guidelines and government laws and regulations are in fact obeyed.

"I suppose that coming here from that same scene in the streets
points out something about the signs that were carried by the trade

unionists there. They said, 'No train, no work.' This is exactly what we are talking about, that we are saying that we desire to be trained, but have never had that opportunity.

"When we look at the signs out in the streets, and they say 'Civil Rights for All,' the very truth is that the sign is ironic in the hands of a trade unionist, because they have been one of the major forces who have seen that there are no civil rights for black people. There have been civil rights for white people, but not black people in the trade unions. Federal money has been spent, but there has been no equal inclusion of black people. Hiring halls, which are against the law, have continued to exist. We have been able to see the seniority system used as a means of keeping us out.

". . . In Chicago, there is a population of 3,600,000 people; 1,173,000 of those are black. That percentage is 32.5. Almost a third. 1950, it was 14 percent. In 1960, it was 22.9 percent. And by 1980, just eleven years from now, the majority of voters in the city will be black people.

"Then you begin to look at another perspective. We are poor. Thirty percent of us have family income of less than $3,000. The average years of formal schooling is 9.3. The large and growing segment of the population suffers from high unemployment. So we begin to deal with this labor figure and with new guidelines. We are talking about the economic survival of black people in this city and cities like this. So our proposal to unions in the city is to try to take into consideration these facts and the reality that we think is basic, by movement to establish alternative training programs that will allow black people to be trained into the unions, into work jobs, into the skills that are basic for the survival of the average man in our society . . . So when we present a proposal, we have said to the unions, let us make no qualifications in terms of age; make them wide enough to fit the realities of a black community that has been pushed out. We dealt with the matter of qualifications in terms of schooling. Our concern was, looking at the figure of 9.3 (average years of schooling in the black community) that we drop any consideration of high school and we deal with functional testing that will see not whether a young person has got the capacity to pass a test, or not pass a test, but whether or not he can do a day's work.

"Another thing we have been saying . . . for there is written in the invisible racism of the trade unions, that a person between 17 and 24. . . not have a police record. The truth of the matter is that the average young black man living in the ghetto with the kind of police action that you saw outside today is harassed all of his life, and that it is unusual to find a young man . . . that has not been in jail for one reason or another. Reasons usually not of his own doing, but reasons that are largely because of police harassment. Or when it's of his own doing they are very minor offenses.

"Let us look at the streets again for clarification of what we are talking about. We have two young men beaten in the streets today by the trade unionists and the police arrested them, those who were beaten. That points up the kind of realities of black life we have to deal with if we are going to construct new kinds of programs that fit the black condition . . . We are asking that black people be trained by black people, or at least the administration of any programs for black people be in the hands of black people. For what the issue is in the street today is not a labor issue; it is a race issue . . . racism was rampant in the street. The signs were trying to say one thing while underneath there was another, and before the morning was over it was very clear they were not talking about labor, they were talking about race. And we cannot allow men like that to be in charge of the training of black people.

". . . We are not asking that our young men come upon those jobs at full scale any more than we would for any apprentice. We are not asking for apprenticeship programs, but for some of the basic kinds of scales that go into it so we can together be able to figure out a means that trains us in and not trains us out . . . For instance, we are asking in the new programs cross training so that if a young man finds . . . he doesn't make a good carpenter, but he'd make a terrific plumber, or maybe the other way around, that he be given the opportunity to cross train without being thrown out of the program.

". . . We are asking to come into an expanding industry, not one that is disappearing. In a couple of trades there are things happening but in another way, in the large picture, all are expanding. Population will be doubled by 2005, and we can't even build enough houses for what we have. We ask for a measly 1,000 training slots. This is to show our interest, not to fulfill the total demand. . . . We are talking to the big three, where justice is decided. We must take action between big business, big labor and big government. What we are saying is that no longer can two of these be involved in producing and training and control of a basic industry. Government must be involved as well. . .

". . . We are saying every black man that comes through our program would know his trade when he's finished. We don't mean we would be putting $200 under the table and getting two people to sign for us, who are also paid. We want to live with pride. We don't want to live with some kind of slipshod method. We want to be on the job now. We want it backed up by the government. We want to learn our trade, and we want it backed up by the black community . . .

"We want to create the Chicago Plan where we work together, all four of us, create the plan that could become the model of the United

States. Out of the midwest can come things for the entire nation. We can do it together, unions, builders, coalition, government—together. Create a model upon which we can deal with racism in fact and deal with expanding economy . . . We can stop the inflation, get rid of a good deal of welfare rolls and instead of creating a culture of poverty, create a condition that takes us out of poverty. We have the opportunity, gentlemen. This is a tremendous moment . . . ''

(A member of the government panel asked Rev. Vivian's reactions to the labor-industry proposals.)

"What we started with was this: We said we want 10,000 training slots now. That's where we started. Because of trying to negotiate and trying to deal as realistically as possible, we said, all right, we'll make it 5,500 a year for five years, and that was negotiable . . . Now, they said, 'we offer 4,000' and this we had at the table. We went on city-wide radio and TV to say, 'let us negotiate, and we'll start at 4,000. We'll accept the 4,000. We are reasonable men.' So we came down to 4,000 in order to negotiate, and then when they go to the table to negotiate, they said their position was non-negotiable.''

(Rev. Vivian then outlined the Coalition's objections to the way the industry's proposal divided the 4,000 jobs, which did not provide for that many new training slots, and to the provision for committees to run the program under mostly-white control.)

". . . They wanted us to have two things: to be advisory, which meant we would not share anything and, on the other hand, to recruit for them, and what that would mean, in terms of everything in the past, would be that we would go out and recruit young black men to be in a situation where their hopes would be destroyed, where they would be trained out instead of in, where motivation would be killed and where white racism such as you saw in the streets today would run rampant. That's why we could not agree with that program. It was not a realistic offer because of all the hookers that went with it.

"When they come back we are willing to talk. We believe that reasonable people can come to a just and reasonable conclusion. We believe that people in this life should not talk about their position being non-negotiable. . . Labor peace is what we desire, not on the old terms, but in a way that deals with the realities of the black community.''

Jo Ann Chandler, third year law student at University of Chicago Law School, who had been studying the apprenticeship system:

"Many of the unions use the facilities of the Washburne Trade School, a publicly financed institution, for the classroom component of their programs. Despite this use of a public facility, the selection of young men to fill the limited slots which are available in these programs is left entirely within the control of the joint apprenticeship committee of each trade — composed half of union and half of contract — or representatives.

"In 1960, these small committees had cumulatively selected 2,700 apprentices, the enrollment at the school at the time, but had included only 26 blacks among them—less than one percent. It has been at least since 1960 that this virtual exclusion of blacks from Washburne had been a cause of concern in the minority community. The minority leadership charged that nepotism was the basis of the selection of apprentices, that racial discrimination was practiced if nepotism was not, that information regarding apprenticeship opportunities was never revealed to non-whites, and that if a black applicant somehow found his way to the correct office, his application was conveniently misplaced and forgotten.

"In the only judicial opinion ever dealing directly with charges of discrimination against a building trade apprentice program in Chicago, Chief Judge Campbell of the Federal District Court for Northern Illinois classified the selection process of the structural ironworkers apprenticeship program as 'invidiously discriminatory.' Since 1963, when that opinion was written, many things have changed.

"For instance, where there was only one percent black apprentices enrolled at Washburne in 1960, there are now six percent black apprentices in the programs—187 men out of 3,070 as of January 31, 1969. Since this increase in participation is often cited as conclusive evidence of the non-discrimination of the joint apprenticeship committees, it might be well to look closely at the performance of the four largest apprentice programs which function at Washburne; the pipe fitters program had no black apprentices in 1963, when the size of the program was 159 men; in 1969, out of 636 participants, still only 12 (2 percent) were black.

"The electricians' program included 12 blacks out of 590 men in 1963 and 37 blacks (6 percent) out of 612 in 1969. The carpenters had 10 blacks out of 166 in 1963 and 26 (6 percent) of 437 in 1969. Finally, the sheet metal workers had no black apprentices in 1963 when the enrollees numbered 235, and still had only 12 (3 percent) of 360 in 1969.

"Other things have changed since 1963. The civil rights act has become law, the department of labor has set up regulations which are intended to keep the stamp of federal registration off any apprenticeship program which does not recruit and select its participants in a totally non-discriminatory fashion, the Apprenticeship Information Center has been established as a clearing house for information to the minority community concerning the opportunities in apprenticeship, the Urban League, under a contract with the Illinois State Employment Service and the Federal Department of Manpower Administration and Training has set up a recruitment and supportive services program which attempts to reach meaningfully into the minority community and recruit and aid young men to qualify for the apprenticeship programs, the Board of Education has at least taken the position that the programs should be non-discriminatory.

"Taking all these accomplishments into consideration, how should the present situation at Washburne be evaluated? My own assessment involves the answers to two questions: Has the recruitment of applicants been rendered effective in the minority community? Does the selection procedure operate on non-discriminatory standards once the minority applicants are recruited?

"Unless both can be answered affirmatively, problems remain.

"Every report which has ever been made on the Washburne Trade School has emphasized that communication must be established with the minority community and that information concerning the opportunities at the school must be widely disseminated in order to meet the mandate of non-discrimination. The Department of Labor regulations and the Bureau of Apprenticeship and Training seem to have eliminated the problem of outright secrecy, but there still are indications that the Urban League, the organization with the most effective contacts in the minority community for recruitment, is not receiving notification sufficiently in advance of the deadline to make its recruiting effective.

"It would not be useful to catalogue here all the agencies which engage in some form of activity which might be classified as recruiting in regard to the apprentice programs. No study has ever been made of the effectiveness of any of these activities. It is worth noting, however, that even the counselors at Washburne, who are responsible for recruiting in the minority community, feel that the job is very difficult and that minority students are not 'sold' on apprenticeship yet.

"In addition, within the Chicago public school system, where recruiting is intended to be at its best, the principal of one almost entirely black high school did not know the basic details concerning Washburne. If the administrators are uninformed, how can the students be reached?

"Yet the major indication of the failure of the recruitment program in the minority community is the continued image of the building trades as discriminators.

"The second phase of my assessment of the present situation at Washburne involves the selection procedures of the joint apprenticeship committees, which may be discovered by a diligent search of the files of the Bureau of Apprenticeship and Training. The standards have been approved as non-discriminatory by the bureau and are designed, in part, to diminish the range of subjective, potentially discriminatory, personal judgment.

"The much-discussed written (objective) examination does play a role in the selection procedures for the building trades. However, five of the programs which employ a written test use it only to give a normative cut-off point below which applicants are rejected, a procedure which minimizes the impact of this non-subjective criteria on the selection process.

"The use of variable awards would diminish the range of subjective evaluation by the selection committee but, unfortunately, such use of the written examination is desirable only if the test has been validated for such scoring—that is, if it has been proven to measure the capability of the examinee to succeed in the apprentice program. Such validation studies have not been completed for variable scoring on any of the written exams which are used, to my knowledge. Therefore, the very use of the tests for variable scoring may be discriminatory, at least under the guidelines of the Equal Employment Opportunity Commission, since the tests are unvalidated and may well have a differential impact upon black and white applicants.

"The high school transcript is another 'objective criteria' which is employed in the selection process by seven of the programs under discussion here. This is also desirable only to the extent that the past academic performance has a demonstrated relation to the performance ot the apprentice on the job. To my knowledge, this evaluation of the educational requirements has not been undertaken by the trades individually nor by any of the various agencies involved in the apprentice situation in Chicago.

"If the validity of the educational requirement could be established, the use of this non-subjective criteria would probably be another step toward assuring the non-discriminatory nature of the selection process.

"The most interesting characteristic of the present selection procedures of the joint apprenticeship committees is the prominence of the oral interview. The interview carries a possible point range of from 24 (of 100 points) for the pipe fitters to 40 for the sheet metal workers.

"The category is certainly a potential vehicle for discrimination and the judgments which must be made in a 20 minute period of the character, cooperativeness, and responsibility of the applicant are virtually unreviewable.

"It remains unfortunately impossible for me definitively to evaluate the selection procedures of each of the apprenticeship programs due to a lack of sufficient records. Each apprentice selection procedure should include a point allotment plan, a situation which does not presently exist.

"For each applicant, records should be made and filed with the Apprenticeship Information Center which would show where in the selection progress an applicant was eliminated. With such information, the policing agencies could perform their function. Other information should also be gathered.

"All written tests used in the selection procedure should be validated and evaluated for their differential impact on the minority versus nonminority applicant. The educational requirement should also be carefully evaluated for relation to performance on the job.

"An intensive study of the success or failure of the recruitment and informational campaigns should be undertaken so that finally an effective and sustained method of communication with the minority community would be established.

"If all these things were done, and done openly and if, in addition, an outside observer were allowed to sit in on the oral interview of the applicants for the apprentice position, even the minority community might begin to believe that discrimination had disappeared.

"It is natural in a situation such as this to look first to those who might be the direct discriminators—the building trades industry.

"However, my study revealed that the agencies responsible for policing the situation and enforcing non-discrimination also share the existing blame. They do not have sufficient information at their disposal to effectively invoke the sanctions which could end discrimination in these apprenticeship programs.

"In addition to the various federal agencies, the board of education has also apparently fallen short of its responsibility in this area. The board is committed to denying the use of Washburne, a public facility, to any apprenticeship program which discriminates. Yet, the Board does not have information such as that discussed above which would make use of this sanction possible. So the procedures of the industry continue and the entire legal arsenal has proven ineffective in the absence of reporting mechanism. Until such information is available no one will be able to say conclusively that racial discrimination is no longer a problem in the building trade apprenticeship program at Washburne."

Ashby Smith, Chicago Urban League:

". . .In 1963, the League played a key role in the establishment of the Apprenticeship Information Center established by the Illinois

State Employment Service. Designed to spread information about apprenticeship in minority communities, it suffered from lack of information, lack of direct contact with apprentice programs, and under-financing—all good ways to kill a program.

"In 1965, an Ad Hoc group known as the Coordinating Council of Community Organizations submitted an indictment of Washburne Trade School to the United States Office of Education . . . (It) produced a document implicating the contruction industry and the Board of Education in a conspiracy to bar blacks from apprenticeship. It took two years for the Office of Education to act . . .

"In late 1965, the United States Department of Labor became disturbed about the small number of minority identity persons in building trades apprenticeships. A Chicago Board of Education count revealed that only 55 minority group persons were among the area's 2,500 building trades apprentices. By 1966, the Chicago Urban League found only 15 of these 55 in apprenticeship.

"In December 1965, the Mayor of Chicago, Richard J. Daley, announced a campaign to bring minorities into the building trades. Surrounded by leaders in the construction industry—both management and labor—and officials of the United States Department of Labor, the Mayor's announcement looked promising.

"In January, 1966, the Chicago Urban League entered into a contract with the U.S. and Illinois Departments of Labor to recruit black youth to become apprentices; to provide whatever support that would be necessary in the way of tutoring and coaching; and to sell the concept of apprenticeship in the building trades to the black community. We felt that we might change a racially exclusive system to a racially inclusive system from inside. The evidence indicates that we were wrong.

" . . . For three years and nine months, the Apprentice Project of the Urban League has worked with and through the United States Department of Labor's Bureau of Apprenticeship and Training, the Illinois State Employment Service and its Apprenticeship Information Center, the Chicago Building Trades Council, the Chicago Building Construction Employers' Association and the Chicago Board of Education.

"With all of this cooperative involvement, only 491 black youth have become indentured as apprentices in the construction industry. Another 41 black youths have passed tests and are waiting for apprentice openings, and 453 are in the process of meeting apprentice program requirements. Eight hundred youth either failed to meet apprentice program qualifications or chose other careers in preference to waiting out the one to twelve month qualification period.

"The apprentices placed by the Urban League during this . . . period represent 11.4 percent of the 3,500 apprentices employed by the construction industry today. Only 2 percent of the apprentices found in late 1965 were non-white. This change may be looked at as progress, but the pace is woefully slow since these men are in programs that last from three to five years.

"Recruiting apprentice applicants is not an easy task. The League had included in the federal contract that we would 'sell' the concept of apprenticeship to the black community. This was necessary because the black community knew that skilled jobs for its members were severely restricted by collusion between the unions, contractors and school systems.

"The black community also knew from experience that this collusion was condoned by government units at all levels and accepted by almost everyone else except those discriminated against and their advocates. It was in this context that the Urban League went out to recruit apprentice candidates.

"The construction industry has not recruited intensively for apprenticeship and building trades jobs in any public way. There are very few printed materials about jobs and apprenticeships in the local construction industry, and none had been made available by the industry . . . The League continues to be the only source for specific information about apprenticeship to the general public.

"The lack of public recruitment activity by the industry and its Joint Apprenticeship Committees is traditional. Over the past eight decades craft unions preferred to secure apprentices and new workers through referral and sponsorship from the current membership or from contractors. With very few, or in some cases, no black union members, black men were effectively kept out by this incestuous recruitment system.

"Some change has occurred in this area, but not enough . . . The Chicago Urban League has learned many things about the workings of the construction industry . . . The most revealing discovery was the fact that the majority of craftsmen working in the building trades in the nation, and in Chicago, became journeymen without having gone through or completed the apprenticeship process. This is the reason so many journeymen are unfamiliar with apprenticeship.

"Blacks and other minorities have always been told that apprenticeship is the ONLY LEGITIMATE WAY to learn a craft. Ray Marshall, in his book called, *The Negro and Apprenticeship*, cited a 1963 Labor Department survey which stated that only 43.9 percent of the construction journeymen had been apprentices. The fact that less than half the workers gained their craft through apprenticeship reveals the existence of many other alternatives.

"The other alternatives are the permit system, the laborer system and the recommendation system. Simply described, all three require the recipient to get a construction job, to 'steal' the craft and present himself and his money to some sort of certifying board.

"The effectiveness of these paths to craftmanship depend entirely on a tight labor market of some duration for a particular craft. While some trades in some localities have chosen to shut off such routes, the same trades in other localities depend almost exclusively on them. These alternatives are open to blacks only if they circumscribe their activities to the ghetto.

". . . Age and education requirements of apprentice programs work against the black youth becoming an apprentice. A man must be between the ages of 17 and 27 years to be considered for apprenticeship. The preferred age range is 17 to 23 years.

"Today in Chicago, there are 65,378 black male youth in the 17 to 23 age group. Of that number 12,000 have a high school diploma (which is required by all but two crafts before one can become an apprentice candidate. [See Appendix A]). These 12,000 have career and education options in addition to the construction industry. Some enter college. Others enlist in the armed forces or are drafted. Many take jobs in other industries at a higher starting rate than is offered by apprenticeship.

"Many of these 12,000 youths would enter the building trades if the construction industry had a real program for recruitment and if black youths believed that equality of opportunity and results actually existed there.

"The other 53,378 black youths from 17 to 23 years of age have no high school diploma. That is one thing they have in common with many white journeymen. These black youths are excluded from all apprenticeship programs except the carpenters and the bricklayers. In these two programs, the requirement for high school graduation has been dropped. The League's apprenticeship program has had no trouble in finding good, trainable young men to qualify and become apprentices.

"When the Chicago Urban League accepted the Apprenticeship Project in 1966, we set out to make changes in an institution. At first, we thought that opening the door to apprenticeship for black youths would rectify the situation.

"We know better now. The whole system surrounding the institution of the construction industry must undergo change. The current confrontation with the black community led by the Coalition for United Community Action is part of that change process.

"This clash with the black community comes at a time when that community had begun to believe that the construction industry was ready to do more than admit a few apprentices to each trade. It was expected that the government-financed construction in the ghetto would mean jobs and training for black people in their own neighborhoods. This was especially implicit in model cities and urban renewal projects. Instead, we find that black people are locked in the ghetto and are not even allowed to build the walls of their prison. The continued lack of sensitivity by the construction industry to the needs of the majority of black people who have been excluded from good jobs is the basic cause of the current clash. The presence of a few black craftsmen, a few apprentices, and fewer black contractors is not enough. The high proportion of black laborers, the semi-skilled and unskilled members of the construction work force, serves only to further pinpoint the exclusion of blacks from the skilled positions in this industry.

". . . The Coalition in its demand for on-the-job training, is calling for a systems change. They are saying that it should not take three to five years to train a mechanic. They are saying that apprenticeship should not be the only recognized route for blacks to journeyman status. They are saying that the industry should take action to afford black workers the same opportunities, exceptions and privileges that white workers now get. And with each of these assertions, we agree. The need for more good jobs for black men is past the point of discussion without action."

Hugh McRae, assistant secretary to the Building Construction Employers' Association of Chicago:

(McRae explained that the association is composed of ten employer groups that deal with individual trades, but that it does not enter into collective bargaining agreements with any union, serving instead as a clearing house for information and participation in general programs. For ten years, he said, the association has tried to interest blacks in building jobs but has been frustrated by apparent lack of interest in these specific trades.)

"An additional matter of concern is the acute lack of skilled craftsmen available for work in the building trades and the consequent pressure on wages and the cost of construction. An obvious response to, and partial solution to this problem, was the recruitment and employment of members of minority groups into these trades, inasmuch as minority groups represent the most logical source of available labor in today's economy.

"We have reservations about a quota system.* . . . Such an approach cannot create additional skilled workmen, either black or white, and

_____

(See Note on following page.)

will, in the end, only foster the concentrated utilization of skilled tradesmen from the minority groups in projects subject to the executive order . . . The aim can best be served by a substantial increase in the present training facilities and programs and by aggressive recruitment for such programs, to the end that the total minority group labor pool will be expanded for all construction work in the Chicago area and not just that in which the federal government has an interest."

(McRae then testified about what he had noticed taking place with the Urban League program designed to prepare recruits for apprenticeship. He pointed out two problems:

1. A recruit signs up for apprentice training and then, while waiting for an opening, perhaps takes a job as a construction laborer. When the slot opens up, he elects to stay where he is because the training period would be at less pay under existing collective bargaining contracts than what he is earning as a laborer.

2. Offers of employment in the construction industry are "frequently" turned down by minority group apprentices because of difficulties in getting to the job sites, which are often inconvenient to public transportation. The recruit may need a car and not be able to get one.)

Fletcher: Has your association any reservations about meeting with the Coalition?

McRae: Our association feels that there are certain members or groups . . . that are not responsible . . . We do not feel that the gangs are responsible groups . . . The gangs who

---

* He was referring to the Philadelphia Plan, widely opposed by the construction industry. The Labor Department fact sheet on compliance, distributed at the federal hearings in Chicago, had this to say about the Philadelphia Plan:

"On June 27, 1969, the Department of Labor announced an important new concept for substantially increasing minority group employment in the higher-paying construction trades in federally-involved construction work. The new concept — which features the government setting acceptable ranges for hiring members of minority groups — was first put into effect in five Philadelphia area counties on July 18, 1969. That program, involving six virtually all-white building trades, is called the Philadelphia Plan.

"Issued under Executive Order 11246, the order establishing the Philadelphia Plan charges the Office of Federal Contract Compliance with setting the acceptable ranges of minority group participation after interested parties – including contractors, unions, and civil rights groups — were given an opportunity to present their views.

"Secretary Shultz has highly praised the order, calling it a 'fair and realistic approach, not an arbitrary formula, to achieve equal employment opportunity in federally-involved construction.'

"The new order requires contractors bidding on federal construction projects exceeding $500,000 to submit affirmative action plans setting specific goals for utilization of minority employees.

"The six trades involved are: iron work, plumbing and pipefitting, steamfitting, sheet metal work, electrical work, and elevator construction work.

"Acceptable ranges of goals will be based upon:
  * The current extent of minority group participation in the trade;
  * Availability of minority group persons for employment in such trade.
  * The need for training programs in the area and/or the need to assure demand for those in or from existing training programs;
  * Impact of the program upon the existing labor force.

"The order has national implications. The Philadelphia Plan, or an appropriate variation of it based on experience in that area and the realistic requirements for equal opportunity elsewhere, will be extended to other areas as soon as practicable."

had their names on the proposal we received were the
Black P Stone Nation and the Conservative Vice Lords.

Menasco: What is the current status of negotiations?

McRae: The current status is that we have said that when responsible people from the black community will come forth, we are willing to discuss this local situation with them.

Menasco: . . . if you could eliminate certain of these that you could identify as being not responsible . . . Do you consider the Rev. Vivian responsible?

McRae: Yes. I have no way of knowing whether Rev. Vivian really thought our proposal was a good one or not because he was the spokesman that particular day and he rejected it, but that was the consensus from their caucus.

Menasco: I'd hesitate to really suggest that the Employers Association scissor part of their people out because of the negotiations or in the union — that part of them be excluded . . .

(When the hearing reconvened the next day, Friday, September 26, members of the government panel seemed to be following a new path in questioning witnesses about the Coalition's refusal to accept the industry-union proposals. They stressed more and more the word "recommendation" in the industry-union ad, which said the Building Trades Council would recommend to member unions that they accept or ratify the proposal, but that that had not actually been done at the time. The government panelists were tending to say that the reason the Coalition turned down the proposal was that a recommendation is not a bona fide offer, that it could not be considered until the unions had ratified it, that had that ratification taken place, the proposal would not have been turned down. That was an idea that had not been pursued by Coalition spokesmen before; perhaps it was a government suggestion of a way out of the apparent impasse.)

Fletcher: It appears to me that the construction industry leadership is saying, "We think the Black Coalition is not credible, not responsible," and the Black Coalition is saying, "We are not too sure that your credibility is good because you haven't spoken to the membership of the locals to find out whether they will buy it or not." And so both sides are claiming the other side is not fully responsible.

Richard Pepper, president of a construction company and past president of the Builders Association of Chicago:

". . . In the November 1969 class (of a carpenters' apprentice program), 20 of the 80 openings will be reserved for hard-core minority youths referred by responsible minority agencies. They will be admitted without interview, without testing, and without screening of any type by the program. We believe that this is indeed a forward looking, challenging approach to the solution of minority representation in the trades."

Arthur F. O'Neil, chariman of the board of a construction company and president of the Builders Association of Chicago:

"For the past nine months management and labor in the Chicago construction industry have been working closely together in the assemblage of manpower surveys and long-range work projections in an effort to determine how much input of manpower the trades in the Chicago area needed to meet the demands of the industry both presently and deep into the 1970s. Months of study and discussion brought to light the fact that rather massive inputs were required into most of the trades, not only to keep pace with the death and retirements of tradesmen, but to keep pace with the construction growth pattern projected for the 1970s. It is estimated that an input approaching twice as much as had occurred in the years 1967 and 1968 would be necessary to accomplish orderly industry growth and to meet the demands of the future.

". . . Although we in the Chicago construction industry concede the fact that there is not only room for, but a very essential need for, improvement and speed-up in the apprentice training program, it is both labor's and management's confirmed opinion that apprenticeship of one duration or another is certainly the best avenue of entry into the trades.

"It is the view of the industry that the suggested new training programs would be more vigorously performed if funded by industry rather than by government grants . . . Furthermore, under a quota system the individual would run the risk of not only losing the teacher-instructor relationship, but would also run the very real risk of having the injection of large numbers of unskilled trainees coming into the system, having a detrimental effect on the productivity of the present journeyman group and quite possibly developing strong prejudices against black workers performing work with a much lesser degree of skill but laying claim to the same high wage scales. It should also be noted that, next to mining, construction is the most hazardous industry on the American scene. It would, in our opinion, be a grave injustice to expose scores of untrained and unskilled young men to the ever present hazards of injury or death.

"Rather than quotas of completely unskilled workers, we believe it would be to the greater interest of the public, the city and the country for the construction industry to intensify its efforts in developing a pool of reasonably skilled manpower rather than to reach into an area of totally unskilled workers in the hope that they shall miraculously and immediately perform various skilled tasks. It is with this thought in mind that we will push with all due intensity the implementation of the plan which was announced by our industry in Chicago on September 4.

Fletcher: . . . I listened to your testimony and I assumed when you made reference to what we call goals you referred to those as quotas. Were you talking about the Philadelphia Plan?

O'Neil: I am in opposition to the theory of quotas for the reasons that I have expressed; namely, that there will be a lot of untrained people that will have to be brought into these trades which have been restrictive up to this point and these people are not going to learn their jobs overnight. It is going to produce a very uneconomical procedure for contracting. Just what its total effect on costs will be is hard to project accurately but it is going to have a very profound effect on the total construction costs if you are going to work with untrained people.

Fletcher: Then you are not familiar with the Philadelphia Plan . . . (He later asked O'Neil about dealing with the Coalition.)

O'Neil: We frankly have been disappointed in relating to the Coalition. It is such a large and complex organization, that we failed to comprehend its operations. We have had a half a dozen meetings with them and it is very difficult — a very difficult bargaining situation. For one thing, they are representing a group that is too large. They come in in a large body of people and we feel that some of their leadership is more interested in their following, which they carry with them, rather than in the issues at hand at times. We also have a very distinct objection to the gang relationship, the street gang identification in the Coalition. We don't care to enter into a contract such as was presented to us, with the Black P Stone Nation or with the Conservative Vice Lords, or these other names listed on a legal document. We are not about to go that route. Therefore, if the Coalition insists on this kind of association, we are not going to relate to the Coalition. It is that simple.

John Wilks, director of Office of Federal Contract Compliance, one of the government panel members:

> Well, it seems to me the problem is that the Coalition has the right to select its own leadership. Now, maybe there should be — it seems to me that you might get some compromise on who does the talking, but I don't see how you can select their leaders for them.

O'Neil: Apparently I am not getting across. I am working under an instruction not to deal directly with the Coalition. This is our committee and I am only one of a dozen men.

Wilks: We understand your position, but I am just trying to interpret what I think is their position, and I don't see how you can ever hope, any more than the Coalition could hope, to determine who is going to be your spokesman.

O'Neil: Rev. Vivian is a very lucid and clear-thinking and articulate fellow and it is good to work with him, but I can't say that for all of the people he is associated with, and some of them are so provocative that our people on our side of the table just don't want to sit on the other side of the table from people like them. They are provocative. They are insultingly provocative. Not that we can't take insult, but we don't come back to it time after time after time. Now, we have had that experience.

Wilks: Have they had experience in working with members of the black community before, your group?

O'Neil: Some of them have, but many of us have not.

Wilks: So they don't know what it is like, working in the black community?

O'Neil: It is something of a new experience, yes, sir. But there are very many reasonable men in the Coalition. It is just the provocative group, I guess, that has perhaps established a tone, you might say, of the meetings which makes reasonable negotiations almost impossible.

Wilks: Now, why, when it comes to a community, can't a group of people who live together decide who they want to be members of their group?

O'Neil: We don't subscribe to the street gangs.

Wilks: Where do you get the prerogative to decide, that is what I want to know.

O'Neil: Possibly we don't have that prerogative.

(Fletcher proceeded to defend the idea of having gangs in on the agreement because "These are the people who need the jobs, who will go into training and gang leaders are the link . . . Don't exclude them just because they don't fit your pattern . . . May I conclude this by saying that I was one of the roughest street gang leaders in Los Angeles?")

The Rev. Jesse Jackson, director of Operation Breadbasket, whose arrival had just caused more trouble on the street outside:

"The existing gap between the greedy and the needy sows seeds for revolution of gigantic and unprecedented proportion . . . Those men downstairs are misdirected, confused, frustrated and exploited because they are insecure. Somebody up above has them there. They have told them: 'There are not enough jobs to go around. Black men threaten your existence.'

"Somebody has forgotten to tell them that the builders in the last three years have had 94 percent net profit while their wages have only gone up 33 percent, and the standard of living 10 percent.

"The poor blacks and the poor whites are not each other's problems. They are each other's alleged stumbling blocks, but the real question is: who puts the stumbling blocks there? Who set the nation up on a collision course so some can ride on boats and in yachts, while others' babies starve . . . and freeze in the wintertime . . . This is not so much the land of opportunity as has been rumored. It is the land of abundance and men have an opportunity to distribute the abundance in such a way until man's age old enemies of poverty and ignorance and disease will no longer be on the face of the earth. We can't merely judge the greatness of a nation by the presence of affluence, but by the absence of poverty. We are here to state that black people in Chicago are determined to build and to participate in the construction boom that brings this city and metropolitan area over $1.8 billion each year.

"We are a new people. We will not be aborted. We will not take a back seat. We will die for what we believe in and we will live for what is already ours. We want to work. We want to be trained. Perhaps we are not qualified but we are qualifiable. Perhaps we are not educated but we are educable. We only need the opportunity . . .

"We realize that our protests create counter-protests. We seek jobs. It is understandable that white workers seek to remain employed, and white workers should be employed, and we were not picketing to take their jobs. We were picketing to challenge the whole labor and government structure to appreciate that there is a little crisis here . . . The jobs that we fight for are for security, protection, opportunity, food, clothing, shelter, education and the necessities of life . . .

"We want a third of the decision making power in the city. We are a third of the population, so if there are 90,000 in the trades unions, we want 30,000 of them. If it isn't but 90, then we want 30. I don't care how much it is. If it is only 15, we ought to have 5, and if it ain't but 3, we ought to have 1, and if it ain't but 1, we ought to have a race and I know we will win then.

". . . We do not want unqualified black men to build houses which we have got to live in, or build bridges we have got to crosss, or build schools which our children will have to attend. We want all of our men to be qualified, but the real issue is that they never have the opportunity to be qualified.

". . . Labor and business now have a marriage . . . the only reason the marriage stuck was because they developed an impersonal third party and arbitrators and mediators and impersonal judges where, when the going got rough, neither party was free to desert the other without being challenged by the government which was the third force — or another force.

"Labor would not absolutely trust business. Business would not trust labor. So they developed the third party, that both had to respect . . . if the black community and labor are to marry and labor and business marry, we must have an impersonal third party, whether it is the government or whatever force, that both parties will respect, so if we don't come up with our end of the bargain we can be called to account. And if they don't come in with their end of the bargain, they can be called to account."

Meredith Gilbert, Coalition negotiator, president of the Lawndale Freedom Movement:

". . . I want to set Mr. O'Neil straight about who is responsible. I am responsible, the responsible leader of and chief negotiator for the Coalition, whether Mr. O'Neil likes it or not. Now he will have to sit at the negotiating table and across from me and whether or not I sit across physically from him at that table, you can rest assured that my influence will be there and in the decision that the Coalition makes, any decision that it makes will be determined in a great degree by me . . ."

The Range of Federal Interest

That was the end of the federal hearings in Chicago but not the end of federal involvement in the city's construction affairs. Further federal action did not await eventual agreement on the Chicago Plan, even though local negotiations were continuing and Labor Secretary Shultz continued to stress the desirability of "home-grown" solutions to the construction enigma. Doubtless the continued involvement served as a spur to the local negotiations.

A wide range of government policies and actions affected the Chicago scene. They centered around three main functions: the engineering of the over-all economy, planning to meet manpower needs, and enforcement of the anti-discrimination provisions of laws and executive orders. The fact that the actions seemed sometimes to be contradictory is due to the complexity of each of the areas, to the political necessities and stresses in each, to the personalities involved in the formulation of policies, and to that basic problem around which this chapter revolves — the difficulty of changing vast institutions.

The first area, that of the over-all economy, was dominated by the inflation that had been building since the expansion of the United States' role in Vietnam in 1965. Curbing the inflation was a major governmental concern by the last half of 1969. One way to halt or slow inflation is to cut back on demand; the administration had sought to do that in private construction earlier in the year by tightening restrictions on credit. The demand for new housing, measured in housing starts, had been dramatically affected. But government building is itself a significant part of the demand picture, and the next administration step was to announce a 75 percent cutback in funds for federal buildings. That was in early September, 1969, a time that could not have been more unfortunate for the Chicago negotiations. The decision threw the construction industry into a turmoil and the trade unionists into panic. It contributed heavily to the heat of the opinions expressed by construction workers on the streets of Chicago during the hectic federal hearings three weeks later.

Another way to put crimps into inflation is to increase supply. In the construction industry, that means increasing the supply of skilled tradesmen. There are two advantages to increasing that supply: it will make enough men available to handle the increased volume of building foreseen, and it will begin to control the spiralling wage costs that have been caused by the tight restrictions the construction unions have been able to impose on the entry of new men into the trades. The unions have been able to regulate the supply of new workers by limiting or expanding the number of apprentices they will admit; the limitations have been designed to provide job security for the men in a notably insecure industry. (The success of union policies is indicated by 1969 wage settlements; construction workers nationally averaged wage increases of 14 percent in 1969, compared with 7 percent for manufacturing employees.)

Increasing the pool of labor has been the concern of the government agencies charged with manpower development. Economists have estimated that at least two million new man-years of work should become available by 1978. If they do not become available, some building needs will not be met, costs will become higher, and the nation's housing problems will be further magnified.

These two aims — anti-inflation measures plus manpower expansion — produced an enigma: growing unemployment in the industry at the same time that great labor shortages were predicted. Both were true.

Compliance with anti-discrimination orders, the third major focus of government action affecting the construction industry, was hampered somewhat, too, by the instability of the industry. Efforts to require an increased proportion of black builders on federally-financed projects are only exercises on paper when the building isn't proceeding. And goals that might work in an expanding industry pose different kinds of problems at times of high unemployment, when more jobs for blacks seems to mean fewer jobs for whites. The construction employment picture, even when the industry is stable, is further complicated by the cyclical nature of building. In good weather, the men work a lot of overtime. Adding people to the labor pool affects both the overtime at peak periods and the amount of work per man at low periods of employment.

All of these aims, sometimes conflicting, were reflected in the federal hearings in Chicago.

APPENDIX

Entrance Requirements for Selected Apprenticeship Training
Programs Affiliated with Washburne Trade School, Chicago

Apprenticeship	Age Range	Educational Requirements	Term of Apprenticeship
Carpenters	17-27	2 years high school	4 years
Cement Masons	17-25	None	3 years
Electricians	18-25	High School grad. or GED	4 years
Ornamental Iron Workers	18-30	High School grad. or GED	4 years
Structural Iron Workers	18-30	High School grad. or GED	4 years
Metal Lathers	17-26	High School grad. or GED	3 years
Painters	18-25	High School grad. preferred	3 years
Pipe Fitters	18-26	H.S. Graduate	5 years
Plasterers	Over 17	H.S. Graduate or GED	4 years
Plumbers	18-25	H.S. Graduate or GED	5 years
Sheet Metal Workers	17-26	H.S. Graduate or GED	4 years
Sprinkler Fitters	18-26	H.S. Graduate or GED	5 years

Footnotes

1. F. Ray Marshall and Vernon M. Briggs, Jr., *The Negro and Apprenticeship*. The Johns Hopkins Press. Baltimore. 1967.

2. Such certification has always come from the joint apprenticeship committees. It is a step in which the federal government has never been involved. The committees have considerable autonomy.

Discussion Questions

1. Which groups operate the labor market in the construction industry? What are the constraints in the operation of the market?

2. What plans could you devise to give black workers a greater share in the construction industry? Consider the structure of the institutions involved and their relationships, authority, and incentives and the changes possible within each of these three potential areas for change.

3. What actions had governments at different levels taken and what was their effectiveness? What other actions might have been taken?

4. What features would you include in a voluntary anti-discrimination plan that would make the plan acceptable to the various parties affected: industry, unions, Coalition, government, public? What trade-offs would be required and how could they be sold?

There can be no doubt that negotiations in Chicago between the construction industry and unions, on one side, and the members of the Coalition, on the other, were influenced by the federal pressures during the extraordinary month of September, 1969. It is apparent that the pressures were felt in two ways, essentially contradictory:

1. They made it clear to all participants that, if they didn't arrive at an effective "home-grown" solution to the problem of black employment in the industry, then a federal solution, perhaps in the form of the much-feared Philadelphia Plan, would be imposed;

2. The very existence of so much heat (Simmons' insistent recommendations for hard sanctions, the reaction of the white workers and the tumultuous days of the federal hearings) made any sort of calm and effective negotiations extremely difficult.

Meetings between the two sides had been held before the federal team arrived to gather facts and the meetings did continue during part of the month while feelings were heating up. But perhaps it's unrealistic to call those early meetings "negotiations." At first, neither side had a clear position from which to negotiate. The builders and unions, concerned primarily with the shutdowns and understandably confused about the nature of the Coalition and what it sought, wanted the trouble stopped and building to continue; many of them were utterly opposed to even meeting with the black groups. And some of the blacks weren't really interested in negotiating either; frustrated and angry about their lack of power to control their own destinies, some were enjoying the heady sense of making people listen. To some at least, the shutdowns were an end in themselves. It is small wonder that the early meetings were tense and confused, with neither side sure of what the other represented or what its power was and with neither side sure, either, of what its own position was. Only gradually, after both sides had submitted proposals that were rejected, could a real process of negotiation begin.

David Reed, the cool-headed man who was a chief architect of the Coalition strategy, has been candid about the bargaining tools the Coalition used and about the problems they caused as well as the successes they achieved.

The Role of the Street Gangs

He has been candid, for example, about the inclusion of the youth gangs that so infuriated the other side and some of whose members served on the Coalition's 12-member steering committee.

"The young brothers played an important role," Reed said. "We could never have closed down the sites without those numbers. But their rhetoric didn't help much in negotiating. So the relationship was both positive and negative."

Reed noted that official Chicago is out "to bust the gangs" and added, "So are a lot of us. Who wants them? But police power is not the answer. Give people jobs, then there is no need to hang on the corner and steal to eat."

But there can be no doubt that presence of gang members at the bargaining table was hard on the process of negotiating.

"Several times our meetings broke down," Reed said, "not always because the other side was stubborn, but sometimes because my team did not have complete understanding of what the problem was and were a bit unrealistic about what to do next.

"The strategy was really rather simple," Reed reminisced. "It's my opinion that the way to really bring about change is to negatively affect those things that people depend on to function economically. The building industry accounts for 10 percent of the Gross National Product. That's a lot of dollars. We knew the unions were the culprits, but we couldn't let the contractors off the hook, because of Executive Order 11246. So we decided to close down the building projects in our community. We did that very successfully — almost $100 million worth. Then some of the brothers began to feel their oats, and wanted to go outside of our community — to Circle Campus — and it was there that we got stopped cold and some of us ended up in jail.

"We entered into a series of meetings that eventually broke down. It was inevitable that they would. The unions, from their position of strength and power, were not about to just give it away. And the contractors have nowhere to go for a labor force but to the unions. If they don't go along, they face extinction.

"The white community suffers, too, because of the union policies. They keep a lid on the supply of labor available and can continue to force wages up.

"The person who loses in the end is the one who has to pay more, to buy a home, for example, because of inflation. On the other hand, we suffer because we don't get to earn a dollar; we can't earn, own, and sustain.

"It's a bad picture for America. The real culprits are the unions, but they're not about to roll over and play dead, and correct all the old wrongs.

"We did have problems in our own ranks. We did have to compromise and not everyone could see that. The real need was to get commitment on the *intent* to increase minority representation.

"So, eventually, we did get an agreement. Some say it's good. Some say it doesn't have enough substance. I agree with both, but we had to start somewhere. It was hard, though, to convince some of the brothers."

Reed's comments, made *after* agreement was reached, help explain some of the difficulties of the protracted negotiations. On at least two occasions, some of the Coalition negotiators including Reed and the Rev. Vivian, were ready to agree but were unable to sell the plan to the rest of their committee.

Mayor Daley's Role

The process of actually negotiating toward some kind of goal acceptable to both sides did not begin until Mayor Daley actively entered the picture, when the arrests of Coalition people at Circle Campus led other black leaders to appeal to the mayor and the growing threat of real violence in the streets added impetus to their appeal. The mayor first approached leaders of both sides.

"We told the mayor if he had the opportunity to get things going again and thought something could be accomplished, then we'd be willing to sit down and talk some more," said Thomas J. Nayder, secretary-treasurer of the Building Trades Council. "We said we didn't want to meet with gangs but left the matter up to his judgment."

Told of the industry wish to meet only with "responsible" leaders of the Coalition, one black minister replied, "That's no problem on our part. I consider all of us responsible."

Nayder had cautioned the mayor, too, that the new talks would have to be limited to how the Coalition could assist in implementing the builder-union plan on an advisory basis. He said the unions and builders were not planning to sign a formal agreement that would interfere "with the historical relationship between labor and management."

Mayor Daley's efforts to bring the groups together again were intensified after the tense days of the federal hearings that brought thousands of belligerent white construction workers into the streets of the Loop. He reacted to that tension and to the threat of federal intervention, for which he had no more desire than the local contractors.

The federal hearings were on Thursday and Friday, September 25 and 26. Late Friday night, in a series of telephone calls, he urged all parties to resume talks. Saturday he met all day in his office with a small group of industry and labor men, plus two prominent black citizens not associated with the Coalition. The two, Alderman Ralph M. Metcalfe and Edwin C. Berry, executive director of the Chicago Urban League, assured the mayor that the Coalition was supported throughout Chicago's black neighborhoods. The mayor urged them to help bring about an agreement, over the weekend if possible. It wasn't, but the Coalition called off a "Black Monday" rally at the Civic Center, a repeat performance of a rally the Monday before that had brought 3,000 people into the center, most of them black and some of them gangs marching in formation.

None of the city officials had any enthusiasm for either large black gatherings or large groups of white construction workers roaming the city streets on Monday.

Thomas Murray, president of the Building Trades Council, told the mayor the 19 building trades unions had forbidden him to negotiate again with the blacks. But he finally agreed, under pressure from Daley, to ask the unions to change their instructions if a preliminary meeting could establish satisfactory ground rules. Arthur O'Neil, head of the contractors' group, was still reluctant to meet again with gangs, but agreed to attend the preliminary meeting on Monday.

Negotiations Resume

The meeting was held, ground rules were established, and the first formal negotiating session under the mayor's auspices was scheduled for Thursday, October 2. Black citizens outside the Coalition were to be present to help facilitate discussions.

All sides met for five hours that day, for almost nine hours a week later and then for five more long meetings through October and part of November until they seemed to be close to agreement. In between, separate meetings were set up for Coalition representatives to talk with union people on a craft-by-craft basis about special training problems in each area.

Many points were at issue during those long discussions and progress in solving some of them often seemed to be ephemeral. The group would seem to reach agreement on an issue at one meeting, only to disagree at the next on just what had been decided. Each side took to preparing statements about what had happened, but those were sometimes disputed too.

Among the issues that plagued negotiators over so many weeks were these:

* The structure of the committees that would administer whatever

new training programs were developed. This was of particular concern to the black people, who are all too used to having majority rule mean that they never have control over anything. When a proposal was for two committee members from the contractors, two from the unions and two from the Coalition, the blacks immediately interpreted it as 2-to-1 against them. Committee structure was much discussed and often altered during the negotiations. The final solution was for operating committees to run the training programs in each craft and an administrative committee to run the over-all program. That sounds simple but it isn't, really. It was never clear just how much control the administrative committee would have, whether it would see that the operating committees actually performed or whether it would just be on hand to offer help if the operating committees asked for it.

*The actual number of jobs the plan would provide for black people. Although the industry and the unions had said in their September newspaper advertisement that they were opening up 4,000 jobs for blacks, they later dropped the actual figure from the offers under discussion, claiming the continued recession in the industry hampered them. That brought a heated reaction. Some of the Coalition bargainers were determined not to settle for an offer of cooperation, but wanted specific numbers of job slots in specific trades written into the agreement. The eventual compromise restored the 4,000 figure of September.

* Auxiliary training, an additional training program outside the traditional apprenticeship program. This was an issue of importance to the Coalition, which continued to insist that apprenticeship just hadn't worked for blacks, that too many obstacles were put in their paths. The unions strongly objected to any route to journeyman status other than apprenticeship. The eventual compromise left the matter vague; it said "Those crafts and industries that can accept . . . auxiliary programs should do so."

* Accelerated training, a companion issue because it was another way of challenging the apprenticeship system. The blacks contended that it shouldn't take three to five years to train a journeyman; the unions contended that it did. The Coalition argument seemed to be one that might appeal to the contractors at the bargaining table, because the industry has said it is very short of manpower and needs more skilled men as soon as possible. But the contractors lined up solidly with the unions in favor of the traditional program. The compromise: the same one as in the issue of auxiliary training, "Those crafts . . . that can accept . . . accelerated programs should do so."

* Financing of training programs. Federal officials had indicated to Coalition leaders that federal funds might be available; the industry initially didn't want the federal involvement, being reasonably certain that it would bring some measure of federal control.

* The Coalition's role. The Coalition had long since given up asking for complete control of training for blacks in favor of a share of control. But it did not clearly accept management's insistence that the Coalition should be responsible for recruitment, for producing the young men to take part in the training programs. (All sides had learned over a period of years that the recruitment task was a difficult one; some of the efforts at expanding apprentice training had floundered because of a paucity of recruits. Blacks always did contend that recruiting would continue to be difficult until changed systems of training could help change the image of the industry as one that discriminates.)

The meetings with the mayor were sometimes amicable but often not. There was tension not only between the two opposing sides, but a certain amount of pulling and hauling within each side. Certainly the contractors and unions, about to engage in a strenuous round of bargaining in their troubled industry, didn't always view the issues as one. Each of their negotiators continued to point out that they could make no final decisions, that they could only recommend to their constituent bodies, the only ones with power to act. (But even that was a concession. The reader will recall that the summertime meetings were characterized by Building Trades Council leaders' insistence that they did not even have the power to recommend action to their member unions. They had been insisting then that the Coalition's efforts were misdirected, that the Building Trades Council itself could not bring about any change, and that the Coalition should approach each union local individually. That was something the Coalition had no intention of doing. It was hunting — and found — a way to gain broad public attention and support, without which its efforts would have been fruitless. Putting pressure on the builders and on the Building Trades Council did turn out to be more productive; whatever the rationale behind the strategy, it worked.)

An Agreement is Reached?

All the hours of meetings, the millions of words, the compromises and the purposeful vagueness, seemed to come to an end on November 6. Verbal agreement had been reached in the mayor's office by all parties to the controversy, they announced to the press; all that remained was for the three lawyers (for the contractors, the unions and the Coalition) to put the agreement into writing to be signed the next week, on November 12.

Thomas Murray of the Building Trades Council said he would recommend that the unions accept the plan. He posed, beaming, for handshaking pictures with Coalition people.

The Rev. Vivian beamed too. "We have agreed, point by point," he said. "All essentials are there. It is an agreement that is fair to all concerned. It is our hope that this will be more than a piece of paper, that it will really be the realization of all our hopes and dreams, not just for ourselves, but for all of the city."

Mayor Daley beamed and said the agreement was "the most outstanding plan in the country to bring in minorities."

Labor Secretary Shultz held a press conference (he was in Chicago to make a speech) and said he, too, was "delighted" because he "has always favored home-town solutions."

The lawyers did put together a draft of the agreement, referring to transcripts of previous meetings, taken by a stenographer. It was ready for signatures when all sides arrived at the Mayor's office on November 12.

But the Coalition refused to sign it.

They gave some reasons, publicly, for their refusal. It is likely there were other reasons, less public.

For the record, the Rev. Vivian said his group could not sign the agreement because it did not contain all the provisions that had been agreed upon during the discussions. Notably missing, he pointed out, was any reference to the number of jobs that would go to blacks under the new plan. There was no mention of the 4,000 jobs that had been specified in the September offer by the unions and industry, a number they had arrived at rather quickly, on their own. He referred, too, to the lack of provisions for training programs to be set up in the black community so young men could get to them and the absence of any indication that auxiliary training programs would lead to journeyman status.

He said the Coalition would need more time to study the new draft and consult with its member groups. "We must be sure," he said, "before we sign our names that it contains all the things we fought for in that room and which we have told our constituents about. The integrity of our people is at stake."

The only reference the draft made to the number of trainees was, "If general business conditions permit, the said parties hope to achieve, year by year, over a period of not more than five years a level of minority group employees proportionate to their percent in the community at large."

A not-so-public reason for the Coalition's refusal to sign the draft apparently was continued disagreement on the steering committee over whether the agreement was worth anything at all without specific commitments from the industry about job slots. The Rev. Vivian and David Reed seemed to feel that the industry's intentions were good and would lead to greatly expanded job opportunities. Others in the

Coalition, Meredith Gilbert among them, didn't trust anybody's intentions and wanted guarantees in numbers. At that moment, Gilbert's position had prevailed.

Mayor Daley expressed disappointment. "I thought all the parties would sign today and we would have this wonderful Chicago Plan in operation," he told the press. "But we still will meet on November 21 when, I hope, we will finally terminate this problem."

O'Neil said the builders and unions would not agree to "substantially change" the document. "The document was drafted by lawyers for labor, management and the Coalition," he said. "Now the Coalition looks at the finished document as if it had never seen such a thing before. The Rev. Vivian's recollection is faulty if he believes the agreements were altered in any way by the attorneys. We have tape recordings and transcripts to prove this."

Dispute Over the Number of Jobs

Murray, the Building Trades Council president, also denied that there had been any agreement on 4,000 training slots for blacks. "We never agreed on such a program," he said. "Economically, politically and logistically, such a program would be impossible."

(To some extent, there was a game of words going on. The September industry offer, referring to 4,000 jobs, never did talk about 4,000 new training slots. It provided for taking 1,000 already-skilled workers into the unions, for taking 1,000 partially-skilled into apprentice programs, for taking 1,000 unskilled into already-existing, pre-apprentice programs, and for starting new on-the-job training programs for another 1,000 unskilled men. In September, the Coalition had balked, arguing that the 4,000 should apply to new training slots. By November, the Coalition was alarmed that the figure was missing entirely. Industry and union people said their original offer had been withdrawn when they started the new round of bargaining in the mayor's office.)

The Coalition later produced a statement by Mayor Daley that did seem to back up their contention that a specific number of jobs had been agreed upon. A transcript of the November 6 meeting, at which agreement presumably had been reached, revealed that the mayor had verbally reviewed what the agreement was. "If you're recapping this," the transcript quoted Daley as saying, "what you do is take the figures that have been put together by the building trades and industry themselves, 4,000 people, who are going to try to be assimilated in the industry and into the respective unions . . ."

To the next meeting, November 21, the Coalition, with Meredith Gilbert, the hard-liner, as the spokesman, brought its own version of what had been agreed upon earlier in the month. It included details about training programs for 4,000 blacks within the next year and set down such details as the pay of trainees, the length of training and the method of certifying them as journeymen.

The meeting collapsed in choas and anger.

Marvin Gittler, one of the union lawyers who had been present at all the negotiations, charged, "The Coalition's document contains matters which not only were never agreed upon but were not even discussed." He said it appears the blacks had "thrown out all the rules of negotiating and are making up new ones as they go along."

The meeting went on for six hours. The Rev. Vivian emerged, tight-lipped. "We agreed upon absolutely nothing in that room today. No progress was made. And we have no comment whatsoever."

"There will have to be continuing discussions which might last, in my opinion, forever," said O'Neil, the builder. "I'm afraid we're in a talkathon."

A new consensus seemed a long way off. And it was. No new big meetings were held for several weeks, although some behind-the-scene maneuverings began that aided eventual agreement.

Some peripheral events affected the progress of the plan:

1. Meredith Gilbert left the Coalition, convinced the industry and unions offered nothing but a run-around. That left the more moderate David Reed in a stronger position.

2. Two developments moved the Rev. Vivian out of the limelight temporarily. One was the establishment of a new Black Strategy Center, funded by big business in Chicago, to produce black-oriented plans dealing with knotty issues of poverty, health and welfare. The Rev. Vivian was to be in charge and he was busy setting up the Center.

A second dramatic event somewhat robbed him of his status for a while. On December 4, State's Attorney's police raided a Black Panther apartment in the middle of the night, looking for illegal weapons. In the process they wounded several Panthers and killed two, including Fred Hampton, the Illinois chairman. The raiders' method produced a fury in the black community and political turmoil in the city. Reflecting black anger, the Rev. Vivian publicly proposed a curfew on entry by whites into the black communities at night, a proposal that led to some public scorn for him.

3. On the same day, Leonard Sengali, one of the controversial negotiators in the Coalition group, was arrested, charged with a month-old murder. Sengali was the Coalition member who was active in the Black P Stone Nation but was also an organizer for the Kenwood-Oakland Community Organization and a trusted associate of many black leaders. The story of the arrest and subsequent developments sound straight out of pulp fiction.

Sengali contended, and highly reputable black people agreed with him, that his arrest was a frame-up, designed to embarrass the Coalition leadership. They suggest it was no accident that the arrest came the same day of the raid on the Panther apartment. State's Attorney Edward V. Hanrahan has built his career on gang-busting and has aimed considerable ammunition at black gangs.

While in jail, Sengali and Hanrahan met together twice in the warden's office. Sengali charged that Hanrahan had questioned him about whether the Rev. Vivian and other civil rights leaders were communists and further charged Hanrahan hinted the murder charge would be altered if Sengali agreed to the communist story. Sengali didn't. Hanrahan said he had met with Sengali, but said it was at Sengali's request; he would not say what the talks were about.

Sengali was in jail for two months before a criminal court judge ruled he should be freed on bond because the presumption of guilt was not great. He later was cleared of the murder charge when the same judge said the state had not proved its case and directed a verdict of not guilty. But Sengali was in jail while Chicago Plan talks got moving again, and it is widely believed in the black community (no one has any kind of proof) that he was a political hostage to force the end of the long construction industry dispute. Chicago is a very political city and there are always a lot of intriguing rumors.

4. Charles R. Swibel, chairman of the Chicago Housing Authority and, as such, a familiar political figure in the city, acted as a go-between in the stalled negotiations, at the request of some of the Coalition leaders who wanted agreement so jobs could become available to blacks. Swibel had worked behind the scenes in September, too, succeeding in getting agreement from Coalition leaders to the original industry plan, but the rest of the Coalition had then refused to go along with their leaders.

Working with the attorneys who drew up the November proposal, Swibel proposed a new version: combining the November proposal with the September proposal (thus putting back into the agreement the job figures missing in November), and eliminating those parts of the September plan that conflicted with November's. Eleven members of the Coalition steering committee signed the document in Swibel's office three days before a public signing ceremony in Mayor Daley's office. Armed with the black signatures, Swibel and the attorneys were able to get union and industry agreement to signing. The official version of the Chicago Plan is dated January 12, 1970, the date of the public signing.

That's how the Chicago Plan was born.

Provisions of The Chicago Plan

"This agreement is entered into on this 12th day of January, 1970, by and between the undersigned, the Chicago and Cook County Building Trades Council (herein called "the Council"), the Building Construction Employers Association of Chicago, Inc. (herein called "Employers Association"), and the Coalition for United Community Action (herein called "the Coalition") for recommendation to their respective members and affiliates.

"WHEREAS, the Council, Employers Association and the Coalition recognize the desirability and necessity of securing a greater minority group representation into the skilled trades of the building industry of Chicago; and

"WHEREAS, if general business conditions permit, the said parties hope to achieve, year by year, over a period of not more than five years a level of minority group employees proportionate to their percent in the community at large; and

"WHEREAS, the parties are agreed that no party will benefit by or has an interest in the destruction or dilution of existing standards and programs; and

"WHEREAS, the parties agree that knowledgeable persons acting in good faith are the most effective and efficient means to achieve these goals;

"NOW, THEREFORE, it is agreed that the Council, Employers Association and Coalition shall affirmatively recommend to their respective members and affiliates the following plan:

I

ADMINISTRATIVE COMMITTEE

A.   There shall be established an Administrative Committee composed of seven representatives as follows:

1. Mayor Richard J. Daley or his designated representative;
2. Two representatives to be selected by the Council;
3. Two representatives to be selected by the Employers Association;
4. Two representatives to be selected by the Coalition.

B.   Duties — the Administrative Committee shall have the following duties:

1. To implement the program agreed upon by each Operations Committee;
2. Where applicable, to seek funds for the purposes of carrying out the directions of the Operations Committees in the

following areas:
a. Recruitment
b. Counseling
c. Physical facilities
d. Teacher recruitment
e. Staffing
f. Motivation and retention
g. Certification of journeymen status

3. Action by the Administrative Committee shall require the vote of at least five members.

4. In the event a complaint arises relating to programs already agreed upon by each Operations Committee, such complaints may be referred to the Administrative Committee for purposes of mediating said complaints.

C. Funding — both public and private funds may be used to accomplish the goals and purposes according to the needs and availability of funds.

II
OPERATIONS COMMITTEES

A. There shall be established an Operations Committee for each participating individual affiliate or member composed as follows:
1. Two representatives selected by the affiliate or craft union;
2. Two representatives selected by the member industry;
3. Four representatives selected by the Coalition.

B. Qualifications — it is expected that representatives selected for the Operations Committees shall be knowledgeable in the particular industry and/or craft.

C. Duties — it shall be the duty and responsibility of each individual Operations Committee to formulate and determine particular programs appropriate to each craft and industry. In formulating and determining such programs, representatives on the Operations Committees shall be guided by the following principles:
1. Those crafts and industries that can accept accelerated and/or auxiliary programs should do so;
2. No program shall in any way affect the integrity of any collective bargaining agreements and/or commitments.
3. Any and all agreements on programs shall be by mutual agreement of all representatives.

D. Filing — programs developed and formulated by each of said Operations Committees shall be reduced to writing and filed with the Administrative Committee for the purposes of implementation as set forth in Paragraph I (B) above.

III

GUIDELINES FOR OPERATIONS COMMITTEES[1]

1. We will endeavor to obtain employment at once for 1,000 qualified journeymen who possess the necessary skills of their respective trades, and look to the Coalition to supply us with such qualified journeymen. Each respective craft union will accept such journeymen into membership within the time period called for in the pertinent collective bargaining agreement, and each craft union will accept its initiation fee or required fees on a partial payment plan to run at least three months.

2. Those persons who possess some of the skills of a particular trade and can furnish proof of employment for two or more years in the particular craft in which they possess some skills will work for a 30-day probationary period, after which they will receive the equivalent of the apprentice's rate for the applicable year of the particular craft, as determined by its Joint Apprenticeship Committee, and will be enrolled as an apprentice. Or a special training program will be set up in those industries where practicable, and each worker will receive special training in the particular craft involved. We will look to the Coalition to supply us with persons possessing such skills.

3. With respect to those individuals who have had no prior training and do not possess some of the skills of a particular craft involved, but who are within the age limits of 17 to 23, or the age limits for the particular craft, we propose an information and recruiting program designed to acquaint all applicants with the trades and the requirements of each trade. We will enlarge upon the present facilities of and combine the efforts of the Urban League and the Apprentice Information Center to implement this program. We believe such a training program would run about one month and could be funded through the government to provide a modest wage during this month period. There would be no prior tests for coming into this program. The program would prepare each applicant for entering the existing apprenticeship programs for all crafts, would explain what each craft does and would determine the aptitude of the applicant with respect to the particular trade and increase the probability of success of the applicant as well as his adjustment into the Construction Industry. From this program the applicant who meets the qualifications would go into the existing apprenticeship program for the

particular craft. The Coalition would be responsible for the recruitment of applicants into this program. We anticipate that at least 1,000 applicants could be accepted into this program.

4. We propose an on-the-job training program for persons who do not wish to take the tests provided for in point 3 above for admission into the respective apprenticeship programs or who fail in such tests. Provided that the necessary funding can be obtained for such a program for on-the-job training, the wage would be geared to the equivalent apprenticeship rate, and provisions would be made for schooling of one day a week or for evening classes as facilities permit. This on-the-job training program would apply in such industries where such trainees could be employed. We believe that at least 1,000 such on-the-job trainees could be placed in those industries which lend themselves to such a training program.

5. These recommendations shall be applicable only with respect to persons who have been residents of Chicago for over one year.

6. We recognize the desirability and the necessity of securing a greater minority group representation into the skilled trades of the Building Industry in Chicago and will therefore seek to establish further programs in keeping with the demands of the industry, and if general business conditions permit, which will hopefully achieve over a period of not more than five years, a level of minority group employees at least proportionate to their percentage in the community at large.

IV
DURATION

The obligations imposed by this Agreement on the Council, the Employers Association and the Coalition shall become effective when signed. There shall be a review of all programs instituted as a result of this Agreement and the effectiveness of the various committees established as a result of this Agreement six months from the execution thereof.

Footnotes

1. This section is almost word for word the same as the September offer, with the elimination of some sentences, most of them referring to appeals committees which were eliminated in negotiations. It was the addition of this section to Sections I and II (the November offer) that made agreement possible.

Discussion Questions

1. In what ways does the case illustrate supply and demand factors in a labor market?

2. What should be the role of law in regulating behavior of the parties? What other tools does society have, besides law, to implement public policy?

3. What parallels do you see between the bargaining process of the Coalition with the industry and unions in Chicago and the bargaining process of the industrial unions during the organizing days of the 1930s?

4. What differences are there between union-management relations in the construction industry and in a private industry like the automotive industry?

5. Labor Attorney Marvin Gittler had originally denied that there was any possibility of bargaining with the Coalition — or any need to. Later, after actual bargaining, Gittler said in exasperation that the blacks had "thrown out all the rules of negotiating and are making up new ones as they go along." What developments in the case made bargaining possible? Was there any change in the power base of any group? What change and when did it take place?

6. Analyze the Chicago Plan in the light of your insights into the entire case:

Preamble

The unions, builders' association and Coalition agree to "recommend" this plan to their members and affiliates. Is this wording meaningful? Would it have been possible to take a stronger stand?

What methods would be available to persuade member groups to follow the recommendations? Would changes be necessary in the structure of institutions and their relationships, in authority, in incentives?

An aim of the plan is to increase minority participation in construction over a five-year period "if general business conditions permit." Who would determine those conditions? What would be the criteria? Does this statement signify that the Chicago Plan agreement has produced any change?

The plan states "the parties are agreed that no party will benefit by or has an interest in the destruction or dilution of existing standards and programs." If existing programs are keeping blacks out of jobs, is it true that no party wants existing programs destroyed? What does "dilution of existing standards" mean? Does it mean changing entry requirements for the trades?

What potential for change is offered by this preamble? What does it offer the black community in specific guarantees? In what respects has this agreement altered black dependency upon the good faith of the white community for performance? Should the black representatives have signed the Chicago Plan? Have any of us, in our system of social organization, ever any more guarantees than the good faith of others? What has the good faith of others produced for black people?

Administrative Committee

The plan states that a vote of five members is needed for action. What kind of combinations of votes are possible under the plan? What is the potential for stalemate? What is the significance of Mayor Daley or his designated representative? What is the potential for change in existing institutions?

Should the duties of the administrative committee be broader? What can it do if operations committees do not agree on programs? What should the administrative committee do if an operations committee decides it's entirely satisfied with the status quo in all areas listed, from recruitment to certification of journeyman status?

What is the relationship between the administrative committee and the operations committees? Is the relationship clear? Which has more power?

Operations Committees

What powers do the operations committees have to bring about change in the construction industry? In what ways are the committees' powers limited?

What is the meaning of the requirement that "any and all agreements on programs shall be by mutual agreement of all representatives?"

What is the meaning of the requirement that "no program shall in any way affect the integrity of any collective bargaining agreements or commitments?"

Since apprenticeship training programs are part of collective bargaining agreements, is it possible for an operations committee to set up an accelerated training program or an auxiliary training program?

Does this keep in effect all the limitations on entry into the trades (length of apprenticeship, pay, rules for qualifying)? Would changes in any of these programs affect existing collective bargaining agreements?

Guidelines

Is adequate machinery provided in the Chicago Plan agreement to put the guidelines into effect?

EPILOGUE

Despite all the public congratulations over the reaching of agreement in January, 1970, the Chicago Plan was in for a stormy history. Countless more hours of frustrating negotiations were ahead in an effort to work out a plan of operation: the agreed-upon plan had included an administrative organization and set some goals but did not include details of how to put the plan to work. There were mutterings of disagreement, too, over the fact that the plan did not include any penalties for those who refused to cooperate with it.

Mayor Daley exuded optimism. "This Chicago Plan recognizes the complete opportunity of young men to participate in the building of this city," he announced. "We know that with the ideas and thoughts written on this paper, we can bring about results. I shall continue my personal interest in this subject."

He did continue his interest and served as the key public member of the seven-man administrative committee. He presided at meetings and worked on details of financing the plan and opening of four recruitment centers. An early action of the administrative committee (which became the board of directors when the plan was incorporated) was to hire Fred D. Hubbard, a black Chicago alderman and former social worker, as project director.

A grant of almost half a million dollars came through from the Department of Labor in May, 1970, with a promise of more as specific training programs were approved.

But the training programs were slow to come. Nineteen operations committees, one for each of the major trades, were set up but these didn't move with the dispatch of the top-level committee, chaired by the mayor.

By the time another summer came, a year after the construction shutdowns brought consternation to Chicago, only one new training program was ready to start and it was a program already in the planning stage when the Coalition began its demonstrations. There were disheartened comments and many black people felt that again their hopes were being dashed by the rigidity of all the old systems. Black leaders called in a team of experts to determine whether the plan was working. The experts concluded that it was not working and that the federal government should write it off, replacing it with a plan with more built-in muscle, such as the Philadelphia Plan, which provides sanctions against contractors who fail to meet goals for minority hiring.

From time to time, some Labor Department spokesman, particularly Assistant Secretary Fletcher (who had conducted the federal hearings in Chicago), did threaten to impose specific goals for hiring in Chicago. But it didn't happen. Nothing much else happened either. The plan simply went nowhere.

In May, 1971, more than a year after the hopeful start and in the midst of general agreement on the failure of the Chicago Plan, Fred Hubbard, the project director, disappeared, leaving behind a record of forged checks amounting to $100,000 made out to him from funds belonging to the Chicago Plan. More than a year was to pass before Hubbard was found, tried and sentenced to prison.

During that year the Labor Department announced that no further funds would be provided for the Chicago Plan and continued to threaten (but not act on) imposition of goals or quotas. Some of the men in charge of the Chicago Plan said they'd go on trying to make it work, with or without federal funds. But again another year passed without much to show in the way of results.

Negotiations between Chicago people and the Labor Department finally led, in July, 1972, to the announcement of a New Chicago Plan, this one to be administered not by a separate committee structure but by the Chicago Urban League. The announcement was made three years, almost to the day, after the Coalition began its building sites protests.

The New Chicago Plan almost died at birth. The Coalition was strongly opposed to it, for some familiar reasons: it didn't assure that black people would oversee the training of young blacks and it still placed too much stress on apprenticeships, which the Coalition insisted worked against blacks. Another important reason for Coalition opposition no doubt was the fact that the Coalition had wanted to be the agency to carry out the plan. Instead the Urban League was made the prime contractor and the Coalition was relegated to the position of sub-contractor, charged with recruiting young men in the community. Another sub-contractor was the Latin American Task Force, which was to seek Spanish-speaking youth for training, an aspect that was missing from the original Chicago Plan.

The New Chicago Plan was finally launched in the fall of 1972, with a Labor Department grant of $1,746,000. Its literature described it as a "voluntary agreement among 12 craft unions and 10 member associations of the Building Constructor Employers' Association to increase the number of skilled blacks, Latin Americans, American Indians, and other minorities in the construction industry. It set a five-year goal of 10,000 jobs and estimated that would bring $100

million in wages into the minority communities. The plan established
a referral committee, charged with accomplishing the goals (including
the development of job opportunties) and a group of craft committees
to review applicants and refer them to appropriate employers for
apprenticeship or advanced apprenticeship training.

The concept of advanced apprenticeship training led to the demise ,
a year later, of the second Chicago Plan. The unions and the contractors
continued to insist that minority members recruited either be ready to
qualify as journeymen or else meet the age and educational requirements
for apprenticeship. The Urban League continued to reply, "The apprenticeship route is too slow and exclusionary; and past prejudice and discrimination has limited the number of minorities who have the experience to become journeymen." The Urban League wanted the Chicago
Plan to provide assistance and on-the-job training to the more than 800
men it recruited for advanced apprentice status but claimed the unions
and contractors failed to produce job slots for these. In the fall of 1973,
the Urban League withdrew from its prime contractor agreement.

The labor department had sought to beef up the lagging plan in the
summer of 1973 by requiring that builders with federal contracts (and
the unions they did business with) either join the Chicago Plan or meet
even-stricter federal goals for minority employment. This hybrid part-
voluntary, part-compulsory provision did not bring any great change
either.

In December, 1973, the labor department released figures showing
only a small gain in minority journeymen over the four-year period, the
period included in the original demands for 10,000 new jobs. Federal
figures showed small percentage increases in some unions: bricklayers,
carpenters, electricians, plasterers, plumbers and ironworkers (the latter
under a federal court order to open up membership ranks). Figures
showed no change at all in the asbestos workers, elevator installers,
glaziers, metal lathers, painters, roofers, sheet metal workers, sprinkler
fitters and operating engineers; most of these still had fewer than one
percent minorities.

At the same time it released the new figures, the labor department
announced a new "imposed" plan for Chicago, similar to the long-
disputed Philadelphia Plan. For any builder with a federal contract,
it set goals for the percentage of man hours to be worked by minorities
in each trade for the following five years.

But the new "imposed" plan covered only federal contracts, not
private building. And the building trade doldrums of 1974 lay ahead.
The keys to greatly expanding minority employment in construction
remained elusive.

Introduction

The Cook County Hospital case, a capstone to the earlier cases, straddles the mainstream of profound changes occurring in the society.

A new idea had been born, the idea that everyone, poor as well as rich, had a right to decent medical care. New medical knowledge and technology was causing another kind of revolution in hospitals, a tremendous expansion of what was possible. Racial compositions of cities were changing; black and brown populations were demanding that hospitals meet their needs. At the same time, spiraling inflation and spiraling demands on public resources brought community concern over climbing tax rates and pressure for control of costs.

Caught in the center of it all, like many other big public hospitals, was Cook County Hospital, a gigantic and aging complex beset with management problems. Along with the sweeping changes in health care and the demands for it, Cook County found itself buffeted by Chicago politics, with no strong governing authority, no personnel system to cope with its high labor turnover and an untrained and in-experienced support work force, little or no coordination of its sprawling medical departments, and a persistent threat that it would lose its accreditation. With a need for millions of dollars in improvements, it had no real control of its own budget and all of its budget was mired in politics.

A massive reorganization attempt brought a changed organizational structure and new leadership. But the changes created tensions and new conflicts, affecting human relationships in many and varied ways; alteration in relations between professional staff and management; unionization spreading to the professional staff which began to engage in sometimes disruptive collective activities to further their own interests; changes in status and power and deep anxieties about the changes; new conflicts with the communities who make up the hospital's patients.

All these strands came together in the firing of five doctors, an event that came close to putting the hospital out of business until the tensions finally began to unravel.

The facets of the case reflect many of the problems and dilemmas facing managers of public sector institutions in the 1970s.

Chronology

Spring 1968	A committee studying reform of Cook County government proposed creation of a Health and Hospital Governing Commission to get County Hospital out of politics, administer it by modern management methods and plan comprehensive health care for the county. The proposal was stymied in the Illinois legislature.
Spring 1969	The Governing Commission's creation was allowed by the legislature but the law was unclear about the commission's powers and duties.
Fall 1969	Commission members were selected and immediately began seeking amendments to the law to give the commission control of its own budgeting and personnel processes.
Spring 1970	Many Cook County Hospital doctors were among those lobbying intensively for the passage of the amendments. Their efforts included overcrowding of the hospital, to call attention to its plight, and threats to close the hospital. On the final day of the legislative session, the amendments were passed.
September 1970	Dr. James Haughton was hired as executive director of the commission and immediately began work on budgeting, staffing and reorganizing to solve dozens of difficult problems.
Spring 1971	Tensions began to develop between the medical staff and the administration over management prerogatives and medical prerogatives. The rumor mill worked overtime and a series of public attacks were aimed at Dr. Haughton by the Residents and Interns Association, which had just been granted collective bargaining rights.
May 28, 1971	The Residents and Interns Association demanded Dr. Haughton's resignation and continued pressuring the administration in a variety of abrasive ways for the changes it felt necessary.
August 1971	The hospital earned accreditation, the object of a concerted effort by Dr. Haughton and his staff ever since his arrival.

For a time, an era of good will in the hospital seemed
possible.

October   The Governing Commission incurred the wrath of the
1971   young doctors by freezing their salaries for two years and
              of senior doctors by challenging them on a touchy ques-
              tion regarding collection of professional fees.

October   A "heal-in" by the Residents and Interns Association led
1971   to overcrowding of the division of medicine, perceived
              by the administration as a direct threat to management's
              rights and responsibilities.

October 29, Five doctors, including the four top officers of two doctors'
1971   associations, met with the hospital director. The director
              claimed they threatened to "close and destroy" the hospi-
              tal unless certain demands were met.

November   The five doctors were fired by Dr. Haughton, bringing
1, 1971   down a storm of protest in the hospital, particularly
              over the procedure followed.

November   A court order reinstated the five doctors and mandated
16, 1971   a disciplinary hearing following due process. The order
              averted the threatened departure of 300 doctors.

Cook County Hospital, in its heyday, was one of the great teaching hospitals of all time. Someone estimated that at least half of all the doctors practicing in the United States have taken some part of their training there, in the massive, ornate yellow brick building or one of the 20 buildings that sprawl around it, serving it, supplementing it, spreading over 20 acres just west of Chicago's loop. It was once the largest hospital in the world.

Young medical students vied to come there to learn from the doctors who donated part of their time to teach the bright young people how to care for the very sick people who filled the more than 4,000 beds. Doctors vied to donate their time; it was considered an honor to be chosen for the staff at County, even though there was no pay. For medical people, County often seemed electric with excitement, with stimulating talk, with pioneering ideas, with the heady sense of doing good things for people, with the bustle of a huge institution that really clicked. Or so it seemed. Or so it seems in retrospect, in the memories of those who talk of County's heyday.

For the patients, the people who couldn't pay the bills in a private hospital, the people who didn't have private doctors and thus were much, much sicker than richer people by the time they finally sought medical care, County wasn't always so stimulating. The poor came, more than 1,000 every day, bringing terrible misery. They provided a ceaseless flow of intriguing diseases, a rich clinical resource for the young doctors. But often, for the individuals, it was disheartening to be part of the ceaseless flow. They came, with their dreadful pains and repulsive sores, and sat for hours and hours on the hard benches, waiting their turns to see one of the doctors. When the turn came for their examinations, there was little or no privacy, even for examinations that the patient, at least, found embarrassing. If the young doctor found the patient less than critically ill, the patient was sent to the clinic, where he would wait some more, perhaps waiting weeks for the results of tests that would show he should have been admitted to the hospital in the beginning.

If he was admitted and put to bed, often that bed would be rolled into one of the miles of corridors, because the wards were already

filled and extra beds already jammed the center aisles in the wards.
There he would wait some more, while the desperately busy doctors
and nurses — never enough of them — would work first with those
even more critically ill. There wouldn't be a bell or a light to signal
one of the frantic nurses. If the patient needed surgery, it would
be in one of the row of operating rooms without any air conditioning.
The windows had to be kept open, to provide fresh air, and the breeze
from the crowded streets outside played havoc with the sterile areas.

Some patients had a chance at some of the finest medical care
available anywhere in the world. Their surgery might be performed
by a man piled high with medical honors — and then again, it might
not. It might be performed by a tired resident, under the direction
of a distracted older physician who was himself terribly overworked.
The patients had no way to choose. And the doctor who cared for
them one day would be off in his own office the next, so another
doctor would come around with the chart but no familiarity with
the patient's particular terrors. (Or he might not even have the chart.
Medical records, and keeping records keyed to patients, were always
a problem at County.)

The fact is that a lot of people, thousands of them, did get care,
some of it first rate, and a lot of people did get well, which they
would not have if there had been no public hospital, like County, to
take them in, penniless. A lot of others didn't get well. Nurses toured
the wards each morning to see which patients had died during the
night. The folklore of the county's poor people said, "Don't take him
to County. They'll kill him there."

That's the way it was in the big charity hospitals of a few decades
ago. No one spent a lot of time worrying about a patient's dignity,
or his rights, or his privacy, or his morale. _

Looking back to, say, 1940, it would seem that there were really
two Cook County Hospitals: the doctors' hospital, with its clinical
riches and its sense of accomplishment, and the patients' hospital,
with its terrible overcrowding and awesome impersonality. When
people talked nostalgically, years later, about the heyday of Cook
County Hospital, they were talking about the doctors' hospital.

Presiding over it all, for an incredible 53 years, from 1914 to 1967,
was a remarkably deft surgeon, a towering figure in the medical world.
He was Dr. Karl Meyer, who had graduated from the University of
Illinois Medical School at 21 and at 25 won a civil service competition
against 80 others to become medical superintendent of the giant
Cook County Hospital. He was a small man physically, but immensely
energetic, up at 5:30 a.m. every day and never late to an appointment
anywhere, despite his own schedule of 10 to 15 operations a day. He
reportedly performed more than 100,000 operations, perhaps a record

in the medical world. He lived right there in County Hospital, in an elegant second floor apartment, right above the main entrance with its carved stone medallions and the fancy stone scrollwork around the big windows. There was never any question about who was boss in that hospital in its heyday.

The Cook County Board of Commissioners knew who was boss there, too. The money to run the giant hospital came from them, from the taxes they collected every year. They were charged by the state with providing medical care for the indigent population of Cook County. There were battles about budgets, of course, and Dr. Meyer always felt he hadn't sufficient funds, but he was canny politically about working with the commissioners to get what he needed for medical service. Perhaps part of the canniness lay in not asking for too much and thus not precipitating a monetary crisis with the county board. Other doctors went along with him to plead with the board for money and some of them developed considerable political skill, too.

The county commissioners also got something out of the arrangement: a myriad of jobs, which usually were distributed with an eye more to the voting booth than to the quality of work performance. Hundreds of people needed to keep the hospital running—along with the doctors and nurses —.were hired not in a hospital personnel office but downtown in the county board's offices. The hospital took what it could get because it was always short of hands, to push sick patients on gurney carts through the endless corridors and tunnels, to pass 12,000 trays a day, to man the telephones, to clean the 20 acres of buildings, to paint and repaint — with the same sickening green paint that came to be called "County green." To reformers, County Hospital patronage was always a scandal. Reformers did succeed in extricating the nursing service from the political patronage system. In 1929, the School of Nursing got its own separate citizens' board and a merit system for the staff; it was an important move because the School of Nursing ran not only its teaching programs but the whole nursing service for County. From that time on there were always some who talked of getting rid of the patronage system for the rest of the employees, too. But this was Chicago and even in the late 1940s, one downtown ward boss chortled, "Chicago ain't ready for reform."

It would, however, be an error to say that the patronage system was the sole cause of the massive problems that began to beset Cook County Hospital in the years after World War II. The causes were far broader than political hiring and would not be solved by putting an end to patronage. Actually, patronage was an easily-identifiable part of the much broader problem of how to administer so vast an institution in a rapidly-changing social and medical climate.

Some of the changes were nationwide, even worldwide, affecting hospitals everywhere:

1. There was a revolution in expectations regarding medical care.

Poor people, the kind who had come to County and waited patiently only to be bedded down in corridors and then often ignored, began to make it clear that "We don't want to be treated this way. We have rights." There began to be talk about every person's right to quality medical care. That's a belief now deeply ingrained in our society but it was revolutionary indeed in the early 1950s and is still a bone of contention among some old-line members of the American Medical Association. These changing expectations about medical care have been closely related to the Black revolution which has wrought so many other changes in American society since World War II. Many once-silent communities are demanding to be heard and considered.

2. There was a revolution in medicine itself.

Greatly expanding medical knowledge led to new medical specialities and to intricate new equipment, making a hospital an infinitely more complex place than a hospital of 30 years ago. Because of the changes, a hospital is more difficult to administer today. This expansion of knowledge has also greatly increased the cost of hospitalization, which helped bring about new programs of hospital insurance, both public and private. And the insurance programs themselves have added to the complexity of administration in hospitals.

3. There is a new breed in the medical profession.

Efforts to provide better, more up-to-date care, have led the big public hospitals like County to hire full-time salaried staff physicians to supervise patient care rather than relying, as in the past, on the part-time volunteer doctors and a staff of residents and interns to do the day-to-day work of caring for patients. These new salaried staff men, many of whom double as faculty in the medical schools, view the public hospitals in a very different way from the voluntary staff and have been outspoken about the defects of the old ways and the second class care the old ways assure. Their efforts at reform have been enthusiastically joined — and often vigorously led — by the young residents and interns who are responding to community demands for better health care for the poor. The social reformers among the young doctors gravitate naturally to the big public hospitals and they are an important part of the medical-political scene in many of these hospitals.

4. A generation of government-endorsed collective bargaining, with its accompanying court decisions broadening the rights of employees in determining working conditions, has helped to change the climate within the hospitals.

Employees simply aren't as docile as they used to be and young residents are nowhere willing to work for $30 a month anymore. Residents and interns have adopted the collective bargaining ideas, not only to improve their own financial position but also to push for reforms in patient care. Although they have adopted the tools of organized labor, they have not yet had time to gain experience in the methods of collective bargaining; as a result, many of their demands for instant change seem unrealistic and impossible to the older administrators with whom they are dealing.

All of these broad changes have been amply reflected at Cook County Hospital over the past two decades and have been complicated there by these additional factors:

1. Dr. Karl Meyer's very long reign.

Where it apparently was once possible, in a different social era, for a busy surgeon also to administer the medical program of a large hospital, it became less possible with the growing complexity of hospital services. Without strong central guidance and administration, it became possible for individual medical chiefs — usually those who had developed some skill in politicking with the county board — to claim considerable independence in running their departments. By the late 1960s, there was much talk of these "fiefdoms" or "dynasties" at County and they complicated the achievement of strong management authority when the need for such authority became great.

As one long-time observer put it, the "result of all of this overlapping responsibility (and) power . . . was that the management of the hospital was, in many areas, without authority, and that decisions could be made as to priorities over which the hospital management had no voice. Cook County Hospital became a congeries of independent feudal baronies, each competing with the other for power and each making demands upon the budget depending upon its own presumed needs or desires. Overall planning was completely lacking."

2. The very size of the hospital complex was another of the complicating factors in administration. There were no other hospitals in the world with 4,000 beds and it was impossible to supervise, even in a calmer era. This, too, contributed to the dynasty system.

3. The increasing age of the buildings, some dating back to the 1890s, was another problem. Because the complex had grown haphazardly, there was poor coordination between services in different buildings.

4. The hospital population was changing, too. As black people came to the city in increasing numbers and whites left for the suburbs, the hospital's patients were more apt to be black. But black people in Chicago — as elsewhere — lacked the political power to effect changes in the early post-war years. Some observers feel that County would not

have lagged so far behind if whites rather than blacks were filling all those beds.

Taken together, these factors added up to a crisis in governance at Cook County Hospital.

Efforts at Reform

In 1967, Richard B. Ogilvie, later to be governor of Illinois, was president of the Cook County Board of Commissioners. Beset by many problems, of which the hospital was only one, he named a Citizens Committee on Cook County Government, charged with making recommendations on reorganization of various areas of county government. One task force worked on health and hospitals and made its report early in 1968.

The report took note of areas of change: changing social and welfare philosophy (the revolution in expectations), changing mechanisms for financing health care, precipitously rising medical costs (the revolution in medicine), and the shortages of manpower for all the developing health specialties. It stated that a comprehensive plan for county health care was needed, to allocate to each sector, public and private, its contribution toward the needs of the community.

The report delved into hard facts (in 1966, admitting-examination room services provided care for more than 438,000 people) and figures (expenditures had gone up in a 10-year period from $16 million to $30 million, while revenues had increased only from $12 million to $15 million). It pinpointed the reorganization required and the new methods needed to improve the financial picture, but then noted that at least $64 million new dollars would be needed to make County meet the lowest standards established by the United States Public Health Service.

Despite the wealth of valuable detail, much of the report's impact was in the statement of what the financial and political problems meant in human terms:

"On the basis of present facilities quality patient care is impossible. The obsolescence . . . has a direct impact on patient care. Large open wards make privacy and the amenities of personal dignity impossible. Inadequate toileting facilities make personal hygiene all but impossible and impose practices wasteful of manpower such as bed baths. Critically ill patients cannot always be separated from those less ill. The lack of adequate environmental temperature control unnecessarily complicates certain clinical problems. The chronic lack of paging system and nurse patient call system guarantee further erosion of patient care.

"Inadequate facilities have other impacts. Working conditions for professionals are uniformly inadequate and result in inefficient performance. Further, because of these working conditions, recruitment of health professionals is hampered and higher attrition rates result. Those factors affect the morale of the whole institution.

"Medical care is largely dependent upon the intern and resident staff. The hospital has over 400 resident and intern positions with approximately 35% filled with foreign medical graduates . . . Ward supervision, and, therefore, medical care depend primarily upon a system of voluntary attending physicians. These visit at intervals to supervise ward rounds and to aid in teaching of both students and the house staff. This voluntary service plan does not function if the attending physician is unable to attend his sessions at the hospital because of commitments to his private practice. Scheduled surgery has been cancelled and the patient delayed in receiving care with consequent increased cost to the patient and the hospital. This voluntary system has the further potential of increasing the work load of the full-time staff. Finally, it has the potential of dangerously increasing the clinical responsibilities of the house staff.

"The lack of a unified administrative authority has further corrosive impact on the quality of care. There is no coordination of inventories and needs. This leads to functional shortages throughout the institution. Since interdepartmental communications are complex they easily break down. The result is a discordinate of services never sufficiently focused or in concert to bring to bear the quality of patient care of which they are capable."[1]

In a series of recommendations for changes, the task force placed its first emphasis on planning, suggesting creation of a Commission on Hospital, Health and Allied Medical Programs, to be composed of a citizens advisory board and professional staff. Among 22 other recommendations were many dealing specifically with internal reorganization of the hospital: strengthening the administrative structure at the top, transferring nursing services back to the hospital from the School of Nursing, improving fiscal operations and controls, instituting a cost accounting system, conducting an intensive management study, and establishing formalized relationships between County Hospital and the medical schools.

Legislative Action

Ogilvie, the president of the county board, acted on the report almost before the ink was dry and his action went somewhat beyond that recommended for an advisory health commission. He began pushing for legislation creating a citizens commission that would take over administrative responsibility for County Hospital, Oak Forest Hospital (its affiliated geriatrics hospital), and the School of Nursing, and would plan for all health care in the public county facilities.

Ogilvie's move for an independent commission probably had political meaning beyond his apparently sincere desire to improve the quality of patient care. He was to run for governor that fall and a record of improving County Hospital would be useful. In addition, it was a way for Ogilvie to strike out against Mayor Richard J. Daley's powerful political organization. The majority of county board members were Daley Democrats and Ogilvie was a Republican; cutting into the hospital patronage would affect the machine and removing the hospital from county board control would be expected to weaken the power of the Democrats. Ogilvie's bills for reorganization of hospital control found few friends among the Democratic county commissioners.

The bills to create an independent commission to run the hospitals didn't get very far the first year. Finally, a year later, it was pressure brought by some of the doctors and nurses within the hospital that led to the change. Some of the medical staff, particularly the relatively new full-time staff members, had been chafing increasingly under county board control, feeling that they were shortchanged in budget and forced to practice 19th century medicine two-thirds of the way into the 20th century.

Much of the story of the considerable political battle of those days has been written by one of the participants, Dr. Harold Levine, then a chest specialist at the hospital and an associate professor of medicine at the University of Illinois. In an article, "County Hospital; Revolution within the Establishment,"[2] Dr. Levine credits the house staff, the young interns and residents, with supplying most of the motive power.

". . . In the fall of 1968, one of our residents returned from a year in a New York hospital. Motivated by what he saw there, he organized the house staff, nursing staff, and the Executive Board of our attending staff to back a projected campaign aimed at the county board. The aim of the campaign was to improve conditions for the house staff and the hospital's patients," he wrote.

". . . The house staff pressed their campaign for higher wages and a general improvement of conditions·at County. Ogilvie was sympathetic but the board's leading Democrat, George Dunne, a protege and possible successor to Mayor Daley, was not. He was chairman of the board's powerful finance committee. The house staff officers met with him privately to underline their determination to force change. He was unmoved. The house staff threatened to release to the press, every day for 50 days, the case histories of patients who died because of inadequate facilities, equipment, or personnel.

"Meanwhile, the gradual retirement of Dr. Karl Meyer as hospital director left a vital position open. The house staff, recognizing the importance of the impending change in leadership, forced the resignation of a non-productive hospital administrator hired by the county board to facilitate Dr. Meyer's retirement. The obvious choice for the job became Dr. Robert Freeark, chairman of the division of surgery, an excellent surgeon and teacher, well-liked and respected, and highly experienced in the internal politics of the hospital. The house staff strongly favored Dr. Freeark. Ogilvie and the dean of the University of Illinois Medical School, both concerned about the future of the hospital, also supported him. But the Democratic members of the county board opposed Freeark, who was a threat to 'their' doctors and consequently county board influence within the hospital. Faced with the intransigence of the county board, the house staff renewed their threat to release to the press horror stories about patients dying. The county board yielded and appointed Freeark as director of the hospital.

"In a few weeks, the board also granted the house staff's pay raise demand. House staff salaries doubled. The house staff was jubilant. But some of us on the full-time staff cautioned them that the county board might be merely buying them off. While appreciating the raises, the house staff began to suspect that this might be true. The board ignored key budgetary demands for major hospital improvements. When Freeark and the hospital staff requested a supplementary budget, the county board resisted.

"The house staff considered a 'heal-in' to pressure the board into granting the extra budget. They invited Freeark to a public meeting to discuss this tactic. Facing almost the entire house staff Freeark warned that if they attempted a heal-in, he 'would see them all in jail for dereliction of duty.' The house staff was stunned. They felt betrayed.

"Freeark later explained to some of us that he felt he had to assert his leadership and that he, at that point, felt the tactic to be incorrect. With Dr. Meyer fading into the background, there was no central authority. Freeark needed to focus power into his office.

"The house staff was distressed for a time. When they recovered, they decided to press their patient care demands by working to help establish an independent governing commission. . . "

Eventually, in the spring of 1969, the legislature did pass the bill creating the new nine-member Health and Hospitals Governing Commission of Cook County, to go into effect on July 1, 1969. The bill provided a method of selection of the commission, fixed terms of office, provided the commissioners would not be paid, empowered the commission to adopt its own necessary rules and hire an executive director and necessary staff, both for the commission itself and for the hospitals. Duties and powers of the commission, which seemed at first to be all-inclusive, were defined:

"The commission shall have the general responsibility of organizing, operating, maintaining and managing the various hospitals and hospital facilities and programs, to make and enter into contracts therefore, and to establish rules and regulations for the use, operation and management thereof. It shall have the power to fix, charge and collect reasonable fees and compensation for the use or occupancy of such hospitals and facilities, or any part thereof, and for hospital, medical and nursing care, medicine or any other hospital or allied medical services furnished by any such hospital or facility."

The commission was charged by the legislation with developing a budget before December 1 each year to submit to the board of commissioners of the county and "the board of commissioners shall appropriate a sufficient sum of money as the board deems necessary to meet the expenses and to carry out the provisions of this act."

Passage of the legislation brought jubilation at the hospital and immediately raised the question of who the new members of the governing commission were to be. The house staff, intrigued with its political victory, wanted a say in the selection process.

Some of that process was detailed in the legislation itself, including careful compromises to assure a balance of power. A five-member selection committee was to be chosen, with two members chosen by the president of the county board, two appointed by the state director of public health, and one selected by the deans of the medical schools in the county. This committee, by majority vote, would choose the nine commission members, for staggered terms of six years. The law required the selection committee to give "due consideration to a fair representation" throughout the county and that not more than five members of the commission shall be members of the same political party at the time of their appointment. No one who held government employment at any level was eligible. The selection committee was also empowered to remove commission members.

For all its attempts at a fair political compromise, the device was a curious one for public administration. It made the commission members responsible for performance of their duties to the selection committee, which was really responsible to no one (there was no provision in the law for removal of selection committee members or any mention of how long their terms should be). Neither the selection committee nor the hospital governing commission were answerable to the voters at election time. And, although commission members were responsible to the selection committee for their appointments and for continuance in office, they still had to go to the elected county commissioners for budget approval. The arrangement made the selection committee, answerable to no one, a very powerful instrument. But if anyone thought that arrangement would keep the selection committee out of politics, it was a mistaken dream; it really led to a new kind of politics.

The selection committee was chosen, and Stuart S. Ball, a Chicago attorney who had served almost 15 years on the School of Nursing board, was elected its chairman. That made Ball the target for any group with a name to propose and he did meet with a number of delegations, some of them from the Residents and Interns Association, some of them from community groups, many of them made up of black and Spanish-speaking residents, who felt they had special concerns with County Hospital because they provided so many of its patients.

Stuart Ball has since talked at length of the kinds of considerations that went into the selection committee's choices of the first nine members of the new governing commission. Among them were these:

*Because the population served in the hospital was primarily black, the committee thought black representation should exceed that of the proportion of blacks in the county as a whole. So four of the nine were black.

*There should be representatives of the "enlightened medical community" to provide needed information on health care delivery. Thought was given to a representative from the County Hospital staff, but that idea was turned down, Ball said, because, "At that time factions in the hospital were so antagonistic that appointment of one would only make an increased problem." Instead the committee named a doctor in private practice, a research pathologist at the University of Chicago, and an assistant dean of the Northwestern University Medical School, a doctor who had trained at County and could serve as a "pipeline."

*Because the governing commission did not yet have its own staff of experts in various fields of administration, certain kinds of expertise were needed on the commission. So a lawyer was chosen. And an accountant who could help solve some of the plaguing budgetary problems.

*Because service on the commission might entail spending a great deal of time working on hospital problems, the committee felt it important to select people able to take considerable time away from their regular jobs. This seemed to rule out working people, those most likely to be patients at County, a factor that was to lead later to considerable turmoil between the management-minded commission and selection committee, on the one hand, and the community people and their Residents and Interns Association advocates, on the other.

The New Commission's Tasks

The nine commissioners chosen by the selection committee took office in the fall of 1969 but it was to be almost a year before they could begin a wide scale attack on the myriad problems that had been mounting for so long.

One reason for the time lag was simply the necessity for the commissioners to find out what was going on. With the exception of the commissioner who had trained at County, none of them had any first hand knowledge of the hospital's problems. And whatever special knowledge any of the commissioners may have had about the administration of other large institutions was destined for challenge, again and again, in the hard reality of running an enterprise like County Hospital. The first need, then, was for information and the commission spent many hours listening to Dr. Freeark and other staff doctors telling it what was wrong. And inevitably it found that one doctor's solutions wouldn't fit another doctor's ideas at all.

Another reason for the time lag in a broad attack on County's problems was the discovery that the governing commission really didn't have the powers it thought it had. Where the legislation granting authority to the commission had seemed clear at first, ambiguities arose in interpretation. There were questions about just how much freedom the commission had in preparing its budget and in getting its funds from the county board, about how free it was to hire and fire and run its personnel function, how free it was to purchase and to operate as a separate legal entity. There was friction between the commission and the county board on many scores. The final blow to the commission's views of its independent powers was delivered in an opinion by the Cook County state's attorney that the legislation had indeed not given the commission the independent powers it thought it had.

The commission was in need of a strong executive director to help it carry out its duties, but it couldn't proceed to hire one until its powers and duties were clarified. Thus the first big task for the new group was to seek amendments in the law to settle the disputes. This process was to be carried out while the commission went on with its job of learning about County.

The clarifying amendments provided that the commission would assume all authority and responsibility for the health facilities but that it would still have to get its total budget approved once a year by the county board. The amendments were sent off to the state capitol, where they promptly met with a storm of criticism from Chicago Democrats and almost got buried in committee.

The governing commission had continued to be under considerable pressure from many members of the medical staff in the hospital, who felt that absolutely nothing was happening to improve conditions there. They were painfully aware, as was the commission, that time was running out on the accreditation of the hospital and that the changes required to gain the vital accreditation were not being undertaken fast enough.

Dr. Harold Levine wrote about this period, too, in his article, "County

Hospital: Revolution Within the Establishment."

"In February, 1970, the house staff began to despair. Their efforts seemed doomed to failure. The new board (governing commission) seemed powerless to correct the hospital's deficiencies. House staff frustrations led to a unanimous decision to attempt an action which would force the hospitals in the area to share the burden. The slogan was 'Practice good medicine.' Without fanfare, patients were kept in the hospital until they were adequately studied or until they were well. In a short time the hospital was overcrowded, even by Cook County standards.

"In a dramatic meeting, the house staff decided to insist on a curtailment of admissions. All agreed to resign should punitive action be taken against any. Freeark's previous threat against drastic actions by the house staff was clearly on their minds.

"But the house staff convinced Freeark of the wisdom of their move. He too had given up hope that the county board would respond to the hospital's problems. Freeark signed the cutback order. The hospital admitting rooms began to accept only dire emergencies. The patient flow was reversed. Instead of the other hospitals shunting all unwanted patients to County, County was sending patients to other hospitals. The house staff was jubilant; they had discovered the extent of their power.

"Meanwhile the county board attacked Freeark for curtailing admissions. But the governing commission stood up for Freeark, passing a resolution forbidding any ward ever again to become as crowded as the medical wards had been.

". . . Thus the crucial struggle to breathe life into the governing commission started . . .

"Full time attending staff and house staff began lobbying efforts. The bill first had to get out of committee. It quickly became apparent that the legislature was going to resist passage of the bill. Chicago Democratic influence was very strong in the legislature. Committee members complained that the bill would give non-elected individuals power over public funds. There were strong innuendoes that the doctors were fighting for control of the budget so that they could misuse the monies for personal gain.

"Hospital personnel chartered buses to lobby in Springfield. After observing and participating in these initial committee hearings, the staff felt almost unanimously that most of the legislators were not evaluating the bill objectively and that they had made up their minds not to pass the legislation. People from the hospital who went to testify or lobby for the bill returned with feelings of anger and frustration.

". . . On May 15, 1970, almost the entire house staff, large numbers of nurses and attendants, administrative personnel, social workers and some attending men (the senior physicians) appeared at a mass meeting. Freeark, informed of the intent of the house staff organization which called this meeting, agreed to address it. Freeark had become the leader in the struggle. Twenty minutes after the announced opening time, with about 600 people packing a large recreation room, a member of the governing commission appeared to read Freeark's resignation.

"It was a total surprise. Freeark reasoned that the politicians were avoiding the real problems by attacking him personally. With his resignation, the genuine issues would come to the fore. The leadership of the house staff was momentarily thrown into confusion. After a brief, intense caucus, they decided to proceed with the meeting. The spokesman of the house staff organization proposed that the hospital be reorganized, or that it be closed. There was loud applause.

". . . Tension began to mount. Despite Freeark's resignation, the county board president continued to blame the trouble on a few doctors. . .

". . . We all looked for new jobs and waited. . . . On the last day of the legislative session a bill granting budget and personnel control to the governing commission went through the state house, 155 to 0, in twenty minutes. It quickly cleared the senate. We had won!"

Dr. Levine's account of the victory is impassioned because he was passionately involved, intimately involved in the "Revolution Within the Establishment." The account itself, as well as Dr. Levine's involvement, will play a later role in this case.

When he speaks of the battle of the "doctors" he is referring primarily to the residents and interns and some of the full-time staff doctors who were, like himself, activists. Other doctors, particularly those with their own bailiwicks or "baronies," went to Springfield to oppose the bill. And certainly many others never got into either side of the political struggle.

But less passionate observers generally agree with Dr. Levine's account. Corbett Long, who had served briefly as the commission's executive director while preparing the legislative amendments, agrees that the revolt of the young doctors and the pressure they brought to bear on the county board were fundamental to the passage of the legislation.

"Back of all the legislation is the question, why?" Long reminisced. "What was the situation over there that even brought about the thought of legislation? Conditions were bad there, yes, but they were also bad in most departments of county government. The difference is that they didn't affect as many people as patient care did.

"It's true that there were changing expectations on the part of the patient population," Long continued. "And it's true that the younger generation of doctors was not going to live with the standards of medical service they saw there. Many of the older ones agreed and joined in. Freeark certainly did, and Freeark knew that hospital—probably knew as much about it, and as many people there, as anyone.

"Freeark was exercising his leadership to bring change. If rules and regulations didn't work, he'd ignore them. By the time I got there, he didn't give a damn about any rules of county government. He'd promote who he wanted and buy what he wanted. The commission was getting in trouble downtown. By violating the rules, Freeark was often making things work. Reclassifying people. Incurring bills without authorization and proper accounting; the commission is still cleaning up some of those bills (two years later). Maybe that went on before, but it was exaggerated under Freeark, The issue was need for control of the budget, personnel, purchasing, if he were to make that place work. Freeark provided intelligent, good leadership in bringing change about—but some waste and irregularities went along with it. The county board tried to pin it all on Freeark. His leaving really did get the legislation passed. It was after that, that Dunne (the county board president) changed his mind and sent down orders to pass the bill."

The passage of the amendments clarifying the commission's powers did breathe new life into the governing commission, and enabled it to hunt for a strong executive and begin to launch more organized plans for change. But passage of the amendments is not the end of the story. The strong executive was soon to come and both he and his organized plans for change were to run into new kinds of trouble, often with the same groups that fought so hard for the legislative changes.

Footnotes

1. The report of the Citizens Committee on Cook County Government. Robert E. Merriam and William G. Simpson, co-chairmen. 1967-68.
2. The New Physician, October, 1970.

Discussion Questions

1. What elements of social change require alterations in political structures? How can necessary alterations be brought about?

2. How should a public institution, such as a hospital, be governed?
    What kinds of governmental structures would best serve the needs
of:
    the publics who use the institution;
    the publics who pay for the institution;
    the management of the institution;
    the employees?
    In what ways do these group needs conflict with each other? With
other political priorities in society?

3. Who is best able to say what is in the public interest?

4. How can the governing commission of a public institution be removed from politics? How would you devise a governmental structure that is essentially non-political but can make political decisions (public policy decisions) in a way that is fair to all parties?

5. In the accompanying diagram, what is the nature of the relationships and responsibilities of each level to the level above it? For example, how is the public represented by the board or commission and which public is represented, those who use the institution or those who pay for it? Who sets the pattern for the relationship of the board or commission to its hired expert and what is the nature of the communication between them? Do employee duties include more than carrying out orders? How can employees affect policy?

Public

Board or Commission

Hired Expert

Employees

6. Are there inherent differences between managing a hospital and managing a private enterprise? Inherent differences between managing a public and a private hospital?

7. What kinds of problems does a union encounter in organizing and bargaining for an employee unit in a public institution that are different from those encountered in private industry?

With its powers and authorities finally established, the governing
commission set about the task of hiring a permanent executive
director, a dynamic leader who could develop a modern health delivery
system for Cook County. It found Dr. James G. Haughton, the first
deputy administrator of New York City's giant Health Services Administration, which included the largest hospital system in the country.
To bring him to Cook County, the commission offered him $60,000
a year, the highest salary paid to any public official in Illinois. Dr.
Haughton accepted in the fall of 1970.

The new executive director seemed remarkably well suited to his
job. He is a medical doctor and practiced medicine for 15 years in the
slums of Bedford-Stuyvesant and Brownsville, in Brooklyn, New York,
learning at first hand the health problems of the poor. He had served
in the Navy as medical and administrative officer of the largest naval
supply depot in the world. Returning to New York and still interested
in medical administration, he earned a master's degree in health administration from Columbia University, and began working for the city
health department, later incorporated into the Health Services Administration.

Dr. Haughton is black, a fact which the commission felt immensely
appropriate for the sprawling Cook County operation, in which about
90 percent of the patients are black. He was viewed—and he views
himself—as a man well suited to battling for the rights of the poor and
black.

"I have always been and will probably always be in the forefront of
controversy because I have always fought to establish the right of the
poor to decent health care," he said later. "The poor have been used
and abused by our health-care system for generations. Many dedicated
physicians, perhaps the great majority of physicians, have, for generations, given of their time and energy to the care of the poor without
compensation. But why, in the richest country in the world, should
any group of citizens have to be dependent upon the charity of others
for their right to health care and life, and why should they have to
receive so much of their care under circumstances which are ineffective,
demeaning and degrading?"

Local governments have done a poor job with their hospitals, Dr. Haughton believes, because there are so many bureaucratic constraints that even the most competent public administrators are frequently frustrated. Nevertheless, he believes that government can be effective and efficient and responsive and he thought perhaps Illinois and Cook County had found the key.

"I studied the law and its amendments," he said, "and came to the conclusion that, at long last, a group of legislators had had the good sense to create a governmental mechanism which could provide efficient management to the institutions entrusted to it."

The news of Dr. Haughton's selection brought rejoicing among the medical staff of County Hospital. The hard-pressed doctors felt that here, at last, was a man who could solve the hospital's depressing problems, and who, with the governing commission, could finally divorce the hospital from the political pressures of "downtown."

For six weeks in the fall of 1970, Dr. Haughton commuted between New York City and Chicago to help in the preparation of the commission's first budget.That first commission budget called for $31,000,000 from the county and estimated collections of about $77,000,000 from other sources, such as private health insurance, Medicare and Medicaid. The collections were to be a prodigious task because of the disorganization at County Hospital, but they were to be a key first step to managerial efficiency.

Dr. Haughton arrived in Chicago to work full-time at the end of November, 1970. Before three months had passed, he was to be lambasted publicly by the Residents and Interns Association for accomplishing nothing. The following few months brought increasing dissension, with broadside attacks on Dr. Haughton and the governing commission coming from many of the same doctors who worked so hard for the establishment of the governing commission in the two previous years. An extensive struggle for control developed, in part because of the developing concept of management in the hospital, in part because the changes threatened traditional structures, and in part because of personality conflicts in a profession admittedly full of prima donnas.

The Developing Concept of Management

Cook County Hospital had never really been managed in the sense that an industrial corporation, for example, is managed, with policies determined at the top and filtered down through levels of responsibility, each accountable for performance to the level above. In a sense no hospital fits this private industrial model. Hospitals traditionally have centered about the medical staff, with the doctors responsible for the quality of medical care and all other administrative units of the hospital

oriented to serving the doctors' needs. Thus, even in the best administered hospital, there is a dichotomy of administration—medical and
non-medical—and there are some inevitable conflicts, if only in the
definition of what is medical and what is non-medical.

It should be noted that this traditional hospital model, in which
most units of the hospital exist to serve the doctors, is derived from the
the private hospital model. In this model, the hospital is an extension
of the staff doctors' offices; the doctors who practice in the hospital
send there the patients they cannot care for in their offices. The sick
patient is not a patient of the hospital's; he is a patient of a doctor
who practices in that hospital. This kind of hospital-patient orientation
is quite different from that of the big public hospitals, like County.
In these, most patients don't have private doctors, either because
there are none in their neighborhoods or because the patient has never
been able to afford to hire one. When he goes to Cook County Hospital, then, it is in a different way from the patient who goes to a private hospital. The public patient is the hospital's patient, where the
private patient is the doctor's. The public hospital, in a sense, then,
serves a different customer. Yet this fact does not seem to be reflected
in a different kind of organization in the public hospitals. Doctors
work in both places—public and private—and they have brought with
them to public hospitals the model established in the private. Doctors
expect to play the same central policy role at County that they do in
any private hospital.

Cook County Hospital embodied all the traditional organizational
problems of any hospital, magnified and complicated by its immense
size, the diffusion of responsibility that had led to all the separate
"fiefdoms" or "baronies," the political conflict over where real control
of the hospital lay, and the exhausting infighting of the years before
the establishment of the governing commission. It was a very loose
structure, exceedingly frustrating to anyone with a task to accomplish.
Those who succeeded in accomplishing anything did not do so by following a system because there was no system; instead, if they succeeded,
they did so by forging ahead on their own despite the lack of system.

Into this loose confusion had come the governing commission, including members accustomed to thinking of orderly processes for
management, with its charge to produce efficiencies and to improve
the quality of care for the county's poor. And into it came Dr.
Haughton, with a background of getting things done in the similar
chaos of New York City. He found himself, he said later, in a "medico-
political jungle." The commission and Dr. Haughton set themselves
the task of managing Cook County Hospital, managing it in a way that
hadn't been tried before. They were dealing with one of the biggest
businesses in the county, with an annual operating budget of more

than $100,000,000, a total of more than 7,000 employees, as diverse as a window washer and a neurosurgeon, and a daily demand for service by more than 3,000 sick and unhappy people.

The problems confronting them were all difficult, all of the highest priority, and all interrelated. Some of these problems were:

1. Accreditation

Cook County Hospital was on probation. It had failed to win complete approval from the Joint Commission on Accreditation of Hospitals in the detailed investigations of 1968 and 1970. It had only until the summer of 1971 to correct the deficiencies or lose accreditation. Without accreditation, it could not function because it could not attract the residents and interns who carry on a major share of the actual patient care in the hospital. Many of the deficiencies were physical, such as proper environmental control for the surgical areas. Others were administrative, such as the need for adequate record-keeping and the requirement for the adoption of bylaws covering the medical staff, its responsibilities and its relationships with the commission. Major emphasis was placed on winning accreditation and the responsibility for following through the details was given to Dr. David MacLean Greeley, a quiet, determined, highly-respected physician Dr. Haughton had hired promptly as his deputy executive director ·for professional affairs. Dr. Greeley had had his own lessons in medico-political jungles; before coming to Chicago he had headed the United Mine Worker hospital system centered in "bloody Harlan, Kentucky."

2. New Emphasis on Patient Care

Traditionally, at County and at other similar big public hospitals, medical supervision of patient care was in the hands of the volunteer physicians who gave their time for half a day a week. In actuality, that meant that all day-to·day care was under the residents and interns; they are graduate physicians, licensed to practice, but they are still learning their specialties. Dr. Haughton believed passionately that this system short-changed the patients, that it placed primary emphasis on training the young doctors rather than on caring for the desperately ill patients. He was determined to hire a greater number of competent, full-time physicians as staff members, to supervise the work of the residents each day all week, not just half a day a week.

"Cook County Hospital will always be a 'teaching hospital,' " Dr. Haughton has said, "but, as long as this executive director and this commission have anything to do with it, it will not be a teaching hospital in the model of the 30's. In that model, the poor and the disadvantaged were the subjects of teaching and research and received their medical care as a by-product of those two activities. During that period and into the 40's, it was felt that paying patients could not be the

subjects of teaching and research because they paid their way. Well,
that model is no longer socially, morally or professionally acceptable;
and those at Cook County Hospital who would have us return to it
are not welcome there."

3. Administrative Control

Cook County Hospital included 20 buildings and dozens of divisions
and departments. There was a medical director, charged with supervision of the medical departments, a director of the nursing service
in all its areas, and an administrator, whose supervisory area included
physical departments as varied as a gigantic laundry, a security system
and the outpatient clinic. But there was no one person responsible
overall for these sprawling operations, who could coordinate what was
going on and find and fill the gaps. Dr. Haughton wanted to find a
director for the hospital but, failing to find one as rapidly as he wanted,
he filled that function himself, as well as acting as executive director
of the governing commission. It may have been an impossible assignment, not only because it was so completely demanding but also because conflicts were to develop between the commission level of administration and the hospital level below it.

4. Fiscal Operations

The governing commission, for the first time in 1971, was to do the
entire job of developing its own budget for presentation to the county
board of commissioners. That project called not only for the mechani-
cal aspect of dealing with great masses of complex figures but also for
determining budget priorities. Other pressing fiscal needs were for a
modern billing system that would allow the hospital to collect fees
from outside agencies such as insurance companies, a process in which
it was woefully behind; negotiating with third party insurers over
categories of charges; and development of a cost accounting system.

5. Planning

Profound changes require extensive planning and planning was
needed not only for changes in programs within the hospital but also
for development of a county health care network that would provide
primary care close to the patient's homes. Many patients at County
travel, often by bus and subway, as much as 20 miles to get to County
for care and, as a result, they are much sicker when they finally get
there than they would be if they could see a doctor in their home
neighborhoods. Since their home neighborhoods, for the most part,
are in one of Chicago's ghettos and there are very few private physicians serving ghetto residents, new emphasis needed to be put on clinic
facilities of some kind in the neighborhoods.

6. Personnel

This was a new function for County Hospital. The nursing service
ran its own personnel office, but other non medical employees had

been hired in county offices. There were few personnel records, no job analyses and no coordinated salary structure. With the county now removed from the business of hiring for the hospital, new personnel administration was needed. One of its tasks would be man-power planning and development. It had nothing on which to build.

7. Labor Relations

This is part of personnel, of course, but is listed as a separate problem here because of the immediacy of the need. Oak Forest Hospital, the geriatric facility also under the mantel of the governing commission, had signed its first labor contract with a union of service employees in 1970, and an election was soon to be held in the larger County Hospital. Contracts with the Illinois Nursing Association, representing registered nurses, and with the Licensed Practical Nurses Association were being negotiated at the time of Dr. Haughton's arrival. The Residents and Interns Association was pushing for recognition and bargaining rights in the fall of 1970, before Dr. Haughton's arrival, and was to push even harder once he got there. Other professionals were considering organizing for collective bargaining. There were no policies and procedures to cover any of these bargaining activities, and very little knowledge on which to draw.

8. Coordination

The charge to the governing commission included consolidation of policies and planning for the three institutions under its control that had previously been somewhat more separate: Cook County Hospital, Oak Forest Hospital, and the School of Nursing, which supplied professional nursing service to each of the hospitals but had had its own separate board of directors since the 1920s. Every effort at reform had recommended bringing the nursing service under closer control of the hospital. Besides this process of consolidation, there was a need for coordinated policies for the hospitals in the areas of planning and budgeting, provisions of services to patients, and administration of personnel services for employees. Largely because of the need for coordination Dr. Haughton began assembling new administrative staff members to serve under him at the commission level, a new level between the operating departments and the governing commission. It was as though, in a private industry with three different plants, a new corporate management level was added all at once. At Cook County Hospital, the addition of the new staff was to lead to considerable confusion and some animosity over just whose job was what.

9. Physical Upgrading of Facilities

Dr. Haughton discovered with horror on some of his first trips through the hospital buildings that they were in deplorable condition. "Most buildings on the Cook County campus are 50 or more years old," he said in a speech about six weeks after his arrival. "There has been no

plan for upkeep except to come around with green paint when someone screams loud enough. Preventive maintenance doesn't exist at
County Hospital." He said his first act as director was to outlaw
green paint and to launch a maintenance program. The broken and discarded equipment that used to litter corridors and tunnels has been
hauled away and all new furniture for patients has been ordered.
Renovation and modernization programs that had been bogged down,
sometimes for years, were redesigned and restarted.

10. Community Relations

Community groups, particularly those representing the minority
groups that are the largest users of patient care at County, were continuing to apply pressure for improvements at the hospital and Dr.
Haughton wished to devise procedures for consulting with the community that would be constructive rather than disruptive. New programs were needed.

11. Medical School Affiliation

This was an old problem, continuing, one that sounds easy to solve,
but isn't. For years, all major recommendations for improvement of
County included stronger ties with the nearby medical schools (there
are six in the county). There is general agreement that affiliation
is required to provide first class training and thus attract a house staff
(interns and residents) that can provide quality patient care.

But there are many problems involved in how to affect affiliation
so that both the medical school and the hospital can profit by the
arrangement, so that patients are not just learning tools. Models
elsewhere provide a variety of patterns, but most of them do not place
primary emphasis on patients and most provide more financial advantages for the medical schools than for the hospitals.

Conflicting recommendations on how to achieve affiliation have
ranged all the way from a recommendation to turn County Hospital
over in toto to the University of Illinois Medical School to a recommendation to include all the medical schools in a training program
at the hospital, with County keeping strong central control over the
treatment of its patients. Dr. Haughton was hopeful of finding an
innovative way for an affiliation that would safeguard the interests
of the patients.

12. Communication

With new programs and new people, combined with the political
traditions of the past and the vastness of the enterprise, communication
loomed as an increasing problem. Sometimes it seemed that no one
knew what anyone else was doing, or how to go about finding it. On
the other hand, the hospital was a gigantic rumor mill: leaked information, often incorrect, preceded every action, feeding discontents and
jealousies and apprehensions. As Dr. Greeley was to say later, somewhat

ruefully, "We don't get the right people in the right room at the right time." Clear channels of communication were desperately needed, but not easily developed.

To accomplish all these changes, people were needed but they were not immediately at hand. There was no executive staff directly account-able to the new executive director, Dr. Haughton, when he arrived. So he began to build one. Even before he arrived, he had drawn up an organization chart of the commission-level staff he envisioned, had defined each job and written job descriptions (See Chart I). But filling the jobs with the right people took longer; commission staff members were still being added throughout most of 1971. And as each arrived, he encountered the immediate problem of trying to learn what was going on in so vast an enterprise, what he was expected to do (even though part of his job was to help develop policies concerning his own job), and how to know and work with each other. In a sense, it was a chicken-and-egg problem. You can't do planning and budgeting without the people but you can't get the people until planning and budgeting help you see what people are needed.

Ideally, of course, staff would have been added in a logical order, hiring directors and then hiring their subordinates, so that training of each subordinate would take place in a logical progression. Practically that didn't always work. Sometimes the subordinates were hired first, because a good person was available or because a need was so pressing that it could not be put off until an organization chart was filled from the top down. And the needs — all of them — were pressing. Everything was a priority. There were pressures from all sides.

As each new commission staff member was added, he found he had to make decisions without adequate policies to guide him, since the policies had not yet been developed and could not be developed until the staff member helped identify what policies were needed.

The process sounds like circular confusion and it was. The new era of management at County Hospital had a difficult birth.

The Threat to Traditional Structures

The addition of a new layer of top management — the commission level staff with a yearly budget of more than six million dollars — brought both confusion and consternation at the hospital level, com-pounded by the fact that there were many changes at the hospital level too. People who had plugged along in their jobs for years found they had new bosses and the new bosses had new bosses too. There were so many changes to be made and change in any large institution is always difficult; inertia stands in the way. It is particularly difficult to introduce modern management to an institution so entirely unaccustomed to any of modern management's techniques. Where a system has run by a patchwork of political accommodations, more organized methods can be perceived as threats.

Each new policy decision by Dr. Haughton and his governing commission echoed down those miles of corridors, with staff members all along the corridors wondering what this policy meant to them, to their accustomed method of doing their jobs, to their prerogatives, to their futures. The rumor mill ran overtime.

A feeling began to develop that the commission staff itself was the enemy. A new staff member would be asked again and again, "Are you hospital or commission?" If he answered he worked for the commission, he became instantly suspect. If he further answered that he really saw his job as one of helping the hospital level people work more effectively, he wasn't believed.

For some employees, changes seemed to come too fast, but there was always a group, mostly of young professionals, who were scornful and scathingly critical because the changes were too slow.

Some of the knottiest problems developed with the medical staff, long used to seeing themselves as the only real management in the hospital, the only group charged with overseeing the medical care of patients. A whole complex of issues arose over what was a medical decision and what was a mangement decision, what a medical prerogative and what a management prerogative.

There was, for example, a heated dispute over a governing commission decision to reduce the number of beds in the division of medicine, the largest single division in the hospital. Dr. Haughton and the commission decided to reduce the beds available to patients in the division from approximately 500 to 400 and gave these reasons: the number of beds was illegally large under the space requirements of the Illinois state hospital code and the number was unnecessarily large anyway because the daily census of patients in the division had rather consistently been below 400. The director of the division, Dr. Rolf Gunnar, and his staff strongly opposed the decision, contending that while the census was below 400, that was seasonal and would increase with the return of cold weather and contending further that the reduction left the hospital dangerously unprepared for emergencies.

A medical decision? A management decision? A little of each perhaps. The decision was made by management and the doctors continued to contend that it should not have been made unilaterally, that they had to have some input into such a decision. Haughton insisted they had been adequately consulted and later added, "To some in this hospital, one is 'not communicating' if one does not say 'yes' to every request — no matter how unreasonable."

Another example: Dr. Haughton and the governing commission decided to change the function of the division of psychiatry and in the process reduced the number of beds in the division from 113 to 26. In the past, they said, the division had been chiefly used for two dismally unproductive functions: as a holding center for persons awaiting court action for commitment to state mental hospitals and as a detoxification unit for chronic alcoholics who often stayed 60 to 90 days, receiving little real treatment. State facilities were available elsewhere for these patients, Dr. Haughton believed, and County's psychiatric staff could be better used in a new crisis intervention unit for disturbed patients who would receive acute care and could then return to their homes. Many of the doctors fought the decision and were joined by the Illinois Society of Psychiatry, who believed County needed more psychiatry beds, not fewer, and needed positive new programs for active treatment of both alcoholics and drug addicts.

Another example dealt with the collection of fees for professional service rendered by physicians to patients. This is a complex problem, made more complex in public hospitals like County by the rules developed for payments on behalf of patients under Medicare and Medicaid, as well as by private insurance companies. Under Medicare rules and under state professional practice laws, no hospital can bill for professional service; it can only bill for the hospital services given to a patient. The doctors' bills are separate and only the doctors can handle this billing, either collecting directly (if they are in private practice) or assigning the collections to another agency if they are salaried by a hospital. No doctor at County Hospital collects for himself any fees for medical service given in the hospital because every doctor there is either a salaried employee or a volunteer who is donating his time without charge.

Before the creation of the governing commission, the County Hospital doctors set up an organization called Associated Physicians and each doctor assigned to this organization the right to collect for him the professional fees for service to patients. Other public hospitals in the area, such as the University of Illinois Research Hospital, have a similar structure. The fees collected by the Associated Physicians were used in two ways: to purchase medical equipment for the hospital, including equipment that the hospital itself designated as needed, and to make small grants to the medical divisions for such purposes as professional libraries for the staff and staff expenses to attend medical conferences.

Some of the governing commission members felt that this was an unbusinesslike arrangement, particularly with the new emphasis on hiring more and more full-time salaried physicians. Since the commission was paying salaries to these doctors, the commission reasoned, fees that were collected for patient care should be returned to the commission to help pay the salaries. Since the hospital was prevented by law from directly collecting these professional fees, the commission set up a fund and decreed that the doctors should assign their fees to this fund rather than to the Associated Physicians. Almost all of the doctors balked, including both the salaried staff and the volunteer physicians. Funds collected for doctors' services, they insisted, should be spent under the direction of doctors. When the commission refused to allow the Associated Physicians access to the records needed for billing, the issue reached a heated impasse and for a time, no one at all was able to collect the thousands of dollars involved.

A management prerogative? A professional prerogative? Some of each, perhaps. It sounds like an issue amenable to compromise, but the tensions and suspicions and jealousies at County Hospital in 1971 did not lead easily to compromises. This was a crucial battle line.

Other examples of medical-management disagreements are legion. In almost every case, there was merit on both sides. In almost every case, the decision — or even the lack of decision — fed the flames of discontent. The era of management, after its difficult birth, was having a difficult childhood.

Personality Conflicts

Doctors are the kingpins of any hospital. Without them, the hospital does not function. All the other employees are there to enable the doctors to do their work, to provide the best care possible for their patients. Every hospital organization, be it a posh private hospital for the wealthy or a big, impersonal and sometimes dismal place like County, places genuine power in the hands of the medical staff. So ingrained is this concept in all our health care institutions that the Joint Commission on the Accreditation of Hospitals absolutely requires that there be bylaws spelling out the powers of the medical staff, its prerogatives and its relationships with other parts of the institution. The bylaws must include "effective formal means for the medical staff to participate in the development of hospital policy relative to both hospital management and outpatient care."

In any hospital seeking to adapt management methods to its hospital needs, a certain amount of conflict seems inevitable between the top management people and the top medical people. Although both groups are concerned with improving medical care, their background, training and methods are very different. Just as there is nothing in the training of managers to enable them to understand all aspects of health

care, there is also nothing in the training of physicians to prepare them
for administering huge enterprises. Students of hospital management
are seeking ways to mesh the kinds of skills needed, but it is not a
simple process.

The process at County Hospital was complicated, of course, by the
previous loose organization of the hospital and by the acrimonious
struggle over the creation of the governing commission, intended to cut
the hospital loose from politics. Feelings often run high at County.

Some of the strongest feelings were most forthrightly expressed by
the young doctors, many of whom have made no compromise with
what they believe are the dreadful standards of the big public hospitals. Throughout the country, and certainly at County, they have used
every device at their command to force their ideas of better care. They've
encouraged dissident community groups to protest and have joined in
the protests — or led them. They've issued newsletters and held press
conferences to advertise the deficiencies of the hospitals where they
worked. They've threatened law suits on behalf of the patients. They've
developed the technique of the heal-in, overcrowding the hospital with
patients, as a pressure tactic. (They've been accused in some places
of toning down the demands for better patient care once they themselves have won salary increases, but they emphatically deny the
accusations.) County Hospital had its fair share of these young activists
and they certainly did stir the pot of discontent during the difficult
year of 1971, earning support of some of the older doctors and thoroughly exasperating others who saw the dissidents not as constructive
reformers but as obstreperous trouble-makers.

Dr. Haughton, as change-minded as some of the impatient young,
found himself tangling again and again with them over their methods.
It was his job to hold the whole rambling structure together and try
to move it forward. In the process, he certainly was no pussyfooter. When
he made up his mind to a course of action, he moved. Then there would
be some who called him an arrogant dictator. Often he found himself
the target of a whole range of complaints from medical staff, some feeling he moved too fast, some that he moved too slowly, some that he
was moving in the wrong direction.

"You have been told of my arrogance, my lack of tact and diplomacy
and my high-handedness," he told a committee of Illinois state
legislators investigating the continuing problems at County Hospital.
"Gentlemen, I am an executive who believes that a leader should lead.
One who does not have the courage to make decisions and to take
unpopular and sometimes controversial positions should not accept
a position of leadership . . .

"There is no 'diplomatic' and 'tactful' way to say 'no' to a division head intent on empire-building at the expense of the taxpayer and whose program promises no visible improvement in the quality of patient care. Firmness and decisiveness were what was required in the medico-political jungle which was Cook County Hospital in 1971. Call that arrogance, if you wish."

Observers who have sought to analyze County's problems have made much of the personality clashes. They did exist. Dr. Haughton did sometimes act precipitously, without the agreement of the medical staff. Some of the young doctors were obstreperous, carried away with the idea that because they provide most of the day-to-day care of patients that they are the heart of the hospital. Some of the older doctors were crotchety and opposed ideas that seemed threatening to them, or to their beliefs about their medical responsibilities. Some of the members of the governing commission were lacking in tact, too, and there are many examples of difficulties over sorting out what is policy-making and what is administration.

But it is simplistic to blame all the problems on personality, as some observers have done. There really were no actual villains in the drama, only groups who found themselves legitimately at odds over issues of genuine concern to all of them. Another cast of characters dealing with the same issues might well have been in similar troubles. The real issue was the knotty management problem of how to run a giant public hospital in this era.

The Management Issue

The management issue is one that is posing similar problems for other management personnel, too, in both public and private institutions. Intricately related with broad social trends in our society, the issue concerns the degree to which top management should consult its employees, particularly its professional employees, in the formulation of policies the employees are expected to carry out. There are guidelines, but they are conflicting.

Guidelines that point toward more consultation include:

— A 40-year trend toward employee organization and to broadening the scope of bargaining, which means opening more and more areas to joint decision-making with employee groups, as opposed to unilateral decision-making. This trend has been fostered by legislation, administrative ruling and court decisions. With this greater sharing of decision-making, management has found it no longer has the power to make decisions unilaterally; there has been steady modification of behavior in business and industry to accommodate this sharing.

— New patterns in the creeping social revolution. Outright authoritarianism is harder and harder to assert. More people are speaking up more often about more things that bother them — and are expecting to be heard and considered.

— Management studies showing that employees work most effectively in carrying out objectives that they themselves have helped to formulate. This kind of consideration is particularly important in dealing with supervisory employees.

— A rather cynical observation, available to anyone willing to look, that no management will have notable successes in carrying out a policy that is actively opposed by a significant number of employees. The policy will be torpedoed somehow, if not outright, then by lack of enthusiasm in enforcement.

— Increased activism by professional groups who claim that allegiance to the profession makes certain claims upon them that may conflict with allegiance to the employing institution.

Conflicting guidelines, those that warn against greater consultation with employees, include:

— Tradition. What is left of the authoritarian structures of society adheres to the principle that he who pays the piper calls the tune. Authoritarianism is everywhere under attack but is still the basis of our public and private structures.

— Management textbooks case studies replete with suggestions that our greatest success models, at least in private enterprise, are those who have managed to reserve a high degree of authority to manage, in order to achieve the overall objectives of the institution.

— Cautions against further broadening the scope of bargaining, lest management find itself completely immobilized between its responsibilities to ownership and its commitments to its employees.

— Political administration guidelines which stress the absolute responsibilities for a governing body to carry out the mission for which it was created — providing police service or library service or education or health care — to the public, rather than operating the agency for the benefit of the service employees it hires.

These conflicting trends pose a management issue everywhere but private, profit-making enterprise at least has its tradition of management authority to lean upon. This is not true of hospitals, which have a different kind of tradition, due in part to the fact that doctors have not usually been employees of the hospital management. The authoritarians in hospitals have been the doctors, and they are certainly unaccustomed to a new kind of authoritarianism being imposed from above.

Hospitals are inordinately complex structures, offering a very wide variety of services so intricate that a specialist in one area can rarely fully grasp more than the essential outlines of another area. Hospitals have a very high proportion of professional staff, whose work involves independent judgment, an allegiance to a professional code, and often a very high degree of prideful independence, which they can afford to assert because they are in demand. A hospital without its professionals cannot function as, say, a telephone company can, with administrative executives filling in for specialists who are temporarily missing. Many a hospital administration has long since discovered that the way to handle its professionals — at least its top professionals — is to give them what they want. Traditional hospital organization accentuates this pragmatic approach. It is simply accepted that, in most matters, the doctors are on top. They are the hospital's customers. The hospital exists to serve them as an extension of their medical offices, and hospital services are organized around the requirements of the doctors. Hospital boards tend to be quiet groups who understand their roles: to raise money to make things work for the medical staff.

Old-line public hospitals — like County used to be — followed the same traditional hospital organization. The doctors ran them. They all had to harangue a bit to get some money from the public purse-watchers, but they learned how to do that in order to get on with their mission: providing medical care to people who needed it and supervising the medical training of the new generation of professionals who would carry on.

It might have all gone on working the same way had not two great upheavals taken place: the revolution in medical expectations and the revolution in medicine itself, which led to the spectacular rise in costs that led in turn to demands for new methods of management.

The revolution in medical expectations meant that suddenly — or at least it seemed to be suddenly — there were voices saying, "Look here. Hospitals ought to be run for the patients. We who use the hospital because we are sick ought to be the prime concern. We have a right to the best medical care available. We don't want to come here to be experimented on." It was a revolution that had to work because almost everyone had come to agree with it. The doctors agreed. "Yes," they said, "medical care for the patients is the primary aim of a hospital. That's what we've always been working for." But the disagreement over how best to assure that aim has been long and clamorous. It is at the heart of the controversy at Cook County Hospital. At County, because of its nature as a public hospital and as a training hospital, a much larger proportion of the medical staff are actually employees of the hospital than is the case in private hospitals but that does not change their view of the prerogatives of the medical staff in making or at least helping to make the basic decisions about the direction of patient care.

CHART I

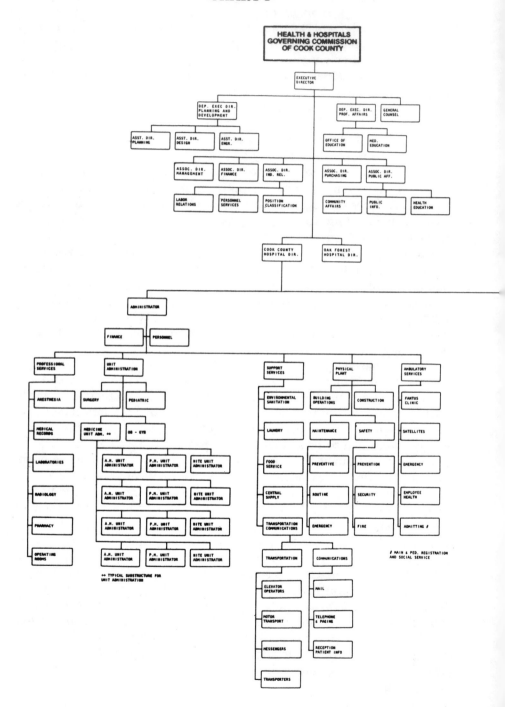

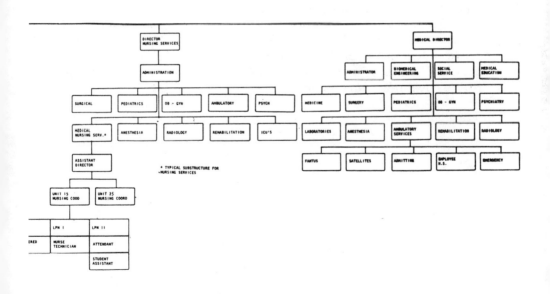

* TYPICAL SUBSTRUCTURE FOR
  NURSING SERVICES

The other revolution, that of new knowledge and new methods that led to spiraling costs, played a major role at County too. The governing commission, in order to solve the myriad problems of delivering health care to the public and to get some kind of planned control over the haphazard cost structure, introduced many modern management methods, often borrowed from private industry. That process didn't work very smoothly.

Some observers of the County Hospital turmoil said it was a struggle for power. That's true, as far as it goes. More precisely, it was a struggle over decision-making: over which groups should make which decision and in what decisions should the power be shared. In this sense, the real issue was the scope of bargaining: the extent of co-determination of policies.[1]

Primarily the struggle was between the new wave of managers brought in by the governing commission — with their businesslike ideas and priorities — and the new wave of young doctors at the hospital — with their commitment to the right of every person to quality medical care and their rather self-centered belief that since they provided the bulk of medical care at County, they should have an important say in its planning and administration.

But gradually, as specific issues and controversies accumulated, other medical staff joined in, until a powerful coalition developed, powerful enough to challenge Dr. Haughton and demand his resignation, and powerful enough to demand basic changes in the make-up of the governing commission.

Footnote

1. Authors' note: It is one thing to agree that there should be consultation with the medical staff and another to figure out how to do it. There are several organizations of doctors within the hospital and they don't all speak with one voice. They don't all represent the same interests and there are shifting alliances and allegiances among them. Among the organizations of medical people at County are these:
   1. The executive medical staff, an official structure provided in the bylaws. It is made up of 26 members; a president and vice president elected by the senior medical staff, plus 20 division and department heads and four representatives of the two full-time staff associations.
   2. Association of Full-time Salaried Staff, reactivated in the fall of 1971 to speak for the group of about 100 full-time senior doctors.
   3. The Residents and Interns Association, representing about 100 interns and 400 residents. They are graduate physicians, licensed to practice, but are in training for medical specialties. The association was formed in the 1960s to bargain for better salaries and for a voice in policy determination; it is the most activist of the groups.
   4. The Voluntary Physicians of Cook County Hospital, formed in January, 1972, because these part-time volunteers felt they were otherwise unrepresented. About 500 physicians perform part-time voluntary services at the hospital and tend to see themselves as the traditional medical group there and an important link with the community and with medical practice elsewhere.
   5. Associated Physicians, an organization of both voluntary and full-time physicians formed for the collection and disbursements of professional fees.
   6. Black Caucus, which also included non-professional but was led by black physicians. It sought, unsuccessfully, to mediate some of the differences between other physicians' groups and the administration. It is significant that black professionals never had many opportunities at County during its long history, just as they had few opportunites at private hospitals; the whole health care industry systematically excluded them. The coming of Dr. Haughton and his integrated administrative staff has changed all that.

Discussion Questions

1. Is there a basic conflict between management knowledge that arises out of technology (as in a hospital) or the peculiarities of an institu-

tion (as in the public sector) and generic types of management which seek to plan, to organize a structure for efficient performance of tasks, to evaluate performance in order to improve future performance? If there is a conflict, how can it be reconciled and what should be the role of each kind of management?

2. Identify the external forces acting upon the management of a large public hospital. Are they conflicting? If so, how can the conflicting pressures be reconciled?

3. Can management techniques developed in private enterprise be successfully superimposed upon existing public institutions? Why or why not?

4. What aspects of organization behavior are illustrated in the management changes outlined in this section?

5. How did the managerial changes discussed in this section affect: losses and gains in power; the concept of the hospital's mission; the demands of the hospital-using public to have a say in its management?

6. What role should doctors play in the administration of a public hospital? In answering, consider the technology, professional ethics, responsibility and accountability to the public, realities of the distribution of power.

7. What kinds of conflict exist between the centralized authority in a system and the sovereignty of its individual units? How much sovereignty can be retained by individual units? How much authority must the central management maintain? What is the effect on this balance of outside intervention such as state legal requirements, federal requirements for equal opportunity or specified safety standards, or a labor organizing drive within the institution? How is the flexibility of the institution affected by the balance between centralized authority and the sovereignty of individual units?

8. Where a hospital issue crosses the line between management prerogatives and medical prerogatives, how can it best be resolved?

9. From a union point of view, what different strategies must be employed if an institution is shifted from political management to professional management?

The spirit of hopeful optimism with which hospital people greeted the appointment of Dr. Haughton as top man didn't last long. Although Dr. Haughton took hold with vigor and promptly began the arduous process of assembling his commission staff to plan and carry out the needed changes, there were no instant miracles.

The Residents and Interns Association, not long on patience, issued a belligerent press release early in 1971, when Dr. Haughton had been on the job only slightly over two months. It was a blast that not only signaled the mood of the young house staff but also identified many of the issues that would come up again and again during the difficult year of 1971.

"Nearly a year ago," began the February 12 press release, "The Residents and Interns Association actively participated in the struggle to remove Cook County Hospital from the political control and corruption which have crippled this hospital for decades. At that time, the association fully supported the concept of an independent nonpolitical governing commission empowered to run this overcrowded and understaffed institution. Hopefully, such a governing commission would have been responsive to the health needs and priorities for those communities served by Cook County Hospital, rather than those subservient to the politicians of Cook County.

"Since the establishment of the governing commission, however," the press release continued, "no improvements in the quality of patient care have occurred. In fact, substantial deterioration has taken place on the crammed, ill-equipped wards. Yet the governing commission has been preoccupied in carpeting and air conditioning its own quarters and hiring a high-powered public relations department. We feel it is necessary to improve Cook County Hospitals as the primary health care institution for thousands, especially the poor and the nonwhite."

The Residents and Interns Association press release announced some targets for further action, among them:

1. A "publicly accountable selection committee" for choosing members of the Governing Commission.
2. Addition to the governing commission of "responsible community

leaders committed to provide decent and quality patient care to all regardless of income and race."

3. All necessary action to bring about "long overdue changes" and improve patient care.

4. Forcing private hospitals and medical care centers "to assume a new attitude of social responsibility" and stop using County Hospital as the "dumping ground for those who are poor, non-white or medically uninteresting."

5. Establishment of a written contract between the association and the hospital to set conditions of employment "conducive to continue to attract top quality foreign and American staff at the resident and intern level, and which provides an official mechanism by which the RIA will actively participate in hospital committees affecting all aspects of patient care."

The news release, although it included other issues that were to go on smoldering, probaby was primarily aimed at the written contract. The Residents and Interns Association had sought a collective bargaining agreement in the previous fall, before Dr. Haughton's arrival, and that was one of the problems awaiting his action. The association represented more than 400 of the approximately 450 residents and interns at County.

Dr. Haughton, in testimony before a court-appointed hearing committee on discipline, has told a rather detailed story of the bargaining that took place:[1]

"The draft contract . . . came to my attention in November or December (1970). I met with representatives of the association to discuss some of the matters raised. The commission at that point was not willing to negotiate, but I felt such a large group in the hospital could not be ignored and that therefore somebody had to sit down with them and try to deal with some of the problems they were raising.

"I therefore finally persuaded the commission to permit me to discuss these matters with them, and I began a series of meetings with the representatives of the house staff. Some of those meetings were quite acrimonious because there were some members of this negotiating team who felt they were not at the hospital for training, that they were there to provide primary care. I rejected that notion because in my experience residents and interns are physicians in a hospital seeking further training. Yes, they provided an important portion of the health service in the process of learning, but I could not accept that our residents and interns were our primary physicians and not there to learn.

"In any case, our house staff insisted that the financial part of the document was their least concern and yet for almost six weeks we talked of nothing else but the salaries and fringe benefits and so on. This was at a time when the commission had already passed a resolution providing a 14½% increase in salaries for residents and interns. I therefore insisted that I had no authority to negotiate additional salary.

"We finally agreed to bypass the issue of salary and get to some of the other questions and problems in the proposed contract. An important part had to do with a grievance procedure, which the representatives felt was important to them, so that they could not be disciplined at the whim of their department chairman or division chairman or by the administration.

"There was a long portion in which they were demanding membership in committees of the medical staff organization. I indicated this was not an issue to be dealt with with the commission, that the medical staff organization was the purview of the medical staff and they should negotiate those membership requirements with the medical staff. They agreed.

"The memorandum of understanding was signed in March 1971. It was to go into effect on July 1, except for a committee on house staff, which was to be started immediately. They indicated they needed a mechanism for communication with the commission, so they could bring their complaints about conditions in the hospital or conditions in their own employment, and I suggested their recourse should be through their division heads and through the administration of the hospital and, at the most, through the medical staff.

"They insisted they had to have their own mechanism, so I suggested the mechanism in this document (the memorandum of understanding), which provided for a committee composed of the deputy executive director for professional affairs (Dr. David M. Greeley), the medical director of the hospital and the administrator of the hospital, to be joined by three representatives of the house staff chosen by the house staff. The committee was supposed to meet once a month, to hear any complaints or problems concerning conditions in the hospital."

The memorandum of understanding, signed March 16, 1971, was in effect a labor contract. It provided for:
— Recognition of the association as bargaining agent;
— Dues checkoff;
— The salary increases already approved by the governing commission, which called for $10,300 a year for interns and a $600 increase

for each year of residency, up to $13,900 for a sixth year resident;
— Benefits including a three-week vacation, housing at small or no cost, meals at no cost, uniforms and laundry, free parking, insurance, and protection against malpractice charges;
— The committee on house staff, to meet monthly;
— A grievance procedure;
— A procedure for disciplinary actions, including the right to a hearing before disciplinary action was taken, written charges, and due process protections during the hearing;
— Continuation of the contract to June 30, 1972.

Dr. Haughton and the president of the Residents and Interns Association, Dr. Ernestine Hambrick, a talented resident in surgery who demonstrated powerful leadership in the hospital, presumably agreed that the announcement of the memorandum of understanding would be made in a joint press release and that there would be no further public statements from either side. But at the press conference, to Dr. Haughton's considerable exasperation, Dr. Hambrick also read a further statement from the association.

She told the press that there was a shortage of house staff and that working conditions at County are "perhaps the most burdensome in the country." She went on to say that there was "little evidence of substantial change at Cook County Hospital, despite a big new commission staff," and that the association would "continue to document specific problems" such as "improper transfers (from other hospitals), faulty equipment, and understaffing." She continued with a new attack on Stuart Ball, the chairman of the selection committee for commission members, whom she called "irresponsible."

Press conferences were to become, increasingly, tools of the residents and interns in pushing for the reforms they wanted. Because they exhibited a flair for the dramatic, they got good press coverage and each new release stirred the pot of discontent always brewing in the hospital. The governing commission, Dr. Haughton, and at least some of the senior medical staff grew increasingly irritable over the barrage of public charges and contended that the residents and interns were not using the channels that existed within the hospital to correct deficiencies. The residents and interns answered that they did use the channels, nothing was accomplished that way, and that it was their responsibility to go beyond the channels to the public to pressure for the changes they felt were necessary. Some of the senior medical staff were in wholehearted agreement with the association's methods and provided not only tacit approval but also specific items that tended to corroborate the charges

Often, during 1971, specific moves by Dr. Haughton or by the governing commission to accomplish the management objectives met with wide medical staff resistance. Each time this happened, the coalition of opposition that the residents and interns had started was widened. This happened, for example, when people both inside and outside the hospital opposed the change in direction for the division of psychiatry. It happened again when the commission cut back the number of beds available to the division of medicine and made other organizational changes in that division which the doctors in the division felt were threatening to patient care.

Another administrative change in the division of medicine produced more heated feelings. Dr. Haughton, following a trend in hospital administration that has been successful in other big hospitals, decided to set up a unit manager system for each division, starting with the big division of medicine. Under this plan, a unit manager — not a doctor — would be placed in charge of nonmedical administrative details; the aim was increased efficiency and freeing the medical staff from problems relating to clerical work, laundry, food service, staff scheduling and similar matters. The medical staff favored the idea in principle but the problem in the division of medicine was that the head of the division, Dr. Gunnar, already had two administrative assistants who were being paid from the professional fees collected by the Associated Physicians. Dr. Haughton informed everyone involved that the two assistants would no longer be needed and that he had appointed a unit manager who would be paid from the regular budget. There was stormy protest, not only over the firing of the two assistants but also over the fact that the new unit manager would report, not to the head of the division, but directly to Dr. Haughton in his role as director of the hospital. Dr. Gunnar and his staff protested that at the very least they should have been consulted about the move. Dr. Gunnar pointed out that the new unit manager, a bright young man with a business degree, had been working in the hospital complex only six months and his service was in the School of Nursing rather than the hospital, so he had no knowledge of the complex needs of the division of medicine.

At about the same time, the governing commission sought to limit the role that community people, representing the consumers of hospital care, were playing in the division of medicine. The division, for some time, had been working with a Consumer Advisory Board. Dr. Haughton and the commission felt it was inappropriate for a consumer group to be involved only with one division of the hospital rather than with the hospital as a whole and announced that this particular consumer group would no longer be able to meet in the hospital. The senior staff of the division sent Dr. Haughton a protest, urging him to "establish forthwith a Consumer Advisory Board" so the commission could have some kind of consulting structure for the community and stating, "Furthermore, the professional staff reserves the right to continue to meet with members from the community to discuss relevant problems."

Each of these specific actions, plus others, kept the rumor mill in full-time operation. Increasingly there was talk of commission meddling in medical affairs that should be left to the medical staff and talk of "overmanagement" without adequate consultation with the medical professionals.

The Struggle for Accreditation

Looming over all the specific problems was the great need to meet, before the summer of 1971, all the requirements of the Joint Commission on Accreditation of Hospitals. If County Hospital did not meet the requirements, its very existence would be threatened. There is general agreement that there was very wide cooperation in the hospital toward accomplishing the changes necessary.

In the midst of these efforts, the Residents and Interns Association dropped a bombshell, in the form of a six-page release which it said was addressed to the accreditation committee but was widely circulated.

"We realize that the executive director has been here only a short time," the release said, "and that in the past few months tremendous effort has been put forth on improvements in hospital conditions." Nevertheless, it continued, many of the accreditation group's 1968 recommendations had not been met. The release proceeded to detail them; among the items listed were:
— Bylaws have not been accepted or approved by the governing commission.
— There has been no move to improve relationships with the medical schools.
— Recommendations for rehabilitative and continuing care have not been met. Instead a medical ward which was a holding area for social service patients and an ambulatory ward have been shut down, with no alternatives provided;
— There is still no adequate provision for patient privacy;
— There have been many improvements in the emergency room but the amount of space has never been increased as recommended, the personnel is still inadequate and patient waiting time is still excessive.
— The number of registered nurses is still inadequate;
— There are still no call buttons for patients;
— Air conditioning in the operating rooms is only partially completed;
— Psychiatric recommendations were not followed.

The report concluded:

The Residents and Interns Association does not direct the attention
of the Joint Commission on Accreditation of Hospitals to the
above points with the idea that deficiencies in these areas should
cause disaccreditation of Cook County Hospital. The experience
at Cook County Hospital has been that the hospital administration
will respond to directives from the JCAH even while remaining in-
sensitive to all manner of pleas from its consumers, community
and medical staff. We therefore believe the JCAH has an important
responsibility to provide such direction and we hope that the data
we have provided will aid you in discharging that responsibility.

That news release was dated May 17. It was followed by a news-
letter a week later, signed by the executive committee of the Residents
and Interns Association, charging that Dr. Haughton's policies are "not
in the best interests of patients, not in the best interests of workers,
not in the best interests of the community and not in the best interests
of the medical staff." It listed details to go with the charges and concluded:

In short, Dr. Haughton is personally responsible for embarking on
a policy of arrogance and manipulation . . . Dr. Haughton has
irrevocably lost the confidence of many of the house staff. Dr.
Haughton has orchestrated the governing commission in such a
manner as to obstruct communication between the governing commission and the medical staff. He has severely set back the progress attained at Cook County Hospital by all of us who work
here. Finally, Dr. Haughton has impaired the ability of the staff to
deliver quality patient care. The medical staff had struggled successfully to eliminate County control of the hospital. That struggle
must now continue to establish a hospital administration which
is responsive and responsible to its patients, workers, community
and staff. Dr. Haughton has not understood. The house staff must
act accordingly.

"Acting accordingly" led later, on May 28, 1971, to a resolution
to Dr. Haughton from Dr. Hambrick, the president of the Residents
and Interns Association, and signed by 340 other members of the
association:

"Be it resolved:

1. That Dr. Haughton has embarked on a policy inconsistent with
   delivery of quality patient care at Cook County Hospital;
2. That Dr. Haughton has dealt with all workers — paramedical,
   nursing and medical—in an unprincipled administrative
   manner;
3. That Dr. Haughton has established a false set of priorities placing

self-interest before the interests of patients at Cook County Hospital;

4. That Dr. Haughton has destroyed the ties between the people who work at Cook County Hospital and the communities served;

5. That Dr. Haughton no longer enjoys the confidence of the medical staff;

6. That Dr. Haughton has made the accreditation of Cook County Hospital a virtual impossibility;

"We therefore demand:

1. The immediate resignation of Dr. Haughton as Executive Director (of the governing commission);

2. Convening of an emergency meeting of the governing commission in order to reestablish viable hospital priorities."

Dr. Haughton did not resign. He did not, in fact, even answer the residents' and interns' blast, as he had not publicly answered any of the earlier charges and demands. But the challenge stayed there in the background; it was to come up again later.

Efforts to win accreditation continued. And they were successful. The Joint Commission made a painstakingly thorough investigation in the summer and finally granted the coveted approval in August, 1971. Many physical improvements had been accomplished and steps had been taken to work out the complicated relationships between the commission and the medical staff; bylaws were adopted and a Joint Conference Committee established, a mechanism by which commission representatives and medical staff representatives would meet to work out their problems.

A new era of good will seemed possible, at least momentarily.

Efforts at Reconciliation with the House Staff

The disgruntled leadership of the residents' and interns' group was by no means ignored. A series of meetings, both formal and informal, was held to listen to their complaints. But the parties to the meetings do not agree on just what took place during the discussions.

Dr. Greeley, the commission's deputy director for professional services, presided over the monthly meetings of the house staff committee established in the memorandum of understanding for regular consideration of problems. He reported later that the meetings were devoted to excoriation of Dr. Haughton and that no specific problems or solutions were brought up. House staff members of the committee claimed they were specific but no reform was accomplished.

Stuart Ball, the chairman of the selection committee, met with a group of doctors from the Residents and Interns Association and reported that he was personally threatened unless he resigned or picked governing commission members they suggested from among a group of community people actively interested in County. He did neither, but said that that night his telephone rang every half hour until 6 a.m. The young doctors said they made no threats but certainly did try to impress upon him their dissatisfaction with the governing commission. They denied knowing anything about the phone calls.

Julian Wilkins, the chairman of the commission, and Dr. James Bowman, a commission member, met with a group of residents and interns but left, they said, after the group heaped invective on Dr. Haughton and called Wilkins and Bowman "Uncle Toms" and "bourgeois blacks."

Perhaps the most talkative at each of these meetings was a young doctor named Nicholas Rango, who had come to County as an intern in the summer of 1970, was active in organizing the interns for collective bargaining, and played an increasingly active role in the Residents and Interns Association until he was elected its vice president in May of 1971. He had been recommended for internship by Dr. Harold Levine, the author of the magazine article that outlined the pressures he and others had brought to bear in getting the legislature to grant the commission its full powers.

After the explosive meeting with Wilkins and Dr. Bowman, the commission members, Dr. Rango wrote each of them a letter, outlining his philosophy. He said he had been committed to radical politics for the last eight years and that "My political diet has been a mixture of Marx and Malcolm X, through which I have attempted to formulate a realistic and humane path towards socialism in this country. As such, I have participated in many struggles relating to the development of social consciousness in our society. . . .

"I am myself from working class, immigrant origins, a family of steel workers, bartenders, and railroad workers. I am the first professional in the family . . . however, ties to my class background are strong, since I understand how working class whites historically have been manipulated and exploited by the white power structure and its representatives in the black bourgeoisie . . .

"Re: Dr. Haughton. Both of you are responsible for creating a Frankenstein . . . You have assigned this responsibility to an individual who has demonstrated a willingness to manipulate and maneuver rather than to establish viable priorities and progressive hospital policies. Within the past six months, Dr. Haughton has succeeded in funneling all information and communications through his office. All concerned parties in and out of the hospital must rely on Haughton and his staff for interpretation of the internal activities of Cook County Hospital . . . There are few avenues of direct communication between the governing

commission and those of us who work in Cook County Hospital . . .
His error has been to move too rapidly towards his self-defined
goals . . . The anger and frustration building up here in the past year
is in large part directed at his office. I fault Haughton not for his ambition (which is considerable) but rather for the way he misuses and
misrepresents people. He has screwed the Community Board which is
composed of decent and principled people. And he lies. Not a little,
but a lot . . .

"Direct and frank communication must be established now, between
the commission and the house staff . . . I want to start a dialogue among
equals . . . Failing that, please understand that I deeply disagree with
your personal style and your politics."

The other residents and interns who were usually present at the
meetings with commission members or commission administrators
included Dr. Ernestine Hambrick, the surgical resident who was president of the association until May 1971, and Dr. William D. Towne,
who took over as president from Dr. Hambrick. Neither is as flamboyant
or as vocal as Dr. Rango, but each has a missionary kind of intensity.

The Tumultuous Month of October, 1971

The governing commission held its regular monthly meeting on
October 2 and passed two resolutions that were to have wide consequences.

One resolution provided a salary freeze for all professional personnel
through 1972 and for all house staff (residents and interns) through
the academic year 1972, terminating June 30, 1973. The basis of the
action, commission members said, was President Nixon's price and
wage freeze of a few weeks earlier. But residents and interns promptly
interpreted the action as retaliation for their behavior. They pointed
out that the action represented a two-year freeze for them, to mid-
1973, even though their contractual arrangement through the memorandum of understanding was due to expire in mid-1972.

The other resolution stated "the commission should receive Medicare
payments for the medical services performed at Cook County Hospital
by its full-time staff in caring for patients" and prohibited the doctors
from collecting and spending fees through the Associated Physicians.
This resolution brought a tremendous reaction from the senior medical
staff, finally unifying it in opposition to the commission and to Dr.
Haughton in a way that it had not been unified before.

The executive medical staff held a stormy five-hour meeting on
October 12. (The executive medical staff is composed of 26 members, all doctors: the elected president and vice president, plus the
heads of all divisions and some major departments within divisions

and four representatives of the Residents and Interns Association.)
The meeting led to the adoption of four resolutions:

1. Calling upon the governing commission to "rescind, revoke and
   withdraw" the October 2 resolutions regarding collection of
   fees by the Associated Physicians and urging the commission to
   find ways to consult the staff to achieve mutual cooperation.
   This resolution was passed unanimously.
2. Stating that "the continuation of the services of Dr. James
   Haughton as executive director of the governing commission and
   as chief administrator of Cook County Hospital is unacceptable
   to the medical staff, and that the medical staff executive committee hereby calls upon the governing commission to remove
   Dr. Haughton from these positions immediately." This was the
   first time that so broad a group of doctors had demanded Dr.
   Haughton's resignation. This resolution was passed by a vote
   of 18 to 8.
3. Calling for the removal of the governing commission and the
   selection committee headed by Stuart Ball because "the executive
   staff lacks confidence in both." It further called for a governing
   commission to include people in the community who use the
   hospital and to include representatives of the medical staff on the
   board as private hospitals do. This resolution was passed by a vote
   of 23 to 3.
4. Requiring the governing commission to "strictly abide" by the
   adopted bylaws, with failure to do so being reported to the
   Joint Commission on Accreditation of Hospitals, which had
   required that bylaws be adopted to clarify the division of administrative responsibility.

That same day, October 12, the resolutions were presented to a
meeting of the joint conference committee, the structure that had
been set up to handle mutual problems of the governing commission
and the medical staff. The doctors pointed out that the joint conference
committee had not heard in advance about the Medicare resolution
and further claimed that the physicians had not been having any input
into the determination of medical policies.

Edwin L. Brashears, the governing commission's new chairman
(Julian Wilkins had resigned during the summer), mandated the
doctors to document the allegations against Dr. Haughton, stating
that the resolution was a slur on his character and personality and
stating that Dr. Haughton was acting under the direction of the
governing commission.

Brashears, the commission chairman, arranged for another meeting
of the joint conference committee, this time with all commission mem-

bers and Dr. Haughton present, for later in the week, on October 16, to hear the documented charges. Normally the committee's meetings were not open to the public, but notices were widely posted announcing the meeting. Because of the open nature of the meeting, the executive medical staff voted to boycott the October 16 session.

Actually, the executive medical staff adopted a series of somewhat conflicting motions when it met on October 15 to review the documentation. The document had been prepared by Dr. Levine, the chest specialist who had worked so hard to establish the governing commission and later so actively opposed it, and one other doctor. They had put together a potpourri of 29 specific charges, most of which had been aired before by one or more groups of doctors. The executive medical staff first voted unanimously to accept the document. Then they voted, almost unanimously, to take it under advisement and refer it to legal counsel. They then voted unanimously not to submit any charges "at this time" until they could be presented at a closed meeting of the joint conference committee. But that is not what happened.

The October 16 session was held and the executive medical staff did boycott it so no charges were presented. Instead, the administration introduced petitions, said to have been signed by more than 1,000 medical and paramedical employees, blaming the troubles at the hospital not on Dr. Haughton but on the complaining doctors. Dr. Haughton, for the first time in public, answered back, accusing the dissenting physicians of being "revolutionaries who are determined to get control of the hospital board."

Dr. James Bowman, one of the commission members, made a widely-quoted statement that further incensed many doctors at the hospital. Claiming that there was an element of racial discrimination in the behavior of the dissenting physicians, he said, "Many appear to feel that because we take care of poor people instead of rich, they can demean them by calling them by their first names, that operations can be performed that they wouldn't dare perform on anyone else and that our people can be packed into the hospital like sardines and can be used as tools of health politics."

At the end of the meeting, the commission members voted confidence in Dr. Haughton and informed the executive medical staff that, in absence of documentation, its resolution calling for Dr. Haughton's removal was rejected. This vote was to be presented to the governing commission's next regular meeting, on October 19.

But October 19 brought a new confrontation. A curious combination of events brought Dr. Levine to the governing commission meeting to present the charges. That afternoon, Dr. Eugene Lutterbeck, the president of the executive medical staff, and the vice president, Dr. George Sutton, who was also one of the voluntary physicians in the hospital, had resigned, in part because they did not agree with the actions against Dr. Haughton. Dr. Collins, the staff's secretary and thus next in line as an official, was out of town. So was Dr. Sheldon Gorbach, the president of the Full-Time Salaried Staff Association. Dr. Levine was secretary of that association and it was apparently his decision to present the charges at the commission meeting, even though the executive medical staff had voted to present them only in a closed meeting.

When Dr. Levine rose to present the charges, he was ruled out of order by the governing commission chairman. Dr. Levine then said he would make his statement to the public and walked out to meet with reporters.

Outside in the corridor, Dr. Levine read his list of 29 charges against Dr. Haughton, which he called a "sampling of pertinent interactions that have led to a mass negative reaction." Among them were these:

— Failure of administrative communication between the governing commission and their executive director with regard to critical problems within this institution.
— Arbitrary reduction of the number of beds available to the division of medicine by about 200 beds against staff advice.
— Arbitrary reduction in number of beds available to psychiatry.
— Failure to develop a program, or even plan for a future program, with regard to alcoholism and drug addiction, two scourges of our patient population.
— Interference with the freedom of assembly of our staff by forbidding us to meet with community representatives.
— Clumsy insertion of administrative personnel into the division of medicine, leading to temporary but disastrous breakdown of communications.
— Violation of the spirit of the joint conference committee by taking unilateral actions on matters previously slated for consideration by them, such as the recent actions on the Associated Physicians and a wage freeze.

"We could go on," the statement concluded. "Some of these matters are more serious than others. None of this background material is being conveyed for debate or refutation, since the refutation of some would not alter the overall balance. They are not charges but our perceptions of interactions between the executive director and ourselves. Based on our experience, we have made a judgment. We have judged performance against deed. That judgment is . . . No Confidence."

A Heal-in at the Hospital?

The wage freeze enacted for the residents and interns reactivated all the old complaints and led to the issuance of two more strongly-worded newsletters, one of them apparently suggesting concerted action to put pressure on the governing commission. It charged that the hospital had always been "controlled by politicians" and that the legislative changes had merely "perpetuated the status quo with some bureaucratic adjustments." It continued:

"The present governing commission and Dr. Haughton will continue to mismanage, to divide, and to deceive until they are stopped. Several months ago a unified house staff brought much pressure to force the creation of the governing commission. The pressure involved 'going to the wall,' being prepared to take any action necessary to win the struggle despite personal sacrifice or professional inconvenience. We stand at a similar juncture now, where only the same kind of unified mass action can rescue Cook County Hospital from the present rapid deterioration into the doldrums of bureaucratic and mediocre health care."

A few days later, in mid-October, the residents and interns held a meeting at which they decided they would no longer turn away people who came to the hospital in need of care and that they would not merely refer these people to the clinic because they couldn't be assured of prompt care there. Instead, the young doctors decided, they would admit to the hospital all who needed care.

While that decision doesn't sound particularly challenging, it was a violation of a governing commission policy. The policy, dating back more than a year and a half to a time of similar overcrowding, stated that when the beds in the division of medicine were 80% filled, there could be no new admissions except for genuine emergencies. Under this policy, the division of medicine was closed during October when the residents and interns held their meeting. But the situation was not unusual; the division had been closed to non-emergencies approximately half the time during the past few months. This was one reason why the division felt so strongly that it needed more beds than the 400 allotted to it by the commission. When a person came to the hospital for treatment during one of these emergency periods, the staff doctors had had these choices available to them:

1. Admit the patient in the case of a real emergency;
2. Send him to the clinic to make an appointment for outpatient treatment, as soon as an appointment was available;
3. Try to place him in another hospital (but other hospitals didn't have a very good record of accepting these poor patients, for whom payment was sometimes unavailable and always slow);

4. Send him home to wait and try again later.

The decision of the residents and interns meant they were closing off some of these options. They said they would no longer send a patient home and they would no longer refer him to the clinic if they felt he needed hospitalization. They would try to place him in another hospital or they would admit him to Cook County, regardless of the crowding. The 400 beds filled up in a hurry.

This kind of action, not unique to Cook County Hospital, has come to be called a "heal-in" and the County doctors had used the tactic before when they were seeking to force the county board of commissioners to turn over real power to the governing commission. Dr. Levine had written an article about it and the hospital management felt (copies of the Levine article had recently been widely distributed in the hospital by the Residents and Interns Association) the residents and interns were following the Levine "script."

The overcrowding in the division of medicine at County during October, 1971, heightened all the tensions; the discontent over the salary freeze and the professional fee problem, the feelings that medical specialists were left out in the cold in the decision-making process, the continuing antagonism between commission level and hospital level personnel, and the animosity toward Dr. Haughton and some members of the governing commission. Some doctors prepared to resign. Among them was Dr. Gunnar, the respected but beleaguered head of the division of medicine, the hospital's biggest division and the focal point of most of the tensions. Dr. Gunnar stated in a letter to the head of the executive medical staff that he would leave the hospital the following July, the end of the academic term. He wrote:

> I think it appropriate that the executive staff be notified of my plans for the future, since the position for which I was employed and the present duties differ so markedly. I find myself in a position where I am unable to develop policy for the division of medicine and must carry out the policy generated in the governing commission office. Many of the programs I initiated have been curtailed or dismantled. I am asked to carry out policy which turns patients away at the door — patients who have no place else to obtain medical care and who are in need of hospitalization. These policy decisions I cannot, in good conscience, abide. My hopes for strong community programs have been totally frustrated by commission inaction.

Meanwhile, considerable administrative pressure was put on Dr. Gunnar to solve the problems of overcrowding in his medical division. He was told that the nursing staff and the unit administrator had indicated to Dr. Haughton's staff that approximately 30 patients were being held who could be discharged. He personally reviewed all the patients on the list, found that most were still acutely ill and renewed his request for more hospital beds to meet the needs.

Dr. Haughton Steps Aside

On October 23, less than two weeks after the medical executive staff voted to ask for Dr. Haughton's resignation and less than one week after the governing commission voted to uphold him, Dr. Haughton relinquished one of his two jobs, that of director of the hospital. He retained the position for which he was first hired, that of executive director of the governing commission. He noted that he had taken on the hospital directorship because the time to achieve accreditation had been so short and he called the accreditation his "greatest accomplishment" so far. (There is a lack of agreement over whether Dr. Haughton's giving up the hospital job was entirely voluntary on his part or whether he was pressured to make the move by the governing commission.)

Appointed as acting director of the hospital was Dr. David Greeley, who had been Dr. Haughton's deputy director for professional affairs and had handled much of the detail of the accreditation effort. Earlier in his career he had managed five hospitals for the United Mine Workers in the Appalachian area and he was not unused to controversy. A quiet, compassionate and dignified man, Dr. Greeley stated it was to be his job, wherever possible, to support the staff, which he called "medically first rate," and said the first step "to get the show back on the road will be to put the past behind us." He said he would be willing to meet with staff members to hear their views on hospital problems. A series of meetings that promptly followed brought the Cook County Hospital crisis to a head.

Dr. Greeley reported to his new job for the first time on Monday, October 25. He agreed to meet the following day with a delegation of staff doctors to hear their problems. Present at that meeting, along with others, were Dr. William Towne and Dr. Nicholas Rango, the president and secretary of the Residents and Interns Association, and Dr. Sheldon Gorbach and Dr. Harold Levine, the president and secretary of the Association of Full-Time Salaried Staff.

Discussed at that Tuesday meeting, which all parties agree was calm and cooperative, was a range of issues: the need to clarify lines of authority in the division of medicine so the director of the division would not again be bypassed in the responsibility for patient care, the need for more beds, new programs for drug addiction and alcoholism, poor morale of the medical staff and threatened resignations, the difficulty of recruiting new residents and interns to come into such a troubled hospital. The meeting ended with an agreement for the group to get together again the following Friday afternoon, October 29.

Before that second session on Friday, Dr. Greeley and Dr. Gunnar had a long conversation. The two men knew each other well and there was considerable agreement on their common problems. Greeley assured Gunnar that he was going to be "my own man" in directing the hospital and that the lines of communication regarding the division of medicine would be clarified to reestablish Gunnar's responsibilities in all patient care matters. The two agreed on the need to act promptly on medical school affiliation and the need to find a way for more adequate representation of community people on the governing commission. Dr. Greeley said it was "unrealistic" for Dr. Gunnar to expect to get the additional 100 beds he said he needed, but that he would explore the possibility of getting 100 beds in local community hospitals to be administered under Dr. Gunnar's division. Then they talked about the overcrowding and Dr. Gunnar said he thought the crisis would be over in 10 days to two weeks; Dr. Greeley indicated he wanted a resolution of the problem that day, even if it meant disciplinary action against some of the staff members. Dr. Gunnar said such action would only make matters worse. Although the two did not agree on how to solve the overcrowding, they parted with assurances of mutual support.

Two telephone calls after the Greeley-Gunnar meeting, however, left that assurance of mutual support in question. In one, Dr. Gunnar said the four officers of the doctors' associations had challenged his right to negotiate with Greeley on anything that affected those associations. In the other call, Dr. Gunnar questioned whether Dr. Greeley really was being "my own man" or whether Dr. Haughton was still calling all the shots in the hospital. In that case, he said, the agreement had been violated.

At 4 p.m. on Friday, October 29, the four officers of the associations (Gorbach, Levine, Towne and Rango) returned to Dr. Greeley's office to continue the discussions started the previous Tuesday. With them came a fifth doctor, Chris Casten, an endocrinologist who had served at County, starting as a student, since 1963. He had not been particularly involved in any of the disputes but was interested, he said, and so came along as an observer. His interest in medical care for the poor dated back, he said, to his own childhood days as a child of Greek immigrants in the slums of Joliet, Illinois.

The meeting between Dr. Greeley, and the representatives of the staff associations was a fateful one, but puzzling, too. It was puzzling because the six persons present in the room do not agree on the crucial details of what took place there. They have repeated the story many times, including twice under oath in court proceedings, and the key details are different.

Here is Dr. Greeley's account, told in essentially the same words in two court proceedings:

"Dr. Gorbach opened the conversation. He said they were very concerned at the morale of the attending staff, that it was a most serious situation, that improvement was needed quickly in order for the hospital to be in a good position to recruit house staff for the next year, to prevent some doctors from leaving the hospital because of the atmosphere, and to meet requirements of the accreditation commission by November 21 (a deadline imposed for workable hospital bylaws). He said he was sorry they had to bring this to me, that they all had high regard for me, but he felt neither I nor anyone else would be able to run the hospital properly, constructively, in the way of good patient care, with the present composition of the governing commission. He said they were not all in agreement with respect to the strategy to follow, but all were in agreement on aims.

"I told him I too was concerned about the atmosphere. Dr. Levine or Dr. Rango then opened the discussion regarding their demands — I think Dr. Rango. He said unless I agreed to persuade Brashears (the governing commission chairman) to obtain the resignation of three commission members — they named the three — and in turn found a way to replace them with three from a list of six which they suggested, they would take measures to close and destroy the hospital. They said this change could be accomplished if I would go to Brashears and indicate the seriousness of the problem. And that Brashears, with Stuart Ball and Mayor Daley even, if necessary, could bring about the necessary changes in the governing commission they were demanding. If those changes were not brought about, they would take measures to close and destroy the hospital, and that the only weapon they had to accomplish this was the disruption of patient care. They said they didn't have legal talents or a large public relations staff and the ability to influence the press — but would use their weapon — disruption of patient care — if necessary.

"My response was that I could support their feeling that it would perhaps strengthen the commission to have additional members, that we could take the legislative route to enlarge the commission, that that was the only legal way of changing the composition. They replied that way was too long, too complicated, too difficult to obtain the proper type of legislation.

"Dr. Rango, principally supported by Dr. Levine, indicated the situation was very serious.

"They said this was the only demand. I had never heard this demand before, and I listened . . . At two points I looked at the five and said, 'Do I understand clearly that you are saying that unless I can find some way to bring about this change, that you will close and destroy the hospital?' I asked twice because I wanted to be sure what they were saying. Dr. Levine and Dr. Rango said yes, that was right. Dr. Casten indicated by his facial expression that he agreed. Dr. Gorbach and Dr. Towne gave no reply and no indication of their feelings. But no one denied this."

Each of the five doctors has denied, also under oath, that they made any threats or any statements that could be interpreted as threats, that they ever mentioned closing and destroying the hospital or disrupting patient care. They denied, too, that Dr. Greeley asked them the specific question about what they were saying or that he gave any kind of indication at the meeting that he thought they were being threatening.

Dr. Gorbach, a 37-year-old specialist in infectious diseases whose work in curbing infections at the hospital (considered the leading cause of death there) had won special commendation from the accreditation team, agreed that he spoke first, as the president of the Association of Full-Time Staff. He told a court-ordered hearing:

"I talked of recruiting problems, said morale was low and the entire staff was beginning to unravel. I said if Dr. Gunnar were forced to resign, there would be tremendous impact on the division of medicine and that others would leave with him. I urged Dr. Greeley to loosen up the pressure, not to force Dr. Gunnar to make these decisions within one or two days, but to allow us to try and settle this over the next two weeks.

"I then told him that I recognized his decisions were controlled and he was not allowed further latitude by the present governing commission and I said that there was an expression among many members of the staff that there should be changes in the composition of the governing commission. He agreed the composition should be altered — and we discussed methods. Dr. Greeley asked who we recommended and Rango gave him a list of six.

"There were no threats. He asked one question which was to the effect, 'Do you mean that if these events proceed' — and I thought that his reference was to the problems with recruitment and the problems with Dr. Gunnar and the morale of the staff — 'Do you mean that if these events proceed, that we will no longer remain a whole institution or no longer be able to give first class care?' — or something along these lines. And it was a rhetorical question; I mean, this is what we have been saying, yes, that we were going to lose valuable staff.

"The discussion of the governing commission took up about 25% of the meeting. It was not the main purpose or the main focus. We knew Dr. Greeley couldn't resolve it alone."

Each of the remaining four doctors agreed with Dr. Gorbach.

The Firing of Five Doctors

At the end of the session with the doctors' association representatives, Dr. Greeley went to Dr. Haughton's office and told him what had taken place. Dr. Haughton later outlined his reaction:

"I have known Dr. Greeley for a number of years. I hold him in high regard and had no reason to believe he was lying to me. He is a very calm and dispassionate man, not one given to uproarious behavior in any way and not one who I feel would misunderstand clear language. He is a very good listener.

"I had to look at his report in the light of what was happening in the hospital, which was that in one division the care of the patient was, in my view, in fact being disrupted. The department was clogged in a way it had never been since I had been there. The senior nursing staff of that division had submitted to the administration a list of patients who, in their view, ought to be reviewed for discharge. They were not making medical judgments, merely saying, 'In our experience patients of this kind would normally be discharged. We would like some medical people to take a look at this.' A senior member of the medical staff had told me undoubtedly some patients were being held who should be discharged.

"Now, in the light of these things, I had to look at this reported threat. It is possible for doctors to disrupt the care of the patient . . . I felt it immoral and unconscionable for any doctor to use patients as pawns, in any political conflict with anyone. When a threat to disrupt care of patients was related to me, I felt some action had to be taken."

Although Dr. Greeley and Dr. Haughton were entirely certain that threats had been made by the four top officials of the two full-time doctors' associations in the hospital, they had no knowledge of the extent of an organized plan, whether the doctors were speaking for themselves or for a much broader group in their associations (about 100 full-time senior doctors and 500 interns and residents). They decided, therefore, that Dr. Greeley would call together all of the doctors in the two groups at a meeting on Monday morning, November 1, to find out.

At the Monday meeting, Dr. Greeley talked of the threats and said, "I can conceive of no more unconscionable, reprehensible, or disreputable act, particularly on the part of physicians professed to be concerned with the health of their patients and the welfare of the employees. And from a practical point of view, I would think that any intern or resident who took overt steps to close and destroy this hospital for the reasons given to me would jeopardize his chances of ever practicing in the United States or his opportunity to continue his medical education in this country.

"I must know and know now," Dr. Greeley continued, "how many of you are going to take the necessary steps to close and destroy this hospital if the demands made of me last Friday are not met. If a substantial majority of you agree that this hospital must be closed and destroyed then I will go the governing commission and recommend a number of alternative solutions. However, if you disagree with this threat and demand then, it seems to me, we have an exciting and challenging future ahead of us to which we can all dedicate our best efforts.

"So, now will all interns and residents who plan to take overt action to close and destroy this hospital if Mr. Brashears refuses to ask for the resignation of three members of the governing commission and then arranges to have them replaced with three of the six names given me last Friday, please stand."

No one stood, including the officers of the Residents and Interns Association who had met with Dr. Greeley on Friday.

Dr. Greeley then repeated the same question, asking all full-time salaried staff members who planned to take action to close and destroy the hospital to stand.

No one stood, including the officers of the Association of Full-Time Salaried Staff who had met with Dr. Greeley on Friday.

"I now know what action to take and I will take it today," Dr. Greeley said and he started to leave the room. He stayed, though, when a chorus of voices asked him to listen. There was considerable turmoil. The five doctors denied making the threats and some of their colleagues chastised them for making threats in their names. Others wanted to talk to Dr. Greeley about problems. It was bedlam.

Dr. Chris Casten, the least involved of the five doctors in the crisis, recalled later, "There were people getting up just shouting for and against such statements and it was crazy. I said to myself, 'This is really crazy.' I was really shocked, totally shocked, by this statement of Dr. Greeley's."

Dr. Greeley left the meeting to report to Dr. Haughton that there was no widespread plot to close and destroy the hospital. Whereupon Dr. Haughton called a press conference to announce that the five

doctors were being fired (he testified a number of times that Dr.
Greeley recommended the firings and Dr. Greeley testified at least
as many times that he did not recommend the firings but concurred
in Dr. Haughton's decision), then telephoned each of the five to report
his decision, and confirmed the telephone calls with a letter.

Dr. Haughton's statement to the press began, "Three weeks ago a
group of doctors at Cook County Hospital, after months of skirmish-
ing with the administration, began a showdown struggle for power.
The showdown began when they demanded both the resignation of
the executive director and the reconstitution of the Health and Hospitals Governing Commission. When the commission rejected these
demands, a crisis condition in one division of the hospital, the division
of medicine, was created. This crisis has continued ever since, and still
exists today. During the past week, Dr. Greeley has applied his considerable leadership skills toward ending the differences between the
medical staff and the administration."

The letters from Dr. Haughton to each of the five doctors outlined
the threats Dr. Greeley had reported after the Friday meeting, stated
that "the threat made by you and the others present on Friday was
completely repudiated by the members of the medical and house staffs
present" at the Monday meeting, and concluded that, because of these
events, "your employment at Cook County Hospital is terminated effective at the close of business today."

At the same time Dr. Greeley met briefly with Dr. Gunnar and told
him his resignation as head of the division of medicine, planned for
the following July, would be accepted immediately.

The Aftermath

The rumor mill exploded. All of the chief elected officers of the
doctor's associations had been fired. Why? For speaking their minds
about hospital conditions that they, as professionals, found intolerable?
For daring to oppose the administration? For threatening dire disruptive action not only against the hospital but against the public it
served? Or were the threats figments of the imagination of worried
administrators, exasperated over the spiraling pressures of the past
few months? What were the doctors' rights? Could they be fired without a hearing and a chance to defend themselves? What about the bylaws? And the memorandum of understanding with the Residents and
Interns Association? Don't public employees have a right to due process
under the constitution? But what if the threats really were made?
Doesn't the hospital have a right to protect itself against disruptive
actions?

Dr. Haughton had said at the press conference announcing the firings, "One cannot administer any organization in the midst of ultimatums and demands. I'll not administer this operation with a gun at my head. I have been trying to make peace for almost 12 months." He added that the doctors had no contracts and could be fired at his pleasure.

Dr. Ernestine Hambrick, the former president of the Residents and Interns Association, moved back into a position of leadership since the new officers had been fired. She told another press conference that the firings were "completely illegal. The association has a memorandum of understanding, and the attending staff has a set of bylaws that have to be adhered to." She announced that 265 residents and interns would resign within two weeks as a protest over the firings. That number grew daily to approximately 300. Ironically, it began to appear that the hospital might indeed be closed and destroyed, with the firings as the trigger.

The executive medical staff met (its numbers somewhat decimated by the firings) and voted a resolution attacking the firings, describing the action as "completely unjustified to the individuals concerned, highly injurious to the interests of the hospital and its patients and establishing a dangerous precedent." Dr. Vincent Collins, acting president of the executive medical staff, and Dr. Ira Rosenthal, acting secretary, said the resolution should be interpreted as showing support for the civil rights of the five doctors and objection to "high-handed tactics."

There apparently was some dissension, too, within the commission staff regarding the firings. Dr. Haughton was advised by counsel that the doctors had a constitutional due process right to hearings. And Brashears, the chairman of the governing commission, was reported to have sent apologies to the executive medical staff for the method of the firings. He said in public that, although he backed Dr. Haughton, the doctors would receive a full hearing on their firings, if they requested such a hearing under the bylaws.

But the question of a hearing raised new legal questions. The five doctors contended that no firings could be legal unless there was a prior hearing, therefore they should be reinstated. Hospital officials contended that the hearing would be in the nature of an appeal and that the firings would stand unless the appeal produced a reversal. That's a "farce," argued Dr. Rosenthal for the medical staff; "The commission appears to have approved the decision to fire. Any chance of a fair hearing has evaporated if the commission already has made up its mind. The commission would be acting as prosecutor, judge and jury."

The medical staff asked that the joint conference committee consider the dispute but Dr. Haughton would not allow that, saying, "The joint conference committee is not the proper place for the matter to be considered. The overriding issue here is whether the medical staff or the Administration is going to run Cook County Hospital."

Outside groups, among them the American Hospital Association, the American Medical Association, and the Council of Deans of Illinois Medical Schools offered to mediate, but these offers were not accepted.

In the midst of the controversy, Dr. Clyde W. Phillips resigned as medical director of County, leaving another important vacancy among top management at the hospital level. His associates said he was frustrated by being asked to carry out administrative policies he didn't agree with. His departure meant there were a dozen vacancies among about 30 top medical staff positions.

A respected science writer for the Chicago Daily News wrote a perceptive background article about the tensions at the hospital:[2]

"If an underlying issue can be isolated, it is the philosophical difference between many of the doctors and James Haughton, himself a practicing physician who switched to hospital administration. The split is over the best way to provide patient care. While goals are similar, their priorities are not.

"Haughton wants doctors at the bedside. He contends patient care is the beginning and the end of medical staff function. The residents and interns, who are physicians taking post-graduate education, believe you can't have good medicine at the bedside unless there is equal emphasis on providing top quality teachers on the senior staff plus the stimulus of clinical research. Haughton concedes some importance to teaching and research but far down the line after effective patient care is achieved . . .

" 'We've gone on the assumption for 20 or 30 years in medicine,' Haughton says, 'that the only way for us to have excellent patient care is to have excellent research and excellent teaching. I wonder whether it's not time for us to question that assumption, because if we focus on the disease rather than on the patient, we begin to find that the patients are falling into the cracks between our specialties.'

"The residents and interns led the fight in bringing about a change in the state law that wrested control of the hospital from the county board and placed it in the hands of a citizens' governing commission. After the commission hired Haughton, the medical staff broke out champagne to celebrate a new era.

"The doctors quickly learned that Haughton wasn't buying their ideas. He said in an interview he was aghast on finding each doctor 'running its own little barony' and involved in administrative matters that could better be handled by laymen. He set out to strip doctors of functions he considered nonmedical and told them to spend their time at the bedside. Physicians viewed his reorganization as interfering with the practice of medicine and good patient care.

"A more resilient administrator might have averted the showdown but Haughton is determined to make his stand on this issue (the firings). To yield, he asserts, is to invite more confrontations later. He has used the analogy of Prime Minister Neville Chamberlain's appeasement of Hitler at Munich in 1938. 'The issue is whether the commission or the doctors are going to run the hospital.' "

Another perceptive Chicago reporter wrote[3], "The power struggle at County is like a life-and-death chess game in which the governing commission controls the board and the rules, and the medical staff controls the men."

The Dispute Goes to Court

On November 12, less than two weeks after the firings, the five doctors started court proceedings, seeking reinstatement to their jobs and an injunction prohibiting the hospital from firing them or otherwise disciplining them without following the procedures in the bylaws and memorandum of understanding and without following the due process requirements of the United States and Illinois constitutions. The governing commission's lawyers argued that the bylaws and memorandum of understanding did not apply in these cases because the documents governed disciplinary action for professional reasons and not a basic conflict in the employer-employee relationship; they argued further that the five had been offered a hearing and had turned it down, so were not entitled to any further relief from the court.

The four days of court hearings before Circuit Judge Donald O'Brien were dramatic because all of the antagonists were always present, studiously not speaking to each other, and everything they did and said seemed charged with tension. They were dramatic, too, because constitutional issues have inherent drama. As Haughton, Greeley, Brashears, Gunnar, Collins, the five fired doctors and others took the stand, one by one, and told their sometimes conflicting stories, the courtroom was crowded, with many of the spectators wearing the white hospital coats of interns and residents. The corridor outside was cluttered with television equipment. Over it all hung the threat of almost 300 interns and residents to quit if the five were not reinstated, a fact of which everyone was mindful.

At the end, Judge O'Brien said:

I have spent the entire week, when not in court, looking up law, thinking about the constitution and studying the facts here. The case is of great importance to the community as well as to the individuals. I have considered the consequences to the community in studying the evidence and attempting to delineate the rights and duties of the staff and the governing commission as stated in the bylaws.

The bylaws and memorandum of understanding do not adequately address themselves to the problem before the court. There is nothing governing the factual situation before the court. Regardless of the fact that there is nothing in the bylaws or memorandum — the question of due process under the constitution requires that certain basic fundamentals be observed — and must be extended to all even though one may disagree with those asserting the right.

I am not expressing an opinion on the truth or falsity of the actions of the plaintiffs. Nor am I expressing an opinion on how I feel about their alleged actions.

Because the bylaws and memorandum are not appropriate or apropos to the matter and because due process requires it, it is the opinion of this court that it will render an order to this effect:

1. The governing commission and the individuals named as acting for it are to immediately reinstate the plaintiffs to their former positions with all the rights and privileges held and possessed before the discharges.
2. I further direct the governing commission to prepare and serve charges, giving notice of time and place of hearing before a committee of five, to be wholly independent of the governing commission and the medical staff; two to be appointed by the governing commission, two by the medical staff and Residents and Interns Association, and one to be appointed by agreement of these four.
3. The plaintiffs are to be paid from the time of termination until final determination on the charges or, if restored, while they are so employed.

With the judge's ruling, some of the tension lifted. There was a sense that part of the crisis, at least, was over because the house staff would not walk out before the conclusion of the disciplinary hearings.

The Disciplinary Hearings

The hearings took a long time, partly because the case became much more complicated. The original charges dealt only with the threats to close and destroy the hospital, but Judge O'Brien granted the governing commission the right to add additional charges:

— That Levine, Towne and Rango engaged in a conspiracy to disrupt the operation and management of the hospital;

— That they failed and refused to proceed through proper channels for suggestions and complaints;

— That they attempted to defeat the vital effort of the hospital to obtain accreditation;

— That they misrepresented conditions at the hospital and knowingly and in bad faith made demands which had no basis in fact;

— That they disrupted orderly patient care by conducting a heal-in to overload the hospital;

— That they failed and refused, as officers of their respective associations, to try to prevent mass resignations;

— That Gorbach and Casten, knowing of what the others were doing, aided and abetted the conspiracy by failing, as spokesmen for the salaried staff, to disavow actions and purposes of Levine, Towne and Rango and others engaged in the conspiracy.

Each of the additional charges required additional hours of testimony, although some of the charges were dropped before the conclusion of the hearings.

The four hearing committee members chosen by the governing commission and by the medical staff chose as their chairman Bernard Meltzer of the University of Chicago Law School, a highly respected arbitrator. Months were spent in hearing testimony (the transcript ran to more than 2,000 pages), and in considering more than 100 documentary exhibits. More months were spent in preparing briefs and in the committee's considerations and writing of its final report, which was itself a long and complex document.

In a summary of its findings, the Meltzer committee stated:

— All charges against Levine, Gorbach and Casten have either been withdrawn or fail for want of proof.

— The evidence sustains the charge that Towne and Rango were involved in an improper change of admissions practices, which led to an unacceptable increase in the bed census in the hospital's division of medicine, involved the risk of reducing the quality of patient care, and threatened the division's reserve of beds for emergency patients. There was, however, no evidence that patients who did not need hospital care were admitted into the hospital. One of the three committee members dissented in this finding.

— All other charges against Towne and Rango (including the threats) have either been withdrawn or fail for want of proof.

— The committee recommended considerations that should be weighed
by the governing commission in determining what discipline, if
any, should be imposed on Towne and Rango.

In an eloquent section of the report, Professor Meltzer wrote:

"The law, reflecting the need for a plenary decision-making body in
a complex organization such as a hospital, confers on the governing
commission and its executive director authority to determine the
policies of the hospital. We recognize that the governors, like the
governed, have no monopoly on wisdom. Nevertheless, a deliberate
overcrowding of a hospital as a means of altering or vetoing decisions
made by properly constituted authorities is an act of grave impropriety.
It is a species of guerrilla warfare that makes force and intimidation,
rather than reason, the ultimate determinant of hospital policy.
It threatens the integrity of the decision-making process established
by law. It converts current and future hospital patients into pawns
of hospital politics and threatens the capacity of the hospital to give
adequate care to those whom it admits and any care to those whom
it ultimately must exclude. It generates distrust between administrators and physicians, who in the end must collaborate and must seek a
rational accommodation of their differences if the hospital is to carry
out its important mission.

"The organization of the hospital reflects the conviction that decisions
are likely to be wiser and staff morale strengthened if decisions take
into account the experience and the recommendations of the attending
physicians, who in the end deliver medical services and, along with
nursing and other supportive staff, are the hospital to the patients.
In order to bring the physicians' insights to bear on policy-making
and administration, there have been established within the hospital
various channels through which criticisms and suggestions concerning hospital operations could be made. We recognize that such channels may look good on paper while being ineffective in practice and
that the attitudes and open-mindedness of policy makers are more
important than formal procedures. We also recognize, however, that
the right to be heard is not the right to be heeded and that in the
end decisions must be made within the framework prescribed by
law. Such decisions will frequently not command unanimous support
and may, indeed, override the strong preferences of a particular
division or group in the hospital. Such difficulties are inherent in
the functioning of all complex institutions, public and private, and
need no further elaboration. It is sufficient for our immediate purposes to reaffirm the point that overcrowding of the hospital is
an improper means for resolving such difficulties or for making

hospital policy, and that that means is not legitimated because it is used for moral and compassionate ends.

"We also recommend that in deciding what discipline, if any, is now appropriate the commission give adequate weight to the following considerations, which we believe mitigate the misconduct involved: the failure of the director of the medical division, among others, to admonish Dr. Towne or Dr. Rango during the 'heal-in;' the potential for future service that they have demonstrated, the educational impact of this proceeding on all the parties hereto, pertinent changes at the hospital, and the deep commitment of Drs. Towne and Rango to the common objective of all parties to this proceeding — the improvement of patient care at Cook County Hospital and associated institutions."

The decision, in late September, 1972, came at a time when greater harmony had already been achieved at the hospital, partly because the long hearings and simultaneous hearings before a legislative committee had helped clear the air through so broad an exchange of views.

Of the five doctors, four — Levine, Towne, Gorbach and Casten — had left to work for other hospitals and medical schools or to enter private practice. Only Rango, by then a second year resident, remained at County. And he was forgiven.

"The question of discipline is moot," said Brashears, the commission chairman. "Dissension has now dissipated, our major departments are now headed by outstanding physicians, and our house staff has begun to realize the aspirations which brought them to our hospital in the first place — the pursuit of a superlative medical education."

Even Dr. Rango had kindly words for Dr. Haughton. "Dr. Haughton and I have had several talks," he said. "The administration's goals are the same as ours."

INTERACTION OF
GOVERNANCE, MANAGEMENT, AND COMMUNITY FORCES

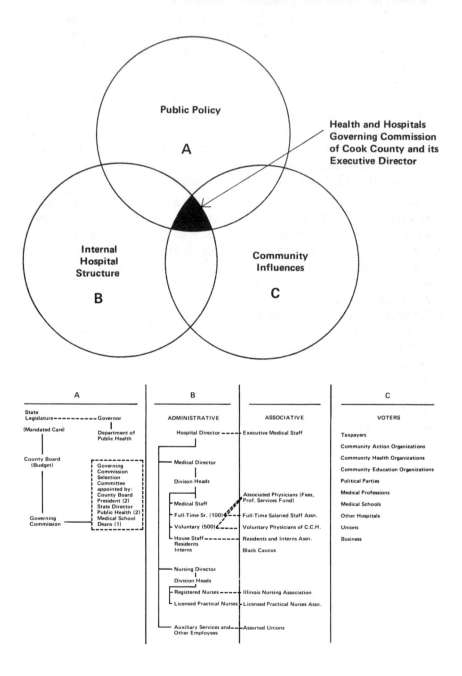

Footnotes

1. Testimony before a committee headed by Prof. Bernard Meltzer, University of Chicago Law School, January 22, 1972.

2. Arthur J. Snider, Chicago Daily News, November 12, 1971.

3. Judy Nicol, Chicago Sun-Times, November 14, 1971.

Discussion Questions

1. From the viewpoint of organization behavior, how does change come about? What organizational elements felt the impact of change in this case and what did change mean to each?

2. What is a union? Was the Residents and Interns Association a union? The Association of Full-Time Salaried Staff? The executive medical staff?

3. What labor-management issues are illustrated in this case? Who was labor? Who was management?

4. Discuss the meaning of scope of bargaining in relation to this case.

5. If you were the administrator of a large hospital, would you bargain with your residents and interns? If yes, what would you bargain about? If no, how would you handle the unresolved issues?

6. Do doctors in a hospital have a professional obligation to use any channel — inside or outside the hospital — to promote their concept of improved medical care? Is their success in doing so related to the power of an employee organization or union?

7. In Dr. Haughton's and Dr. Greeley's positions, would you have fired the five doctors? What reasons did they have? What other actions were possible?

8. Dr. Haughton said several times, "The issue is whether the medical staff or the administration is going to run Cook County Hospital." Was this a genuine issue? Does Professor Meltzer, who played the role of arbitrator in the disciplinary dispute, shed any light on the handling of the issue?

9. What rights does the management of a public institution have to act when it believes the institution is directly threatened by actions of its employees?

10. Do public employees have job protections that private employees do not have?

11. How were these elements of bargaining power exhibited in the case: the ability to withhold labor; the impact of collective bargaining on hospital issues; the effort to pack the governing commission; diversionary tactics such as the attacks on Haughton and the selection committee; and the impact of radical politics on bargaining?

12. Did the advent of the Governing Commission take Cook County Hospital out of politics?

A Renewed Search for a Method of Governance

The well-publicized fracas at County brought the Illinois legislature back into the picture. Shortly after the firings of the Cook County five, the general assembly, meeting in Springfield, passed a resolution directing the Legislative Investigating Commission to look into the "continuing state of administrative turmoil" at the hospital and to report back to the legislature with recommendations for action.

The Legislative Investigating Commission is composed of six state senators and six representatives; it has a three-member investigative staff. The group held a series of seven public hearings in Chicago, staff members conducted some additional interviews, and the staff and a couple of legislators visited public hospitals in six other cities to see how comparable problems were handled elsewhere. The hearings proceeded during the first third of 1972, at the same time that Professor Meltzer's court-mandated committee was conducting hearings on discipline.

Oddly, the public hearings helped both to clear the air and to cloud it further. About 30 witnesses, from the medical staff, from the governing commission and from outside groups, appeared to present their problems and ideas. Because many of them stayed to hear each other, the result was a vast interchange of opinions and reactions regarding the knotty problems between the commission and the staff. As a result the actual participants in the controversies at County seemed, by the end of the hearings, to have reached greater understanding of each other and their respective roles and some sense of renewal of their abilities to work together. The anger and animosity often expressed when the hearings started in January had given way to an aura of seeming good will by April.

But the hearings clouded the atmosphere in other ways, raising new issues that had not been problems and interjecting some new personality clashes. Most of the legislators did not play an active role in the investigation. Only one of them, for example, attended all the hearings and he tended to switch sides on the issues as the hearings progressed. Some of the other legislators came for a session or two and they each had their own political axes to grind. One of them was consistently incensed at the nerve of the staff doctors — particularly the younger ones — in challenging authority. Another, from Cook County, was chiefly concerned with the rising costs of hospital care, which he blamed on the governing commission; he repeatedly reminded witnesses that he had opposed the creation of the commission and that matters were a lot better off when the county board ran the hospital. One of the witnesses, a long-time county board member, emphatically agreed, adding that "this politico-medical group is a pain in the neck."

Running through all the testimony were the familiar recurring themes that had been so heatedly disputed within the hospital during the turbulent year of 1971:

1. The composition of the governing commission.

Some of the witnesses vehemently supported having more community representatives — representatives of the hospital's users — on the commission; others opposed, stating that the commission should represent a range of expertise rather than special community segments. Medical staff spokesmen argued that medical representatives from the hospital should sit on the commission; others, non-medical people mostly, said that would be comparable to having employees of General Motors sit on the GM board of directors.

2. The question of who should collect the fees for professional services and how they should be spent.

Dr. Haughton and other commission members argued eloquently that the doctors earned good salaries for services including patient care and that the fees earned from public or private insurance programs for this care should be returned to the commission. Doctors — from other hospitals as well as from County — contended that the fees should be under the control of those who earn them, but agreed that none of these fees should go to the doctors themselves.

3. Medical school affiliation.

Almost everyone agreed that formal affiliation with one or more of the county's six medical schools would enhance the quality of medical training in the hospital. But they disagreed widely on the nature of the affiliation, the form it should take, and what it would mean in terms of patient care. Some said it couldn't help but improve patient care; others said medical schools have traditionally had a "parasitic" relationship with hospitals, in which the schools gain clinical resources for their students but are not primarily dedicated to the patients.

4. Decision-making on hospital policies.

Commission members were adamant about their public charge to manage the hospitals under their jurisdiction; they said they felt there was ample opportunity and structure for consultation with the medical staff. Medical people for the most part contended that the commission and its new staff were "overmanaging" the hospital and leaving medical opinion out in the making of decisions.

5. The spiraling costs of medical care and the accompanying burden on the taxpayers, who pay one-fourth of the governing commission's budget of about $125 million a year.
6. The relationship of the governing commission and the county board of commissioners, particularly regarding the budget.

Legislative Investigating Commission Recommendations

All of these issues, plus others, figured in the report of the Legislative Investigating Commission. The report, printed in a hefty and handsome volume, appeared in November, 1972, after the County Hospital "turmoil" seemed to have largely dissipated.

The report included proposals for radical changes in the role of the governing commission, the administration of Cook County Hospital, and the political relationships between the governing commission, the county board and the state of Illinois. It also included proposals for changes in the law to accomplish these alterations. Taken together, the recommendations seemed to raise a whole new set of unanswered questions on how to govern County Hospital.

The Role of the Governing Commission

"We have mapped out a radical departure for the commission from its former role as the administering agency of Cook County Hospital," the legislative group stated in its report. The "radical departure" includes a four-way split in administrative authority, increasing the power of the state, the county board, and the hospital staff and decreasing the power of the governing commission.

Part of the specific recommendation states:

"The Health and Hospitals Governing Commission . . . should cease its involvement in the daily administration of Cook County Hospital. It should instead function as a broad policy-making body for Cook County and Oak Forest Hospitals as well as the . . . School of Nursing. Its primary role should be that of comprehensive health and hospital care planning for Cook County. This latter function should be undertaken in cooperation with state, regional and local health planning agencies."

"In our view," the legislative group wrote, "the removal of the governing commission from the direct supervision of Cook County Hospital would clear the air of oppression that currently pervades much of the staff. The redirection of the commission toward a general function of coordinating health care . . . would place that agency in conformity with the role intended for it by the legislature when it established the commission in 1969."

(The report does not say how the legislative commission established the intent of the legislature in 1969. The law written in that year states the responsibilities of the commission to be "organizing, operating, maintaining and managing the various hospitals and hospital facilities owned by . . . (the) county and the hospital, medical, nursing, health and allied medical programs related thereto.")

Other proposals return a certain measure of power to the county board, reaffirming its right to approve or disapprove of the governing commission's total budget and adding a new power, the power to "veto or reduce any item of the budget that it deems contrary to the powers of the commission, unnecessary or unwarranted." The change is significant because it would allow the county board to pick and choose among the priorities established by the commission; this is not possible where a total program budget is approved and the commission is empowered to do its own picking and choosing within the allocated funds.

The commission's powers would be further diluted by the recommendation that there be a strong affiliation with the University of Illinois Medical School, apparently meaning that the Medical School will determine medical policies of County Hospital, as long as they do not conflict with the "broad policies" established by the governing commission.

The final step in dismantling the governing commission's power to manage is a proposal that a strong administration be developed at the hospital to oversee the actual operation of the day-to-day work there.

"We have found," the report continued, "that much of the dissent among the physicians at Cook County Hospital is attributable to the fact that in the past they have not had access to a hospital administration which is both sympathetic to their needs and neutral in its position regarding the governing commission . . . In our view an empathetic, professional hospital administrator answers all legitimate criticism by the staff that they are not being heard prior to the formulation of hospital policy. We are confident that the pursuit of an 'open door' policy at Cook County Hospital by its chief administrator will go far in restoring confidence among the staff that they have someone who will act as an advocate for their needs."

Taken together, these proposals suggest that day-to-day decisions on operating the hospital should be made by the hospital administrator responding to the interests of the medical staff.

As for the medical staff, the legislative group urges "a spirit of harmony, cooperation and optimism" with the hospital's administration and the governing commission.

Medical School Affiliation

At several points in its 172-page report, the legislative group laments the decline in County's prestige and refers to the "humiliation" of having so many foreign medical students filling the house staff positions that American medical graduates used to seek out.

"We soon recognized . . . that the deplorable morale and quickly sinking academic reputation of the hospital were due primarily to confusion regarding the relative functions and goals of the . . . governing commission and members of the medical staff. We also realized that many of the positions taken by certain individuals on the governing commission and on the hospital's medical staff were inconsistent with Cook County Hospital's function as a public teaching hospital," the report stated. "It was apparent that the academic program at Cook County Hospital needed revitalization in terms of personnel and programs."

The legislators therefore determined that the "best medicine" they could prescribe for County was an immediate affiliation with the University of Illinois Medical School; "In time," they said, "this would restore the atmosphere of academic excellence that the hospital once knew and would provide a major drawing card for an American-trained house staff."

They spelled out some of the details of the prescribed affiliation: "Under this affiliation all members of the medical staff would enjoy faculty appointments at the medical school. The operations and techniques employed at the hospital would be consistent with the educational program offered by the university and the general policies set forth by the governing commission. The Cook County Hospital administration would have the responsibility to carry out these policies and to ensure the affiliation agreement is being carried out."

But the recommendations do not answer all the questions raised by affiliation. They do not deal, for example, with who will hire the faculty members-hospital physicians and who will determine the criteria. They do not deal with which institution will determine salaries, nor even within which budget these salaries will be included. They do not resolve the question that has so plagued the hospital and commission: Whether primary emphasis must be on patient care (with attendant benefits for teaching purposes) or whether primary emphasis must be on teaching (with attendant benefits for patient care). They do not resolve the question of establishment of priorities and whether they will be determined by the university or the governing commission.

In its insistence on affiliation with the University of Illinois, the Legislative Investigating Commission disregarded the strong pleas of both Dr. Haughton and Dr. Thomas Ainsworth, assistant director of the American Hospital Association, that the governing commission and hospital officials be left free to bargain with medical schools in order to gain the best deal for patients. Both felt that affiliation was essential but that forced affiliation closed off options that the hospital desperately needed.

Composition of the Governing Commission

"There should be no modification of the membership of the governing commission to include members of the medical staff or members of the communities served by Cook County Hospital," the legislative group recommended. "In our view it is a wiser course of action to provide the governing commission with varied expertise rather than varied constituencies."

That is the only reference in the recommendations to the issue of community representation that had been so fundamental a cause of the 1971 turmoil in the hospital, including the dramatic confrontation in Dr. Greeley's office that led to the firings of the five doctors. To many observers the knottiest public administration problem of the 1970s is to devise adequate methods for community participation in the decision-making that affects their lives.

Collection of Professional Fees

At the opening of the public hearings, legislators had been extremely sympathetic with the doctors who had complained that the governing commission was trying to force them to assign their professional fees to the commission, thus doing away with the Associated Physicians and its program. Before the issuance of the report, however, the legislators changed their minds. They recommended that the Associated Physicians be phased out and that the commission should collect the fees until affiliation with the university is accomplished. At that point, the professional fees earned by County doctors would be assigned to a similar fund operated by the University of Illinois Medical School and its doctors. The legislators did not resolve what may be a conflict over the use of those funds; University of Illinois spokesmen told the public hearings that most of that money is used for "salary supplements." Such use has been ruled out by the governing commission which contends that its salary schedule for physicians is generous and there should be no supplements. Also unresolved, if Cook County rather than the University of Illinois is to continue paying physicians' salaries, is the validity of assigning the professional fees earned to the university rather than to the county to help lift the burden on the county taxpayers.

Budgeting

The proposed legislative changes leave with the governing commission the responsibility for preparing a budget covering its income and expenses. But the suggestions for a changed role for the governing commission leave unclear just what its budgeting function will include. Normally, a budget for an institution like County Hospital grows out of an interchange between the policy-making board and the operating departments; the operating departments present their needs and recommendations and the policy-making board consolidates the recommendations, assigning priorities and approving amounts that seem best designed to carry out the aims of the board.

But the recommended changes state that the governing commission will be responsible only for "broad policies" covering County Hospital and its other institutions. "Broad policies" are not anywhere defined. Presumably they include budget allocations, but the links in the development of those allocations are missing if the commission is to be divorced from close supervision of the hospital. There are suggestions, at least, that priorities and policies should be developed by the University of Illinois Medical School. If such is the case, what is the power of the governing commission to control the hospital budget?

An example would be the by-now-familiar case of the number of beds in the division of medicine. The number is a policy decision but there are attendant budgetary problems: additional medical staff if the number is to be increased, additional nursing and clerical staff, more hospital aides, more sheets, more laundry and dietary employees, more social service workers, more medical supplies and equipment. If the University of Illinois makes the policy decision, or if the staff doctors working through the hospital administrator make the decision, is the role of the governing commission only to approve the larger budget? And, finally, if the governing commission does approve the larger budget and that additional item is axed by the county board using its newly-recommended powers, what is the result? Would that not resurrect all the hospital politicking in the county board that the creation of the governing commission was designed to correct?

Unresolved Questions

Some of the complex issues that affect the governing commission and health care in Cook County received little or no attention in the legislative report.

Oak Forest, for example, the geriatrics hospital also operated by the governing commission, was left in limbo. There were no suggestions regarding how it would be governed if the governing commission loses some of its administrative powers.

The need for more help from the private hospitals of the city in caring for poor patients received scant attention, too, although it is a question that has led to some of the strongest feelings among the house staff at County and thus was a component of the "turmoil." The legislative group merely said:

"Private hospitals have not shown the degree of commitment necessary to provide health care for the poor. Because of their disinterest, Cook County Hospital has been used as a dumping ground for patients unable to afford health care. We deplore this condition and call upon all private hospitals in the Chicago area to assume their fair share of the responsibility of promoting the public health."

This recommendation does not take into account the fact that priorities are established in different ways in the private hospitals and in a public hospital. Private hospitals have no funds to provide for care for indigent patients and must be concerned about how such care will be paid for. Although state welfare funds in Illinois can be used to pay for welfare patients' care in private hospitals, experience has shown the private hospitals that the money is slow in arriving and often does not entirely cover the cost of care. The public hospital, on the other hand, is charged by the state with caring for indigent patients and probably will continue to be the dumping ground until a more adequate fiscal arrangement is provided by the state.

But the most pressing of the unresolved questions probably is related to the hospital's relationship to the community it serves. It is from the community — chiefly the black community — that much of the pressure for change has come. Nor has the pressure been for change alone; it has included demands for a voice in determining both the rate and the extent of change. These demands, by any of the varied accounts, were at the heart of the confrontation in Dr. Greeley's office that led to the firing of the five doctors. The legislative proposals deal with the problem only peripherally. They recommend no change in the composition of the commission and include a brief reference that some of the commission members have been trying to set up a community advisory group. The commission chairman "anticipated that the input from this group will be very effective in bringing the thoughts and desires of the community to the attention of the governing commission."

Doubtless it is noteworthy that none of the 30 witnesses that appeared before the Legislative Investigating Commission hearings was a representative of any of the community organizations that are seeking a voice in the management of County Hospital.

Commentary

The method of governance of Cook County Hospital seems still to be evolving. Whether or not the recommendations of the Legislative Investigating Commission are adopted by the legislature, certain changes in the nature and the method of governance will continue to take place, if only because of the need for adjustment to the powerful intrusion of the social environment of a big city.

Reflection indicates that for a large public institution like County, the method of governance must develop to suit the particular needs. Trying to fit it into an alien mold or trying to transfer models from other institutions doesn't seem to work very well. The other alternative is a special sort of evolution that will accommodate all major interests in each particular institution; apparently the evolutionary process is rather slow and painful.

Transferring models from other institutions offers these examples of failure to accommodate all major interests. The traditional private hospital organization, in which the medical staff is the power, was borrowed by the big public charity hospitals and worked only until the revolution of expectations on the part of the patients served, who began to speak up and insist "We don't want to be treated this way." The business management model, in which efficiency is the aim and an authoritarian hierarchy carries out policies aimed at efficiency, didn't work very well either because it clashed with the professional views and responsibilities of the medical specialists, failing to accommodate their legitimate interests.

The evolution of a new method of governance at County apparently is continuing. The evolution started, rather abruptly, when the end of the long autocratic reign of Dr. Meyer happened to coincide with a period of intense community pressure — particularly from the black community — and with a period of sharply rising costs due both to the revolution in medicine and to the inflationary spiral. Rather simplistically perhaps, the politicians of the county board were made the scapegoats; the rallying cry became, "Let's get politics out of the hospital." Proposals for a new kind of governing body were made, with the intent to remove or isolate political pressures so County Hospital could get on with its important function.

The proposals were simplistic because it is not really possible to remove politics from a public institution. Decisions to be made, just because it is a public institution, are by definition political. What was accomplished instead was the transfer of decision-making authority from one kind of political body to another kind. In the process, it is true that some political pressures were removed, such as patronage hiring of hospital employees. A complex method of appointment to the new governing body assured at least consideration of many segments of society, cutting down the possibility of domination by any one particular political group. The decisions the new governing body had to make were still, however, political. Determining priorities and allocating funds are political decisions in a public hospital.

With the new governing commission selected, great effort was made to bring business management methods to bear on problem solving. These methods included the hiring of experts in various phases of management, planning for future needs, new personnel policies including collective bargaining structures lacking in the past, cost accounting and up-to-date billing techniques, and the inclusion of a corporate staff level for coordination and administration.

Some real successes resulted from these modern management methods. Accreditation was achieved, physical facilities and the fiscal operation were vastly improved and there were important efforts toward a new and higher standard of patient care. But the management methods led to storms of protest, a clash between the new experts and the old experts, with neither entirely understanding the importance of what the other had to contribute or of the new reality that neither could any longer accomplish their aims alone. Since the "turmoil" there has begun to be an accommodation of these varying interests and a possibility for much better cooperation.

But the public, the communities who use the hospital, has not yet been accommodated, at least to the extent it wishes. There are profound differences between the ways in which priorities are set in a private sector business (according to profits) and in a public institution. The powerful trend of history is toward greater consideration of the community in decision-making, providing it a strong voice in the process. That pressure continues at County and was largely disregarded by the Legislative Investigating Commission.

The legislative group, deeply concerned about the reputation of the hospital, did not seem to deal basically with the evolution of a management method particularly suited to County. Instead, it searched among other models. In the end, it placed strong reliance on the University of Illinois Medical School, another new set of experts, to correct the dislocations of the last set of experts (actually faulting the last set of experts for trying to carry out governing commission policies). While bolstering the power of the medical staff, of the county board and of the state-operated university, it essentially disregarded the pressure of the community to be heard and to have a major say in running its institutions.

Probably what is evolving is some kind of colleague management, a consultation of equals to produce services that will be responsive to public pressures and needs. Colleague management is not new to hospitals; really it's the traditional method but the colleagues in that tradition are the doctors. The evolving system will increasingly make colleagues of the specialists in modern management and it will begin to be successful when the relationship between the medical staff and the management staff changes from an adversary to a collaborative one.

It will not be sufficient, however, for the doctors and the managers to accept each other as equals because other evolutionary pressures will continue:

*There will be continued pressure to include as colleagues representatives of the communities that use the hospital. Some adjustments have been made in response to community demands; patients are treated with greater dignity and consideration. There is certainly a movement away from the paternalistic operation of the old charity hospital with its attendant philosophy, "Well, after all, these are poor people." But representatives of the community have not yet been allowed a responsible share in decision-making.

* The environment in which colleague management will have to operate will be political, simply because the hospital is public, a part of government, and decision-making in a public institution is political.

*Pressures from employees, many of them organized into unions or bargaining associations for the first time at the hospital, will continue. Collective bargaining means that the unions will have something to say about the way the hospital operates because any alteration in the delivery of patient care affects conditions of employment. Conditions of employment are bargainable. In addition, the work force at County is increasingly black and, as blacks, the employees are also responding to community pressures.

*While a new model of colleague management is evolving, there are still old traditional forces at work, meaning that the evolution must take place in a push and pull kind of atmosphere. All the participants in the evolving system of governance, the doctors, the business managers, and the legislators and county officials, bring with them to the new task all their old traditional attitudes, ideas and biases. Thus in a sense the new systems compete with the old ones.

INDEX